SOMETHING
WICKED

SOMETHING WICKED

The Lives, Crimes and Deaths of the Pendle Witches

By CAROL ANN LEE

First published in the UK by John Blake Publishing
An imprint of The Zaffre Publishing Group
A Bonnier Books UK company
4th Floor, Victoria House
Bloomsbury Square,
London, WC1B 4DA
England

Owned by Bonnier Books
Sveavägen 56, Stockholm, Sweden

www.facebook.com/johnblakebooks
twitter.com/jblakebooks

Hardback – 9781789465839
Ebook – 9781789465853
Audio – 9781789465822

A CIP catalogue of this book is available from the British Library.

Designed by Envy Design Ltd
Printed and bound by Clays Ltd, Elcograf S.p.A

3 5 7 9 10 8 6 4 2

John Blake is an imprint of Bonnier Books UK
www.bonnierbooks.co.uk

'I care not for thee . . .'
Elizabeth Southerns

'A sense of righteousness is not incompatible
with doing terrible things.'
J. K. Rowling

CONTENTS

Part III: THE KAGE

Part IV: PARLIAMENT OF ROOKS

KEY SITES IN THE PENDLE WITCH TRIAL

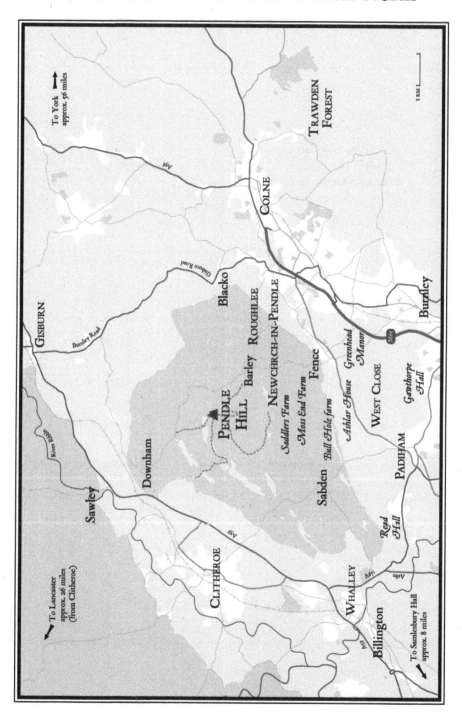

SOUTHERNS-DEVICE FAMILY TREE

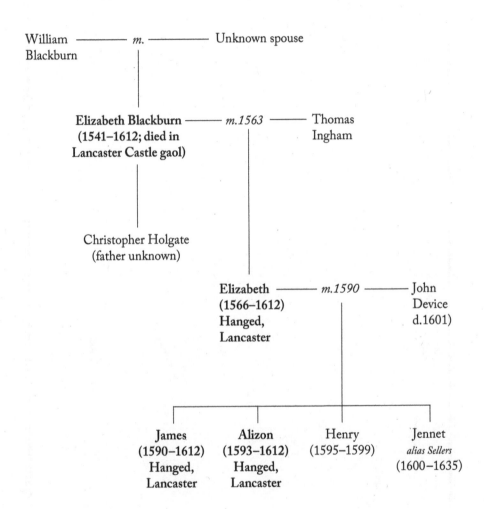

William Blackburn ———— *m.* ———— Unknown spouse

Elizabeth Blackburn ——— *m.1563* ——— Thomas Ingham
(1541–1612; died in
Lancaster Castle gaol)

Christopher Holgate
(father unknown)

Elizabeth ——— *m.1590* ——— John Device
(1566–1612) d.1601)
Hanged,
Lancaster

James | Alizon | Henry | Jennet
(1590–1612) | (1593–1612) | (1595–1599) | *alias Sellers*
Hanged, | Hanged, | | (1600–1635)
Lancaster | Lancaster

WHITTLE-REDFEARN FAMILY TREE

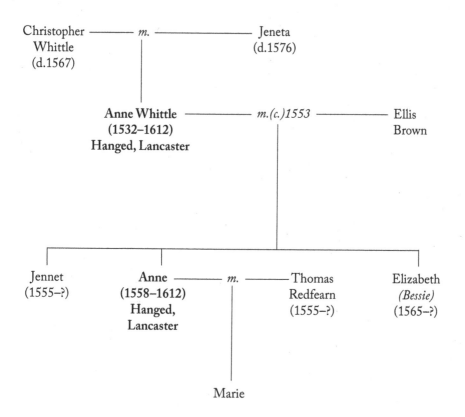

Christopher ———— *m.* ———————— Jeneta
Whittle   (d.1576)
(d.1567)

Anne Whittle ———— *m.(c.)1553* ———— Ellis
(1532–1612)   Brown
Hanged, Lancaster

Jennet   Anne ——— *m.* ———— Thomas   Elizabeth
(1555–?)   **(1558–1612)**   Redfearn   *(Bessie)*
                  Hanged,   (1555–?)   (1565–?)
                  Lancaster

Marie

SOUTHERNS-DEVICE FAMILY TREE*

Based upon the family tree compiled by Gladys Whitaker in

Roughlee Hall: Fact and Fiction (1983)

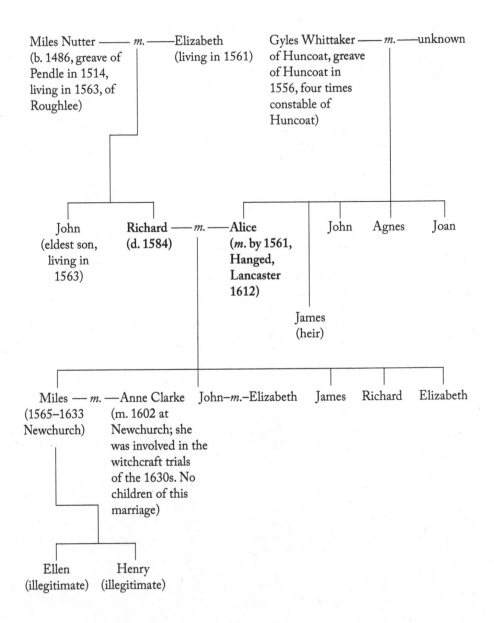

Miles Nutter ——— *m.* ———Elizabeth
(b. 1486, greave of   (living in 1561)
Pendle in 1514,
living in 1563, of
Roughlee)

Gyles Whittaker ——— *m.* ———unknown
of Huncoat, greave
of Huncoat in
1556, four times
constable of
Huncoat)

John   Richard ——— *m.* ———Alice   John   Agnes   Joan
(eldest son,   (d. 1584)   (*m.* by 1561,
living in   Hanged,
1563)   Lancaster
                                                1612)

                                        James
                                        (heir)

Miles — *m.* —Anne Clarke   John–*m.*–Elizabeth   James   Richard   Elizabeth
(1565–1633   (m. 1602 at
Newchurch)   Newchurch; she
              was involved in the
              witchcraft trials
              of the 1630s. No
              children of this
              marriage)

Ellen   Henry
(illegitimate)   (illegitimate)

Miles' children inherited the Nutter family estates upon his death

DRAMATIS PERSONAE

GISBURN: CONDEMNED AS A WITCH:

Preston, Jennet – executed at York, 29 July 1612

PENDLE: CONDEMNED AS WITCHES:

Bulcock, Jane – executed at Lancaster, 20 August 1612

Bulcock, John – executed at Lancaster, 20 August 1612

Device, Alizon – daughter of Elizabeth Device, executed at Lancaster, 20 August 1612

Device, Elizabeth *nee* Ingham – daughter of Elizabeth Southerns, executed at Lancaster, 20 August 1612

Device, James – son of Elizabeth Device, executed at Lancaster, 20 August 1612

Hewitt, Katherine [*wife of Old Mouldheels*] – executed at Lancaster, 20 August 1612

Nutter, Alice – executed at Lancaster, 20 August 1612

Redfearn, Anne *nee* Brown/Whittle – daughter of Anne Whittle, executed at Lancaster, 20 August 1612

Robey, Isabel [*Windle Witch*] – executed at Lancaster, 20 August 1612

Whittle, Anne [*Chattox*] mother of Anne Redfearn – executed at Lancaster, 20 August 1612

And:

Pearson, Margaret [*Padiham Witch*] – found guilty of bewitching and
   killing a horse, sentenced to a year's imprisonment and the stocks

Southerns, Elizabeth [*Demdike*] – charged with witchcraft, but died in
   prison before trial, c. May 1612

SAMLESBURY: ACCUSED OF WITCHCRAFT:

Grace Sowerbutts, chief prosecution witness, accused the following:

Bierley, Jennet – found not guilty

Bierley, Ellen – found not guilty

Southworth, Jane – found not guilty

*Five defendents in this case were released by Judge Bromley before the trial,
   with a warning about future conduct:*

Astley, Elizabeth – accused of witchcraft, released

Gray, Alice – accused of witchcraft, released

Hay, Lawrence – accused of witchcraft, released

Ramesden, John – accused of witchcraft, released

Sidegreaves, Isabel – accused of witchcraft, released

OTHER CHARACTERS:

Alker, William – Southworth family retainer

Altham, James – judge at the Lancaster trials and at Jennet Preston's
   trial in York, both 1612

Anderton, James – magistrate from Clayton, Lancashire

Assheton, Richard – of the Downham Asshetons; Anne Whittle
   claimed that he had been murdered by Elizabeth Southerns

Baldwin, Richard – owner of Wheathead mill, father of child allegedly
   murdered by Elizabeth Southerns

Baldwyn – schoolmaster in Colne who was friendly with the
   Redfearns

Bannister, Nicholas – of Altham, justice of the peace who assisted
   Roger Nowell in bringing the witches to trial

Booth, Jennet – wife of James Booth of Padiham

Boothman, Jane – friend of Anne Whittle

Bromley, Edward – judge at the Lancaster trials of 1612

Bulcock, Henry – accused Alizon Device of bewitching his child

Bulcock, Christopher – farmer at Moss End, husband of Jane
    Bulcock, father of John Bulcock, both executed for witchcraft

Chaddock, Peter – of Windle, claimed to have been bewitched by
    Isabel Robey

Chisnal, Edward – of Standish, justice of the peace

Covell, Thomas – Lancaster gaoler, coroner, magistrate and mayor

Crooke, Margaret – sister of Robert Nutter the younger

Crouckshey, Anne – of Marsden, known to the Pendle accused

Device, Jennet – daughter of Elizabeth Device, she accused her
    grandmother, mother and two siblings of witchcraft; chief
    prosecution witness at Lancaster Assizes 1612

Device, John – husband of Elizabeth Device and father of James and
    Alizon, who believed that he had been murdered by Anne Whittle

Deyne, Jennet – wife of John Deyne, of New Field Edge in Middop,
    Yorkshire, allegedly bewitched by Jane and John Bulcock

Dodgson, Thomas – son of Edward Dodgson, allegedly murdered by
    Jennet Preston

Duckworth, John – of the Laund, allegedly murdered by James Device

Foulds, Anne – of Colne, allegedly bewitched to death by Katherine
    Hewitt

Gerard, Thomas – of Windle, justice of the peace who investigated
    Isabel Robey

Gray, Alice – of Colne, known to the Pendle accused

Halseworths – cunning man of Windle, consulted by Peter Chaddock

Hargreaves, Blaze – of Higham, allegedly murdered by James Device

Hargreaves, Christopher – [*also Christopher Jackes*] of Thorniholme

Hargreaves, Elizabeth – of Higham, wife of Christopher Hargreaves

Hargreaves, John – of Goldshaw Booth, allegedly murdered by James Device

Hargreaves, Henry – constable of Pendle Forest, conducted search of Malkin Tower

Hargreaves, Jennet – wife of Hugh Hargreaves of Under Pendle

Hay, Grace – of Padiham, known to the Pendle women

Heyber, Jane – wife of Thomas Lister the younger, daughter of Thomas Heyber

Heyber, Thomas – magistrate of Marton, father-in-law of Thomas Lister the younger, prosecuter in Jennet Preston's trial 1612

Holden, Robert – of Holden Hall, Haslingden, justice of the peace and son-in-law of his colleague on the bench, Nicholas Bannister

Holgate, Christopher – of Pendle, son of Elizabeth Southerns, half-brother of Elizabeth Device

Holgate, Elizabeth – wife of Christopher Holgate, daughter-in-law of Elizabeth Southerns

Knyvett, Elizabeth – wife of Thomas Knyvett, close acquaintance of Thomas Potts

Knyvett, Thomas – Baron of Escrick in Yorkshire, close acquaintance of Thomas Potts, made famous for his arrest of Guy Fawkes

Law, Abraham – Halifax clothier and son of John Law, who pursued the charge against Alizon Device

Law, John – petty chapman whose encounter with Alizon Device sparked the trials

Leigh, William – rector of Standish and justice of the peace

Lister, Leonard – brother of Thomas the elder, allegedly bewitched by Jennet Preston

Lister, Thomas – the younger, son of Thomas Lister of Gisburn, pursued charges against Jennet Preston

Lister, Thomas – the elder, allegedly murdered by Jennet; his corpse was said to bleed at her touch

Loomshawe's wife – friend to Anne Whittle

Lyon, Margaret – of Windle, wife of Thomas Lyon and friend of
    Peter Chaddock's wife

Moore, Hugh – of Pendle, allegedly murdered by Anne Whittle

Moore, John – gentleman of Higham, father of child allegedly
    murdered by Anne Whittle

Moore, John – infant son of John Moore of Higham, allegedly
    murdered by Anne Whittle

Mitton, Henry – of Roughlee, allegedly murdered by Elizabeth
    Device, Alice Nutter and Elizabeth Southerns

Nowell, Roger – of Read Hall, justice of the peace who investigated
    the Pendle accused

Nutter, Christopher – father of Robert Nutter the younger, allegedly
    murdered by Anne Redfearn

Nutter, Elizabeth – wife of Robert Nutter the elder

Nutter, John – brother of Robert Nutter, the younger

Nutter, John – of Bull Hole Farm in Goldshaw Booth, whose cows
    were allegedly bewitched to death by Elizabeth Southerns and
    Anne Whittle

Nutter, Marie – wife of Robert Nutter, the younger

Nutter, Robert, the younger – of Greenhead, allegedly murdered by
    Anne Whittle

Parre, Margaret – of Windle, acquaintance of Isabel Robey

Pearson, Edward – husband of Margaret Pearson, the 'Padiham witch'

Potts, Thomas – clerk of court at the Lancaster trials and author of
    The Wonderfull Discoverie of Witches in the Countie of Lancaster

Preston, William – husband of Jennet Preston, of Gisburn

Redfearn, Thomas – husband of Anne Redfearn

Robinson, Anne – family retainer of the Listers, who gave evidence
    against Jennet Preston

Robinson, James – stepson of Robert Nutter the elder of Greenhead

Robinson, James [*alias Sawyer*] brother of John Robinson, allegedly murdered by Elizabeth Device

Robinson, John [*alias Sawyer*] brother of James Robinson, allegedly murdered by Elizabeth Device

Sandes, William – Mayor of Lancaster in 1612

Shuttleworth, Richard – Master of Gawthorpe Hall, employer of Robert Nutter the younger

Singleton, John – family retainer of the Southworths

Southworth, Christopher [*alias Master Thompson*] – of Samlesbury Hall, Jesuit priest, son of Sir John Southworth; he indoctrinated Grace Sowerbutts to accuse three women of witchcraft

Southworth, Sir John – of Samlesbury Hall

Sowerbutts, Grace – fourteen-year-old girl who claimed to have been bewitched at Samlesbury

Sowerbutts, Thomas – father of Grace, tenant of the Southworths

Sawyer, Christopher – of Barley; his sheep was stolen by James Device for the Good Friday meal at Malkin Tower in 1612

Towneley, Anna – of Carr Hall, wife of Henry, allegedly murdered by James Device

Towneley, Henry – of Carr Hall, husband of Anna Towneley, nephew of Jane Southworth

Walshman, Hugh – father of Thomas Walshman and boatman on the River Ribble

Walshman, Thomas – yeoman of Samlesbury, son of Hugh, father of child allegedly murdered by Ellen and Jennet Bierley and Jane Southworth

Wilkinson, Jane – of Windle, allegedly bewitched by Isabel Robey

INTRODUCTION

Cornwall, 1976

'I don't believe in witches.'

I am seven years old, standing with my parents in the shop attached to the Museum of Witchcraft and Magic in Boscastle. No sooner have I finished speaking, than a book on a nearby carousel sails through the air and lands at my feet.

The man behind the till looks amused and perplexed. He comes out from behind the counter to pick up the book. Replacing it on the carousel, he leans down and whispers theatrically, 'Oh, they heard you.'

I vow to never doubt the existence of witches again.

We all encounter witches in our childhoods. From fairy tales to films, they are almost always figures of fear or derision, offering enchanted apples to unsuspecting maidens and transforming from cantankerous, bicycling spinsters into green-skinned hags on broomsticks. The Cornish village where I spent my earliest years was rumoured to host a coven that met in the woods to do unspeakable things.

The 1970s were so saturated with the supernatural that anything seemed possible. Not least because my family lived in a succession of very old, very haunted houses. Even our holidays were strange: we once rented a farmhouse in Yorkshire for a week and, every night at two o'clock, a cuckoo clock struck loudly. We invited relatives over one evening and went on a cuckoo clock hunt but couldn't find 'the damned thing', as my father kept referring to it. But on the day we left, as he began reversing the car down the lane, we hit a large pothole, blowing a tyre. We got out to look at the damage and there, in the hollow, bobbing about in the rainwater like a bath toy, was a broken cuckoo clock.

Inevitably, ours was a superstitious household. At Christmas we hung 'wessel cups' on the tree, but cards with robins on them had to be thrown away because they were bad luck. We saluted and greeted magpies but dreaded a robin (again) hopping indoors in case it brought death. Hair was never cut on Friday nor washing done on New Year's Day – both were ill omens, along with peacock feathers used for decoration, or an umbrella opened indoors . . . on it went.

My father had a keen interest in nature, history and the paranormal. His idea of a bedtime story was to pick a tale from the *Reader's Digest Folklore, Myths and Legends of Britain*, while a precarious tower of books by M. R. James, Daphne du Maurier, Peter Haining, Margaret Baker, Dennis Wheatley and Harry Price took up permanent residence on his bedside table. Day trips revolved around the esoteric, with the most startling involving a time-slip experienced by the whole family in the ancient woodlands below Castle Drogo. Every outing had its intrigues, whether it was the wave 'gathering half the deep' and 'full of voices' that deposited a pile of mermaids' purses and marbles at my feet in Merlin's cave at Tintagel, to the invisible, book-flinging witches three miles along the coast in Boscastle.

My perception of witches began to change as I neared double figures. First came the BBC drama *Lizzie Dripping*, with a witch as schoolgirl Lizzie's imaginary friend. She materialised at odd moments and, in one memorable scene, appeared at the beach, shrieking with joy as she paddled along the seashore. A little later I discovered Susan Cooper's *The Dark Is Rising* and became obsessed with the third novel in the series, *Greenwitch*. Set in an imaginary Cornish town (but clearly based on Mevagissey, which I knew well), the title refers to an annual offering to the sea formed of twigs, created by women and cast off the headland.

But the mournful effigy is also a living being with a long-held secret, which she relinquishes to the character of young Jane, who has shown her compassion.

Then along came the extraordinary Kate Bush, whirling and witching the words of 'Wuthering Heights' on the weekly BBC1 chart show *Top of the Pops*. Dubbed 'the White Witch of Pop', she was (and is) beautiful, arcane and beguilingly brilliant. Her music, played on my tinny cassette player until the tapes snarled up, provided the soundtrack to my much-loved weekly read: a comic fronted by an elegant, raven-haired witch with ice-blue eyes. Her name was *Misty*.

Marketed as 'a great mystery paper for girls', *Misty* had no equal.[1] In each issue, our eponymous heroine ('*Misty* – your friend of the mists') introduced lurid tales of horror in the form of groovily Gothic comic strips. There were boarding schools run by demonic staff; evil dijnns lurking in fish and chip shops; paintbrushes that would only obey a long-dead, criminally insane artist; and a Northern mining town with a cursed jukebox. 'Winner Loses All', the most popular long-running series, featured a schoolgirl who made a pact with the devil to become a show-jumping champion and to save her father from alcoholism.

A sizable portion of *Misty*'s stories were witch-centric, most often dispatching some well-deserved tit-for-tat sorcery to school bullies. 'The Tale of Little Wytching' is different. It opens with Jennie and her auntie Pat arriving in Little Wytching, a village associated with the witch trials. This troubled past is being mined by the villagers in the pursuit of tourism: 'Years ago, the craft shop sold little handmade peg doll witches on broomsticks, lovingly made by the local gypsies. Now they were all plastic and mass-produced in Hong Kong or Taiwan.'[2] Pat informs her niece that strange things are happening in Little Wytching: endless thunderstorms, soured milk, even a plague of toads. She suspects it is all the doing of Old Meg, a seventeenth-century witch who had terrorised the village with her 'wicked spells' until being burnt at the stake.[3] In the final frames of the comic strip, a young descendant of the witchfinder sets fire to a building where Old Meg crouches unsuspectingly behind the chimneypot, clutching her broom. I remember feeling helplessly complicit as she was once more condemned to a terrible end.

But I forgot about Old Meg for years. Thirty years, to be precise; she returned to my thoughts during another family holiday. I was the parent now, staying with my twelve-year-old son and our energetic little dog in the Lancashire village of Gisburn. The handsome estate was once owned by the Listers, lords of the manor, but I knew nothing about the area and had made the booking on a whim.

It was mid-August, and the rain was incessant. We decided to explore further afield by car and turned off the main road, travelling under dripping trees until the way ahead widened out to a spectacular, sweeping view.

Pendle Hill appeared through the low-lying mists like a sleeping giant, alive with the elements. As we drew closer, the grey swathes of mist thinned to reveal a branding on the giant's shoulder: *1612*. We agreed that it had to refer to a date, but had no idea what was being commemorated, or that it was a temporary installation, moulded from a material used to protect crops. We took a few photographs then headed down into Barley, a small village with two pubs and well-kept stone houses along a narrow, double-parked road. There were witches everywhere: skimming the open doors of a Land Rover dealership, appearing in green profile on an estate agent's board, and flying by moonlight on a pub sign. There were even witches advertising a local brewery, on rain-sagged parasols, where people sat nursing pints at picnic tables.

The road out of Barley curved steeply upwards, bordered by high hedges before opening out into fields. The long hump of Pendle Hill loomed behind us, and a perfectly symmetrical line of trees graced the horizon. A reservoir below resembled a scrying mirror, its black, still waters reflecting the trailing mist.

Dropping down into Newchurch-in-Pendle, we found a parking spot by a pair of old weavers' cottages. On a wooden waymarker, next to an uphill path through thick shrubbery, sat two tiny plump witches astride their broomsticks, pointing in opposite directions. 'Witches Galore' read the sign across one of the three-storey weavers' cottages. A bay window teemed with gothic trinkets, suncatchers and fairies on fishing-wire. A life-sized papier mâché witch in cloak and hat slumped against the wall as if slightly inebriated, a faint smile on her crumpled face.[4]

The doorbell tinkled as we entered the shop. Inside, every surface, shelf and ceiling was festooned with witches, cauldrons, broomsticks, black cats and black hats, sage sticks, tarot cards and spell books. Pewter witches pirouetted on keyrings; moon-bound hags zipped by on coasters, and a handful of miniature, glass-blown crones 'made by a real Pendle witch' lay flat on the shop counter as if struck by lightning.

White-haired Maureen Stopforth, owner of 'Witches Galore' for over forty years, answered my question about the numbers on the hill: 'It's four hundred years this week since the witch trials. A big group of people from Pendle – mostly women, of course – were hanged in Lancaster. There's no end of things going on to mark the occasion. We've had people from all over the world stop by. Have you seen the statue of Alice Nutter in Roughlee? It's just gone up. I think it's rather splendid.'

We had a last look around the 'little shop with the big reputation' as 'Witches Galore' bills itself. Drawn to the cheerful chaos of the bay window display, I gazed at an array of wooden witches in flight, and a half-remembered line surfaced in my memory: 'Years ago, the craft shop sold little handmade peg doll witches on broomsticks . . .'

The sky darkened. As we left the shop, I looked up at the chimneypot, almost expecting to see Old Meg there, waiting.

The Da Vinci Code was published a few years before my first visit to Pendle. A global phenomenon, Dan Brown's fast-paced thriller has sold around eighty million copies to date.

It contains a passage replete with widespread misconceptions about the 'witch craze' in Europe, courtesy of the novel's lead character, a Harvard professor, who declares that the Catholic Inquisition was behind 'the most blood-soaked publication in human history'. This is the *Malleus Maleficarum*, or 'Hammer of Witches', which the professor summarises as having 'indoctrinated the world to "the dangers of freethinking women"' and which instructed the clergy how to locate, torture and destroy them. He explains that those deemed witches by the Church included 'all female scholars, priestesses, gypsies, mystics, nature lovers, herb gatherers', and any woman 'suspiciously attuned to the natural world'; while midwives were killed for 'their heretical practice of using medical knowledge to ease the pain of childbirth . . . During 300 years of witch-hunts, the Church burnt at the stake an astounding five *million* women.'[5]

It is indeed astounding, and utterly incorrect but for a kernel of truth: the *Malleus Maleficarum* is an actual text ascribed to two inquisitors, although none of the quotes within the professor's unedited speech originate from it. The remainder of the passage is as fictional as the plot, but *The Da Vinci Code* enjoyed a huge reach in circulating delusions about the witch-hunts, while similar misapprehensions and wildly inflated figures appear frequently elsewhere.

In reality, approximately 90,000 people were prosecuted as witches in Europe during the period 1482–1782, many in ordinary secular courts. Around 50,000 were sentenced to death and an estimated 25–30 per cent of those were men. England's witch trials were few in comparison, and the probability of acquittal was high; approximately 500 executions took place on English soil.

The entire country was therefore completely unprepared for the scale, drama and impact of the trials held at the Lancaster Assizes in August 1612. In his landmark study of English witchcraft, American historian Wallace Notestein refers to the case as 'the most remarkable event of the sort in James's reign'.[6] The hearing of nineteen people (fifteen of them women) from Pendle and Samlesbury constituted the largest number of defendants on witchcraft charges at a single assizes until that time. Perhaps most startling of all was the presence of the chief prosecution witness, Jennet Device, an eleven-year-old girl who looked smaller and younger due to her circumstances. Jennet gave crucial evidence against her mother, brother and sister; her grandmother, who had been accused with them, died in gaol.

All eight of the Samlesbury accused walked free from court, while a woman tried alongside the Pendle group was sentenced to a year's imprisonment and punishment in the stocks. The remainder – eight women and two men from Pendle – were condemned to death, the same fate meted out to their female 'co-conspirator' from Gisburn, who had been executed at York one month earlier. The ten from Pendle were hanged in Lancaster on 20 August 1612, before a vast crowd on the moors overlooking Morecambe Bay.

An official account of the case was published the following year, written by Thomas Potts, the clerk of court, at the instigation of the trial judges. All were motivated by political necessity, self-preservation and personal gain; as a result, *The Wonderfull Discoverie of Witches in the Countie of Lancaster* remains a poisoned chalice for readers. No other written works are ascribed to Potts, but his confidence in demonstrating the righteousness of the verdict reverberates in every line. We will come to recognise him as a frustratingly untrustworthy source, his pen guided by the hand of its editor-in-chief, Judge Bromley. Their combined efforts produced a potent draught of hateful hags, multiple murders by witchcraft, uncontrollable familiar spirits, wicked enchantments and a diabolical sabbath attended by the region's shape-shifters – all fermented in a pot of political anti-popery with a dash of *Macbeth* thrown in for good measure.

Although it is easy to be scathing about *Discoverie*, without it we would know nothing of the 1612 trials, for Potts leaves us with the only substantial documentation about the case. At the time, he must have felt deeply gratified when his work was not only well received but went on to have a significant influence on the legal system. Excerpts from *Discoverie* were included in barrister Michael Dalton's *The Country Justice*, a handbook for justices of the peace and local magistrates. First published in 1618, *The Country Justice* ran to many editions, shaping court process throughout England and the colonies. Its guidelines on the use of child witnesses, adapted from *Discoverie*, later came to the attention of an eminent Puritan clergyman named Cotton Mather.

Grandson of a Lancashire preacher, Mather was a prolific author whose best-known work has obvious parallels with *Discoverie*. Published in 1693, *The Wonders of the Invisible World* is a court-sanctioned account of an American case in which Mather had some involvement. Like *Discoverie*, Mather's book is a 'propaganda piece' endorsed by the chief trial judge.[7] Like Potts, he worked from the original trial transcripts and court documents. And like Potts, he depicted the judiciary as irreproachable and the ghastly outcome of the case unavoidable. But while Potts was unabashedly in favour of the 1612 hangings, Cotton Mather has been somewhat less fairly portrayed as the 'architect and executioner' of the 1692–3 trial with which he was concerned: Salem.[8]

When the British government rejected the idea of a pardon for the Pendle witches in 1998, they issued a statement. Reasoning that 'the Pendle witches were apparently convicted according to the law of the time', a pardon would only be granted 'if evidence came to light which showed conclusively that the Pendle witches did not commit the crimes with which they were charged'.[9] The then home secretary, Jack Straw, conceded that it was 'particularly difficult to obtain conclusive evidence that no offences were committed and to apply modern morality and criteria' to the case, but stood by the decision.[10]

Under those terms, a pardon for the Pendle witches seems impossible – although at the time of writing, another attempt is underway. But how does one present evidence, conclusive or circumstantial, to show what cannot be seen? Which then might legitimately lead to the question of whether this book can realise its intention: to present a true crime study about a crime that most people would argue cannot be true.

Nevertheless, the story of the 1612 trials is one of crime and punishment, a brutal depiction of how 'justice' was meted out in its day. Apart from several popular novels, including two modern classics, *Mist Over Pendle* and *The Familiars*, there have been a great many books published on the case. Leaving aside those that might be categorised as local studies – and which therefore provide the backbone for the body of the subject – most are academic, written to explore new scholarly theories, and are aimed at readers with a penchant for the minutiae of such discussions. *Something Wicked* is written from a different perspective in the hope of achieving something different.

Despite our primary source, Thomas Potts, being a far from reliable narrator, and the fact that all the original, trial-related documents have been lost, we can pry out small but incredibly useful gems from *Discoverie*, and work with an array of other material to untangle myths and make the truth accessible, engaging and personal. For while there are elements in the case that sit completely alien with us, ultimately the strands of the story that the authorities were able to exploit are ones that we instinctively recognise: family relationships, power imbalances, neighbourhood feuds, money struggles – and those close friendships unique to women that are life-affirming when good but can be ruinous if they turn sour.

Through all of this, I've sought to make those at the centre of the case as visible and heard as possible; too often, the voices of the less literate and chronically poor have been lost to us, with no wills, diaries or any form of written account to speak across the centuries. But I think we can occasionally hear them, faintly, in those sinister documents from the witch trials, albeit through the distorting filter of other voices who sought to silence them forever.

All we have to do is listen.

Part I:

STICK AND STAKE

Thursday, the Twentieth Day of August
in the Year of Our Lord 1612

PROLOGUE

Gallows Hill, Lancaster

England does not burn its witches.

In Scotland and overseas, many pyres are lit in the pursuit of justice. But in England, under our Scottish king, a person found guilty of witchcraft will hang. Burning is reserved for the woman who compounds her witchcraft conviction with another of petty treason; a witch who has killed her husband and master is burnt at the stake. The fortunate ones are strangled by the executioner before they hear the kindling crackle.

On this summer's day, ten bodies hang from the gallows on the windswept heights of Lancaster Moor. Two are those of young men: an itinerant labourer and a farmer's son. They grew up more or less together; this time last year, they were busy with the grain harvest, hoping for a run of dry days, sun-browned arms gathering up bundles of yellow stalks to prepare for threshing and winnowing, sifting and sieving. Not dangling at their sides like that, pale and lifeless as stillborn lambs.

Their mothers hang next to them on the scaffold. The sister of one of them too. And another mother and daughter, once friends of theirs, close as kin, but hated in the end. Two of the three remaining women are acquaintances of the rest, but not the last, who turns slowly on her rope like a broken marionette. The one from Windle has known them all only a month, during incarceration in the prison deep below the castle grounds.

Years from now, the yawning creak of the ropes will be replaced by the thump of leather on willow and ripples of applause in many a grammar school cricket match. The ground that bears the heavy imprint of the dungeon cart and horses' hooves will disappear under an immaculate green lawn and a white sports pavilion with its view of the glittering bay beyond the castle. The crowds that gather will not be the vast, unruly hordes who walked all night to watch the witches hang, but instead boys in blazers calling to classmates, and a schoolmaster biting back exasperation at a poorly bowled ball.

All of them unaware why the soughing of the wind in the woods nearby sounds like a woman whispering in an ancient tongue, and that below their feet lie the blackened bones of the ten who hanged on another English summer afternoon.

'*Crucifixus hoc signum vitam Etername. Amen.*'

A SHORT HISTORY
OF WITCHES

Witch. A small word on quickened breath, yet it carries an unfathomable weight of meaning. Its connotations shift in droves, like cattle through the purifying needfires of old. Today the witch stands before us transformed, divested of the shroud she wore for almost 2,000 years, loathing and revulsion in its folds. A century of cultural alchemy has given her new robes; freed from patriarchy, she is now admired as fearless, possessed of secret knowledge, rebellious yet inclusive, and a fundamental part of the natural world. The rehabilitation of the witch from a despised, half-human creature to a figure as sympathetic as she is inspirational has been described as 'one of the most radical and unexpected developments of modern Western culture'.[11]

But this is not the witch we are going to meet in the villages of woodsmoke and whisper below Pendle Hill. To better understand who she – and he – is, we have to leave the era of the hashtag witch and unfold the map of the past, entering a world lit only by sun, moon and fire. The absence of artificial light gives the shadows more substance in this realm: at night, the strange shrieks and cries in the fields and hedgerows seem more unearthly, while movement – those quick, half-glimpsed flickers in the furrows – might be witches disguised as hares, or boggarts, spirits native to Lancashire and neighbouring Yorkshire.

For in this world, the supernatural is as real as the grass between your toes and the air on your face. Spirits, fairies, angels, demons, imps and numerous other beings populate the land, sea and ether. The spiritual and the corporeal are divided by a gossamer thread, with the astrologer regarded intellectually in much the same way as the astronomer.

Nothing happens here by chance or coincidence, but science is not yet able to provide explanations or solutions for disease and disaster, personal tragedy and widespread catastrophe. Nonetheless, answers are sought, and, in the absence of rationality, the devil is thought to be at work. And while evil may take many forms, its preferred shape is the witch.

The malevolent omnipotence of the witch is 'but one facet of the devil's activities upon earth. In early modern England he was an all-pervasive force and his influence was seen everywhere, in murders, war, papistry, gluttony . . .'[12] The belief in witches as a supernatural, demonic force is all-encompassing. If you believe in God – and very few do not, regardless of their denomination – to deny the existence of witches is tantamount to blasphemy: 'For if witches did not exist, some would take the next step and say the devil did not exist. And, if the devil did not exist, perhaps neither did God.'[13]

Purging society of such evil, in the form of organised witch-hunts, is mostly the work of men. Four centuries on, they will be decried as misogynists, religious fanatics or motivated by greed, but in their own time they, 'like the justices, clergymen and other notable inhabitants, really believed that they were performing a public service, dealing with a public menace'.[14] Horror-struck by the conspiracy of witches in existence, they feel compelled to act out of 'a combination of curiosity, bewilderment, and anxiety, with a desire to exercise power and to perform a useful public duty'.[15] What emerges is a collective tyranny that sees potential diabolism everywhere, dividing communities and destroying lives in an atmosphere of overwhelming terror and 'the fear of hell – the fear of absolute evil upon the earth'.[16]

The first laws against witchcraft date back more than 4,000 years. Hammurabi, king of the fabled city of Babylon, created a set of rules for his people which are among the world's earliest and most complete written legal codes. Inscribed on a colossal stone pillar (discovered by archaeologists in 1901), the 282 decrees laid out rules, fines and punishments for crimes such as stealing and murder, and legal guidance for marriage and commerce.

Witchcraft was covered in the initial decrees; Babylonians were strong believers in demons and the supernatural. Hammurabi, who assumed all witches to be male, dictated that any man who placed a 'death spell' on another should be executed, while another law foreshadowed the 'ordeal by water' that was meted out during the European witch trials: 'If a man has accused another of laying a spell upon him, but has not proved it, the accused shall go to the sacred river, he shall plunge into the sacred river . . .'[17] If the suspect drowned, his home would be given to his accuser. If he survived, his accuser would be put to death and his home would be given to the accused.

Hammurabi's laws echo those passages within the Hebrew Bible dealing with witchcraft. Although Exodus 22:18 is the most well known – 'Thou shalt not suffer a witch to live' – the exact meaning of 'witch' in its original Hebrew (*mekhashepha*) has been lost. Attempts have been made to define it, ranging from 'a magic associated more often with women', to 'cannibal' and 'vampire'.[18] In the Greek translation of the Bible *mekhashepha* became *pharmakous* (poisoners), but was replaced with *maleficos* in the Latin Vulgate Bible, which broadly translates as (male) 'wrong doers'.[19] The alteration came to dominate how medieval people understood witchcraft and had long-term implications. One twelfth-century writer clarified that *malefici* were 'those who use the tricks of the art of magic and devilish illusions. They are heretics.'[20] He believed that it advocated excommunication for heretics, not execution.

The word 'witch' appears in the earliest authorised English trans-lations of the Bible, long before King James I of England commissioned an updated version of the text, which was published in 1611. Matthew Hopkins, the self-appointed Witchfinder General, shrewdly chose the line as a preface for his 1647 book, *The Discoverie of Witches*, written to quell the rising criticism of his methods. Hopkins' book was an exercise in damage limitation; in citing the line, he implied that his activities were guided by divine power.

While the earliest translations of the Bible, like Hammurabi's laws, envisaged witches to be male, ancient Greek literature burgeons with bold, wild women who cast spells and are capable of great wickedness. Circe, Hekate, Medea and their kind have stalked the imaginations of writers and artists ever since, yet at the time there were few prosecutions in Greece of those regarded as real-life enchantresses. The execution of Theoris of Lemnos, deemed a 'filthy sorceress' and convicted of using harmful potions and casting incantations, was unusual.[21]

The Romans, who were heavily influenced by Greek culture, made use of magic in the form of amulets, charms and curse tablets (private prayers inscribed on small sheets of lead or pewter) but thought of them almost as devotional items. A distinction between charitable and malicious magic was made around the first century BC. Intention was key, followed by the question of whether the magic performed had the ability to defy the gods and change nature's course.

Thereafter, magicians were increasingly looked upon as harmful users of *veneficium* (magic or poison) and witches as users of *malefica* (harmful magic). A woman named Numantina, accused of using incantations and potions to compel her former husband to kill his second wife, was among the earliest to be prosecuted within this framework. Numantina was acquitted, but following the conversion to Christianity of Roman Emperor Constantine, the demonisation of magic deepened. The interlocking laws of Church and State led to witch-hunts, prosecutions and the murder of a remarkable woman named Hypatia, daughter of Theon of Alexandria.

Hypatia had initially followed in her father's footsteps as a brilliant mathematician and astronomer, but became an even more accomplished scientist, philosopher and teacher. Orestes, a Roman state official, began consulting Hypatia on ethical matters, which enraged the Bishop of Alexandria, with whom Orestes often argued. Rumours began to circulate that Hypatia had bewitched Orestes and 'beguiled many people through her Satanic wiles'.[22] Rumblings of discontent among the bishop's followers erupted one day in 415 CE: Hypatia was seized, tortured and mutilated, in a church. The men who had defiled Hypatia left her body parts strewn outside the church. Her remains were cremated.

Few records exist of witch trials in central Europe during the Middle Ages. Moreover, in 1080, Pope Gregory VII wrote to King Harald of Denmark that holding witches responsible for storms, illnesses and other natural disasters was tantamount to heresy. Such matters were Acts of God, the pope insisted, and to punish witches for them could only inflame God further and cause suffering to the blameless.

But in October 1347, twelve ships from the Black Sea sailed into the Sicilian port of Messina with an unknown and terrifying cargo: the Black Plague. Most of the crew of each ship were dead; the rest were dying, covered in seeping, bloody boils. Around twenty-five million were killed during the next five years as the plague raged through Europe, the Middle East and Asia, leaving widespread poverty and infertility in its wake. Pernicious rumours began to be disseminated, insinuating that the deadly outbreak was caused by Jews contaminating the water supply to 'punish' Christians. As retribution, thousands of Jews were tortured and burnt to death.

One scapegoat was not enough for the clergymen who claimed to have a unique insight into God's will. They insisted that witches were to blame: acting in their capacity as agents of the devil, witches had sought to bring fresh hell upon mankind by unleashing the plague. The theory gained traction and was soon harnessed to other calamities. In August 1428, a series of witch trials began in the mountainous Swiss canton of Valais. Many of the accused were male peasants who confessed under torture to multiple meetings with the devil, who had promised them the power of flight. Further brutalisation led some to claim that they were werewolves. Admissions of murder soon followed, with almost four hundred suspects executed over an eight-year period.

Some were beheaded; others had bags of gunpowder tied to their necks before being cast into a blazing pyre.

In 1484 – six years after the Roman Catholic Church established the Spanish Inquisition – Pope Innocent VIII issued a new decree that all witches making pacts with the devil would henceforth be tried and punished as heretics. Among the men officially empowered to identify and punish these servants of Satan was one Heinrich Kramer of the Dominican Order.

Educated in the Alsace and renowned for his fire-and-brimstone sermons, in 1485 Kramer's inquisitorial commission arrived in the Austrian city of Innsbruck. Bishop Georg Golser allowed Kramer to search out witches but was soon appalled by his methods and condemned his pursuit of Helena Scheuberin, the outspoken wife of a wealthy townsman.

Helena had made no secret of her loathing for Kramer. She refused to attend his sermons except to disrupt them and encouraged others to follow her example. On one occasion she spat at Kramer in the street, hissing, 'Fie on you, you bad monk, may the falling evil take you!'[23] Kramer eventually succeeded in bringing Helena to trial but his questioning of her was so sexually fixated and rambling that the case was dismissed. The scandal saw Helena walk free from court and Golser taking great satisfaction in expelling Kramer from Innsbruck.

Returning home to Cologne, Kramer's thoughts were in turmoil. Disgraced and humiliated but not yet defeated, he sat down to write a treatise on witch-hunting that would ensure few of Helena's kind escaped justice as he saw it. He warned that women in general were easy prey for the devil due to their physical, emotional and mental inferiority, while their lustful nature compelled them to surrender their souls quickly to Satan in the pursuit of sexual pleasure. Witches were suffused with wicked ambition: killing infants, preventing conception, inflicting physical harm, destroying harvests and raising storms.

In Kramer's view, demons were also omnipresent, taking the form of *succubi* to seduce sleeping male witches, and then as *incubi*, using purloined semen to impregnate female witches; these nefarious activities increased the ranks of the Satanic army. Nevertheless, female sexuality was problematic: in both spinsters and married women, 'the mouth of the womb' was never fully satiated; mortal man was inadequate and carnal cravings could only be relieved by virulent demons.[24] Midwives, too, had furtive motives, delivering babies safely in order to kill them. The limbs of an unbaptised infant were an essential element in the creation of a flying unguent, which when slaked on a broomstick or chair then mounted by the witch, would ensure that she was 'immediately carried up into the air, either by day or by night and either visibly or, if they wish, invisibly'.[25]

In one particularly notorious passage Kramer described how witches were partial to thieving great numbers of penises to hoard in a box or bird's nest, 'where they move themselves like living members, and eat oats and other feed'.[26] He cited a 'case' in which 'a man reported that he had lost his member and approached a certain witch in order to restore his health. She told the sick man to climb a particular tree where there was a nest containing many members and allowed him to take one he liked. When he tried to take a big one, the witch said you may not take that one, adding, because it belonged to a parish priest.'[27]

The passage is often misinterpreted as an example of Kramer's untrammelled misogyny. In reality, although his pathological loathing for women is undeniable, he attempted to show that such acts were illusory works of the devil, writing: 'It must in no way be believed that such members are really torn right away from the body . . . they are hidden by the devil through some prestidigitatory art so that they can be neither seen nor felt.'[28] By stating that the biggest penis belonged to the parish priest, Kramer hoped to demonstrate with a little humour how people might be fooled by their own eyes.

Central to Kramer's entire argument was a prevailing notion that it was heretical to doubt the existence of witches when the Bible had insisted that they should be executed. Pre-empting the conundrum of why witches were not able to overrule all attempts to apprehend them given that they were invested with diabolic powers, Kramer outlined how those men who sought, prosecuted and administered justice against witches were protected by the highest authority of all: God himself. Kramer nonetheless advocated self-protective measures of any kind. He further stated that because witches were wily and sorcery was difficult to detect, the use of torture was not merely permitted, but advised. Naturally, because witches were heretics by nature, they should expect the same fate: burning at the stake.

Kramer instinctively believed that his doctrine would meet with the approbation of the pope, but the Inquisition condemned the book. Nonetheless, when the *Malleus Maleficarum* was first published in Germany in 1486, Kramer reproduced the papal bull of two years earlier as a frontispiece to imply approval. He also added a second inquisitor, theologian Jacob Sprenger, as his co-author. Sprenger's role, if any, in the production of the *Malleus* remains in dispute, but he appears to have been vehemently opposed to Kramer's activities.

The invention of the Gutenberg printing press helped the *Malleus* find a substantial readership from 1500 onwards. Extensively circulated across Europe in its original Latin, Kramer's work ran into fourteen editions between 1487 and 1520. Yet while the *Malleus* was undoubtedly influential, it was also widely disparaged by inquisitors, critics and secular courts as 'ridiculously paranoid about male sexuality'.[29] There were no further reprints until 1580 and the book itself was 'slow to impinge upon England'.[30] Intellectuals obtained copies for their private libraries, as they habitually bought and read foreign books, but the absence of a German or English translation until as late as the 1920s is significant. Nevertheless, there were sixteen reprints in Germany before 1700 and eleven in France; together with previous editions, Kramer's vision of the witch as the devil's earthly representative was certain to find a wide audience. And it was this correlation above all else that fanned the tinder of suspicion into a conflagration of savagery.

In 1534, less than fifty years since the *Malleus*'s first publication, a German translation of the entire Latin Vulgate Bible and the Greek language version became a bestseller. The book was a collaborative effort headed by Protestant Reformer Martin Luther, whose criticism of the Roman Catholic Church created the foundations for Protestantism. In 1526, Luther had given a sermon in the German town of Wittenberg, declaring: 'It's a very just law to have the sorceresses killed because they do a lot of damage . . . If you see such women, they have evil forms. I have seen some. That's why they should be killed.'[31]

Luther's words heralded one of the many revisions he made to the Bible; the male noun 'maleficos' became the female 'maleficas' at Exodus 22:18, 'Thou shalt not suffer . . .' The altering of a single word would have catastrophic implications, with theologians confirming that it led directly to the 'concentrated attack on female witchcraft over the next 150 years'.[32]

In England, the legal framework regarding the prosecution of witches was rickety from the beginning. Prior to 1500, anyone practising maleficent magic would likely receive a minor punishment. But by the late fifteenth century, witches had come to personify evil; witchcraft now stood revealed as 'the greatest crime of all', and its practitioners were enemies of God and a threat to the entire fabric of society.[33]

Henry VIII passed the first law defining witchcraft as a serious crime in England. The 1542 Act Against Conjurations, Witchcraft, Sorcery and Enchantments covered everything from treasure-hunting to maleficium, all of which warranted the death penalty. The Act remained law for five years before being repealed by Henry's son, Edward VI.

In 1558, the daughter of Henry VIII and Anne Boleyn became queen. Elizabeth I, a Protestant, succeeded her half-sister Mary – known as Bloody Mary due to her aggressive attempts to convert the whole of England to Catholicism. Among those Protestants returning to England after fleeing under Mary's rule was John Jewel, who began regaling the new queen with tales of witchcraft in England. In 1562, the Act Against Conjurations, Enchantments and Witchcrafts was passed, imposing the death penalty on anyone found guilty of using, practising or exercising any form of witchcraft, enchantment, charm or sorcery that resulted in the loss of life. However, distinctions were made between lesser and capital offences, with a year's imprisonment and a stint in the pillory for a first or minor offence. The Act took witch trials away from the church and into regular courts.

In Scotland, the Witchcraft Act of 1563 declared both the practice of witchcraft and consulting with witches to be capital offences, punishable by death. The Irish Witchcraft Act of 1586 was almost identical to the one passed by Queen Elizabeth in 1562. The first legal case of witchcraft in Ireland dates back to 1324, when Alice Kyteler of County Kilkenny was accused by her stepchildren of using witchcraft to kill four husbands. The local bishop supported the allegations, which were classed as crimes of heresy due to an absence of witchcraft legislation. Seven charges, including consorting with demons, were eventually brought against Alice and others, but she was able to escape the country with the help of some well-placed friends. While Alice died in obscurity, her maidservant, Petronella de Meath, became the first person in Ireland flogged and burnt at the stake for heresy.

Despite the notoriety of a handful of cases, Ireland – like Wales and the Scottish Highlands – experienced few witch trials in comparison with other regions. Long-established beliefs in other forms of the supernatural may be a factor; misfortunes in more remote areas were often attributed to fairies – larger, bolder and considerably more spiteful than the sweet, ethereal beings of children's literature. Otherwise, although Scotland was sparsely populated in comparison to England, the proportion of witch trials was considerably higher. Continental legislation was enforced, leading to the trials of around 4,000 people; approximately 67 per cent were executed by strangulation or suffocation before being burnt at the stake.

Hanging remained the preferred method of execution in England, where witch trials were 'essentially local and erratic'.[34] Prosecutions amounted to no more than 5 per cent of all surviving English assize indictments between 1558 and 1680. The first major trial was staged in Chelmsford: three women from Hatfield Peverel were charged with witchcraft before the attorney general. Agnes Waterhouse, sixty-three, pleaded guilty to save her daughter Joan from execution, but the testimony of a twelve-year-old girl saw Agnes hanged on 29 July 1566, along with other felons at the Midsummer Assizes. The Chelmsford trial became the subject of a popular pamphlet; precedent plays an important role in English justice.

Historian James Sharpe describes England as a place 'where witchcraft was an endemic rather than an epidemic problem, where witch trials were sporadic and few, where accusations were usually levelled against individuals or groups of three or four suspects, and where the acquittal rate was high'.[35] Nevertheless, the idea that witches and demons roamed the earthly realm preoccupied many leading thinkers. In 1580, another immediate bestseller appeared: *De la démonomanie des sorciers* ('On the Demon Mania of Witches'). Author Jean Bodin, a French professor of law, public prosecutor and royal adviser, essentially elaborated on theories put forward by Kramer in the *Malleus Maleficarum*. Bodin's witches were never at rest, continuing their traditions of sexual intercourse with the devil, raising storms, spoiling crops, meeting by night in great assemblies and murdering newborns.

Four years later, an opposing voice made itself heard. Kent MP Reginald Scot's *The Discoverie of Witchcraft* largely panned the views of Continental demonologists. But sceptics were outnumbered for the time being; by 1600, there were at least forty-five popular texts on demonology in print across Western Europe, with a ready audience in university professors, churchmen, nobles, kings and queens. The availability and quantity of Continental works resulted in such views having been at least potentially 'more important to educated English witchcraft belief' than homegrown demonology.[36]

One English language book on the subject defied this generalisation, proving not only influential but also 'among the most widely cited witchcraft treatises published in England. No doubt the status of its author has much to do with this.'[37] The book was *Daemonologie*, and its author was King James VI of Scotland who, within a year of publication, had been crowned King James I of England.

Born in 1566 to Mary, Queen of Scots and Lord Darnley, James was only eight months old when his father was murdered. He had scarcely celebrated his first birthday when he became king: his mother had remarried and was forced to renounce the throne; she fled to England, where she was executed in 1587. Orphaned as an infant, James was raised as a Protestant at Stirling Castle. He grew up to be complex, erudite, sensitive and vain, bisexual but eager to create a traditional family life. At the age of twenty-three, he was betrothed to Anna of Denmark, who was then fourteen.

After a proxy marriage in Copenhagen in 1589, Anna set sail for Scotland, but her fleet was embattled in raging seas and winds, necessitating a diversion to Norway. With Anna delayed in Oslo, James set out to collect his bride. As they prepared to return to Scotland, treacherous storms blew up again, delaying embarkation and plaguing the crossing. The couple and the royal fleet arrived safely, but rumours soon arose that witchcraft in the homelands of both parties had created the life-threatening storms.

Consequently, several people connected to the Danish court were arrested on suspicion of collaborating with demons to wreck the vessels. Ane Koldings confessed under torture that it was true; she and twelve others were executed.

The first whispers of witchcraft in Scotland were attached to a servant girl named Geillis Duncan, whose employer had grown suspicious of her. Like Ane, Geillis was tortured into submission, implicating several people, including a senior woman named Agnes Sampson. King James demanded that Agnes be brought to him at Holyroodhouse; despite the overwhelming strangeness of the situation, and her own gnawing fear, Agnes steadfastly refused to answer questions. Dismissed from the king's presence, she was then subjected to extreme sleep deprivation and various methods of torture: her head was shaven and clamped into the Scold's Bridle, an iron instrument bolted to the wall of her cell. The head cage was furnished with four sharp prongs that inserted into the mouth, two against her tongue and the others inside her cheeks. Agnes endured unimaginable pain until she broke down and began telling her interrogators stories of visiting the haunted church of North Berwick. She and other witches had gone there to meet the devil; they had all kissed his buttocks and vowed to kill the king, then danced down the aisle while the devil looked on triumphantly from the pulpit.

Her story was too far-fetched even for King James. He declared that Agnes and her fellow suspects were 'extreme liars' until she was apparently able to tell him, word for word, what had passed between him and his child bride on their wedding night.[38] Whatever the truth of that part of the tale, at least seventy people are believed to have been charged in Scotland's first major witch trial. Geillis and Agnes were convicted, strangled and burnt; schoolmaster Dr John Fian underwent severe torture before suffering the same fate, while the Earl of Bothwell – whose uncle had been the chief suspect for the murder of King James's father – was banished from Scotland and died penniless in 1612.

The 1591 pamphlet *Newes from Scotland, Declaring the Damnable Life and Death of Doctor Fian*, remains one of the most well-known chapbooks. In 1597, it was added as a final chapter to *Daemonologie*, penned by the king himself. Written in the form of a theological dialogue between two characters, the book outlines James's belief in Continental ideas of demonology while examining aspects of magic and different forms of sorcery and witchcraft. The royal author also provided his readers with a list of demons and spectres, alongside their individual characteristics. The fact that their king had written such a book impressed upon many the idea of witchcraft as a real and immediate threat of Satanic heresy. *Daemonologie* sold better than any other volume on the subject in England and Scotland, and was subsequently translated into Latin, Dutch and French.

Six years after *Daemonologie*'s publication, James's aunt, Queen Elizabeth I, died without issue. Years before, he had responded with extreme caution in the form of a single protest, when Elizabeth had signed his mother's death warrant; he already had one eye on the greater prize. Shortly after being given the news that his aunt was dead, James left Scotland with his family and entourage to set up a new court in London. Finally enthroned as King James VI of Scotland and James I of England, he hoped to unite his two kingdoms and protect his people from the greatest threats to their safety: papists and witches.

To that end, James sanctioned the reissue of *Daemonologie* in 1603 to mark his second coronation and endorse the witch-hunts taking place throughout the land. James, in common with other heads of Europe, regarded magic as a dark correlation between humanity and the supernatural realm of evil. Those agents of the devil who practised witchcraft had been invested with its heinous power and were so corrupted by it that no crime was beyond them. He did not question why an omnipotent God could allow such evil to flourish, for he knew there was but a simple answer: God allowed the devil to exist in order to tempt the weak and punish the wicked.

And there was reason enough for England's four million inhabitants to fear a period known as the Little Ice Age. In 1607, the first Frost Fair was held on the frozen River Thames; the ice was so thick that people lit fires on its bluish surface. The cost of food kept rising, leaving families struggling to afford bread while wheat rotted in the fields because of the weather. The harvests of 1593, 1594, 1596 and 1597 were desperate failures. France, the Netherlands and the Holy Roman Empire were relentlessly stricken by plague, deadly influenza and religious warfare.

Unsurprisingly, the majority of England's witchcraft executions occurred during the second half of the sixteenth century and the first three-quarters of the seventeenth.[39] It seemed to those who took a particular interest that the numbers of witches had begun to multiply unstoppably during the last few years of the sixteenth century.

'The land is full of witches,' declared Lord Chief Justice Anderson in 1602, adding grimly, 'they abound in all places.'[40]

Part II:

SICKLE, HORSESHOE AND HOLLOW FLINT

'. . . In puppets' wax, sharp needles' points,
We stick, to torture limbs and joints . . .
We'll sell you winds, and ev'ry charm
Or venomous drug that may do harm;
For beasts or fowls we have our spells
Laid up in store in our dark cells
For there the devils used to meet
And dance with horns and cloven feet . . .
We grasp the moon and scale the sun
And stop the planets as they run . . .'
The Lancashire Witches from *Lancashire Folk Lore*,
Harland and Wilkinson, 1867.

Chapter One

FIREBRAND
or
ELIZABETH SOUTHERNS

Hill, hill, hill: if you refer to Pendle Hill, you're using 'hill' three times. Once from its original British name of 'penno' – a prominent, steep-ended hill; secondly, the Saxon suffix 'hill', which gives us 'Pennehill'; and a final 'hill' added simply for clarity, or so it seems.

The hill is what remains of a great plateau of sedimentary rock – seven miles long and shrouded in a deep blanket of peat, its distinctive whaleback shape forged from millstone grit overlying a series of ancient limestone beds. At 1,827ft high, it falls just short of the 2,000ft that makes a mountain. Even so, some believe it inspired Tolkein's Lonely Mountain, towering 'grim and tall' in *The Hobbit* and *The Lord of the Rings*, some of which was written when Tolkein stayed in the area during the Second World War. During the eighteenth century, *Robinson Crusoe* author Daniel Defoe travelled through Lancashire and was struck by how 'monstrous high' the hill appeared, in possession of 'a kind of an unhospitable terror . . . all barren and wild'.[41] In contrast, preacher George Fox felt irresistibly drawn to the hill when visiting the area in 1652 and was 'moved of the Lord to go up to the top of it'.[42] His vision at the summit inspired the Quaker religion, while his more practical legacy is refreshment for hikers at Fox's Well –

a trapdoor in the hillside has a tankard chained to the lid, for dipping into the water below.

Nine years after Fox's spiritual epiphany, mathematician and astronomer Richard Towneley visited the hill with his friend and family physician, Henry Power. Using a home-made barometer, the two men conducted experiments and discovered that atmospheric pressure decreases with altitude. Towneley's fellow science buff, Robert Boyle, reported their breakthrough and, as a result, is often credited with its detection.

The hill is rarely alone – there are always those who want to climb it, regardless of the weather. And when the air is clear and pin-sharp, the views from the summit are reward enough for the long climb. In summer, the fields are a tide of purple heather moving on the whim of a warm breeze, white cotton grass bobbing among the ling. On dark winter days, snowfall is common, ribboning the drystone walls as lights burn in the villages below. A cloudless moon turns the reservoirs into unsettling black ovals, and casts sharp shadows from the holly and hawthorns planted by farmers to protect against witches. Animals and birds remain throughout the seasons: sheep dotted like paint blots about the fields, tail-twitching cattle standing idle in the meadows, quicksilver hares loping down lanes, and kestrels and curlews wheeling gracefully overhead.

Locals regard the hill as a reliable weather gauge. One adage advises: 'When Pendle doth wear a woolly cap, the farmers may all take a nap; when Pendle Hill doth wear the hood, be sure the day will not be good.' Another: 'If you can see Pendle, it's going to rain; it you can't see Pendle, it's raining.' But when there is no rain, or cloud, or mist, beyond the wild beauty of the moors lie the Lakeland Fells, Welsh hills and Irish Sea. Even Blackpool Tower can be glimpsed on occasion, but the assertion that York Minster is visible from the summit belongs firmly to a Victorian writer's imagination.

The top of the hill is known as the Beacon, in recognition of bonfires lit there throughout history. From the thirteenth century until the time of the witches, conflagrations on the hill warned inhabitants of the surrounding countryside that they were under threat from Scottish border raiders. A crowd of over one thousand gathered on the summit in summer 1887, after twenty horses dragged combustibles there for the lighting of a beacon in honour of Queen Victoria's Golden Jubilee. A similar celebration took place in June 2012 to mark Queen Elizabeth II's Diamond Jubilee, part of a 4,000-strong chain of beacons across the kingdom.

That the summit also served as a meeting place for covens was the suggestion of William Harrison Ainsworth in his 1848 Gothic bestseller, *The Lancashire Witches*. The Victorian novelist attributed the deep clefts on the sides of the hill to an irate wizard smashing a wooden staff against the ground, forcing water to burst forth in a deadly flood. In reality, the pressure of water within the hill has erupted in three violent 'brasts'. The 1669 brast created an unstoppable wall of black water that surged past trees to Worston, flooding the cottages in the tiny village. The last brast occurred in 1870, breaking forth on the Burnley side of the hill, in a mass of stone-filled, saturated peat that clattered into the mills with 'tremendous force'.[43] Smaller waterquakes have left shallower scars.

Across the southern end of the hill is a road colloquially known as the Nick o'Pendle, once the haunt of weary traders and packhorses. Apronfull Hill, with its large cairn of stones, lies near the snaking road. Its name relates to an incident when the devil lost his temper with the occupants of Clitheroe Castle: he leapt onto a large boulder (leaving two impressions on the stone, known as the Devil's Footprints), hurling the rocks he had collected in his apron, whose strings snapped, causing the rocks to tumble where they remain today. One rock found its target, however, and the hole in the castle keep can still be seen.

Yet for all its arcane presence, Pendle Hill is never mentioned in Potts's *Discoverie*. For much of his life, Thomas Potts lived and worked across the border in Yorkshire, around seventy miles from Pendle. With withering contempt, he referred to the place he had probably never visited as 'fit for people of such condition [as witches]'.[44] In a less churlish sense he was right, given that the setting is integral to the story, as much a part of it as any person. Events surrounding the 1612 trials can only truly be understood by exploring the landscape and the turmoil that enveloped it. For a time, the horrors visited on its people were such that it seemed as if the devil himself was guiding proceedings from the summit of the hill.

In his annotations to the 1845 reprint of *Discoverie*, editor James Crossley describes the two families at the heart of this story as the Montagues and Capulets of Pendle. It was an apt analogy, for although the love between the two lead families was not romantic in nature, its outcome was more violent and tragic than *Romeo and Juliet*. A true friendship of many years sustained two households through poverty, personal loss and poor health. But when it rotted, there followed bitter recriminations, antagonism, jealousy and a thickly twisted vine of rumour that grew, unstoppably.

The lives of the two matriarchs – Elizabeth Southerns and Anne Whittle – were remarkably similar, but in common with almost every individual we will meet in these pages, their ancestry is difficult to trace. A faultless line back through the generations is impossible: records are often incomplete or indecipherable, names are spelt in a multitude of ways (often in the same document or even on the same page), and details may have been carelessly transcribed. All we can do is bring together the best available evidence with the most likely scenario and combine the two as rationally as circumstances allow.

Beginning with Elizabeth Southerns, the Newchurch-in-Pendle parish registers provide reliable evidence from the 1590s onwards, which then enables us to work backwards into her past. We also have William Harrison Ainsworth's notes from his research for *The Lancashire Witches*, published in 1848; these are less dependable but useful, nonetheless. He spoke to many locals during his trips to Pendle. Among the tales he recorded was one declaring that Elizabeth Southerns was the daughter of an Elizabeth (Bess) Blackburn and that as a child she was sent away from home to live with 'two peasants in Barrowford'.[45]

Tendrils of truth emerge from the roots of local lore: the child who was fabled to grow into 'that wicked firebrand of mischief' was baptised Elizabeth Blackburn on 18 April 1541 at St Mary and All Saints Church in Whalley, a Domesday village some three-and-a-half miles south of Clitheroe. Her parentage remains somewhat obscure but there is a strong possibility that she was the daughter of George Blackburn and Elina Nuk, who had married at the same church three years earlier.[46] The couple had several children and were tenant farmers on the Braddyll estate at Billington, on the outskirts of Whalley. Among the principal tenants was their son William Blackburn, who married Jennet Singleton in 1568, and again it is highly probable that he was Elizabeth's brother; they were baptised within six years of each other, and their children would bear the same names, suggesting a strong familial link.[47]

Thus, the tale told to Harrison Ainsworth is a tangled version of reality. However, it is doubtful that Elizabeth Blackburn spent her childhood in Barrowford, given that all the important events in her life prior to reaching middle-age were associated with Whalley and, specifically, its picturesque church.[48] Her ancestors had worshipped at St Mary and All Saints, and Elizabeth had entered its doors as a baby in her mother's arms, then as a bride and, later, a young mother. She had attended the weekly services with her family after walking a mile from Billington, in the shadow of the Nab and the 'gray, embattled towers' of the nearby churches, before crossing the ancient bridge over the river Calder.[49]

It was then but a short walk to the thirteenth-century church, which remains little changed since Elizabeth's time, from its priest's door with an elaborate bronze knocker representing the head of Christ, to the intricately carved, caged pew that sparked a war of words between two land-owning families. Elizabeth knew of the furious dispute, in which the Shuttleworths of Gawthorpe objected to the overbearing structure, while the commissioning family spent years obsessing over its wrongful use. The man at the centre of the row is remembered among the names carved into the pew: magistrate Roger Nowell. Chillingly, he and Elizabeth attended the same church, worshipping the same God and observing the same religious rituals, until shadows gathered and whispers flew, and he stepped forward to lead the 1612 witchcraft investigations against her.

Elizabeth had been born into deeply troubled times. Henry VIII was king; his union with Katherine of Aragon had produced a daughter, Mary Tudor, but no male heir, and he was determined to marry his wife's handmaiden, Anne Boleyn. When the pope refused to annul the existing marriage, Henry overrode his objections, establishing the Church of England as a new religious authority: laws made it a treasonable offence to deny the validity of the king's second marriage and his position as the head of the Church.

Prior to the Reformation, Catholicism was the largest religion across England and Europe, but in 1536 Henry ordered the dismantling of its wealthiest and most powerful structures. Over the next four years, the Dissolution of the Monasteries resulted in the destruction of hundreds of England's monasteries, abbeys and priories. By seizing their treasure, properties and land, the king was able to resolve his financial worries and build great wealth, while those who had supported his break with Rome were able to purchase confiscated buildings and ground. The religious orders who lost their homes and livelihoods were offered money or pensioned off, but many refused to accept what was happening. Protest marches and armed uprisings melded together under the leadership of the Catholic gentry. Their ranks were increased by the less affluent, who feared life without the existing religious framework and its traditions of providing alms, shelter, medical assistance and labour for the poor and sick.

The Pilgrimage of Grace was the largest rebellion of Tudor times, encompassing 40,000 souls from Lincolnshire, Yorkshire and Lancashire who marched below a banner depicting the Five Wounds of Christ from the crucifixion in a protest filled with symbolism, prayers and ritual. Beacons were lit across the north, which was said to be 'one loud storm of bells and blaze of bonfires from the Trent to the Cheviot'.[50] Negotiations with the king brought the uprising to an end, but fresh outbreaks of revolt led to arrests and executions. Whalley Abbey, founded in 1296, had been ransacked and its abbot,

John Paslew, was executed in Lancaster with two fellow monks. There are different accounts of what became of his corpse: in one version his remains were brought back to Whalley and kept in a gibbet overlooking the abbey, while another holds that his body was hanged in chains on the abbey gates before being interred in the churchyard.[51] The last monks of Whalley were banished without pensions for their part in the Pilgrimage and could be seen wandering about the ruinous buildings 'like a few surviving bees about a suffocated hive'.[52]

Whalley Abbey remained in Crown ownership until the site and its properties were sold in 1553 to landowners John Braddyl and Richard Assheton. They and other prominent local families, including the Nowells and Towneleys, benefitted from the loss of the old abbey estates in no small way.

We know from parish registers that Elizabeth married a man named Thomas Ingham, and on 15 June 1563 there is an entry for a wedding at St Mary and All Saints for a couple bearing the right names.[53] Their daughter, also Elizabeth, was born a couple of years later and the same register records the baptism of an Elizabeth Ingham on 29 September 1566. By the mid-1570s, the family of three had left Whalley to settle ten miles east, in the Forest of Pendle, probably for economic reasons.

Wild boar, red deer and wolves roamed the wooded regions of the Forest, for it comprised around 25,000 acres of royal hunting ground and was home to punitive laws that made it a criminal offence to lop a holly or fell an oak, and 'more penal to kill a stag than to murder a man'.[54] Punishments were inflicted 'with no sparing hand' and the penalties for anyone caught poaching were castration or blinding.[55]

Cattle farms or 'vaccaries' within the Forest were leased to farmers for a nominal rent. Most inhabitants lived in thatched, timber-framed dwellings scattered about the five clearings known as 'booths'. When the laws changed and the Forest began abiding by the same rules as regular land, fixed rents were set and those who inherited land were subject to entry fines of a year's rent. Tenant farmers became copyholders, allowing them to farm on their own account.

The English agricultural landscape was undergoing sweeping change due to the rapid spread of enclosure.[56] Land that was 'waste' or for common use, where people could collect firewood, cut turf or let their livestock graze, was increasingly converted to private land. Some people reaped the benefits: those who could afford to do so acquired newly enclosed land on lifetime leases; new farms sprang up and landowners profited from subletting. Farms often remained within families for over a century: tenant lists show the same names again and again, including several of those involved in the 1612 trials – Bulcock, Robinson, Hargreaves, Moore and so on. But for many, enclosure proved catastrophic, with evictions and disputes over land rights that rumbled on for years. Those who had relied on common land for grazing and other uses were unable to access the newly fenced-off ground. They were lost, turned into vagabonds and beggars by a law that made agriculture a capitalist venture affecting every aspect of life, creating 'a major realignment of social priorities, norms and values'.[57] Revolts against the new social order were plentiful, with women taking part in protests that saw them tear up the fences around the old common land, but the only gain was in knowing that they had briefly demonstrated their fears and frustrations.

In Pendle, people lived close to the land, dependent on the turning seasons and the vagaries of the weather. Short, dark winter days were only sustainable by work completed earlier in the year, and for many, disaster might be little more than a downpour away: 'A spell of bad rain, or a drought, or the loss of the family's pig, or a rise in prices, could tip a household into debt or difficulty.'[58] The region relied on livestock, making it much less economically resilient than regions in the south of England, where the constant cultivation of arable land provided a more regular living. Other trades were essential to the local economy and provided a lifeline for those struggling to subsist, particularly quarrying, brewing and tanning, but cattle was the mainstay, along with cloth. Nearby mills flourished: Colne enjoyed strong trading relationships with Halifax, Heptonstall and other textile towns, while Burnley and Padiham produced linen and woollen cloth. Many homes in Pendle at this time contained handlooms and spinning wheels. As the cloth trade continued to prosper, wealthy families who had bought properties confiscated from the Church converted them for use in the industry. From the 1540s onwards, England's countryside seemed to be a surfeit of 'ruins, adapted ruins and sheep'.[59]

Land and property transactions help us place some of the families we meet repeatedly in this case: the Nutters were clustered around Roughlee, Newchurch-in-Pendle, Old and New Laund, and Sabden Fold; the Robinsons farmed mostly at Thorneyholme (Roughlee), Barley, Wheatley Lane and Old Laund; the Hartleys and Hargreaves were scattered; the Holgates farmed at Barley (Black Moss and Under Pendle); and those named Ingham can be found in Whalley, Colne, Read and Padiham. They worked as woollen merchants in Padiham and Burnley but were mainly occupied in farming land south of Higham (West Close, Hunterholme, Filly Close, Ightenhill). One of the area's many listed buildings from this period is Ingham's Farmhouse, in Reedley Hallows.

As to our own Inghams – Elizabeth and Thomas Ingham and their young daughter Elizabeth – there have been debates about the location of their home, Malkin Tower, ever since the reissue of *Discoverie* in 1845. The unearthing of a cottage near Barley in 2011 led to global media speculation that Malkin Tower had been found, while organised archaeological digs have failed to provide a definitive answer. The issue will be explored in a subsequent chapter, but this book takes the view that the lost building with its mythical status has been hidden in plain sight all along: Malkin Tower was built by Elizabeth and her husband on the outskirts of Newchurch-in-Pendle. It stood in the fields that now lie south of Well Head Road, in what used to be referred to as the 'Saddler's Farm triangle' because it encompasses farms of great importance to the story of the 1612 trials: Bull Hole, Moss End and Saddlers. Tynedale Farm and Lower Well Head are also within the triangle, and are often mentioned in relation to the trials, but with no clear indication why – other than location – they have any relevance.

That, too, will be considered in another chapter. Not far from Tynedale is another farm, Rigg of England, whose name tells the traveller much about the district, as a local author writing at the time of *Mist Over Pendle*'s release explains:

'Rigg' is an expressive word, full of high winds in exposed places. Rigg of England lives up to its name for the bare hill-top sweeps up and down to the Big End of Pendle deeply fissured and rough from this angle, with many square miles of country stretched below, fertile and sunlit, while up here it is a grim twilit world – witches' country. Climbing still further along the narrow-edged lane from Rigg there is Tinedale on the left. Cappers and Saddlers follow . . .[60]

Newchurch was then Goldshaw Booth, at the centre of Pendle Forest and its highest settlement, with homes 'cut into the living bed-rock of the hillside'.[61] Steep, twisting roads converged in the middle of the tiny village, but the inhabitants did not have to walk far for their water supply, with a number of wells and springs nearby. The main one ran from the precipitous fields on the Barley side; it then passed under the road and emerged on the other side of the churchyard before forging on to Spen Brook. Water collected in a stone trough that provided the villagers with their daily supply. Another well was set back into the stone wall at the village end of the narrow lane dropping down to Dimpenley Clough. It was – and is – said to be haunted by a lady whose spirit inhabited an old stone nearby at the summit. Occasionally she would emerge to drink at the well, but when a priest heard about her, he took a heavy object to the stone and smashed it in half. When the spirit lady next emerged, her head was gone; in breaking the stone, the priest had decapitated her. In some versions of the legend, the spirit is called Jinny, after whom the lane is named, but in others, she is Jennet.

In the thirteenth century, a chapel of ease stood on the land later occupied by the church of St Mary and All Saints. A second chapel was consecrated on the same spot in October 1544 by the Bishop of Chester; it was here that Elizabeth Southerns and her relatives worshipped. In those days, horse-drawn carriages would rumble up the lofty roads and families would traipse through the fields and footpaths to reach the services while bells rang out across the valley from church to chapel. Most clergymen remained only two or three years before being posted to another parish, but during Elizabeth's time, a local farmer's son named Thomas Varley served almost forty years, leaving in 1607. There is some confusion regarding whether Goldshaw Booth actually had its own clergyman during the period of the witchcraft investigation; John Town is listed as incumbent from 1610–11, but there appears to be no name on record then until 1620. Perhaps Town remained in his position nonetheless, or the church was served by a locum clergy; otherwise, we are left with a curious interlude where witchcraft was rumoured to be rife in a village whose church was devoid of spiritual leadership.

All that remains of the last chapel are the lower courses of the tower. Twice restored, that part of the building is said to house a stone – now hidden by the roof of the existing church – inscribed with the date 1544. Precisely when the village's most curious and commented-upon feature was added to the west side of the tower is a mystery, but the Eye of God is an enigma in itself. Viewed from the outside, it does resemble a cloudy eye, formed of blue slate set in sand and cement with two separate stone pieces shaped like an almond, finished with a rectangular drip stone. Inside the tower, however, its appearance is more mundane, as Newchurch's historian, Clifford H. Byrne, explains: 'The eye is actually a blocked-up window, below which the sexton once stood peering out to watch the now unused gate just to the side of the present churchyard gateway. This gate, wide enough to allow a cortège to enter, was the earlier entrance to the churchyard. On spotting the funeral procession, the sexton would inform the bell ringer below him, who would commence to toll the passing bell.'[62] Another local writer disputes this, musing that 'its low situation obscures a clear view over the hills. It is more likely a representation of the all-seeing eye of God, a protection against the dark forces which are known to have been active in the churchyard.'[63]

Precisely how Thomas and Elizabeth made their living has not come down to us, but in all probability they managed a smallholding or worked in the cloth industry. We do know that after relocating to Newchurch-in-Pendle, Elizabeth had a second child who was baptised Christopher. But his surname presents us with another puzzle, since he was born a Holgate, not an Ingham.

A number of explanations present themselves, with the most logical being that Thomas Ingham died before Christopher was born to Elizabeth and a man named Holgate.[64] Two Thomas Inghams appear in the burial registers of St Mary and All Saints in Whalley for the relevant period, raising the possibility that he was laid to rest in a family plot. The two entries are dated ten months apart, in February and December 1573. Neither is without problems if we try to make them fit our premise, but we know such documentation is inherently challenging and it may be that one of them is the 'right' Thomas Ingham, nonetheless. Elizabeth would then have been widowed in her early thirties and gave birth to her son Christopher after 1573.

The Newchurch-in-Pendle registers show that Christopher married in 1590, while the trial evidence further identifies him positively as uncle to his half-sister Elizabeth's children; her youngest daughter, Jennet, declared Christopher to be 'of Pendle' to distinguish him from another man of the same name living in Colne, who was also known to them. But who was Christopher's father?

Curiously, early twentieth-century writers on the case refer to Elizabeth as 'Widow Holgate', but there appears to be no records of her marrying a man of that name. It may simply be that she had a relationship that resulted in her son and named him after his father, as was common then among women with illegitimate children.[65] We know a Christopher Holgate lived in Colne and others sharing his surname lived and farmed in nearby Barley, one of whom is named as

Richard Holgate in various land transactions. One of these may have fathered Elizabeth's son.[66]

This leaves us pondering one other mystery regarding Elizabeth and names associated with her: why does Potts repeatedly refer to her by the surname Southerns, or variations of it, in *Discoverie*? Southerns was an uncommon surname in Pendle yet found more frequently in the district of Whalley among the lower gentry. We also have to bear in mind that clerks of this period wrote phonetically in Latin or English, thereby muddling the appearance of names. This was also true of magistrates taking statements, who were often unable to understand the local dialect of the impoverished; one such example is Roger Nowell's detailing of Isobell Holgate (Christopher's wife) as 'Elizabeth Howgate'. None of which resolves the mystery of 'Elizabeth Southerns'. Local historian John Clayton suggests that it may be more colloquial – perhaps even a variation of 'Sathan' (meaning 'evil'), bestowed upon Elizabeth either by locals or Nowell in his preparing the case for court.[67] What we can be sure of is that by the 1580s, Elizabeth was widowed and living as a single woman in Pendle with her two children, Elizabeth and Christopher. And that left her extremely vulnerable.

In mid-seventeenth-century England, the general life expectancy among men was between thirty-two and forty years. One author remarked in 1635 that more people died *before* thirty-five than past it, and those who survived frequently suffered a chronic illness or untreatable affliction.[68] The greatest threats to a woman's longevity were pregnancy and childbirth, otherwise she might expect to reach sixty or above. Nonetheless, the advanced ages of Elizabeth Southerns and Anne Whittle in 1612 often provoke comment, not least from Thomas Potts, who viewed both women as 'decrepit'. Despite his callousness, the two women may well have looked older than their years, given the harsh lives they had endured and their circumstances. However, Potts was very aware that by emphasising the women's ages, he was also inferring guilt: 'The wrinkles of an old wife's face is good evidence to a jury against a witch. And how often will the common people say, "Her eyes are sunk in her head, God bless us from her."'

This was a notoriously merciless era for women. Until she became a wife, virtually all the decisions of a woman's life would be made by her closest male relative. Twenty-six was the average age for a woman to marry, and once she was betrothed, her husband would assume legal control of any money and possessions. Pre-nuptial agreements were very rare, and a woman could expect to have very few individual, financial or property rights. The wealthy widow was the exception to this rule, and if she had riches before her betrothal these would revert to her, together with a dower (a share of her deceased husband's money and property) for spousal and child support. But if she remarried – as many did, given that men had a tendency to die first – then everything passed to her new husband.

For impoverished women like Elizabeth Southerns and Anne Whittle, the situation was incredibly bleak. Prior to the Reformation, and under the old Charter of the Forest, a widow was entitled to a portion of her husband's land, either to cultivate it herself or to let it be done by a younger family member who would safeguard her livelihood. But those days and guarantees were gone: 'For all the era's professed charity and alms, the poor were constantly being demonised and legislated against.'[69] Under escalating new laws, beggars had to be licensed or face being whipped for a first offence, maimed for a second (usually losing an ear) and hanged in the third instance. Other forms of identifying vagrants included branding and badges. In 1563, the Relief of the Poor Act made it compulsory for every household earning above a certain income to contribute to a fund for the poor. Yet until the turn of the century, vagrants were still subjected to a range of punishments, such as being burnt through the ear or compulsory labour in houses of correction.

In 1601 the Act was updated, and would serve as the foundation of the English Poor Law Administration for the next two hundred years. Vagabonds remained largely in the same legal position as before, but there was a new category of the 'deserving poor' for whom individual parishes were required to provide financial assistance, work and apprenticeships. Their numbers were swelled by destitute families arriving in towns and villages in search of work, leading to an onslaught of anger from those paying poor relief tax, and the needy who feared being ousted by the newcomers.

Potts informs us that Elizabeth Southerns was a habitual beggar, presumably without a licence, who would walk many miles in search of alms. Her poverty, age and widowhood would have made her liable to accusations of witchcraft. In his study of witchcraft in Essex, Alan Macfarlane notes that any or all of these aspects were solidly contributing factors, and that age brought with it the notion of an intrinsic 'mystical power which could be used for good or evil. Just as suspected witches seem to have been old, so they were almost always "wives and widows" rather than unmarried women.'[70]

In Elizabeth's case, there was a further element that caused the dust of suspicion to swirl, eddying at first before being swept up into a funnel that whirled from one village to the next, gathering more substance as it spun: she was a cunning woman.

'Shadow clergy' is how one historian refers to cunning folk, and with good reason.[71] Following years of plague and famine, economic upheaval and societal discontent, the Church was no longer seen to be fulfilling the needs of its people, who were told that such disasters were God's punishments for their sins. The Church itself had been torn apart by the Reformation and new legislation, leaving it unable to provide alms and welfare as it had always done, at a time when people were more in need than ever before.

Cunning folk had long been part of community life and they were many: anthropologist Alan Macfarlane calculates that no one in Elizabethan Essex lived more than ten miles from a known cunning person, while historian Owen Davies estimates there were about 200,000 cunning folk plying their trade in England around the time of the witch trials. Ecclesiastical courts occasionally referred to cunning men as 'wizards', and they were known as healers, white witches, wise men and wise women, but mainly as cunning folk. For the most part, they were ordinary villagers, if occasionally prickly and temperamental, but their skills were regarded as otherworldly.

For a little pecuniary aid, they offered practical assistance, support and guidance. Fees 'related to the type of activity undertaken and the degree of success. Some cunning folk refused payment.'[72] Most were readily available and performed tasks that were otherwise scarce and expensive, especially in areas like Pendle, where communities valued them too highly to support any attempts at prosecution. There were instances of cunning folk being held to account in ecclesiastical courts, but unless something else was at play, or they were suspected of defrauding clients, harsh sentences were rarely issued. Where punishments were given, these were generally a penance of some kind, which involved making a humiliating public apology but no worse.

Nonetheless, the Church and puritanical members of society viewed cunning folk as practising a form of witchcraft, albeit 'white' magic; in their eyes, all magic emanated from the devil and this 'lesser' magic was actually worse. Theologian William Perkins declared that the so-called 'good' witch was 'the most horrible and detestable monster' who 'struck a mortal blow' to a person's soul.[73] It would be, he opined, 'a thousand times better for the land if all witches, but specifically the blessing witch, might suffer death'.[74] His words were echoed by other writers, including John Brinley in *A Discovery of the Impostures of Witches and Astrologers* who warned that 'ignorant and narrow-sould' people consulted cunning folk who 'do evil that good may come of it, that is use charms, spells and incantations . . .'[75]

Their revulsion was all the greater in the knowledge that some of the methods employed by cunning folk seemed to mimic those of the Church. Additionally, those who sought such people often saw little difference between the vicar standing on the edge of a field to pray that the newly sown crop might grow well, and the charms provided by the local cunning man or woman. The latter was often less intimidating too, and less likely to admonish the person consulting them or to regard their problem as trifling; many requests for help concerned small or intensely personal matters. Magic 'responded to the needs of the individual just as it worked through the individual's intent. It recognised the importance of small things in people's lives, to help a person achieve what mattered to them. Magic declared and demonstrated the importance of the individual.'[76] It also caused significant consternation among the clergy, who viewed it as a direct challenge to God's authority, as did the liberal mixing of herbs, charms and religious terminology.

Lost property and love affairs, ale that had gone bad and animals with distemper – all were problems for the local cunning person to resolve. Although most remained in their home village or town, some travelled to other areas in search of more success, setting up markets stalls to offer their services in exchange for food or money. Some also worked as fortune tellers, using astrology, cards and other forms of divination such as animal entrails, mirrors and crystal balls.

Unfortunately, a full understanding of their work is unfeasible, since most of it was conducted in secrecy and left no record. But some of it has survived in various accounts and forms. Attempting to locate something that had gone missing was easily one of the most common tasks for cunning folk. People had so little that to lose anything, particularly money, could be disastrous. There were no banks, leaving people to bury or hide their valuables, which they might require assistance with finding again. The 'sieve and shears' method was often employed for this undertaking: a sieve would be balanced on a pair of shears, which would spin if the correct place was mentioned. A similar method involved a Bible, a key and a wedding ring on a piece of string for use as a pendulum. Both means were also used in trying to identify a thief.

Health was often a cause for consulting the local cunning person. Transference was one of the most common ways of getting rid of an illness and could also be employed for banishing other problems too. A 'get lost box' was a popular means of achieving one's aim: items of any description belonging to the sufferer were placed in a box, which was then left somewhere public; the first inquisitive person who picked up the box and opened it would then fall ill or take on the specific problem of the box's owner. With medical treatment still in its infancy and inaccessible for the majority of people, other cures were sought.

In Lancashire, a widespread remedy for whooping cough involved popping a live furry caterpillar in a pouch that was then attached to the client's neck; as the caterpillar wasted away, the cough diminished accordingly. Nine knots on a rope placed about the neck was another attempted cure, as was spitting in a frog's mouth. Moles' feet were also hung in a pouch about a person's neck, but to cure toothache or cramp. Scrofula was a throat infection that required a more gruesome method: the sufferer was told to attend an execution and request of the hangman a moment to stand by the gallows in such a way that the hand of the dead criminal could touch the person's throat.

A hand cut from an executed individual could be mummified for other purposes. If used to hold a candle made from a felon's fat, its powers included the ability to immobilise a person instantly. The 'Hand of Glory', as it was known, appears in many tales of folklore. Similarly, a candle composed of human tallow, lodged in the crook of a hazel branch and set alight, was said to extinguish itself when near treasure. A noose was thought to cure toothache or consumption when placed around a patient's neck while mandrake roots were given as good luck charms due to their habit of growing below gallows, where dripping waste was believed to be responsible for their distinctive human form. Ropes, too, were often used in knot magic, but these tended to be ordinary lengths of rope, rather than those used to end a felon's life.

Preventative magic was widespread in an age where disease was too often untreatable in humans and livestock. Iron was believed to have protective powers; thus, many homes and farm buildings bore horseshoes nailed above door lintels, or an old key hung with hagstones to represent heaven's door key. Written charms were another means of protecting a home and its inhabitants. Talismans inscribed with words or symbols are often associated with love magic, but they were just as likely to be employed as a defence against fire and theft, or to rid a building of mice, fleas and other infestations. During renovations at a house in the Pendle hamlet of Coldweather, a piece of vellum was discovered tucked between two panels of the front door. Secured with a red wax seal, it unfolded to reveal a charm featuring a 'magic square',

Greek letters and ciphers. Thought to be around two hundred years old, its presence shows that anti-witchcraft charms were still in use around Pendle even in the nineteenth century.

Recent discoveries of long-dead, shrivelled cats bricked into walls or shoes laid under floorboards often likewise attest to the strong belief in preventative magic (occasionally, however, these are poor animals who simply got trapped, and shoes that were lost). The same can be said of other written charms tucked inside stone cavities and symbolic carvings on or near fireplaces, where witches were thought to enter a home. It is also worth noting that while the frequent use of animals or animal parts in magic seems to indicate that their lives were thoughtlessly expendable, in fact the opposite was true. Cunning folk held all creatures in high regard and believed the natural world overflowed with magic and an unseen, unassailable force entirely of its own creation.

For those who believed themselves already bewitched, counter-magic was often regarded as their best option. This usually necessitated taking a strand of hair, a nail or some piece of clothing from the offending witch and then setting it alight. The belief lingered into Victorian Lancashire, with the saying, 'draw blood of a witch and she cannot harm you', accompanied by scratching the witch to break the spell. Suspicion fell on cunning folk when they failed to achieve their brief. For instance, if he or she failed to halt the spread of disease among cattle, that left them open to accusations of fraud or deliberately bungling the task.

Sometimes, cunning folk were called upon to curse an individual or cattle. This was usually a temporary measure designed to prevent matters escalating, and to cause minor difficulties rather than permanent harm. Such curses were meant to be reversible, to allow the targeted person to show sufficient remorse or to have suffered enough. Infidelity was often the root of such curses; wives who suspected their husbands of having been unfaithful would request a spell of impotence. The placebo effect could be witnessed in many of these cases, since it was often enough for a man simply to believe he had been cursed with lasting impotence for it to have the desired result. This demonstrates, too, how magic in all its forms depended upon the active party's intention and the personality of their target, who was probably already weakened due to poverty, malnutrition and exhaustion. On the other hand, a sick person might recover swiftly after being told they had been treated with healing magic. We know now that the mind can instigate profound physical effects on the body and that the immune system can break down under psychological stress.

As far as the Pendle accused were concerned, only Elizabeth Southerns and Anne Whittle appear to have been consulted regularly as cunning folk, although James Device (Elizabeth's grandson) and Anne Redfearn (Anne's daughter) were also known to be part of the family business, as it were. Their elders passed on their cunning skills and charms, which they themselves referred to as 'prayers', teaching them purely by oral means, since none of them could read. Powers granted by a spirit was something quite different.

The two matriarchs clearly considered themselves to be adept cunning folk who were regarded as such by their neighbours. They were proud of their gifts and of being called upon as healers, even though in *Discoverie* all their methods fail and they were evidently unable to make a decent living from the cunning trade. Even just a hint of dwindling belief from a client was cause for concern, especially if the same client had come to realise that one woman was more naturally gifted than the other. That sort of remark sparked professional jealousy, anger and fear. For a cunning person was only as good as their last task. If the promised outcome failed again, their intentions might be called into question – and from there sprang rumours of inverted magic or witchcraft.

Chapter Two

THE HEART, ILL EYE, ILL TONGUE
or
ANNE WHITTLE

What might Elizabeth Southerns have told us truthfully of Anne Whittle, and vice versa, while the two of them remained close? Or even after their friendship curdled like milk? Thomas Potts gives us not so much a character sketch as a scribble, revealing little of Anne's personality or her background, providing only a derisive mention of 'a very old, withered, spent and decrepit creature, her sight almost gone . . . her lips ever chattering'.[77] He refers to her throughout as Anne Whittle or Chattox, but the scarcity of the Whittle surname in the region, coupled with fragments of information elsewhere, leads us to her beginnings.

She was born around 1532 to Christopher and Jeneta Whittle, tenant farmers in Newchurch-in-Pendle. Documents from 1562 refer to transactions between Anne's father and Edmund Stevenson, who had farmed land at East Delph, adjacent to Bull Hole Farm, in the village for several years. Bull Hole had been in the tenancy of the Nutter family since the turn of the sixteenth century. The papers confirm that Christopher Whittle rented an area of land known as Red Moss and a further 'parcel of land in Goldshaw [*Newchurch*], probably part of the Bull Hole estate' from Stevenson.[78] The land was around two acres, 'sufficient for a fire to be spent and burnt on said parcel to the use of Christopher Whittles and his assigns for 29 years at £0.7s.4d per year'.[79] This gave the family the right to dig peat for their own use, providing they kept only one fire per dwelling. The agreement strongly suggests that the Whittles lived on land just below the village, between Bull Hole Farm and Moss End, from 1562 until the end of the lease in 1591.

At the age of twenty, Anne married Ellis Brown, head of a farming family in nearby Barley. They had at least three children: Jennet was born in 1555, Anne in 1558, and finally Elizabeth (Bessie), born around 1565.[80] Potts refers to Anne and her daughter Bessie using the surname Whittle; to her daughter Anne by her later married name (Redfearn) and to Jennet not at all. To avoid confusion, we will do the same. Where the family lived is uncertain, but it was most likely either in Barley or Newchurch. Given the events about to follow, the latter seems most likely.

Two years after his granddaughter Bessie's birth, Christopher Whittle was hauled into court with James Moore of Higham, both charged with causing an affray. The Moores reappear in the lives of the Whittles over forty years later, when Anne would be charged with having bewitched the family. It may be that the accusation had its roots in this or another much earlier disagreement, given that the 1567 court case avows that the two men had been brawling. No further information is imparted, other than that they were each fined 20d for being disruptive, but Christopher Whittle died later that same year, and one obvious inference is that he had been seriously injured in the fight.

Anne lost the second of the two most important male figures in her life when her husband of fifteen years also passed away in 1567. Now a widow in her mid-thirties, she had three daughters aged twelve, nine and two, depending on her. Given that both she and her mother were widowed in the same year, it may be that Anne and her daughters moved in with her mother at or near the Whittle homestead in Newchurch

– or she may have lived there all along, even after her marriage. If that supposition is correct, then we might also have an explanation for the origin of her friendship with a woman not quite ten years her junior: Elizabeth Southerns.

The lives of these two 'notorious witches' now converge. We know that the Whittle home lay somewhere between Bull Hole Farm and Moss End; under the terms of their lease, it would remain in their hands until 1591. In the mid-1570s or thereabouts, Elizabeth arrived with her husband and young daughter to settle within close walking distance of the Whittles and built Malkin Tower. And so a friendship that would end in unimaginable horror began in a very ordinary, mundane manner: the two women were almost certainly neighbours. What drew them together may well have been what would eventually tear them apart: magic.

Their friendship suggests that Elizabeth's arrival on Anne's 'patch' pre-dated the former's activities as a cunning woman, or perhaps the other way around. It seems unlikely but not impossible that one woman imparted her knowledge to the other, but more doubtful that they shared a 'patch' or worked together. Particularly since Elizabeth was also soon widowed, and became even more impoverished than Anne.

They had much in common, and more so as time went on. Being widowed rendered them – and their families – vulnerable to predatory, avaricious men. *Discoverie* unwittingly reveals that Elizabeth and Anne fought such men courageously, mostly due to being fiercely protective mothers. Loving, strong-willed and far from easily intimidated, they were quick to deliver threats, curses and reproachful looks. Deliberately fostering reputations as witches safeguarded them to some extent, but in the end it proved their undoing.

Both women battled equally to keep their families afloat, taking any work available. Certainly their cunning skills, whether perceived or genuine, were something of a lifeline. They both worked within roughly the same area, walking from one farm to another, primarily to heal livestock. At some point, surely, this would have been unsustainable for the two of them, particularly since Elizabeth had the stronger reputation. Once they were in direct competition with each other, the animosity may have begun.

In 1576, Anne Whittle's mother Jeneta died and was buried at Newchurch-in-Pendle.[81] The daughter Anne had named after her disappears from the story even before then, although there are tenuous links to her marrying and bearing a child. But there is no mention of Jennet in *Discoverie*.

Anne's second daughter married Thomas Redfearn in 1583 at the church in Newchurch-in-Pendle. Potts then consistently refers to her as Anne Redfearn, and tells us that the couple settled at West Close with their daughter Marie. Anne Whittle's 'witch name', Chattox, is often taken to be a reference to her 'ever chattering' lips, but in all probability it came from 'chattocks', an old word meaning waste wood or sticks, with bundles of ash or beech referred to as ash chats or beech chats.[82] Elizabeth Southerns' moniker, Demdike, is more uncertain. One local reporter mused in the 1930s that within the Saddlers triangle 'there is a stream that can be diverted and made to reach the sea via Barrowford instead of via Sabden. This stream can be demmed and diverted by a single sod and has caused trouble and lawsuits for over 300 years. There is another due this autumn to decide whether this dyke be a demmed dyke or not a "demdike".'[83] Apart from the old English word for a ditch, 'dyke' appears as a surname in Cumberland, derived from the two lines of Roman wall in Burgh. Despite claims to the contrary, it does not translate as 'demon woman'. However, the Greek goddess of justice was named Dike and, as a noun, the word refers to justice in a formal sense and fairness in common sense. But it is unlikely that neighbours and friends would have referred to Anne Whittle as 'Old Chattox' or to Elizabeth Southerns as 'Old Demdike'. The names may have been an inventive flourish added by Potts, given that within the pages of *Discoverie*, only he and the magistrates use those derivatives.[84]

The Whittle-Brown family history suggests that the youngest and most troublesome daughter, Bessie, also wed and that her husband was Thomas Elliot, but we get no sense of her being married from *Discoverie*, and only during the writing of this book has new information come to light that supports that possibility. At some point, Anne Whittle began living permanently with her daughter and son-in-law, the Redfearns, perhaps due to the lease concluding on the Whittle home in 1591.

Housing was a problem across Pendle at this time, due to a substantial increase in the population: from 100 inhabitants in 1527 to about 1,620 by 1650. This had its advantages, but not for the poor, who had no choice but to either rent or squat in cottages with hardly any land, regardless of an Act passed in 1589 which forbade the occupation of any cottage with less than four acres attached. By now, the old thatched and timber-framed dwellings were being replaced by houses built in stone with slate roofs.

High inflation from the late sixteenth century into the seventeenth piled yet more misery on families who were already struggling and those without land. They took in whatever work they could, either carding and spinning wool for local weavers, as Anne Whittle did, or labouring in the fields like James Device, son of Elizabeth Device and grandson to Elizabeth Southerns, who had no permanent job. As the need for land grew ever more keen, younger family members would create small farms on the margins of the land owned or rented by their parents but this proved unsustainable. Without even the smallest plot of land to feed themselves and their families, people struck out to find other work or ventured to other towns. Copyholders were able to exploit this desperation for land. In 1600–19, copyholders charged their sub-tenants twenty-five times the rent they themselves paid to the Duchy of Lancaster; during the 1620s and 1630s, this rose to nearly forty-three times as much. Matters were made even worse by the fact that the leases were often for a period of less than one year and a day and therefore had to be documented in the halmote rolls (Forest courts), with an entry fine of a year's rent payable to the Duchy. The situation was tolerated by the authorities as long as the money rolled in each month.

This is the tenuous existence in which Thomas and Anne Redfearn found themselves. They were sub-tenants of Robert Nutter of

Greenhead, who rented his land and property from the Shuttleworths of Gawthorpe, a family as wealthy as they were influential, with many properties and vast acreages in their portfolio. Nutter threatened the Redfearns with eviction on at least one extremely ugly occasion, no doubt leaving them feeling even more insecure than they were already. The Devices, the family that Elizabeth's daughter married into, also appear to have been living on a smallholding of some sort, though neither of the families dwelt in the hovels of popular perception. More than one commentator on the case has noted that Potts records how both families had lived in their homes for several years prior to 1612, suggesting either a secure tenancy or ownership, which we will return to in a later chapter, and that these dwellings may have been textile workers' cottages, or farm buildings, disused water mills or converted malt kilns.

Unwittingly, Potts does provide us with a sense of family cohesion among the group at West Close, and it is clear that Anne Whittle maintained a good relationship with her son-in-law, daughters and granddaughter. How the family supported themselves is unknown, but Anne was an adept wool carder and still worked as such from time to time. Carding was an arduous and time-consuming task, part of the process of preparing wool for sale. Raw wool was liberally greased with butter, then 'carded' until it was ready to be spun, usually by women, with the fastest capable of producing between forty and one hundred metres of cloth an hour. Five or more workers were needed to keep a weaver fully supplied with yarn, which was then woven in lengths on narrow looms at home. Carding was done using a pair of wooden paddles and best achieved by holding one paddle on the knee and drawing the other across it, pulling a quantity of greased wool between the two on hundreds of tiny wire hooks set into the paddle backs until the soft fibres lay symmetrical.

Apart from her work as a wool carder, Anne was primarily known as a cunning woman until the rumours began that she, like her close friend Elizabeth Southerns, was a witch.

*

In 1612, when Elizabeth Southerns and Anne Whittle were individually brought before magistrate Roger Nowell to answer charges of witchcraft, they each stated that spirit encounters had led them down that particular path. All testimonies were transcribed by either the magistrate or his assistant, hence the third person narrative. Elizabeth dated her beginnings as a witch to around 1592, stating that, 'As she was coming homeward from begging' she was met at 'a stonepit in Goldshaw' (Faugh's Quarry) by 'a spirit or devil in the shape of a boy, the one half of his coat black, and the other brown, who bade [her] stay, saying to her, that if she would give him her soul, she should have anything that she would request. Whereupon [she] demanded his name and the spirit answered, his name was Tibb. [She] in hope of such gain as was promised by the said devil or Tibb, was contented to give her soul to the said spirit.' This agreement seems to have been in name only, for Elizabeth then states that for the next five or six years, 'the said spirit or devil appeared at sundry times . . . about Daylight Gate [an ancient term for Dusk], always bidding her stay, and asking her what she would have or do'. Having apparently agreed to give him her soul, and despite her hand-to-mouth existence, Elizabeth said her reply was always: '"Nay nothing" . . . for she wanted nothing yet.'

After six years or so had passed, the pact with Tibb was formalised one Sunday morning, when Elizabeth was still half-asleep, dressed only in a smock and holding her youngest grandchild, Henry, on her lap. Tibb suddenly appeared 'in the likeness of a brown dog, forcing himself to her knee, to get blood under her left arm'. Tibb succeeded in drawing blood from her. Elizabeth was then fully awake, and feared for her grandson, calling out, 'Jesus save my child!' She found that she had 'no power' to call upon Jesus to save herself. 'Whereupon the brown dog vanished out of [her] sight: after which, [she] was almost stark mad for the space of eight weeks.'

Anne Whittle gave conflicting accounts of how she became a witch. Initially, she makes no mention of Elizabeth Southerns having played a role in her 'conversion'; only weeks afterwards, when her former friend has passed away awaiting trial, does Anne then tell

57

her captors that it was through Elizabeth's 'wicked persuasions and counsel' that she was 'seduced to condescend' into 'that devilish abominable profession of witchcraft'. Clearly, she felt safer blaming Elizabeth, who was no longer there to suffer punishment, than bearing the brunt of responsibility herself.

Curiously, she refers to both events to being 'about fourteen years past', but this would date them to around 1598, which seems a little late. However, dates and timings within *Discoverie* are often hopelessly vague, and therefore we can with some degree of confidence assume matters to have taken place some while before.

Anne told magistrate Roger Nowell how 'a thing like a Christian man' appeared to her 'sundry times' over a period of four years, requesting that she should give him her soul. 'In the end', she agreed and was 'contented to give him her said soul, she being then in her own house, in the Forest of Pendle'. The devil again assumed the form of a man, telling her, 'Thou shalt want nothing; and be revenged of whom thou list.' He then 'commanded' her to call him Fancie, adding that 'when she wanted anything, or would be revenged of any', to call on him 'and he would be ready'. He then vanished but reappeared 'not long after, in man's likeness', and argued with her to let him 'hurt the wife of Richard Baldwin of Pendle'. We know that Elizabeth Southerns and her daughter had had issues with Baldwin, the Wheathead mill owner, but we learn no more about Anne's issues with him or his wife, and in any case, she 'would not then consent unto him'. Apparently annoyed at being thwarted, Fancie 'would then have bitten her by the arm; and so vanished away, for that time'.

Anne then provided a second account of how she met her familiar, which resembles a sort of 'mini sabbath' in her description of consenting to letting the devil take her soul at Elizabeth's urging. She told her captors how, while the two women were at Malkin Tower, 'the devil appeared unto her in the likeness of a man, about midnight'. He remained outside and the two women went out to him. 'Whereupon the said wicked spirit moved [her], that she would become his subject, and give her soul unto him.' Anne apparently grew frightened and refused, but 'by the great persuasions' of her old friend, she acquiesced. The spirit then told her 'that he must have one part of her body for him to suck upon' and again Anne refused. Then she asked him 'what part of her body he would have for that use' and he replied 'a place of her right side near to her ribs'. She then agreed.

Immediately afterwards, Anne saw 'a thing in the likeness of a spotted bitch' which spoke to Elizabeth, telling her that she should have 'gold, silver, and worldly wealth, at her will'. They were then presented with a feast of 'victuals, viz. flesh, butter, cheese, bread, and drink' and told to eat as much as they wished. Elizabeth's familiar, Tibb, then appeared and joined Anne's familiar, Fancie, and the two of them 'gave them light to see what they did, although they neither had fire nor candle light'. Afterwards, the two spirits 'carried the remnant away'.

There is an anomaly in Anne's description of her spirit: although Fancie first appears to her 'in the likeness of a man' at the end of her tale, she refers to him and Elizabeth's spirit as being 'both she spirits and devils'. She had, in fact, referred to Tibb as being like 'a spotted bitch' although Elizabeth only ever refers to her spirit as a male creature, whether in human or animal form. Thus, it seems that familiars could both shape-shift and alter their sex at will.

We will discover in due course how Elizabeth's grandchildren James and Alizon Device similarly described their 'initiation' into witchcraft – curiously, we are told nothing of Elizabeth Device's initial meeting with her familiar, for when Ball comes into the story, the two are already acquainted – but how typical are these encounters?

Certainly, the role of the familiar spirit demonstrates how the concept of witchcraft differed between Continental ideas and its development in England during the second half of the sixteenth century onwards. The familiar represented a merging of perceptions, spiritual beliefs and phenomena in which the relationship between human and animal, particularly the domestic pet, played a vital part.

Continental witch trials had already been taking place for over a century when in 1566 the first English case to be documented in a contemporary pamphlet was tried in Chelmsford. One of the most sensational aspects of both case and pamphlet was the shape-shifting demonic white cat named Sathan, the familiar spirit of Agnes Waterhouse, who was subsequently executed. Following Sathan's unholy adventures, familiars began making regular appearances in England's witch trials, but not so much on the Continent, where animals most often featured as the devil or witch in disguise, or to carry witches to sabbath meetings.

Despite the popular perception of familiars as the witch's companion, evident from the pamphlets, plays and stories of the period, there was no legislation against familiars until the Witchcraft Act of 1604, when it became a felony punishable by death to 'consult, covenant with, entertain, employ, feed, or reward any evil and wicked spirit, to or for any intent or purpose'.[85] Fourteen years later, Michal Dalton's *The Country Justice* informed magistrates and judges that witches generally had a familiar or spirit 'which appears to them, sometimes in one shape, sometimes in another; as in the shape of a man, woman, boy, dog, cat, foal, hare, rat, toad, &c. And to these spirits they give names.'[86] Lawmen tasked with investigating witchcraft during the seventeenth century habitually questioned suspects about familiars to the extent that it became 'an almost mandatory part of the judicial process'.[87]

One of the theories put forward regarding why Continental ideas about witchcraft differed from ours regarding the role of the familiar suggests that England was more 'pet-friendly' in general. A better explanation seems to be that the demon-worshipping sabbath was deeply ingrained in the Continental concept of witchcraft and took precedence. The *Malleus Maleficarum*'s bestial blueprint of women's relationship with animals underpinned many a Continental trial, whereas the English perception of the 'pet-keeping habits of socially isolated women' contributed at least a fraction to the idea of the witch's familiar. Those people, but especially women, who had been 'scorned and shunned by their neighbours' were 'inclined to make friends with animals . . . or more unusual pet . . . No doubt they were often heard talking to their favourites and on the principle that birds of a feather flock together, the animals soon came to be looked upon as devils or familiars.'[88]

People such as Elizabeth Southerns and Anne Whittle shared their lives more closely with animals. Even larger animals – cows and donkeys particularly – often shared a space with their human companions, frequently only separated by a partition wall. The poor huddled up to their animals for warmth as well as comfort; cats were valuable in hunting rats and mice; dogs would hunt rabbits and birds and guard the home. In all probability, the poor especially understood animals better and respected them more; for those who lived in remote areas, animals would have provided precious companionship. Once the witch trials were under way, domesticated pets were viewed with suspicion, almost regardless of their owners' standing: Boye, a white poodle belonging to Charles I's nephew Prince Rupert was the subject of much speculation after he was known to sit with his master at council meetings and ran alongside him at the head of the Royalist army during the Civil War.

Dogs and cats were frequently proposed as familiars, along with small creatures such as moles, snails, ferrets, polecats and the ubiquitous toad. Occasionally there was a crossover with animals from folklore, with the black dog being perhaps the best-known example. Featuring in several witch trials, including that of 1612, the black dog was regarded as an incarnation of the boggart in Lancashire and known colloquially as 'Black Shuck' in the north, where it was sometimes feared as an omen of death. In Yorkshire, the black dog is often referred to as the Padfoot, and again in Yorkshire, but also in Northumberland and Durham, its warning form is known as the Barguest. Not far from Pendle, at Hurstwood near Burnley, there were tales of a black dog that turned into a scrap of white linen if someone tried to catch it. Eventually, it was laid to rest at Hoggarths Cross, having agreed 'never to trouble mortal man again as long as a drop of water runs through Holden Clough'.[89] The black dog can be found in Suffolk too: during a terrible storm of August 1588, a black dog tore into St Mary's Church at Bungay; it ran down the nave and killed two parishioners at prayer. Another is more compliant, guarding gold in Stowmarket. Newgate Prison had its own black dog legend: in 1596, a scholar was gaoled for witchcraft but was murdered and eaten by starving prisoners. A black dog then appeared and, despite the cannibals managing to escape the guards and the prison walls, they were each brought down and killed by the black dog. In literature, similar dogs abound, from the Hound of the Baskervilles to the Guytrash that haunts the solitary paths of northern England and is mentioned by Charlotte Brontë in *Jane Eyre*.

The sudden appearance and disappearance of such animals is a recurring feature in witch trial documents. The witch – or cunning person, for they too often shared their lives with a familiar more helpful than the witch's companion – could usually remember with pin-sharp precision the exact circumstances of their initial encounter, whether they were out in the country or occupied in some mundane household task. This was of great assistance to the person interrogating them afterwards, who were never anything less than keen to extract the exact details of that first meeting. The juxtaposition of the ordinary (the magical practitioner engaged in some domestic or very normal duty) with the extraordinary (the animal having the power of human speech) was an ongoing feature of the relationship between witch and familiar. Although some familiars later took on a demonic form or behaved demonically, usually they first appeared like domestic pets or animals of the field. Very often, the manner in which they made their entrance mirrored the moment in many fairy tales when the protagonist is at their lowest ebb and an elf or fairy-like being materialises, offering exactly the assistance they require.

Habitually, the familiar would introduce itself, and whatever forms it later adopted, the name would always remain the same. Most had typical pet diminutives, although the witch trials instigated by Matthew Hopkins and John Sterne are notable for the unusual names of the familiars that feature in them, such as Blackfast, Sydrake, Pyewacket, Peck in the Crown, Griezel Greedigut, Jamara, Pease, Germany, Vinegar Tom, Hangman and Holt. Unsurprisingly, given the unscrupulous nature of some of those leading the investigations, a few names recur in separate trials, such as the mouse familiar Prickeares. Witches could have more than one familiar: Ursula Kemp, hanged for witchcraft in 1582, had four: Pigin, a black toad; Tyffin, a black lamb; a black cat called Jack and another cat-like creature with grey fur, called Titty. Five familiars appear in the 1612 trials: Anne Whittle's Fancie, who appears as a man, a female spirit and a bear; Elizabeth Southerns' Tibb, who takes the form of a boy, a spotted bitch, a black cat, a brown dog and a hare; Elizabeth Device's familiar Ball, who appears solely as a brown dog; James Device's spirit Dandy, a brown or black dog; and Alizon Device's familiar who appears as a black dog without a name but who was – very unusually – due to be 'christened' during a meeting at Malkin on Good Friday of 1612.

The first conversation between witch and familiar was something of a sales pitch, with the witch as customer and the familiar offering something that would be of use. Usually, the familiar made a promise that would prove hard to resist, being what Scottish witchcraft expert Christina Larner termed 'the freedom from want'. However, where the familiar who became attached to a cunning person would then go on to prove useful, in helping to find lost items and heal those who visited needing medical assistance, the witch's familiar could just as readily offer to harm, maim or kill. The Pendle familiars were very much in this vein: offering food and drink but then eager to both offer harm or to instruct in methods such as fashioning and then destroying clay pictures of the person who was the witch's target. If the witch wanted her familiar to assist, she frequently had to perform some sort of ritual, but we are told that the Pendle folk simply called for theirs. Nonetheless, 'the popular magical practitioner's simple process of "asking" or "demanding" that their familiar come to them may have masked powerful, but externally minimalist, invocatory techniques'.[90]

For Puritans, there was no such divide between the benevolent or the malicious familiar. Such creatures were not part of Christian doctrine and therefore could only be associated with the devil. They argued that the rituals set out by familiars 'were associated with the devil and beliefs concerning the use of spirits to perform magic were obvious targets . . .

Theologians argued that the devil, always eager to capture human souls, saw witches (with their taste for magic and their corrupt natures) as an easy target.'[91] In essence, this was the reason the familiar was so necessary a part of the evidence against the suspected witch: with Satan preparing for a war against humanity, the witch was, in effect, his recruitment officer and thus, 'the practices of the witch threatened not only the local community but the whole of Christendom.'[92] With this in mind, historians have pointed out those sections of trial records that show evidence of intervention on the part of the investigator; those parts of the confession where allegiance to Satan and his demons is believed to have been falsely introduced by magistrates etc., simply in order to secure a conviction.

How far Pendle magistrate Roger Nowell potentially manipulated the evidence is something we will never know. But there can have been no doubt in his mind that the familiars working with the people who came before him in March and April 1612 were demonic, regardless of their ability to do good as well as bad. The Pendle familiars seem somehow morally ambiguous or outside that particular realm, in the same way that fairies of the early modern world would help, but only if they were given something in return.

In the case of the familiar, however, that 'something' was part of the witch themselves. Trial documentation shows a marked development from the idea of rewarding a benevolent spirit with a mere drop of blood. At the trial of four witches in Windsor in 1579, one woman declared that she fed her toad familiar with blood 'from her own flank'.[93] Three years later, this has progressed to something more vampiric, when the court at the trial of Ursula Kemp in 1582 heard how she let her toad suck blood from her thigh. After that, the practice became excessively overstated with lascivious and lingering bloodsucking scenes inserted into hearings.

Then came the search for proof of where the familiar had drunk its fill, which subsequently became muddled with the search for the devil's mark, inflicted by Satan on his followers to create heretics out of witches. There may have been some deliberate thought in confusing the two, since the devil's mark was one of the few 'proofs' that could be likened to exhibits at a modern trial. Otherwise, there were few items of physical evidence when the case concerned witchcraft: charms were rarely written down and never left simply lying about a place; wax or clay pictures had to be destroyed by the witch for their magic to work; and locks of hair belonging to victims were of little use hundreds of years before the discovery of DNA. The scene of crime officer would have been sorely tested – but for the devil's mark, which was described as early as 1579 as 'a common token to know all witches by'.[94]

Almost a century later, the 1697 edition of *The Country Justice* advised judges to seek out both extra nipples and blemishes, with the former linked to the familiar and the latter to the devil. Dalton described how the witch 'hath some big or little teat upon their body, and in some secret place, where he sucketh them. And beside their sucking, the Devil leaveth other marks upon their body, sometimes like a blue spot or red spot, like a flea-biting . . . And these the devil's marks be insensible and being pricked will not bleed, and be often in their secretes parts and therefore require diligent and careful search.'[95]

Dalton's words echoed those of King James in *Daemonologie*, who described the devil bestowing his mark 'upon some secret place' which remained 'thereafter ever insensible', how it was 'nipped or pricked'.[96] Given that the mark was supposed to remain insensible to being nipped or pricked, the only means of testing out that theory would be an attempt at causing pain or drawing blood. This was a common feature of witchcraft enquiries in Reformation Scotland, where witch-prickers established a professional guild and charged clients enormous sums for providing the service. In Newcastle-upon-Tyne, the arrival of a commissioned Scottish witch-pricker was preceded by the magistrates' bellman striding through the streets, throwing the bell up and then down, following each clang with a shout: that anyone who had a complaint against a woman 'for a witch' should make themselves known and that woman would be sent for and tried. Thirty women were duly dragged into the Town Hall, divested of all their clothing and then 'openly had pins thrust into their bodies'.[97]

The majority were found guilty of witchcraft. The most well-known proponent of the procedure was Matthew Hopkins, who was paid per head in witch-pricking sessions. After opposition to his work forced him to retire, a needle with a retractable point was found among his belongings.

A jury at a 1579 witch trial in Southampton asked if half-a-dozen 'honest matrons' could be found to divest the suspects of their clothing and find the spot where the bloodsucking had taken place.[98] Usually, something suspect could be found upon a person's body, often near the 'secret parts'. In 1593, after the elderly Alice Samuel was hanged as a witch in Warboys, the gaoler and his wife removed her clothing to look for the telltale nipple. Finding a small lump of flesh about half an inch long on or near her genitals, before a crowd the gaoler's wife squeezed the lump and from it came forth 'beesenings', something resembling milk and water, then blood. They were all then satisfied that Alice had indeed been prudently executed.

The drawing of blood from the witch by the familiar was, nonetheless, invested with purpose: the sealing of the pact between the two, which simultaneously signified allegiance to the devil. This was often carried out, as it was in Pendle, in conjunction with the witch agreeing that her familiar should possess her soul. Sometimes, this required what amounted to a 'topping up', with the familiar taking blood from the witch a second, third and fourth time, etc.

What are we to make of these encounters and the ongoing relationship between witch and familiar? Are the accounts we find in trial materials mere inventions on the part of the accused, or did they genuinely believe they had interacted, often on multiple occasions, with supernatural beings? Or were these sections of the evidence manipulated by magistrates who had read the Continental accounts of witch trials and wanted to make a name for themselves by foisting such ideas on terrified suspects – who then acquiesced from surprise or fear or a desperate willingness to please? Or were they simply mistaken? Was the familiar apparently masquerading as a small boy or a dog no more than they appeared – just a boy and just a dog?

As with other aspects of witch trials where the accused behave in ways the majority of people cannot understand today – such as Elizabeth Southerns discussing her interactions with Tibb in the same way we might mention something our dog or cat has done, or Alice Nutter, another of the Pendle accused, seemingly remaining silent throughout her interrogation, trial and execution – we are offered reassuring if unhappy explanations such as undiagnosed dementia or delusions caused by extreme stress. But as author Emma Wilby points out in *Cunning Folk and Familiar Spirits*, in any such debate there is almost always a spiritual element missing, underpinned by a form of snobbery. For while historians readily acknowledge that learned and highly intellectual magicians performed rituals to facilitate mystical experience or revelation, the magical beliefs and practices of ordinary folk in this period are largely dismissed. 'Scholars often make passing comments which reveal their personal opinions as to what was actually going on during a familiar encounter,' Wilby explains. 'Most of these comments pertain to the general view that the encounter, if not wholly a fiction created in the courtroom, was likely to have been a mixture of fact (involving remembered events involving "real" humans and animals) and fantasy (involving fiction, distorted memory, suggestion, self-delusion, hallucination and so on).'

Historian Marion Gibson makes a similar argument regarding the passage in Alizon Device's confession about the black dog who offered to lame the pedlar John Law when he refused to give her some pins:

Readers of such a story will divide into two main groups: those who accept that the magical details in the story are probable, and those who do not believe in magic. There will be farther divisions within the second group, for example, those who suggest that the talking dog was an hallucination of Alizon's, those who believe that she was pressed by the prosecuting authorities into creating a folktale-like story, those who read her story as a voluntary adoption of the powerful mythic status of the witch. Some will see the whole story as a fiction, while others content that the pedlar really did fall ill, or that Alizon really saw a (mute) black dog.[99]

Returning to Emma Wilby, she describes these encounters as 'actual psychic events which occurred in historical time and geographical space'.[100]

The concept of the familiar, of attributing supernatural agency to animals who suddenly appear in this fashion, and the existence of malevolent, otherworldly beings or spirits are widespread among shamanistic cultures. Contemporary Mayans in the Mexican province of Chiapas believe that everybody possesses a 'soul animal' that exists 'independently of the body', indistinguishable from a real animal but in some way existing on a supernatural plane.[101] One explanation they have for illness is that witchcraft has been inflicted on one's soul animal or the soul animal has been mistaken for an ordinary one, then harmed. The traditional remedy is to employ a shaman who will use rituals and his own more powerful soul animals to find the source of the problem and counteract it. Mayan folklore holds that shamans and witches can adopt the material form of their soul animal to access the supernatural realm. This idea is unique to the Mayan culture and not a model for beliefs in earlier times elsewhere, but there are similarities.

The first readers of *Discoverie* would have had little difficulty in believing that Elizabeth Southerns and her family and neighbours worked with familiars. For theirs was a punitive world of plague and famine, but one of magic and superstition too, full of enchantment where 'powerful occult forces permeated life at every level. The air teemed with invisible supernatural entities which constantly influenced the natural world and the lives of men. A prayer could be answered. A spell could cure. A look could kill. A spirit or deity could be at your ear at any time of the night or day ... Everyday life was sympathetically linked to the heavens and even the smallest event could possess a cosmic significance.'[102]

And it was, increasingly, a world where witchcraft was deemed to be rife.

Chapter Three

THAT FRIDAY SPELL
or
ELIZABETH DEVICE

Scratch, scratch, scratch . . . the quill that Thomas Potts wielded so determinedly against Elizabeth Southerns left its inky marks, describing how she had acted as an agent for the devil in the Forest of Pendle. But like all books purporting to bring the truth to light, it left behind a complex shadow: those stories that an author doesn't tell, either because they don't fit the narrative or would reveal a reality that the reader does not want to be told: that the bad can be good, and the good much worse than the bad.

As agents for the devil go, Elizabeth Southerns was not the accomplished evil-doer that Potts would have us believe. She and her family were regular churchgoers, and not simply to avoid the compulsory fines for non-attendance. Their religious sensibilities went far deeper than that.

The Newchurch-in-Pendle parish registers provide valuable information regarding Elizabeth's family. In 1590, both her son and her daughter married at St Mary's Church; it may even have been a double wedding. Christopher's bride was Isabell Robinson, and although we know nothing of her background, she was very probably a member of the local Robinson family, who farmed at Barley, Black Moss, Foothouse Gate and Whitehough.

Elizabeth, Christopher's half-sister, married John Device, whose origins are as obscure to us now as those of his new sister-in-law. There is an assumption that he was older than Elizabeth, since he is believed to have already had a son named William.[103] Baptisms soon followed for the newlyweds: Christopher and his wife welcomed a daughter, Alicea, while Elizabeth Device gave birth to a son, James. In 1593, the Devices also had a daughter whom they too named Alicea, but everyone knew her as Alizon.[104] The couple's third child, Henry, was born in 1595.[105]

Where the Devices lived prior to mid-1612 is not recorded, except that it was very near to Malkin Tower. James Device provides us with the little detail there is, via his interviews with magistrate Roger Nowell: he recalled heading home and encountering a brown dog loping away from his grandmother's house; on another occasion he heard a horrible noise emanating from Malkin Tower; and finally, he estimated the distance between his mother's home and his grandmother's house, Malkin Tower, as '20 roods', or 'rods'. An archaic English measurement also referred to as a 'perch' or 'pole', the average length of a rod was a little over five metres, with a contemporary definition being that it was the equivalent to the left feet of sixteen men lined up heel to toe as they emerged from church. What it tells us is that the Device home and Malkin Tower stood around 110 metres apart and that it would have taken about a minute and a half to walk between the two.[106]

Elizabeth was twenty-four years old when she married John Device. Until then, she probably remained at home with her mother and worked whenever the opportunity presented itself. This later included working at the Baldwin mill in Wheathead, but from the argument that arose as a result of the mill owner failing to pay her, it seems the arrangement was casual rather than regular employment. Potts, as ever, gives no real insight into the woman he witnessed on the eve of her certain hanging, describing Elizabeth instead with a vicious flourish: 'O, barbarous and inhumane monster, beyond example . . .'

He presents her, through the distressing scenes in court, as someone who 'was not able to contain herself within the limits of any order or government', while failing to consider what last, terrible thing had caused her to lose control after months of being pushed beyond the limits of endurance. He warns that 'no man near her, neither his wife, children, goods or cattle should be secure or free from danger', mostly on account of Elizabeth being the daughter of Elizabeth Southerns. That alone emboldened Potts to declare that there 'amongst all these witches there was not a more dangerous and devilish witch to execute mischief'. In the end, of course, it was Elizabeth who was executed.

Potts adhered to the practice of equating physical 'otherness' with moral deformity, telling us that the 'odious' Elizabeth 'was branded with a preposterous mark in nature, even from her birth, which was her left eye, standing lower than the other; the one looking down, the other looking up, so strangely deformed . . .'[107] It may be that Elizabeth was born with her distinctive features, but it is also possible that this was a result of the brutality meted out to prisoners awaiting trial. Potts knew Elizabeth only from her appearances in court, and even if it occurred to him that she had been the victim of judicial violence, he would have kept silent about the matter.

Repulsed as he plainly was by Elizabeth Device, Potts nonetheless believed that she was fated to end up as she did on account of her parentage. He places Elizabeth Southerns firmly at the head of his list of wicked women, telling us that although Chattox was likewise charged with murder, she was more likely to damage goods than people. Elizabeth, by contrast, was a 'damnable and malicious witch, of so long continuance' and a 'sink of villainy' who, by the time of the trials:

. . . had been a witch for fifty years. She dwelt in the Forest of Pendle, a vast place, fit for her profession. What she committed in her time, no man knows. Thus, lived she securely for many years, brought up her own children, instructed her grandchildren, and took great care and pains to bring them to be witches. She was a general agent for the devil in all these parts: no man escaped her, or her Furies that ever gave them any occasion of offence, or denied them anything they stood need of: And certain it is, no man near them, was secure or free from danger.[108]

Potts believed that Elizabeth followed the path set for her, encouraging her own children to give their souls to the devil 'into mischief and bondage'. There are no examples in *Discoverie* of Elizabeth being called upon by neighbours as a cunning woman, but Potts includes two charms she had taught her children to demonstrate her witchery. These are of real value to us, both as historical items in themselves and for their revealing insight into the accused. The two Device charms show that Elizabeth and her family believed that people, animals and innate objects were liable to bewitchment and that the most effective means of release combined elements of the spiritual or supernatural. Their antidote was a much more esoteric counter-measure than the healer's use of plant medicine.

Joyce Froome, assistant curator of the Museum of Witchcraft and Magic in Cornwall, believes that the Devices and their matriarch, Elizabeth Southerns,

> . . . openly practised magic. Their lives and values were shaped by a complex magical culture – a strange fusion of Christian and pre-Christian elements. Magic gave them practical ways to deal with everyday problems – illness, bad luck and unhappiness in love. But it also had a profound effect on their spiritual beliefs. There was very little evidence that they had committed any of the crimes they were accused of, but their magic called on the help of supernatural forces that Roger Nowell sincerely believed were evil.[109]

The two charms Elizabeth Device taught her children were in all probability ones she had learnt from her own mother and may have been part of an older family tradition. The Devices referred to them as 'prayers', although the longer charm identifies itself as a 'spell'.

In common with other 'rural magicians', the family made use of the principals and rituals of the medieval Church in their charms, basing them on 'centuries of Catholic teaching'.[110]

The shorter charm appears in the evidence against Elizabeth's son, James Device, aiming to damn him as a Catholic sympathiser and he-witch: '*Crucifixus hoc signum vitam Etername. Amen.*'

The Latin is garbled – 'crucifixus' means 'crucified' and appears in both the Nicene Creed and the Apostles' Creed, as declarations of faith during the Catholic Mass. Otherwise, the correct translation of the charm would be: 'The crucifix is the sign of eternal life. Amen.' Elizabeth Device would have been familiar with spoken Latin, and the charm resembles the catechism taught to deprived children in pre-Reformation 'petty school' classes where chanting replaced reading. Curiously, the catechism still used today by the Church of England was devised by Alexander Nowell, who was Dean of St Paul's during Elizabeth I's reign, the inventor of bottled ale – and half-uncle to magistrate Roger Nowell.

Elizabeth Device's younger daughter, Jennet, later told a crowded courtroom that she and her family used the charm mainly 'to get drink'. She recalled a time when her brother had said the charm and 'within an hour . . . drink hath come into the house after a very strange manner'. A charm was frequently meant to be repeated, like a mantra, and to give the reciter confidence in its efficacy.

Crucifixus hoc signum vitam Etername: the Latin in the Device charm is garbled, as we know. The obvious inference is that one of the family muddled the line, suggesting that they were cobbling together bits of liturgy with a feel for the words but a poor grasp of grammar. The phrase *hoc signum* occurs in the liturgy as *hoc signum crucis erit in caelo* or 'this sign of the cross will be in the sky'. The Device charm connected the cross with drink, perhaps equating the flow of blood and water from Christ's side as a means of ensuring the charm 'would bring drink as miraculously as water bursting from Christ's pierced side'.[111]

However, there may be a far more insidious explanation. Historian Diane Purkiss suggests another explanation for the Devices' garbled

Latin: that it was potentially 'tactical' and not so much an error as 'a sign of magical (mis) use of words as things'. Garbled and gabbled Latin in charms of this period is often used as a prompt for the 'enduring association between "mindless" recitation and diabolical agency', merging Catholicism with concocted phrases or words taken from ancient languages which unlock spells and invocations.[112] Abracadabra is probably the best-known example.

For most of us, the only time we might hear Latin spoken is in the cinema or on television – in stories of witchcraft or diabolism. Then, too, the Latin is often garbled or recited at speed. Perhaps the most famous example is *The Exorcist* (1973), in which a Catholic priest is tasked with driving an ancient demon from a young girl. Latin is used in the film partly to lend historical weight and authenticity to the events taking place. Unsurprisingly, following the success of *The Exorcist*, Latin has become shorthand 'evilspeak' in other forms of drama.[113]

Purkiss's theory is that the Devices may in fact have used Latin correctly and that Thomas Potts garbles the Latin to make us believe that the family got it wrong, thereby insinuating that the charm was part-papist and part-Satanic. Purkiss clarifies: 'We may be able to acquit Jennet and her brother James of intending this garbling in their testimonies, or of being too uneducated to say a charm straight; the garbling could well be part of Potts's polemic.'[114]

The other Device family charm is far longer and filled with Catholic symbolism:

A Charm
Upon Good Friday, I will fast while I may
Until I hear them knell
Our Lord's own bell,
Lord in his mess
With his twelve Apostles good,
What hath he in his hand
Ligh in leath wand:
What hath he in his other hand?

Heaven's door key,
Open, open Heaven door keys,
Steck, steck hell door.
Let Crissom child
Go to it Mother mild,
What is yonder that casts a light so farrandly,
Mine own dear Son that's nailed to the Tree,
He is nailed sore by the heart and hand,
And holy harne pan,
Well is that man
That Friday spell can,
His child to learn;
A cross of blue, and another of red,
As good Lord was to the Rood,
Gabriel laid him down to sleep
Upon the ground of holy weep:
Good Lord came walking by,
Sleep'st thou, wak'st thou Gabriel,
No Lord I am sted with stick and stake,
That I can neither sleep nor wake:
Rise up Gabriel and go with me,
The stick nor the stake shall never deere thee.
Sweet Jesus, our Lord, Amen.

Jennet Device told Roger Nowell that her mother had taught her the charm, but Nowell credits James Device as its author, probably because he recited it for the magistrate's benefit. The charm itself suggests it should be passed from one generation to the next ('Well is the man/ That Friday spell can,/His child to learn'), but the Devices made it their own, and we learn more about them by looking at its origins.[115]

In a staccato but weirdly hypnotic fashion, the charm tells the story of the crucifixion, via the Last Supper and Jesus in the Garden of Gethsemane, using several words that are now obsolete. The identity of the narrator is uncertain until the halfway point, when the viewpoint becomes that of Mary, mother of Jesus. The charm opens with the narrator intending to observe the obligatory Catholic fast on Good Friday. That particular holy day appears to have been something of a motif for the Devices and their friends, not least because the 'witches' sabbath' which they were later accused of organising was held at Malkin Tower on Good Friday, 10 April 1612. In religious terms, Good Friday is the day of the crucifixion. The Roman Catholic Church does not celebrate mass on that day, although a liturgy is performed; church bells fall silent, altars are left bare and pilgrims fast. In Sweden, the period between Christ's death and His resurrection on Easter Sunday was considered especially vulnerable to evil, with witches emerging to create chaos, often on purloined broomsticks or cattle.

The charm then refers to Christ and his twelve apostles at the Last Supper before asking of an unnamed figure – probably Saint Peter – 'What hath he in his hand, / Ligh in leath wand . . .' Given that leath can mean supple or flexible, the line may refer to the figure securing the door to hell with a staff while holding the keys to heaven in the other. 'Steck' was to fasten, and Jesus gave Saint Peter the keys to the kingdom of heaven, which then became a symbol of papal authority.

A 'Crissom child' is an archaic term, with chrisom being the cloth in which a baby was swaddled following its baptism for a period of seven days or until the mother was churched (a thanksgiving service for the birth of the child and survival of its mother). If the infant died before then, it became known as a chrisom child and was buried in its white baptismal cloth. Bills of mortality record these as 'chrisom' babies. In this context, and if the speaker is Mary, then it may be a reference to her son's death; He remains an infant to her but she is unable to protect Him. She then wonders about the source of a beautiful ('farrandly') light, and realises that it is her son, upon the cross, nailed to it by his feet and hands, with thorns about his skull. Hence: 'He is nailed sore by the heart and hand, / And holy harne pan . . .' In the Yorkshire district of Craven, where another accused woman, Jennet Preston, lived, it was common to refer to a skull as a 'harn-pann'.[116]

Mention of 'that Friday spell' brings in the supernatural before reminding us again that Christ is on the cross ('As good Lord was to the Rood' – at one time, 'rood' was the only Old English word for the cross to which Jesus was nailed). 'Upon the ground of holy weep' appears to refer to the Garden of Gethsemane, where Jesus broke down and cried while his disciples slept. He was comforted by an angel, unnamed in the Bible but often believed to be Gabriel. 'Sted with stick and stake' means 'beset with stick and stake' and finally 'shall never deere me' is equivalent to 'shall never harm me'. Christ then told his sleeping disciples to awaken 'and go with me', reassuring his followers before the charm ends with a customary 'Sweet Jesus, our Lord, Amen.'

The charm incorporates small sections of older charms that reference the White Pater Noster.[117] 'Our Father' in Latin, the Pater Noster became known as the Lord's Prayer after the Reformation and begins, 'Our Father, Who art in heaven, hallowed be Thy name . . .' Regarded as the most profound of all ritual prayers, for believers it is 'a magical prayer of immense power', used by Christ to teach His followers how to pray.[118] Elizabeth Southerns and her family were as familiar with the Pater Noster as with their own names, for it accompanied all stages of life within the Church, from baptism onwards, and parishioners were taught to recite their prayers, including the Pater Noster, in Latin.

One section of the charm in particular has several parallels:

What hath he in his hand
Ligh in leath wand:
What hath he in his other hand?
Heaven's door key,
Open, open Heaven door keys,
Steck, steck hell door.'
Let Crissom child
Go to it Mother mild . . .

The earliest extant example of this appears in the *Enchiridon Leonis Pape*, a 1523 grimoire ascribed to Pope Leo III:

> White Paternoster, Saint Peter's brother,
> What hast thou I' th' t'other hand. Heaven-Yate Keyes.
> Open Heaven-Yates, and steike Hell-Yates.
> And let every crysome-child creepe to its owne mother.
> White Paternoster! Amen.[119]

One expert analysis of the Pater Noster points out that although these lines bear little resemblance to the original prayer, the 'main theme of the authorised prayer, the desire to be delivered from evil and to enter heaven, is also explored in this text. The reference to St Peter holding the keys to the gates of heaven derives from the gospels ["Matthew 16: '. . . *upon this rock I will build my church; and the gates of hell shall not prevail against it. And I will give unto thee the keys of the kingdom of heaven* . . ."].'[120] Both versions of the prayer stress the concept of salvation. This particular version is also of interest because of its use of the word 'yate' in place of 'gate', a common occurrence in old Lancashire dialect, with a 'Yate House' standing at the crossroads to Newchurch-in-Pendle and Barley.

A very similar version appears in *The Way to the True Church*, published in 1608. The author, John White, worked for a time as a vicar in Eccles, some thirty-five miles south of Clitheroe. A committed Calvinist, he was repelled by the superstitious beliefs of many Lancastrians, deriding them as 'addicted to Papistry'. He included a prayer 'they call the white Pater Noster' to serve as an example of their 'prodigious ignorance', which runs:

> White Pater noster, Saint Peter's brother,
> What hast i'th t'one hand? White booke leaves,
> What hast i'th t'other hand? Heaven gate keys.
> Open heaven gates, and streike hell gates:
> And let every crysome child creepe to its own mother:
> White Paternoster, Amen.[121]

This second rendering has very significant parallels with the Device family charm. There are three charms with notably similar elements, all included in Joseph Ames's 1749 *Typographical Antiquities*, a history of English printing. The first is a 'popish white pater noster' dated 1624 and known as *The Spell of Edmonds Bury*:

> What hast in thy honde? Heauen keyes.
> What hast in thy tother?
> Broade booke leaues.
> Open heauen gates,
> Shutt hell yeates.
> Euerie childe creepe christ ouer
> White Benedictus be in this howse
> Euerye night.[122]

The second:

> What holdest thou under thy belt?
> Heaven keys, heaven keys.
> Open, open heaven gates,
> Steike steike hell gates . . .[123]

But it is the third and final version which is most like the Device charm. Borrowed from 'a great papist' in Norfolk in 1637 it reads:

> Tomorrow is good Friday
> We'll fast while we may
> Till we hear the knell
> Of Our Lord's bell
> Our Lord stands at his mass
> With his 12 Apostles
> Fair lady what's yonder bright?
> Fair lady what's yonder bright?
> Yonder's mine own dear son

Nailed to the holy roode tree
Through hand through foot
Through holy heart roote
Through the hard brayne panne
Well them that this Friday's spell can
Say it in the morn
Seven times forborne,
Say it at noon,
Seven times fore doom,
Say it in the evening
Seven times forgiven
All the day of our doom than
Wells they this Friday's spell can.[124]

A little later, writer George Sinclair added lines very like those of the Device charm to a version of the Pater Noster which features in his 1685 book, *Satan's Invisible World Discovered: Detailing the particulars of Strange Pranks Played by the Devil, together with a Particular account of Several Apparitions, witches and Invisible Spirits*:

. . . Open, open, Heaven's Yaits,
Steik, steik, Hell's Yaits.
All Saints be the better,
That hear the White Prayer, Pater Noster.[125]

Sinclair believed this text to be connected to witchcraft due to its crudely and irregularly fashioned verse and its humorous nature. His belief was supported by a clergyman who referred to 'the Witch's Pater Noster', quoting a fifteenth-century text that warned witches would rot a man's feet by dripping candle wax in his footsteps while 'saying their Pater Noster'.[126] But Sinclair also included another charm, of Irish origin, in *Satan's Invisible World Discovered*. This tells the story of Christ's injuries from the crucifixion and was used, Sinclair explains, 'at night, in the time of Popery, when folks went to bed, they believed the repetition of the following prayer was effectual to preserve them from danger and the house too'.[127] It runs:

> What is that, what I see
> So red, so bright, beyond the sea?
> Tis he was pierc'd through the hands,
> Through the feet, through the throat,
> Through the tongue,
> Through the liver and the lung.
> Well is them that well may
> Fast on Good-Friday.[128]

Although these texts feature in books published after the 1612 trials, that is not to say that the charms themselves post-date them too. Which begs the question: which came first – these charms, or the one used by the Devices? Were the Pendle folk taking elements from charms already in existence, or was theirs the original source?

'That Friday spell', far from being garbled or gibberish, was exact and its vocabulary ancient. It tells us, hundreds of years after the family recited it, that they had deep-seated Catholic beliefs. Incorporating aspects of religion and magic meant that when they recited their charm they then felt the power of both mediums, putting ritual and prayer to a single use in order to achieve a specific aim. They were certainly not the first or last to fuse religion with the occult; the Pater Noster has been melded into charms since the Dark Ages. Many have been lost due to being part of oral tradition, but the British Library has some examples, dating from the twelfth century and used to cure warts and heal boils. There was a time when the Church actively encouraged its followers to recite prayers, including the Pater Noster, while gathering herbs or healing the sick. This led to a belief among the laity that reciting prayers in Latin could achieve a desired outcome, depending too upon the individual concerned. After the Reformation, the Protestant Church was vehement in condemning this and actively discouraged the use of prayer in 'non-Christian' rituals, fearing that it led the ignorant to dabble in the occult. The Church then prohibited the use of some Roman Catholic prayers, especially those recited in Latin, including the Pater Noster, but without great success. The continuation of this tradition led to terrible consequences for those who 'sought to flout the Church's ruling'.[129]

Hence one of the 'proofs' of witchcraft: if a suspect was unable to recite the Lord's Prayer without stumbling over the words, then he or she was likely to be a witch. But equally, this demonstrates 'a contemporary concern about the remnants of Catholic practices in England after the Reformation'.[130] The Pater Noster became increasingly associated with witchcraft and the devil, especially when recited in Latin, which was believed to be the devil's method of tricking the unwitting into summoning him.

George Sinclair cited Agnes Sampson, executed in 1591 after being caught up in the North Berwick Trials, as an example, adding that she seemed 'not so much a white witch as a holy woman. She also used nonsensical rhymes in the instruction of ignorant people and taught them to say the white *and* black Paternoster . . .' Sinclair then recites Agnes's own version:

> God was my foster,
> He fostered me
> Under the book of Palm tree.
> St Michael was my dame,
> He was born at Bethlehem.
> He was made of flesh and blood,
> God send me my right food;
> My right food, and dyne too,
> That I may too yon kirk go,
> To read upon yon sweet book,
> Which the mighty God of heaven shook,
> Open, open, heaven's yaits,
> Steik, steik, hell's yaits,

All saints be the better,
That hear the white prayer, Paternoster.[131]

Once more, we see the lines from the Device family charm bringing another charm, similarly, to its conclusion.

Another Agnes – Waterhouse this time – executed at Chelmsford in 1566 was said to have recited the Pater Noster whenever she wished her familiar to work on her behalf: 'She said that when she would will him to do anything for her, she would say her Pater Noster in Latin.' In sixteenth-century Somerset, too, it was noted that one healing technique necessitated taking a girdle from the sick person and cutting it into five pieces, 'then say five Paternosters and five Aves, and then bury the pieces of the girdle in separate places'.[132] A popular divination technique was the aforementioned use of sieve and shears, accompanied by 'the invocation of the names of the Father, Son and Holy Ghost, or of St Peter and St Paul. Creeds, Paternosters and Ava Marias were repeated; the sign of the cross and the name of Jesus was employed'.[133]

The *Malleus Maleficarum* defined expectation as a crucial difference between prayers and charms: the former asked for God's help but understood the outcome was dependent upon His will, whereas a charm fully anticipated the granting of a request. For cunning folk, the expectation that their charms would work was essential; their livelihoods depended on a client's faith in them.

As late as 1904, writer E. C. Vansittart referred to 'the White Paternoster [sic], a strange remnant of superstition which, under the form of an evening prayer, is still used as a charm or incantation by the illiterate in at least five European countries . . . the White Pater Noster occurs in many different forms, but all take the tone of a magic incantation or charm; some are so weird and strange as to border on blasphemy.'[134] It was a view no doubt shared by Thomas Potts, whose inclusion of the Device charms in *Discoverie* was a clear demonstration that the tales of rampant popery in the north were not mere rumours at all, but a disturbing reality.

Chapter Four

MUCH BLOOD SPILT
or
ANNE REDFEARN

The Redfearns had lived at West Close since around 1591, with five family members under one roof: Anne and her husband Thomas Redfearn, their daughter Marie, Anne's sister Bessie and her mother Anne Whittle. Now attached to the parish of Higham, West Close was located west of the Old and New Laund deer enclosures, hence its name. In Anne Whittle's time, West Close was part of Gawthorpe Estate, owned by the Shuttleworths who had lived there since at least the fourteenth century. Richard Shuttleworth was appointed Chief Justice of Chester in 1589 and began work on Gawthorpe Hall in 1600. He passed away before building was completed in 1605; the first residents were Colonel Richard Shuttleworth and his wife Fleetwood Barton, who married in 1608. Their first child was born in 1612. Today Gawthorpe Hall stands in vastly reduced grounds due to parts of it being sold off to developers. It is still a striking home, nonetheless, created from golden stone and overlooking the River Calder at the southern foot of Pendle Forest. Through advantageous marriages, the Shuttleworth fortune accrued, with the Towneleys being their only rivals in terms of influential families in the district; Sir Richard Shuttleworth's daughter, Eleanor, went on to marry Roger Nowell's son Christopher.

Around eighty people called West Close home; some were yeoman farmers and others high gentry. It was a thriving area: apart from the usual farm workers and labourers going about their daily business, it was also something of a thoroughfare for traders and cattlemen heading to the nearby towns of Burnley and Clitheroe, and further afield to Blackburn, Preston and beyond.

The exact location of their home is uncertain, but it stood near a track, around ten feet from a ditch, and cannot have been far from Anne Whittle's childhood home since she called regularly at Bull Hole Farm, in Newchurch-in-Pendle. Due to its name, when West Close Farm was put up for sale in 2017, local and national newspapers ran stories on the home of two Pendle witches coming onto the housing market, declaring, 'You can still imagine Old Chattox and her daughter making potions in the ancient-looking farmhouse kitchen.'[135] A far more likely site is the old Heys Farm, now a ruin, off Foxen Dole Lane, where in past times a track ran directly from the lane to the farm. The ruin stood on the old Higham Lane and comprised two dwellings: Heys Farm and Heys Farm Cottage, occupied in the 1890s by a gamekeeper and a weaver, respectively. The homes are later than 1612 but were almost certainly built on the footprint of an older building and using the materials from it to construct the farm and cottage. Medieval ditches formed the enclosure on three sides with stone walls on earthen banks; the track formed the remaining side. Nearby was a spring, since diverted, but which would have provided a perpetual source of fresh water for inhabitants and animals alike. The Ightenhill track connected Heys Farm with the homes of John and Hugh Moore, who came to play a significant role in the story.

The old ruin on the site of an earlier building thus fits what we know of the Redfearn home perfectly. The family certainly kept hens, and therefore there was land attached to their home, which would then have been a small cottage of wattle and daub with a fern-thatched roof, not far from a main thoroughfare. Like Elizabeth Southerns' home, contrary to popular belief, the house would not have been a hovel by any stretch of the imagination, but instead a smallholding with some land to cultivate, and perhaps a pig or two. The dwellings would be fairly small and draughty, with beaten earth covering the floor and a 'carpet' of straw. The wind also got in through the windows – or wind-eyes, as they were then known – which were not glazed but covered with sacking or shutters. They would have slept on straw pallets over which lay a sheet, and with a rough cloth coverlet. Many people used a log as a pillow. They most likely ate from wooden platters, although the more moneyed used pewter or tin. They had few utensils or bowls and would have huddled near the fire on the coldest of nights; a simple hole in the roof let out the smoke.

Women like Elizabeth Southerns and Anne Whittle, together with their daughters, had busy lives within the home. They cooked on open fires with few pots, fetched water, baked, made butter and cheese and salted bacon. They had little meat, depending on what they were able to catch. Sometimes they might have bacon if a better-off neighbour had killed their pig and hung it in the chimney to be preserved by the smoke. Beggars often lived on leftover food from the kitchens of various houses, and we know that the Devices later worked for the Towneleys and may have been given or filched from their kitchen. Bread was the most important food, but when they were unable to afford wheat, they used oat or barley flour. The rest of the food came from the garden: vegetables, fruit and herbs, or was foraged. Town markets often sold cheaply at the end of the day, especially those foodstuffs liable to go off, such as butter and fish. Mostly they did their own brewing and drank a watered-down version of beer called small beer, and ale and milk. But living poorly meant they were likely to fall ill. Their homes were often crammed so infections spread, and when they begged food it was often on the turn.

Elizabeth and Anne, and their daughters, had little time to themselves. They looked after their children, did the laundry and sewing, swept the floors, collected firewood and made their own candles and rushlights out of wax and tallow. Elizabeth Device and Anne Redfearn might have helped with their husbands' work, or they went to work themselves in the fields, mills and private houses. Sometimes they took in sewing, or prepared wool or flax, spinning it into yarn for sale or to weave.

As far as it is possible to tell, both Elizabeth Device and Anne Redfearn appear to have had stable marriages. Reading between the lines of *Discoverie*, John Device and Thomas Redfearn seem quite similar in character, seemingly acting as peacemakers when necessary and enjoying good relationships with their mothers-in-law. However, where Thomas Redfearn was alleged to have participated with his wife and her mother in making wax poppets, John Device appears to have shrunk from such things, and was clearly fearful of Anne Whittle, despite his mother-in-law Elizabeth's reputation and his wife and children's involvement in cunning folk activities.

The Redfearns were sub-tenants of a prosperous yeoman family, the Nutters, who rented their land and property – Greenhead Manor in the village of Fence, near to West Close – from the wealthy Shuttleworths of Gawthorpe Hall. The relationship between the Redfearns and the Nutters was troubled due not only to the imbalance of power, but to Robert Nutter's attempts to exploit that. The surname of Nutter was a common one in the Pendle region and features throughout our story, with Alice Nutter at the head as one of those executed in 1612. To complicate matters further, there was a habit in and around the area of using one or two of the same Christian names for eldest sons. For several generations, the Nutters of Greenhead called their sons Robert, then Christopher, then Robert again, and so on for years. Christopher Nutter was the head of the family and lived at Greenhead with his sons John and Robert, who was the retainer of Sir Richard Shuttleworth, essentially his right-hand man.

The Nutters had connections with others who feature in the story. The Christopher Nutter of Greenhead who sublet to the Redfearns was named in 1562 as a co-trustee in the estate of Henry Mitton, who was allegedly bewitched by Alice Nutter, Elizabeth Southerns and Elizabeth Device. A portion of Christopher Nutter's land and property deals were drawn up with indentures made between him, his wife and magistrate Roger Nowell. Christopher Nutter's daughter Margaret married a man whose cousin, John of Old Laund, left a grey coat in his will to Thomas Redfearn, Anne Whittle's son-in-law, and it seems that he, at least, was on good terms with the Nutter family.

Whether or not those good terms outlasted what happened next is another matter.

Tenants usually paid their rent at Michaelmas and Easter, with sub-tenants often struggling with the latter due to prices frequently being higher and work on the wane in comparison to harvest time. Perhaps it was to discuss the rent – and to make a suggestion about another method of payment – that shortly after Easter 1594, Robert Nutter visited Anne Redfearn at her home in West Close. Anne Whittle disclosed what had taken place: that while Robert Nutter was with her daughter, he desired 'to have his pleasure of her'. She refused, 'whereupon the said Robert, seeming to be greatly displeased therewith, in a great anger took his horse, and went away, saying in a great rage, that if ever the ground came to him, she should never dwell upon his land'.[136] In other words, Robert Nutter had attempted to rape Anne Redfearn, who had fought him off. Furious that a woman he regarded as very much his social inferior had refused him, he threatened that if ever the land on which she and her family lived came into his possession, he would evict them.

Anne told her mother of the encounter with Robert Nutter, and now Anne Whittle was enraged. This was the motive, the authorities later claimed, for her seeking to kill Robert Nutter by witchcraft. Anne Whittle made a confession to that end, but not without countering that she had been approached by three other women who also wanted to see Robert Nutter dead, 'which time of request, was *before* that Robert Nutter desired the company of Redfearn's wife'. One of the women, according to Anne, was Elizabeth Nutter – the second wife of Robert Nutter the elder, grandfather to the aggressive Robert.

Anne Whittle stated that Elizabeth Nutter had approached her and two other cunning women with her murderous request. These were identified as 'Loomeshaw's wife' and Jane Boothman. Both women were from Burnley, and both died prior to the 1612 trials. Little is known about them, unfortunately. Potts tells us no more, although records appear to show that Jane Boothman had an illegitimate son whom she named Thomas in 1571 and there is a burial at Newchurch-in-Pendle for a woman of that name in 1602, but no further information.[137]

'Loomeshaw's wife' is equally shadowy as far as facts are concerned, although local historian John Clayton makes a solid claim for her being married to a man whose given name was John Hargreaves; he became 'alias Lomeshaye' due to being part of the Hargreaves family who owned the small estate of Lomeshaye that lay between Barrowford and Reedley Hallows. If Clayton's theory is correct, then Lomeshaye's wife was a Robinson by birth and married in Newchurch-in-Pendle. This would also mean that Lomeshaye's wife was related to Robert Nutter the elder's wife – perhaps even her sister, and there may well be a further familial link to Jane Boothman. If the three women had been alive at the time of the 1612 trial, they would surely have been charged alongside those condemned as witches.

Anne Whittle later told Roger Nowell that Elizabeth Nutter wanted her step-grandson murdered so that 'the women, their cousins, might have the land'. This is curious, for as the laws stood, there seemed little possibility that they should inherit anything, and there must surely have been other alternatives to murder, however covert the means. However, there may well be interpretations that are now lost to us. What it does suggest is that, if true, there were undeniable tensions within the family, caused at least in part by the behaviour of Robert Nutter the younger, who may have been as odious at home as he was on its peripheries.

Anne Whittle's extraordinary claim about the three women reveals that she not only believed that she had the capacity to kill a man using supernatural means, but that others in the neighbourhood shared her belief. Or it may simply have been a desperate attempt on her part to lay the blame for Robert Nutter's death elsewhere; certainly, she brought Elizabeth Southerns' name into the alleged plot once her former friend was no longer alive either to be affected by it or respond to the claims. Curiously, Anne Whittle went on to say that although she and the other women had been fully prepared to go ahead with the murder plot, she subsequently refused due to the intervention of her son-in-law, Thomas Redfearn, who 'did persuade [her], not to kill or hurt the said Robert Nutter'. This again, speaks volumes both about Redfearn's character and the relationship he had with Anne Whittle – that he was able to dissuade her from continuing with the plan.

Yet in so doing, he infuriated Lomeshaye's widow. She was incensed at the loss of potential income from what was a very strange and unusual contract killing. As such, she let it be known that she would 'like to have killed the said Redfearn'. But Anne Whittle recalled that Nicholas Baldwin 'did by his learning, stay the said Lomeshaye's wife'. Baldwin was schoolmaster at Colne Grammar and resident of Greenfield, who passed away two years before the 1612 trials. Where he came into the story is unclear, although there have been suggestions that he was a magical practitioner and certainly would have been able to read and speak Latin. Suffice to say that he did Thomas Redfearn a great favour; in return, the much-relieved Redfearn presented the placating schoolmaster with a capon (a small chicken) in gratitude.

Nowell also went on to question Margaret Crooke – Robert Nutter's sister. Now married, it was her husband's cousin who was on such friendly terms with Thomas Redfearn that he left him a coat in his will. In the interview she later had with Roger Nowell, Margaret Crooke said nothing of the attempted rape – which no doubt Robert would not have spoken of to her anyway – stating instead that around the middle of 1594, her brother had told her that 'upon some speeches' between himself and Anne Whittle they 'fell out'.[138] Margaret told Nowell that 'within some week, or fortnight, then next after, [her] said brother fell sick, and so languished . . .' She stated that throughout his illness, 'he did a hundred times at the least say, that the said Anne Redfearn and her associates had bewitched him to death'.[139]

A James Robinson was living at Greenhead with the Nutters at the time. He and Robert Nutter the younger were good friends, and it would also appear, from the available evidence, that James was

Elizabeth Nutter's son from a previous relationship; he was named in a land surrender as Robert the elder's 'second son'. James later told magistrate Robert Nowell that he had seen Robert the younger fall sick 'in the summertime'. Several times his friend complained that he had been harmed 'by them'. Robinson asked him who he meant, to which Robert had replied 'that he verily thought that the said Anne Whittle, alias Chattox, and the said Redfearn's wife, had bewitched him'.

In her examination by Roger Nowell, Elizabeth Southerns discussed how she was passing near the Redfearn home on a midsummer day that same year, 1594. She was carrying milk in 'a can or kit'.[140] When she came within three yards of the east end of the building, she saw her former friend Anne Whittle and her daughter Anne Redfearn on one side of the ditch and the other opposite. Two 'pictures of clay or marl' lay beside them, and each woman was busy with the clay or marl to make a third. As she passed very near them, but apparently unseen, her spirit familiar, Tibb, appeared in the shape of a black cat. He told her, 'Turn back again, and do as they do.' Elizabeth responded, 'What are they doing?' Tibb told her they were making three pictures and when she asked who the pictures were meant to represent, he told her, Christopher Nutter, Robert Nutter and Robert's wife Marie. Elizabeth recalled that she refused Tibb's instruction to retrace her steps and help them. Tibb then became angry and 'shoved or pushed' Elizabeth into the ditch, making her spill the milk she had in a container. He then vanished from her sight but returned soon afterwards 'in the shape of a hare' and followed her about a quarter of a mile, but neither she nor he spoke a word.

James Device told Nowell a remarkably similar tale in which he claimed to have witnessed Thomas Redfearn, his wife 'Anne Redfearn the Witch' and their daughter Marie with 'three pictures of clay, of half a yard long'. Each family member held a clay image; Anne Redfearn 'was then crumbling' the one in her hands. James was unable to work out who the images were meant to represent and was prevented from moving closer when 'some ten roods off' from the three Redfearns 'a thing like a hare' appeared and spat fire at him. James dated the sighting to around 1610, but the parallels between his statement and that of his grandmother suggest they occurred around the same time.

The hare is significant: in his grandmother's telling, the hare is Tibb in another guise, in which case it might be inferred to be protecting James from the Redfearns; however, the implication in James's statement is that it was in fact protecting the Redfearns. Hares were and are closely associated with witchcraft. In 1662, Isobel Gowdie told a court in Scotland that she could change her shape at will by reciting: 'I shall go into a hare, With sorrow and sych and meickle [much] care; And I shall go in the Devil's name, Ay while I come home again.'[141] More than likely, James's statement was a simplified copy of the other, changed enough to further incriminate Anne Whittle and her daughter. The incident is one of very few mentions of Anne Whittle's granddaughter Marie; in 1609 she married Richard Clayton at St Mary's and seems to have escaped unscathed from the witchcraft charges that befell her mother and grandmother.

But it may be that Elizabeth Southerns was being truthful in her statement about having spotted the two Annes busily making clay pictures. Image magic has been a universal practice for thousands of years, based on the ancient belief that there is an unseen correlation between things or people that look alike or have been in contact with each other. Palaeolithic hunters would mould clay into shapes representing animals such as bear and bison, then spear them ritually to ensure a fruitful expedition; the remnants of those shapes have been discovered in caves in southern France. In ancient Egypt, likenesses of enemies of the state were stabbed, burnt or buried, with whatever was left then dissolved in urine.

King James refers to image magic in *Daemonologie*, stating that 'the Devil teacheth how to make pictures of wax or clay, that, by roasting thereof, the persons that they bear the name of may be continually melted or dried away by continual sickness'. There were various methods and different materials used in the process, whose appeal lay partially in the fact that it was 'not difficult to construct a rough effigy of wax or clay, name it for the detested enemy, stab it with thorns, or nails, or pins, and then destroy it slowly by roasting or melting it before a fire, or burying it and leaving it to rot in the ground. No great skill or long practice in magic was needed for this work, only strong hatred, and enough determination to carry the rite through to the end.'[142] For someone nursing a grievance and feeling ineffective, the act of creation was satisfying in itself, and offered a means of retaliation against those who were otherwise unassailable, as we see with Anne Whittle and her family.

In Scotland, the maker of a 'clay corpse' would utter a charm and pierce the small figure with pins where they wanted their victim to feel pain. The clay was then placed in a stream or river and, as it crumbled, the victim would weaken. One Scottish account tells how one young woman, discovering that she had a love rival, crafted a clay image of her that she left in a stream for the inevitable to take place. The other woman duly fell ill but recovered when a shepherd saw the crumbling clay figure and plucked it from the water. The maker of the image began creating another but was caught in the act and punished.

In Ireland, likenesses were often fashioned from wheat, with hearts of plaited straw and pins in the joints. The ritual involved its creator visiting a church to recite a charm or prayers while facing away from the altar, then burying the flaxen doll near their victim's home in wet soil to hasten death or dry soil to make the end protracted and painful. Sometimes the wax or wheat image was replaced by a lit candle in which pins were stuck; the victim wasted away as the candle burnt down. On other occasions the victim's name was written on paper, which was then attached to a tree and left to rot. Clay was put to other uses by cunning folk: if someone wanted to know the identity of a thief, names of possible suspects were written on paper, then rolled into clay balls and submerged in water; the first to fall open would reveal the guilty party.

Several witch trials refer to image magic. In 1570, a group of Windsor women created figures from red wax, which they pricked with hawthorn spikes through the heart. Twenty years later, Agnes Sampson described making an image from yellow wax, which she then conjured in the victim's name and placed on a fireside to melt away. Crumbling a clay image is less common but is recounted in several instances by those involved in the Pendle trials. Elizabeth Southerns described with great eloquence how it was done, telling Nowell that 'the speediest way to take a man's life away by witchcraft, is to make a picture of clay . . . and dry it thoroughly'. To inflict pain 'take a thorn or pin, and prick it in that part' of the clay picture. To cause that part of the body to waste away, 'take that part of the picture, and burn it' or, to kill them outright, she suggested burning the image entire 'and so there upon by that means, the body shall die'.[143]

Anne Whittle was a proud cunning woman who appears to have taught her married daughter the trade. Given Robert's behaviour and his threat of eviction, practising image magic against their landlord's son might have seemed a feasible means of self-protection. Anne Whittle told Nowell that although she had withdrawn from the murder plot with the other three women, after Robert Nutter had assaulted her daughter, she 'called Fancie to her; who came to her in the likeness of a man in a parcel of ground called, the Laund'. Her familiar asked what she would have him to do, to which Anne 'bade him go revenge her of the said Robert Nutter'. Clearly, the intimation is that Fancie did as she had bidden him, with irreversible consequences.

Robert remained ill. His brother John recalled later to Nowell that around Christmas 1594, he and his brother were returning from Burnley with their father Christopher when Robert suddenly said, 'Father, I am sure I am bewitched by the Chattoxes – Anne Chattox and Anne Redfearn, her daughter. I pray you, cause them to be laid in Lancaster Castle!' Christopher frowned at his son, responding, 'Thou art a foolish lad,' adding that it was all in his son's head. To the surprise of both men, Robert then began to cry, insisting, 'Nay, I am sure that I am bewitched by them.' But in a flash of his old temper, he added that if he were to return from his imminent business trip, he would ensure that the two women would be put in such a place 'where they shall be glad to bite lice in two with their teeth!' In other words, he would have them thrown into prison, where they should starve.

The story behind Robert's insistence that he had been bewitched was very possibly local knowledge – and scandalous at that. His was a family of good standing and Robert himself was the right-hand man of the most eminent local landowner yet had attempted to force himself upon a married woman – who also happened to be the daughter of a notorious cunning woman. His father, Christopher, seems to have been a reasonable man and of good temper; he still welcomed Thomas Redfearn to Greenhead Manor and probably found his son a great embarrassment. He did not believe him to be bewitched, except perhaps in the way in which he had thought about Redfearn's wife. He told him to desist from making such claims, but to no avail.

When the season's somewhat muted festivities were over, Robert prepared to accompany his master, Sir Richard Shuttleworth, on a trip to Wales. Shortly before the two men were due to leave, Thomas Redfearn visited Greenhead. John overheard his brother talking to the older man in a state of fury, shouting, 'If you ever come here again, I shall have my father put you out of your house – or I myself shall pull it down!' Redfearn replied quietly, 'When you come back again, you will be in a better frame of mind.' The conversation ended there, and Redfearn departed. Soon after, Robert left for Wales with his master and told him, too, that he believed himself bewitched.[144] When the trip ended, the two men began their journey home. But Robert was ailing fast. They had just reached Cheshire when, on the eve of Candlemas (2 February), he finally succumbed to his long, nameless malady. He was buried at the ancient St Peter's Church in Burnley.

For Christopher Nutter, his son's death was a cause of grief but not of vengeance, despite the wild claims he had made about Anne Whittle and her daughter; there was no suggestion that he would turn them out, even after his son's passing. But there would have been rumours. Particularly when Christopher, too, fell sick. By Maudlintide (22 July) 1595, he was very seriously ill. Languishing in his room at Greenhead Manor, Christopher was visited by his daughter, Margaret. 'He did sundry times say,' she later told Roger Nowell, 'that he was bewitched.' But when asked who had caused him to be so ill, 'he named nobody that should do the same'. Whatever rumours there had been about Robert Nutter's source of sickness, and now that of his father, it was not Christopher Nutter who fostered any belief that Anne Whittle and her daughter were to blame – perhaps out of respect for Thomas Redfearn.

Christopher Nutter died at Michaelmas (29 September) 1596. But their troubles did not end there. Marie, Robert Nutter's widow, survived any bewitchment that might have gone in her direction; a year after her husband's death, and following the finalising of the business of his will, she married their neighbour, Henry Robinson of Old Laund. Henry moved into Greenhead Manor, but, within a year, Marie too was dead and he was in St Mary's Church again, in Newchurch-in-Pendle, where they had married only a few months before. Henry could not dismiss the rumours of a curse on the family into which he had married; he decided to leave the area completely. He bought a handsome home, Swinsty Hall, in Yorkshire, for a good sum due to its owner being severely in debt. He married a woman named Jennet, with whom he had two sons and three daughters. Shortly thereafter, Jennet fell into depression, refused to leave her bed and began threatening to kill their children.

Jennet was probably suffering from undiagnosed post-natal depression, but Henry could not forget what had happened to his first wife and family; he began to wonder if Anne Whittle and her daughter had such powers that they were now afflicting his second wife. Hoping another woman might help her feel less isolated, he engaged young Bess Foster to help with the children and to spend some time with Jennet. Henry must have felt himself to be living in a strange world indeed when his neighbour, poet Edward Fairfax, claimed that Bess was bewitching his own daughter in some way after she began acting strangely following Bess appearing to her in a dream. Matters worsened and came to a head in August 1622, when six women whom Edward Fairfax had accused of witchcraft were tried at York. The case collapsed when a friend of Fairfax's daughter confessed that her own father had invented the whole scenario. The man was imprisoned, and Edward Fairfax wrote a book about the affair, *Daemonologia*. Fairfax died ten years after the trial. His home, New Hall, now lies beneath the waters of Swinsty reservoir.

In his writings, Fairfax noted that his neighbour, a Mr Robinson, had lost his first wife to the maleficium of the 1612 witches. Today the case is all but forgotten, but it demonstrates how even 'in an intellectual and social milieu . . . gossip about witchcraft, knowledge of witchcraft and worry about witchcraft were commonplace'.[145] Henry passed away in 1639, still haunted by his past. Swinsty Hall still stands on the banks of the reservoir, above the submerged ruins of New Hall; it is currently occupied by the former manager of the English national football team, Gareth Southgate, and his family.

Chapter Five

HE WERE BUT YOUNG
or
JAMES DEVICE

'A monster in nature', 'dangerous and malicious' and a 'wicked and miserable wretch' were just some of the terms Thomas Potts used to describe James Device, grandson of Elizabeth Southerns. James has fared no better in the books published since his death: writers have been almost unanimous in believing him to have had some form of learning difficulty; one asserts that he was suffering from schizophrenia; writers Peel and Southern refer to him as 'evidently half-witted' and whose evidence was 'inexplicable nonsense and triviality', while eminent Burnley historian Walter Bennett claimed that James – as the offspring of a woman who was 'mentally unstable and prone to fits of uncontrollable passion' – was 'a youth of weak and childish intellect . . . inclined to be vicious but frightened by authority . . . incapable of working, always begging, and a thief'.[146]

These later twentieth-century pronouncements are not simply harsh, baseless and untrue; they are alarming in that they suggest, even in our own time, hundreds of years after James Device was hanged for witchcraft, he is still regarded as someone so easily dismissed as to be worthless. The sole voice of reason is writer Jonathan Lumby, who describes James as 'a callow country lad . . . but this young man was no simpleton. He had religious scruples, was a Christian and, clearly, no demonist.'[147]

Born in 1590, the year of his parents' marriage, James was the eldest of their children. He seems to have been close to the women in his family, perhaps especially because by the time of his fifth birthday, he had suffered two catastrophic losses that left him the only male in the household. His younger brother, Henry – to whom James was close in age – died at the age of four. Then, a few months later, James's father, John Device, became seriously ill. Once again, the finger of suspicion pointed very emphatically at Anne Whittle, whose former friendship with Elizabeth Southerns had become so badly fermented that other members within both families were drawn into their feud.

Alizon Device later explained to Roger Nowell that her father 'being afraid that the said Anne Chattox should do him or his goods any hurt by witchcraft' made an arrangement whereby 'if she would hurt neither of them', he would pay her an 'aghen-dole' of meal each year. 'Aghen' meant 'in hand', and used with 'dole' referred to a handout. Thus, John Device had agreed to pay Anne Whittle what would now amount to eight and a half pounds of oatmeal every year.[148] However, in the year prior to his death, he either failed or refused to continue with the arrangement.

Nonetheless, the spoken contract belies understanding and something must be missing from the account of it given in *Discoverie*, for why would John Device be so frightened of Anne Whittle when he had, apparently, married into a family of cunning folk, with a mother-in-law who was not scared of confrontation, particularly when it concerned her family. Perhaps, given the Nutters' run of tragedy, he feared that Anne Whittle was capable of anything and might have been more powerful than they suspected? Perhaps he was not willing to take the risk? In that case, he may have kept the arrangement from his wife and mother-in-law to protect them all. There is another factor, too, not previously considered: in the year that John Device failed to make the payment to Anne, his young son Henry passed away. It isn't too difficult to imagine that John Device believed this was Anne's doing too – although he again said nothing to his own grieving family about his suspicions – and his probable guilt and heartache caused him to sicken physically as well as psychologically.

And there was, it seems, another reason for him to be deeply troubled that year, which must have been one of the most difficult of his life. Around the time of their younger son's death, his wife fell pregnant again. It is hard to imagine the emotional strain the two bereaved parents were under, but to make matters even more complicated, there were rumours that the child Elizabeth Device was carrying was not fathered by her husband. We can never know now whether the rumours were true or not, and certainly when the child was born, in 1600, she was given her mother's married surname. The baptismal register of St Mary's of Newchurch-in-Pendle lists the baby as Jennet Device, but the burial records hold an entry that corresponds with other information we have about her life, and this tells us that a woman named 'Jennet Seller als [also known as] Devis' was buried on 22 December 1635, with the entry being added at a later date.[149] Local historians have discovered that Sellar was common enough surname in the area of Whalley where Elizabeth Southerns had grown up, but there were fewer in Pendle: a handful of people named Sellar/Seller farmed at Newchurch and Barley, and another family of the same name lived at nearby White Moor. The probability that the entry in the burial register references 'our' Jennet is fairly high; we know that Jennet was the only survivor of the 1612 witch trials, and it is a definite possibility that she took her father's surname afterwards, either to distance herself from events, or because she found a new home with him.

Although it has been said that 'so many of the leading gentry of the county had bastard children that illegitimacy carried no social stigma', in fact it did matter, very much, to women like Elizabeth Device.[150] The Poor Law Act of 1576 named 'bastardy' as 'a great dishonour' to the nation generally. Quite apart from the effect such rumours would have had on her husband and children, it mattered because a woman's reputation was often the catalyst for how she and her family were treated. Women were forceful in defending their own characters in this regard;

the Church Courts of York in the 1590s show that most defamation cases were brought by women suing those who had referred to them as whores. And a reputation for having a less than circumspect attitude where the number of sexual partners was concerned was also frequently regarded as a potential indicator that a woman might be a witch.

A woman giving birth outside wedlock was required to identify the father under the Poor Law Act of 1576. He was then obliged to pay a weekly fee to the parish, but in practice, that often failed to occur. It was easy enough then for a man to deny fathering a child, while a woman had no such recourse to escape the consequences. The revised Act of 1598 decreed that illegitimate children would be forced to work if their parents did not support them financially, and while the birth rates among unmarried women in Newchurch-in-Pendle (and Padiham, Colne and Burnley) were high at the time, it was not only impoverished, unmarried women who had children; as we already know, illegitimacy was also high among the financially comfortable and gentry.

Unsurprisingly, then, Elizabeth Device was pained and enraged when 'John Robinson, alias Swyer, of Barley' (not to be confused with the Robinsons who were related to the Nutters of Greenhead) began spreading rumours about her during an already excessively turbulent period for her family. The Robinson family lived at Foothouse Gate Farm, which still stands, adjacent to Black Moss reservoir, off the track leading to the Pendle sculpture trail, which commemorates the trials. Elizabeth later told magistrate Roger Nowell that 'Robinson had chidden and becalled [her] for having a bastard-child with one Seller' and there would be comments from other men, too.

The ongoing tensions did nothing to help John Device, who became paranoid that his first suspicions were right, and that his mother-in-law's rival was to blame for his family's troubles. Alizon, his daughter, recalled for Roger Nowell that 'her father, upon his then deathbed, taking it that the said Anne Whittle, alias Chattox, did bewitch him to death, because the said meal was not paid the last year'. We must bear in mind that accusations of witchcraft from a person on their deathbed were not uncommon with most due to fevers, rather than a stone-cold certainty of bewitchment. But John Device had clearly feared Anne Whittle for some time and believed that in the end she had carried out the threat that lay behind their previous agreement. He was buried in St Mary's churchyard in Newchurch-in-Pendle.

Anne Whittle's daughter Bessie was in her thirties at the turn of the new century. We know so little of her from *Discoverie*, and there is no sense of her having taken part either in cunning work or the creation of clay images, despite living with her family at West Close. It has always been believed that Bessie was unmarried and childless, but during the writing of this book it was discovered that Bessie had a child and may well have been married as the parish registers suggest.

During recent research into the household accounts of the Shuttleworths of Gawthorpe by current staff members, it was discovered that parts of the previous transcription had been misinterpreted. An entry that was once believed to refer to clothes in Bessie's possession (and therefore regarding the following event) was both misunderstood and wrongly dated. The text actually tells us that four days after the trial, the Shuttleworths made a payment to the parish in Padiham 'towardes the bringing upp of Besse Chattocks childe'.[151] The Shuttleworths had a moral responsibility towards the child's care because the mother, Bessie, lived on sublet land at West Close belonging to them. There is no mention of a husband or the father of her child, and it seems reasonable to assume that Bessie was quite alone at the time.

Frustratingly, for now at least, the trail ends there, but the correction gives us a fraction more insight into Bessie's life, which remains otherwise largely obscure. Our only other glimpse into her character is from an incident recounted in 1612 by Alizon Device, which despite its solitary nature conveys across the centuries that she was an audacious woman with a distinctly mischievous streak, capable of causing deliberate provocation to those whom her family regarded as enemies.

In the months following John Device's death, Bessie left home to walk the two miles or so to the home he had shared with his wife and children.[152] Finding it empty and no one nearby, she forced her way inside. Alizon later referred to Bessie having broken into their 'firehouse', which simply meant a dwelling with a fire – their home – rather than a non-residential building. Bessie moved quickly about the place, collecting clothing and food, and was gone before anyone spotted her.[153]

Elizabeth Device and her family were devastated when they returned home and discovered the burglary. Alizon later recounted what had been stolen: most of their linen clothes, 'half a peck of cut oatmeal' and a quantity of meal, amounting to a loss of twenty shillings or more. Today's equivalent would be around £100, and for the Devices, that was a huge sum. To lose so much food and clothing was ruinous, when even the loss of small items could tip the balance between existence and collapse for a family.

Nor was this a theft that Bessie hoped to keep quiet, but quite the opposite: she fully intended to bait the Devices with it when the time came. The Sunday after her daring mission, she headed into church, wearing 'a band and a coife' that she had taken from Elizabeth Device. A coife covered the hair and was worn by married women to show their status; removing the coife to give the impression that one was single, was known as 'letting your hair down'. Bessie undoubtedly wore the ribbon and coife purely to needle the Devices. She succeeded in causing a row before the entire congregation, who heard how she had stolen those items as part of a bigger theft from their home.

Bessie remained unbothered. After all, the two families had been at each other's throats for years now, in a game of attack and retaliation, but it was always kept between them. They were, simply, not the sort of people who liked to involve the authorities in their grievances, no matter how severe. But the incident added further kindling to the fire that both families were tending and sent a message to Elizabeth Device that she and her children were fair game now that John was dead.

Whatever their relationship had been at the time of his demise, Elizabeth Device must have felt fearful and alone without her husband after ten years of marriage. She was now responsible for three children: James, Alizon and Jennet, while mourning a fourth, Henry. Her mother, although seemingly indomitable, would also need her help more as the years went by too. Elizabeth's brother, Christopher, and his wife and children lived nearby but it was usually the daughter who took on the greater share of care for an ailing parent. But like her mother, Elizabeth was resourceful and strong and had endured a great deal; her determination and willingness to take on whatever work became available kept the fragile thread of survival from fraying.

As her eldest child – and indeed, like all children from an early age – James would have been expected to help in the home, doing chores and tasks set for him by his mother. He would have had little education; rather than attend school, some impoverished children were provided with apprenticeships by their local parishes in an effort to prevent them from becoming burdens on their communities. Most apprenticeships were in 'humble' work, such as labouring. James may well have been given some form of help in this regard, working as a child and then a young adult as part of that 90 per cent of people who toiled on the land, joining the ranks of the poorest who worked as labourers and 'owned nothing but rented themselves out daily for a fee. A life spent working the land was hard, physical and precarious.'[154] He would have been physically strong – and we know this from his carrying home a stolen sheep across the steep hills between his home and the farm where he had purloined it – and was clearly, despite his earlier biographers' claims, not afraid of hard work.

Like all labourers, he would go where the work took him, walking home hot and bone-tired at the end of a long day's labour. Keeping clean was a challenge, although standards were different then and natural odours were regarded as less offensive. Most labourers would jump in a stream or pond to wash the grime from their skin, but cleaning clothes was more difficult and usually it meant turning them inside out every now and then – although white clothing was often cleaned with urine. Bedding and other materials could be aired and woodsmoke tended to overpower most unpleasant smells. In the morning, if he was fortunate enough to have another day's work ahead, he would rely on the sounds outside, particularly the crowing cockerel, or the rising sun to know when to leave home, and church bells were the shared timepiece of all inhabitants of a community.

Those periods in the agricultural calendar where more hands were needed were James's best, but the more fallow periods between would have caused anxiety. The average farm worker's wage rose between 1550 and 1603, but prices climbed at a more rapid rate, and in order to survive and help his family, James went poaching and begging. He at least had a roof over his head, parents and other family who loved him, and if he were anything like his peaceable father, he would have preferred to avoid trouble in an area that was regarded by the government as feral and lawless, 'where the church was honoured without much understanding of its doctrines by the common people'.[155]

The lands that made up what would later become the county of Lancashire were collectively known as the Blackburn Hundred. It was one of the most impoverished regions in England. Many shared the opinion of Lord Strange, who in 1583 described his native county as 'so unbridled and bad a handful of England'.[156] The Council in the North complained that it was impossible to maintain good order in Yorkshire, because its people couldn't be 'insulated from the evil influence of Lancashire'.[157] The men of the Blackburn Hundred were notorious even among their own as having a propensity for 'theft, violence and sexual laxity'.[158] The Duchy of Lancaster established a commission to investigate the 'detestable crimes and offences of adultery, incest, fornication and bawdry' in the region and to clamp down on the 'unusual sexual delinquency of Lancashire men'.[159]

The Forest of Pendle itself was wild and remote, its poor roads frequently impassable, the moorlands desolate and marshy, and its rivers given to bursting their banks. Most of the inhabitants were self-sufficient, illiterate and suspicious of outsiders. They lived scattered in small, isolated homesteads with little communication with the world beyond their everyday reach. The area's gentry was a relatively small group, less wealthy than their southern counterparts, and relied on patronage and connections to ensure the survival of family names. 'Social inferiors' were not admitted, resulting in the leading families all being related in some way. Marriages between relatives were arranged in order to keep estates together, rather than splitting them among inheritors. The county's ruling group 'formed a compact and inter-related coterie'.[160] Strong alliances and settlements were of equal importance; unions were negotiated while children were still of school age, with records revealing that couples could be as young as five years old. Child marriages were common among poorer families too. Lancashire appears to have been 'unusual in this respect', although such unions were not against the law.[161]

But there were as many conflicts between families as there were mergers. Those at the top of the social scale were said to maintain their position through intimidation and violence. Physical altercations frequently took place in church, where rivals were certain to meet, and the clergy themselves could occasionally be found brawling in the aisles. The enmity between families, especially among the better off, would spill over into other areas of worship, such as conflict over the size, placement and ownership of pews, as was the case with the Nowells, who spent years quarrelling over the imposing and richly carved 'Kage' in St Mary's and All Saints Church in Whalley.

The local church or chapel was at the centre of village life. It was regarded by parishioners as a suitable place to buy and sell goods, with the atmosphere on Sundays often resembling that of a street market. Church attendance was compulsory; those who refused or failed to appear were known as recusants and threatened with fines and even imprisonment. Hefty penalties were also in place for anyone who attended Catholic services, while Catholic priests were hunted and executed, while those who had harboured them faced prosecution and forfeiture. Small groups of devout Catholic recusants survived nonetheless and were at their strongest in Lancashire, headed by the gentry class but also among yeomen and farmers.

Because parishes were often substantial in size, the ecclesiastical authorities struggled to establish control. It was therefore 'a much more formidable task to enforce laws and detect offenders in Lancashire than in most other parts of England'.[162] By the end of Elizabeth I's reign the numbers were increasing, from 498 detected recusants in 1598 to almost 2,000 in 1603 – the largest Catholic community in England, albeit still a minority overall. King James I recorded that: 'At our first entering to this Crown and Kingdom we were informed, and that too, truly, that our county of Lancaster abounded more in popish recusants than any other country of England.'[163]

James Device, in common with the rest of his family, was an avid churchgoer. However, he later claimed that Anne Whittle had partaken in some particularly unusual activity at St Mary's around the time of his father's death, when James would have been about ten years old. Despite the animosity between the two families, James insisted that Anne herself had told him how, following a burial, she had taken 'three scalps [skulls] of people, which had been buried and then cast out of a grave'. From these, she removed 'eight teeth . . . she kept four to herself, and gave the other four' to his grandmother, who apparently buried them 'at the west end' of Malkin Tower, her home, 'about half a yard over in the earth' with a picture of clay, 'almost withered away', which was a representation of a girl Anne was later accused of murdering by witchcraft. These items were later found after James led a police constable to them during the investigation of 1612.

This strange story is given credibility by several factors. First, that James himself led the constable to Malkin Tower, where they were subsequently discovered, and secondly, because teeth were often used in magic, together with human bones, skulls, nails and urine. Teeth were especially useful in medicinal magic, and a teething child was said to be soothed by hanging a pouch containing a human tooth about its neck. Witch bottles too – usually for the protection against witchcraft – often utilised human teeth: in 2019, an ancient bottle containing fish hooks, glass shards and a human tooth afloat in an unidentified liquid (probably urine) was unearthed during work on a family home in Watford; it was the 1761 birthplace of Angeline Tubbs, who later emigrated to America where she became known as the Witch of Saratoga for telling fortunes. Another bottle found in 2021 by a metal detectorist had been buried in woodland near Oswestry in Shropshire and contained hair, urine and a human tooth. Perhaps more in keeping with the cunning magic performed by the two Pendle families was the belief that the teeth had occult properties having lain in churchyard earth, which Catholic priests would consecrate with salt and water.

James was careful to relate that Anne Whittle had not dug up the teeth – which was illegal – but had discovered them 'cast out of a grave'. The oldest building in Newchurch-in-Pendle is thought to be that in the churchyard near the main gate. The windows and fireplace are thought to date from the seventeenth century with considerable renovations at a later date, or dates. Its upper floors once served as a school, and it is believed to have been the home of the minister for a time. But it was also used as a charnel house, where bones unearthed by gravediggers when the ground became too full would have been stored. It was common then to excavate the early graves that had no headstones, or those whose families were impoverished and could afford only the simplest of grave-markers and to remove the bones and use the plots again for the recently deceased. Over the course of time, the bones of those related to the 1612 accused would be dispersed, lost, and all memory of them gone.

There are problems with James's story, nonetheless. His grandmother and Anne Whittle had long since ceased to be on the terms that would allow for sharing of elements for use in magical craft by the time of the incident. In all probability, it was his grandmother who had acquired the teeth for her own purposes, but by incriminating Anne Whittle, James would also provide Roger Nowell with apparent corroborating evidence against her. This was especially so with regard to the withered clay image, which James used as a means of demonstrating that his grandmother had attempted to 'unwitch' Anne Whittle's victim.

It seems that Anne Whittle was being increasingly viewed as less a cunning woman and more a potential witch. In 1606, she was employed to card wool, which was something of a regular income for her. Somewhat puzzlingly, the woman who asked for Anne's help in this instance was the wife of James Robinson, who had lived with the Greenhead Nutters and would later give evidence that Robert and his father Christopher believed Anne had brought about the sickness that eventually killed them. Nevertheless, 'upon a Friday and Saturday, she came and carded wool' alongside James's wife. They worked together perfectly well and thus 'the Monday then next after she came likewise to card'. James's wife had brewed some ale, a staple drink in almost every household of the time and usually the drink that accompanied meals as well as an ingredient in many: 'great quantities of ale . . . were drunk on dusty harvest days and mulled in winter chimney-corners for heartening effect'.[164] Most of these cheaper ales were thick and cloudy with a taste depending on the herbs added to the brew; small ale was weak enough for children to drink safely. The ale was housed in a vessel next to where Anne worked with her paddles and wool. Having a thirst from the dust and effort, she took 'a dish or cup . . . drawing drink several times'. Unfortunately, the ale spoiled and was undrinkable 'for some eight or nine weeks'. James Robinson was certain the drink had been ruined 'by the means of the said Chattox' rather than any fault with the ingredients of the ale itself, or with the brewer – his wife.

But more serious claims yet were being made against Anne Whittle. In 1612, Alizon Device stated that 'about six or seven years ago', her grandmother's former friend 'did fall out with one Hugh Moore of Pendle' about 'certain cattle' belonging to him; Moore claimed that she had bewitched his livestock. He and his family lived at White Lees, on a farm whose fields adjoined the Redfearn property; the cattle would have been, quite literally, on Anne's doorstep. Hugh's wife happened to be Mary Nutter, the sister of Christopher Nutter, head of the Nutter family, whom Anne Whittle was rumoured to have murdered through witchcraft.[165] According to Alizon Device, Anne now turned her attention to Hugh; she 'did curse and worry' him and warned that 'she would be revenged' of him. Hugh then 'fell sick, and languished about half a year, and then died'. In what was now a familiar pattern, 'Moore upon his death-bed said that the said Chattox had bewitched him to death'.

Alizon also related for the benefit of Roger Nowell another incident from around this period involving Anne Whittle. The two families – in particular, the matriarchs, Elizabeth Southerns and Anne Whittle – were frequent visitors to Bull Hole Farm and had been so for many years. Elizabeth remained a neighbour of farmer John Nutter, while Anne and her family had lived close by for a long time before relocating to West Close. John Nutter occasionally employed Elizabeth and Anne in their capacity as cunning women, and in turn they would call in to see if he could spare them a little sustenance. On this occasion, as Alizon told it, Anne's younger daughter, Bessie, had visited John Nutter 'to beg or get a dish full of milk, which she had, and brought it to her mother, who was about a field's breadth of the said Nutter's house'. Taking the milk from her daughter, Anne poured it into a can 'and did charm the same with two sticks across in the same field'. But as Anne was reciting the charm, John Nutter's son appeared and was incensed by the sight of the elderly woman crouched over the can, quietly reciting words of enchantment. 'Misliking her doings', the young man marched across and kicked the can across the grass. It isn't difficult to imagine how Anne and her daughter reacted, watching their precious milk sink into the soil. Alizon does not recount the immediate events, but 'the morning next after, a cow of the said John Nutter fell sick, and so languished three or four days, and then died'.

Evidently, John Nutter's son did not share his father's magnanimity towards the two women. His reaction was swift and aggressive, but many farmers feared attracting negative magic into the dairy and its environs; the often-careless hygiene, bacterial issues and temperature was believed to create a petri dish for witchcraft. A witch could 'dry up' cows, bewitch cows and prevent butter from being made. One solution was to plunge a red-hot iron poker or, best of all, a horseshoe, into the cream. This was believed to reverse the spell and might burn the witch, 'who is actually or mystically present in the churn – in the form of a hare, it may be'.[166] If a known or suspected witch appeared during churning and was sent away without a little milk or pat of butter, farmers were led to expect 'many a weary hour of labour' when they next came to churning.[167] As a precautionary measure, they were advised to carve a churn-staff from the wiggan tree (rowan), 'and you will be effectually freed from her further interference'.[168] Likewise, milk pails were safest when fashioned from ash wood and hazel sticks were favoured for stirring milk in cooling troughs to save it from fairies. Across the border, in nearby Yorkshire, dairymaids prepped a 'churn spell' of their own to ensure the butter would come, by leaving a crooked silver sixpence on the witch post near the hearth. Plunging a glowing poker or horseshoe into the cream was believed to 'kill the witch' but actually simply produced the 60°F required for making butter.[169]

But it was not only Anne Whittle around whom whispers of witchcraft had begun to swirl faster. Elizabeth Device's anger towards John Robinson of Barley for his cruel taunting had scarcely diminished, if there is any truth in what she and her children told magistrate Roger Nowell in 1612. She describes how Ball, her familiar or spirit, had appeared to her for a third time 'in shape of a brown dog' at Malkin Tower. The phrasing of the examination makes it seem as if it had been Ball's idea to initiate what followed, for he had instructed Elizabeth to 'make a picture of clay after the said John Robinson, alias Sawyer'. Elizabeth had done so, 'at the west end' of Malkin Tower, which clearly was the place where the family carried out their magical practices. After she had moulded the clay picture, she dried it against the fire 'and crumbled all the same picture away within a week or thereabouts'.

Elizabeth's son confirmed to Nowell that he had been with her in Malkin Tower when 'there came a thing in the shape of a brown dog', whom his mother called Ball. James's account follows Elizabeth's version of events, namely, that Ball had 'bade her make a picture of clay like unto John Robinson . . . and dry it hard, and then crumble it by little and little, and as the said picture should crumble or mull away, so should [John Robinson] decay and wear away'. Ball had insisted that 'within two or three days after, the picture shall so all be wasted, and milled away; so then, the said John Robinson should die presently'. The dog then 'suddenly vanished'. James watched her mother 'take clay' at the west end of Malkin Tower and 'make a picture of it after the said Robinson'. About two days after the drying process was complete, James had watched his mother crumbling the picture of clay, 'every day some', for three weeks in all. He confirmed that 'within two days after all was crumbled or mulled away, the said John Robinson died'.

Prompted by Nowell about the matter, Elizabeth's youngest child, Jennet, made it clear that her mother, rather than Ball, had been the instigator of Robinson's murder. She recalled having seen her mother's familiar, or spirit, come to the house 'sundry times . . . in the likeness of a brown dog, which she called Ball'. On one occasion, Jennet had heard Ball ask what Elizabeth 'would have him to do, and [she] answered that she would have the said Ball help her to kill John Robinson of Barley, alias Sawyer'. Whatever the circumstances of his death, the registers record that John Robinson passed away in 1609 and was buried at St Mary's in Goldshaw Booth.

Jennet went on to tell the magistrate that 'about a year after' Robinson's death her mother had again 'called for the said Ball, who appeared as aforesaid'. When Ball asked what she wanted of him, her mother had replied that 'she would have him to kill James Robinson, alias Sawyer, of Barley aforesaid, brother to the said John, whereunto Ball answered, he would do it'. There was no known motive for this second 'killing' within the Robinson family, but within three weeks, James Robinson too was dead. He was buried in May 1610 in St Mary's alongside his brother.

Despite Elizabeth's efforts to insinuate that she had acted on the instructions of her spirit, Nowell had her young daughter's testimony, which was more damning. For as far as Jennet was concerned, Ball, the faithful familiar, simply did as his mistress bade him. But by then, another canine spirit was circling the family; this time, with its sights set firmly on her brother.

In the hilltop village of Goldshaw Booth, the New Church prepared to observe Eastertide of 1610. On Shear Thursday, the last before Easter, Elizabeth Southerns called for her grandson James and bade him not to eat the bread at the communion service but to 'bring it and deliver it to such a thing as should meet him on his way homewards'. James dutifully attended the service. He listened as the rector reminded the congregation how Christ had shown his humility and service by washing his disciples' feet at the Last Supper; afterwards he queued at the altar rail next to people he had known all his life as they shuffled in a line past the rector, who handed out tablets of unleavened bread and sips of wine to represent the body and the blood of Christ. If James remembered his grandmother's wishes, he chose to swallow the bread anyway.

Later that April day he must have wondered what to expect as he headed up the slope away from the church. He was some 'forty roods' away from the church when there suddenly appeared, he later recalled, 'a thing in the shape of a hare', who boldly asked whether he had brought the bread as his grandmother had instructed. James answered that he had not, and the hare-like thing flew into a temper, threatening 'to pull [James] to pieces'. James stood his ground and made the sign of the cross over his chest. The creature immediately sprang away.

Why had his grandmother told him to keep the Eucharist host for the hare-like creature? Evidently it was for some magical purpose. There was a common belief among the populace generally that anyone leaving church with the Communion bread in their mouth had taken possession of a powerful source of magic, with which they could cure ailments, reverse blindness, sate a fever and use as a charm of rare luck, both ill and benevolent. A cunning person who enjoyed gardening might also crush it into a powder and scatter it over the earth to ward off caterpillars. Accordingly, the Church had long been worried about potential thefts of the host; it represented the body of Christ and as such was a powerful signifier of protection in many forms. The *Malleus Maleficarum* refers to a woman who stole the host and hid it in a jar with a toad, ready to make it into a powder for use in her enchantments. In Lincolnshire, folklore held that if a woman kept the communion bread in her mouth, then fed it to a toad in a churchyard, the man she loved would want to marry her. Another version suggested that a young girl at her first communion could be made a witch if she kept half of the bread in her mouth. Other witches who managed to make away with the host would hide it in bedchambers to make people fall sick, or in stables to afflict cattle and in fields to ruin crops and cause drought. In addition, anyone suffering from fits could try effecting a cure by creeping three times under the communion table at midnight on Midsummer Eve, while it was also said that placing a bit of the consecrated wafer in a beehive to increase the supply of honey in one instance resulted in the pious bees building 'a little church of wax about the wafer, with towers, windows, altar, and all'.[170]

James's disobedience in the face of his grandmother's request, together with his behaviour before the hare-like thing plainly suggests that he wanted no part of her plan, or that he simply dare not try to hide the bread upon his person while in such close quarters with the minister. But in making the sign of the cross he had acted in such a way that would bring him approbation if seen, since that was now frowned upon as superstitious nonsense.

On Easter Monday, according to James's examination, 'hard by the new Church in Pendle' he was met by 'a thing like unto a brown dog'. The creature offered that James should be 'revenged of any whom he would' in return for his soul. James replied that his soul was not his to give but belonged to 'his saviour Jesus Christ'. Nonetheless, he decided that he was content to give the dog 'as much as was in him [he] had to give'.

There are points of contention here. If the hare-like spirit was so frightened or repelled by James making the sign of the cross that he sprinted away, then it does not follow that the creature would want the host. Nor could James have argued with his examiner that his grandmother wanted the consecrated wafer for 'good' magic, since Nowell regarded all magic as evil. Shear Thursday, the day James was asked to steal the communion wafer, was immediately followed by Good Friday, which was a significant day for the family both in terms of religion and cunning-wise.

And despite having told Nowell that he had given the brown dog part of his soul, when James was questioned again during his imprisonment, he stated that the spirit had told him that he was 'above Christ' and therefore James 'must absolutely give him his soul'. The brown dog had appeared to him 'sundry times' and always in the likeness of a dog, 'and at every time most earnestly persuaded him to give him his soul absolutely'. James insisted that he had always replied as before, that at this point he was adamant that he would give him his own part and no more.

If James hoped to convince Nowell that he had resisted as much as was in his power to do so, and that he had in some sense done the right thing, he was bitterly mistaken.

Chapter Six

BROUGHT UP IN THIS DETESTABLE COURSE OF LIFE
or
ALIZON DEVICE

Most accounts of the 1612 trials begin with Alizon Device. Her plea – or demand, if you believe the official account – for some pins is regarded as the catalyst for the events that took place in Pendle and Lancaster. She was nineteen years old. What might her life have been if she hadn't encountered the pedlar John Law on the sun-dappled lanes through Trawden Forest?

Marriage and motherhood were the expected map of Alizon's future; like her brother, she would have had no schooling as such but had learnt to live on her wits. Like James, too, she would have helped out at home from a very early age, particularly with household chores and looking after her younger siblings. She would have mixed in the same circles as her brother, who was a similar age to John Bulcock, of Moss End Farm within their immediate neighbourhood, and she enjoyed a lifelong friendship with Anne Nutter. Two years Alizon's junior, Anne lived in Newchurch with her mother Elizabeth and yeoman farmer father Anthony, who was closely related to the Nutters of Bull Hole Farm.

But death was never far away; Alizon was still a child when her father and younger brother died within a couple of years of each other. She would have been aware of the rituals of death within her home: the washing and winding of the bodies and her mother and grandmother, at least, sitting up all night to watch the corpse by flickering candlelight, murmuring prayers. There were no coffins; Alizon's father and brother were buried in their shrouds within a day or two of dying.

She witnessed the birth of two siblings: Henry, the brother who died, and Jennet, the sister who lived to become a pawn in a game that would destroy them all. Living in such close proximity, she would have had some understanding of how her siblings came to be; her mother's only practical means of avoiding pregnancy was abstinence or withdrawal. Most women could expect a high number of pregnancies in their lifetime, with six or seven reaching full term, but a less than favourable chance of more than two children reaching adulthood. Most parents experienced the unrelenting agony of losing one child or several. Alizon's mother may well have suffered miscarriages or still-births that went unrecorded. Pregnancy was rarely spoken about until after the fourth month, known as the quickening, when the possibility of miscarriage was smaller. In the absence of medical assistance, many pregnant women relied on charms of some sort to help with any issues during the gestation period. A wealthier mother-to-be might wear an eagle-stone, bought from abroad, in a small silk bag about her neck in the belief that this would eventually lead to an easier delivery. It was common among female relatives to pass written charms to each other during pregnancy too. Midwives were chosen with great care, not simply in terms of medical skill but bearing in mind that she was well-placed to cause harm if they so wished; Elizabethan midwives had to take an oath that they would refrain from using 'any kind of sorcery or incantation in the time of the travail of any woman'.[171] There were many superstitions, nonetheless, which often varied from one neighbourhood midwife to another.

Every birth carried a substantial amount of risk for both mother and child. Most women had someone ready to give whatever support they could; in all probability Elizabeth Southerns was present at the birth of her daughter's children, but such things could not be scheduled; labour began whenever and wherever the baby was ready. It was not until the nineteenth century that Caesarean sections were performed successfully, and pain relief came only in the form of prayer, herbs and wine. Chewing willow bark was believed to help and played a role in the development of aspirin. The high rates of infant mortality saw babies baptised within a few days of birth and wrapped immediately afterwards in the white chrism cloth mentioned by the Devices in their family charm. If the mother suffered ill-health or postnatal depression there was again no means of medical assistance. If the baby was illegitimate, or rumoured to be illegitimate, as was the case with Elizabeth Device's last surviving child, then her ordeal was intensified: magistrates were within their rights to order punishment for breach of the peace against a woman whose child was born out of wedlock, or to a man other than her husband. The law looked unfavourably on the mother, rather than the father, if she could not financially support her child. The man might be prosecuted to force him into a form of maintenance, but a woman could expect to be whipped, have her hair forcibly cut off or sent to gaol.

As Alizon grew up in the expectation that her life probably would not be so different from that of her mother, she would have had to cope with changes in her own body in ways that seem foreign to us now. The average age for the menarche was fourteen, but that depended on the health of the girl concerned. If she failed to begin her periods, she was believed to be suffering green-sickness, a condition peculiar to adolescent females, with a range of physical and psychological symptoms. Often known as 'the flowers', this led to a seventeenth-century adage: 'Where there are no flowers there can be no fruit.' Scraps of old cloth were used to absorb the blood flow, as they had been since Biblical times. The view of menstruation was virtually unchanged since then too; women were regarded as inferior to men partly because they bled each month. It was not yet understood how or why menstruation occurred; one seventeenth-century theory held that women had an excess of blood that had to be expelled each month. It was regarded widely as foul or filthy and sought by demons. Other strange beliefs held that a child conceived as a result of sex during menstruation would be born red-haired and weak of limb or deformed. Simply by her presence, a menstruating woman was thought to be capable of causing mirrors to become cloudy, filling the air with a sulphurous stench, forcing bees to abandon their hives and crops to die.

By the time she was in her late teens, Alizon would have been familiar with her surroundings in a way that most of us cannot comprehend. There was a world beyond hers that she would never see; prior to 1612, her entire life was measured by how far she walked. But she would have known every bleat, cry, bark and rippling note of the creatures in that world; and its smells, from the fatty tallow candles and simmering pottage with stolen meat on the fire at home to the sweating flanks of cattle at the markets where she begged; and its weather, from thunder rolling in across the valley and the snow waiting in a sky pink as a pig's backside; and time, measured by the failing light and the crowing cockerel, by the church bells tolling a death or calling worshippers to prayer and the more joyful peals of celebration.

As for Alizon herself: Thomas Potts would have been incensed to realise that something of the real character of the people he so despised is revealed in *Discoverie*; from the little we can glean, Alizon leaves an impression of a young woman who was obedient and kind, believing that her family had supernatural powers and that she had them too, but was not yet able to control them. If she did any form of paid work, we don't hear of it from Potts; she walked long miles to beg at places where her chances of scraping together some coins were most favourable. When confronted with an alleged misdemeanour, she would cry and plead forgiveness, either from remorse or fear, or in the expectation that her tears might stem the situation from escalating unstoppably. But the circumstances in which she found herself being accused were never in regard to small issues or ones that she could actively disprove; equally, she knew that neither society nor justice was on her side.

Above all, Alizon's love for her grandmother survives Potts's best efforts to efface the true nature of their relationship. Elizabeth Southerns lost her sight later in life, probably because of cataracts, which left the sufferer 'stone blind'. Alizon was her grandmother's eyes when needed, accompanying Elizabeth wherever she asked to go and for whatever reason, even if it meant more confrontation. Alizon appears to have been her grandmother's closest companion and clearly held her in the highest regard. Once the wheels of the witchcraft investigation began to revolve, the authorities appear to have cast the two women in the role of the witch and her apprentice; as a result, Alizon and her grandmother were in the first group from Pendle to be dispatched to Lancaster and endured the entire experience together. The subsequent impact of Elizabeth's death during imprisonment must have brought Alizon close to breaking point. But it was in her grandmother's defence that Alizon took centre stage, when in court she was asked whether she could reverse the 'curse' placed on the pedlar John Law. No, she replied, but if her grandmother had lived, 'she could and would have helped him out of that great misery'. In that one instance, Alizon showed the great courage and loyalty of which she was capable, standing defiant against the authorities as they stared back at her in the small, stone courtroom.

At the beginning of the investigation, Alizon had provided magistrate Roger Nowell with several examples of her grandmother's magical abilities. One of these took place 'about two years ago' when Alizon had succeeded in begging 'a piggin [small wooden vessel with a handle on one side] full of blue milk' from a farm. She carried it into her grandmother's house, where Elizabeth lay in bed, and then left for about half an hour. Returning, Alizon was astonished to find 'butter to the quantity of a quarter of a pound' in the milk, which had not lessened in volume. She was certain there had been no butter in the house beforehand, and her grandmother still lay in bed. But she was certain the very welcome pat of butter was her grandmother's doing.

A more recent example concerned their near neighbour John Nutter of Bull Hole Farm, who requested Elizabeth Southerns' help with an ailing cow. At about 'ten of the clock in the night', Elizabeth called on Alizon to 'lead her forth'. They followed the familiar track to Bull Hole Farm with the land rising like a black wall on the horizon. It seems that Alizon left her grandmother at the farm, for she told Nowell that Elizabeth 'did remain about half an hour' and that it was her sister, Jennet – then ten or eleven years old – who 'did fetch her in again'. Alizon could not tell Nowell what had transpired at Bull Hole Farm that night, but the next morning she heard that the cow had died. Prompted no doubt by the magistrate, Alizon did 'verily thinketh, that her said grandmother did bewitch the said cow to death'. Whether John Nutter shared that view at the time is not recorded.

A far more immediately serious argument occurred as a result of Alizon's mother agreeing to 'help Richard Baldwin's folks' at his mill in Wheathead.[172] Elizabeth Device appears not to have been questioned about this issue by the magistrate in 1612, most probably because she wasn't present when the row unfolded. However, that leaves us wondering why she pressed her mother into visiting Baldwin at home to 'ask him something for her helping of his folks' rather than speaking to him herself. Alizon again accompanied her grandmother to the Baldwin home, which would have been some distance on foot for the two of them if it were near the mill, over Roughlee way.[173] Elizabeth Southerns recalled that 'near to the said house' they encountered Baldwin, who roared at them, 'Get out of my ground, whores and witches – I will burn the one of you and hang the other.' But she was not afraid of him. Seething at his inclusion of her granddaughter in his offensive spite, she replied, 'I care not for thee, hang thyself.' With Alizon close by her side, Elizabeth turned away. In her examination before Roger Nowell, she recalled how 'over the next hedge' Tibb then appeared. What form he took and whether her granddaughter could see him or not, she did not recount, declaring instead that Tibb had spoken to her, urging, 'Revenge thee of him.' Still incensed, she claims to have responded, 'Revenge thee of him, or his', letting Tibb know that he had her consent to harm Baldwin or those closest to him. Her familiar then vanished. It was their last meeting.

Elizabeth Southerns' account of the row with Baldwin ends there. But Alizon made a further statement, parts of which appear to be copied directly from her description of the visit to Bull Hole Farm. She told Nowell how, 'about four or five days then next after' her grandmother had come to ask her to 'lead her forth'. Again, this foray took place around ten o'clock at night, but Alizon does not say where they went or with what purpose, only that Elizabeth 'stayed forth about an hour' and Alizon left her there. As before, Jennet 'fetched her in again' and once more it was the following morning when Alizon learnt that Ellena, one of Richard Baldwin's young daughters, 'was fallen sick'. Although echoing how she came to 'verily thinketh' that her grandmother was the cause of the girl's languishing, here her account deviates, as she recalls hearing Elizabeth Southerns 'curse the said Baldwin sundry times'. Her last comment on the matter is a curious one, recalling how her grandmother said 'she would pray for the said Baldwin both still and loud'. No caveat is given, leaving us wondering whether Elizabeth Southerns intended to pray for Ellena to recover, knowing that suspicion would fall on her – and Alizon – if she passed away, or was 'pray' meant in the sense of saying a charm, for good or ill?

This period saw an escalation in tensions between the two families and their neighbours, with the already swirling rumours eddying only to return twice as volatile. For Alizon, it was marked by the death of another person close to her, apparently at the hands of her grand-mother's nemesis.

Anne Whittle later told magistrate Roger Nowell that she believed her gifts as a cunning woman were being compared, adversely, to those of her former friend, and named Anthony Nutter as having begun to 'favour Elizabeth Southerns'. Anthony was the father of Alizon's friend Anne, and a close relative of John Nutter of Bull Hole Farm. Anne Whittle had upset John Nutter's son when he found her 'muttering' over the milk her daughter Bessie had begged from his father and was believed to have killed one of their cattle in anger. Nevertheless, the Nutters were naturally closer to Elizabeth and her family, although Anne

Whittle had worked for them in the past using her cunning skills. If Anthony had employed her in the past, he may have felt uncomfortable about continuing to use her services after the trouble at Bull Hole Farm. But choosing to work with his daughter's friend's grandmother instead was certain to cause further disruption, for as Potts succinctly phrased it: 'Whom the one favoured, the other hated deadly.'

Writing up his examination of Anne Whittle, Roger Nowell stated that upon sensing betrayal, 'she called Fancie to her (who appeared like a man) and bade him go kill a cow of the said Anthony, which the said devil did, and that cow died also'. Thus, Anne had apparently confessed to killing two cows belonging to the Nutters' herds. She knew that cattle were extremely valuable, and for poorer families, the loss of a single cow could prove catastrophic. Farmers used many means of protecting their herd from witches, including plaiting sprigs of rowan around their horns or nailing the plaits above the cattle stalls. Witches were suspected of stealing milk by means of their own plaited ladder, such as the ancient one discovered in a Somerset farmhouse in 1887 during demolition; entwined with cockerel feathers, the 5ft-long rope would have been hung from a witch's window in order to magically steal from the cows at milking time. Cows' horns were also adorned with wax dripped from Easter candles and even the droving sticks used by farmers were chosen with protection from witches in mind, thus rowan and hazel were popular and believed to fatten the cattle. Cows were also said to do well in fields where hawthorn grew. Many charms and cures were utilised in Northern England and Scotland from the tenth century until the eighteenth, especially where 'elf-shot' cows were concerned. These were cows that failed to produce milk and were said to have been shot at by elves with sharp arrowheads. One way of countering the problem was said to be borrowing a blue bonnet from the eldest woman in the family and rubbing it all over the cow until the wound showed itself.

But according to Alizon and her brother James, Anne Whittle was not yet done with Anthony Nutter. Nowell duly wrote up that Alizon had recounted for him a visit to her friend Anne Nutter's home when 'the said Anne Whittle, alias Chattox, came into the said Anthony Nutter's house'. Whether the older woman had been invited or not is impossible to determine, but her gaze fell immediately on the two girls, who were laughing, and accused them of laughing at her. 'Well then,' the woman said darkly, 'I will be meet with the one of you.' This was an unguarded threat, as the girls would have known, and when Anne Nutter 'fell sick' the following day, Alizon knew what to expect: 'within three weeks' her childhood friend was dead.

Alizon's accusation of murder by witchcraft received some corroboration from her brother, James, when he was questioned during the 1612 investigation. He referred to the picture of clay discovered by himself and a constable at Malkin Tower, adding with deliberation that 'about half a yard over in the earth, where the said teeth lay, which said picture so found was almost withered away, and was the Picture of Anne, Anthony Nutter's daughter; as [his] grandmother told him'.

If Alizon truly believed Anne Whittle was responsible for the death of her father and friend – and it certainly seems that she did – then her willingness to share with Nowell more incidents painting the older woman in a poor light becomes more understandable. She offered him the story of how Anne was suspected of 'bewitching the drink of John Moore of Higham' in 1610. This in itself was a serious matter, for brewing was as important to households as baking bread or making butter, and only the most malicious of witches would ruin it. Agnes Waterhouse, one of the Chelmsford women hanged in 1566, was said to have caused 'Satan (her imp) to destroy the brewing'.[174]

Questioned about the matter by Nowell, Anne confirmed that John Moore's wife had requested her help with drink that was 'forspoken or bewitched'. Anne was a very strange choice, given that John Moore's wife Elizabeth was the daughter of Robert Nutter and the granddaughter of Christopher Nutter. Elizabeth had been a child when her father was alleged to have been bewitched to death by the woman she then selected to assist with some turned ale.[175] Even if Elizabeth had been unaware at the time that Anne was regarded by her family as having murdered father and son by witchcraft, she would have known once she reached adulthood. Clearly, there was more to the situation than met the eye, for at Elizabeth's request Anne made her way to one of two neighbouring properties owned by the Moores just north of Higham.

When Nowell confronted Anne Whittle with Alizon's claims, she responded that John Moore's wife had indeed sent for her help with drink that was 'for-spoken or bewitched' and she had recited 'this prayer for the amending of it':

> Three Biters hast thou bitten,
> The Hart, ill Eye, ill Tonge;
> Three Bitter shall be thy boote,
> Father, Sonne, and Holy Ghost,
> A God's Name
> Five Paternosters, five Avies,
> and a Creede,
> In worship of five woundes
> of our Lord.[176]

This solitary example of the prayers/charms in Anne Whittle's cunning repertoire has remarkable and palpable similarities with those used by the Devices. King James regarded such things as the work of women, or 'daft wives', but they are 'tweaked prayers' in Diane Purkiss's phrase, representing 'a set of hopes that are difficult to remove, a set of ideas about the body and how it can be controlled'.[177] Reverend Jonathan Lumby agrees, regarding them as texts of flawless Catholic orthodoxy that would not have been out of place spoken by priests in a church setting during the medieval period, such is the archaic quality of their content – and the fact that the prayers at the end were meant to be recited in full. He adds that we can be certain the women who spoke words infused with such strong faith were no Satanists. Equally, historian Keith Thomas declares that these prayers/charms 'reflected the idea that the resources of the Christian religion, if properly mobilised, were sufficient to deal with the powers of darkness'.[178]

The text itself bears little or no relation to the problem Anne Whittle had been asked to resolve, albeit accepted that charms/prayers could be applied to diverse issues. In this context, the words make it appear as though Anne is 'scolding the bad beer for being more bitter than an evil tongue, and imposing a penance as the priest would do when she was confessed'.[179] Taken at face value, the first line appears to address someone who has been harmed or bewitched; the second line refers to three sources of witchcraft: veiled ill-will in the heart, bitter words on the tongue and the evil eye. The speaker then invokes the Holy Trinity ('three bitter/better') to vanquish the affliction, with 'boote' meaning help. Reassurance is given that this is being done 'in God's name' before instructing the subject to recite their prayers. The last line refers as the Device prayer/charm did to the five wounds of Christ that had appeared on the banners of the Pilgrimage of Grace and would have evoked an immediate reaction to those who feared and loathed any sign of 'popery' or Catholic mutiny.

Like the longer Device charm, too, similar versions of Anne Whittle's charm can be found, with the redoubtable Keith Thomas informing us that hers was an old charm, of 'a standard formula and many examples of its use survive'.[180] In 1538, Agnes Robson admitted to healing animals with the use of a charm which is recited in full in the *Bishop of Lincoln's Visitation Book*:

John is thy christen name, John,
And thre bytter bytter hathe the bytten,
Thre bytter bytter hathe the nyppen,
And thre bytter bytter hathe the stryken,
Beeschyng almighty god, whedder itt were
eye or tong or hert, the better shall be your heale
and boote, the father the son and the holy gooste.[181]

A woman named Johanna Connyngton confessed to reciting a similar spell for sick children: 'Three byttes haue ye bytten with hert and tong and eye.'[182] In 1616, Isobel Harvie of Kirkcaldy admitted using a version of the charm which she had learned from 'a way-fairing man.'[183]A fascinating 1622 manuscript held by the Bodleian Library entitled *A book of experiments taken out of diverse authors*, has several versions of the charm under the section heading 'Bewitched, Forspoken or Enchanted':

> If any three biters have thee forbidden
> With wicked tongue or with wicked thought
> or with wicked eyes all ye most, I pray God be thy boot
> In the name of the father, & of the son, & of the holy ghost.
> God that set virtue between water and land,
> be thy help and succour with this prayer that I can,
> for Jesus' sake and charity.
> Amen.[184]

Another version begins similarly, but is listed as used for a 'horse or beast bewitched':

> Three biters have bitten thee,
> Three betters have betters have bettered thee,
> In the name of the father, the son and the holy ghost,
> Three persons and one trinity stand in a god's name.[185]

Beneath this was the instruction: 'Say this three times and make three crosses on him with your hand and he shall be cured.' Another version followed:

> Three times wert thou
> Bitten though the lyver &
> Through the lungs through
> The hart & through the
> Tonge & by the power of
> Almithye god in trinitie, so
> Shalt thou never more bitten

Be. *In nominee patris et filii &*
Spiritus sancti. Amen. Then
say 5 pater nosters 5 Avies & Creede.[186]

The final version runs:

If any 3 byters have thee bitten with wicked tonge or with wicked
thought or with wicked eyes at the most,
    I pray God be thy boote in the name of the father, the son &
the holy ghost
    God that set virtue between water and lande by thy helpe &
succour with this prayer that I can, for gods sake & St Chairitie
    Say this 5 tymes thrice over & at every 5 tymes a pater noster
an Ave. & a creede.[187]

Whether these charms pre- or post-date the one used by Anne
Whittle is impossible to know, but in 1622, London doctor Richard
Booker anointed a patient whom he believed to have been bewitched,
pronouncing: 'Three biters have bit him – heart, tongue and eye; three
better shall help him presently – God the Father, God the Son, and
God the Holy Spirit.'[188] A Dutchman taught the father of Lancashire
cunning man Henri Baggilies a very similar 'multipurpose' charm: 'Tell
thee thou forspoken toothe and tongue: hearte and hearte alike: three
things thee boote most: the father sonne and holigh hoste with the
lordes praier and I believe three times over.'[189]
    Other interpretations of the charm were used in Scotland for ailing
horses, specifically in 1641 and 1656, and in Wales and Kent. There
is also the 1653 case of Anne Greene of Gargrave who used the word
'boote' in her cure for a man's earache. The remedy failed and she
was charged with witchcraft. But versions of the Whittle charm were
still being used in the Orkney Islands in the late nineteenth or early
twentieth century.[190]
    Following Anne's recital of the prayer/charm, the Moores' drink
'was amended' successfully, yet Elizabeth Moore then 'did chide' Anne

and was 'aggrieved at her'. This response again suggests there was more to the story than we are being told, for why would Elizabeth be annoyed with Anne for correcting the 'forspoken' drink as she had asked her to do? Unsurprisingly, Anne's reaction was one of greater fury; despite no longer being on good terms with her, Alizon later claimed that she had been in Anne's presence and heard the older woman state that she would 'meet with the said John Moore, or his'. To 'meet with' in this context was to threaten retribution. Anne confirmed to Nowell that she had 'called for her devil Fancie, and bade him go bite a brown cow of the said Moores by the head, and make the cow go mad'. Anne ended her version of the story with how 'and the devil then, in the likeness of a brown dog, went to the said cow, and bit her: which cow went mad accordingly, and died within six weeks next after, or thereabouts'.

Alizon, however, had an extended version to share with Roger Nowell, which concerned a much graver accusation regarding the Moores' son, John, who was three years old in 1610. Alizon informed the magistrate that after Anne Whittle had proclaimed her warning, young John Moore fell ill. During the weeks while he 'languished' she, Alizon, had come upon Anne sitting in her own garden, with 'a picture of clay like unto a child in her apron'. When Anne realised she had been seen, she hid the clay image in her apron. Alizon afterwards mentioned the incident to her mother, who replied that the picture probably represented little John Moore. A short while later, in August 1610, the little boy passed away and was buried at Padiham's St Leonard's churchyard.[191]

Scarcely a month later, following a long illness, the young daughter of Wheathead mill owner Richard Baldwin died. As the family gathered for Ellena's funeral in Colne on 8 September, Richard Baldwin's grief was shot through with a deep anger borne of his belief that Elizabeth Southerns was responsible for her death.

To magistrate Roger Nowell, Alizon described how she had resisted her grandmother's attempts to follow in her footsteps and become a witch. 'Sundry times' when the two of them were out walking or had gone begging together, her grandmother tried to 'persuade and advise' her to 'let a devil or a familiar appear to her, and . . . let him suck at some part of her' to give her anything she desired. The fact that the two of them were often begging when her grandmother, already a witch, attempted to persuade her no doubt demonstrated that submitting to a familiar was not guaranteed to realise her dreams. However, the timing of what then occurred is of interest; if Alizon believed everything she told Nowell, was it the escalation in tensions between the two families, and especially the loss of her friend, that in the end made her more receptive to the idea of becoming a witch? It seems she had finally agreed in principle, for 'not long after these persuasions', Alizon was walking towards Roughlee, 'in a close of one John Robinsons', when 'there appeared unto her a thing like unto a black dog'.

If she was frightened, she does not say so, instead describing how the creature spoke to her, asking 'her to give him her soul' and in return 'he would give her power to do anything she would'. Alizon, enticed by the offer, sank down on the ground and the black dog 'suck[ed] at her breast, a little below her paps'. She remembered that the spot where the creature had drawn from her 'remained blue' for the next six months and that the black dog had vanished from her sight once the pact was sealed. There were no further encounters until that day in March 1612, when Alizon met pedlar John Law, and the black dog offered to lame him, sparking a tumultuous trial that would live long in the memory and for centuries thereafter.

Chapter Seven

DRAWN TO FALL
or
ALICE NUTTER

The blame lies largely with the man they called 'the Northern Dickens'. William Harrison Ainsworth's *The Lancashire Witches* is the primary source for a stream of myths about Alice Nutter, with Robert Neill's *Mist Over Pendle* acting as something of a tributary. The real Alice, much like her Wonderland namesake, became lost within a folklore that has taken on a life of its own.

Nowhere is this better illustrated, in a very literal sense, than in the fact that for the better part of a century, virtually every book or article about the 1612 trials was accompanied by references to Roughlee Hall as Alice's home. A typical newspaper column from 1963 refers to it as having belonged to 'a beautiful girl called Alice Nutter . . . known for her benevolent ways and her reputation was unblemished until lying witnesses implicated her when giving evidence against the hated Lancashire witches . . . even a vicar from a neighbouring parish swore that he had actually seen Alice riding through the air on a broomstick . . . Alice Nutter was taken to Lancaster for trial, convicted of witchcraft and burned in 1612.'[192] Meanwhile, another references Roughlee Hall as the home of Alice who gave birth shortly before her trial and whose husband 'fearing that the child would be a witch, threw it upon the fire, whereupon another raked it out, leaving it on the hearth. A mark on the floor is supposed to show the place.'[193] Needless to say, there are no such stories otherwise attached to Alice or Roughlee Old Hall. Local historian Gladys Whittaker was eventually able to prove that Alice had never lived at the Hall but the misapprehension is still frequently repeated, along with the image of Alice as a recusant and the victim of a boundary dispute with magistrate Roger Nowell. The former is a result of Alice's distant kinship through marriage with two well-known Catholic martyrs and the latter stems again entirely from Ainsworth's imaginative pen.

In his annotations to *Discoverie*, James Crossley rightly laments that on the subject of Alice Nutter, 'Potts is singularly meagre, and it is to be lamented that the deficiency of information cannot at present be supplied. Almost the only fact he furnishes us with is, that she died maintaining her innocence. It would have been most interesting to have had the means of ascertaining how she conducted herself at her trial and after her condemnation; and how she met the iniquitous injustice of her fate.' Indeed, Potts provides us with no more than a pithy paragraph for Alice's biography: 'For it is certain she was a rich woman; had a great estate, and children of good hope: in the common opinion of the world, of good temper, free from envy or malice; yet whether by the means of the rest of the witches, or some unfortunate occasion, she was drawn to fall to this wicked course of life, I know not: but hither she is now come to receive her trial, both for murder, and many other wild and damnable practises.'

In truth, Alice was not the wealthy heiress of Potts's retelling. Born around 1540, she was one of five children – three girls and two boys – brought up on her father's farm in the village of Simonstone, south of Pendle Hill and about a mile from Padiham. Gyles Whitaker, originally of Huncoat, was financially comfortable, but certainly not rich by the standards of the county's gentry. At this time, however, while gentlemen 'of lower rank' were many and influential, the yeomanry also prospered and the wealthiest among them began to acquire 'gentle status'.[194] This group enjoyed a new degree of social mobility, despite the isolation of the county itself. At the highest social levels there remained an insularity with the gentry marrying within the county, but there were signs of change with contact with London increasing and Lancashire men making 'mercantile fortunes' and occasionally holding 'legal, ecclesiastical or government offices. Many of these features were to be seen especially clearly at an early date in the eastern part of the county, which included the Pendle Forest district.'[195] [196]

Alice's father was held in extremely high regard locally: four times constable of Huncoat, Gyles Whitaker was elected by his fellow townsfolk to the position of greave in 1556, which saw him acting as an intermediary with the lord of the manor and shouldering responsibility for the smooth running of the community. The Whitakers in Simonstone have a long history stretching back to the thirteenth century; their coat of arms is set in stone above the door of Simonstone Hall. The major landowners in the area were the Starkies, whose lives were also touched by witchcraft; their family seat, Huntroyd Hall, was completed in 1576. There was a great deal of land trading between the different families, several of which involve the Whitakers and Roger Nowell of neighbouring Read; it may well be that when William Harrison Ainsworth visited to research his novel, these land disputes were part of local lore and gave him the idea for a plot line which was subsequently taken as fact.

Alice married into the sprawling clan that was the Nutter family of Pendle Forest. Her father-in-law, Miles Nutter of the Roughlee branch was, like her own father, a comfortably off yeoman farmer. Although there is no trace of Alice's wedding to Richard Nutter, the Clitheroe Court Rolls provide information regarding the settlement of her dower in 1561. It seems that her brothers James and John acted as representatives, arranging that she should have 'one fourth part' of her husband's property in perpetuity, which was the same agreement her brothers made for their own wives. It may be that Alice's marriage was an arranged one, with her brothers or father in the role of matchmaker. There was also a land transaction in 1561 between the Whitakers and Nutters, concerning a farm in Roughlee, which would ensure that after

Alice's parents-in-law died, a quarter share would pass to Alice, 'now wife of the said Richard Nutter for life, in the name of her dower' and the rest to Richard and his heirs.

The Rough Lee, as it was then known, lay quietly in the green valley bowl, among woods and the fast-running Pendle Water, between Blacko Foot and the climb to Newchurch, with Pendle Hill rising in the near distance. Living at Roughlee Hall at this time were the Smith family, with two daughters, Alice and Alison; folk memory later confused them with Alice Nutter, worming into the imaginations of novelists William Harrison Ainsworth and Robert Neill, who also gave 'our' Alice an illegitimate son, which again has been repeated as fact. A datestone on the west gable of the Old Hall bears a scarcely legible inscription that is believed to read: 'This house was built by MN in the year of Our Lord 1536.' However, the stone was transferred from another building, invalidating the theory that the initials refer to Miles Nutter, Alice's father-in-law.

Further research suggests that the home of Miles Nutter, which was inherited by his son Richard and wife Alice lay between Dam Head, Crowtrees and the present Judson Fold within the village, half a mile from the Hall. Surviving copyhold rents of the Honor of Clitheroe show that the family property passed during 1527 to 1609 from Miles to his younger son Richard and thence to Richard's son with Alice, also called Miles. The Hearth Tax returns show that their home was taxable with two hearths and therefore much smaller than Roughlee Hall, which had six hearths. They were also less prosperous than their second cousins, the Nutters of Greenhead.

Throughout her marriage to Richard Nutter, Alice lived a comfortable but far from wealthy life in the heart of the Roughlee with a growing brood of children. Then in 1584, when Alice was in her mid-forties, Richard passed away, leaving her with five children: Miles (the eldest at nineteen), John, James, Richard and Elizabeth. We know virtually nothing of Alice's life from this period until she appears as one of the accused in the 1612 witch trials, except that she remained living at the same property. Far from being the beautiful young heiress of popular imagination, the long-widowed Alice was around seventy years old in 1612 and it no longer becomes such a puzzle why she might have been on good terms with Elizabeth Southerns, who lived not so far away in Goldshaw Booth and was of a similar background to Alice, albeit far more impoverished in later years particularly.

While it cannot be said with absolute certainty, it seems likely that Elizabeth Southerns and Alice Nutter were also of the same religious faith. Newchurch-in-Pendle historian Clifford Byrne reflects: 'A Newchurch tradition of the witch trials related that the so-called witches were actually practicing Roman Catholics . . . [Alice Nutter] refused to say anything incriminating at the trial, which traditionally was because she had a son training as an unlawful priest, and was protecting the others.'[197] Silence may have been Alice's only recourse in attempting to shield her family from the shame of her trial, and while there is no evidence that one of her children intended to join the priesthood, there is some truth in a familial connection to Catholic martyrdom. Alice's husband was related to Ellis Nutter of Waterside, Reedley Hallows, whose sons Robert and John travelled to Douai in Northern France to train as priests. Robert was ordained at Rheims in December 1581 and was sent on the English mission within a fortnight, having assumed the surname Rowley in a nod to his home. Following his capture, Robert spent many years in various prisons, including the Tower of London where he was manacled and tortured for forty-three days in 1584. While there, he learnt that his brother John had also been detained and was hung, drawn and quartered at Tyburn. Eventually released, Robert was banished from England with other missionaries but returned to England in 1585. Apprehended again, he enlisted as a Jesuit while incarcerated at Wisbech Gaol and managed to escape in early 1600. Having reached Pendle Forest, he was arrested in May 1600 and dispatched to Lancaster Castle. In July 1600 he suffered the same fate as his brother, being hung, drawn and quartered. Ellis Nutter, nephew to Robert and John, studied at the English College in Rome around 1603 and was probably the person mistaken for Alice Nutter's son.

In *Discoverie*, Potts concedes that Alice was 'in the common opinion of the world, of good temper, free from envy or malice'. Yet he then goes on to inform us that she collaborated in the murder of a man for a pittance, admitting to being baffled by the crime himself: 'yet whether by the means of the rest of the witches, or some other unfortunate occasion, she was drawn to fall to this wicked course of life, I know not'.

The alleged victim was a man named Henry Mitton, whose father held around forty acres in the Roughlee; Dam Head was among the Mitton property holdings. Henry inherited only six acres of this land on his father's death, when a board of trustees was set up to safeguard his interests due to his young age; coincidentally, Christopher Nutter of Greenhead Manor was one such trustee. As a young man, living at Ridge Farm, on the Blacko side of the Rough Lee, Henry became involved in the first of a series of land disputes with members of Alice's extended Nutter family, whom he blamed for not having gained all the land he felt was owed to him. This may provide a tenuous explanation for Henry blaming Alice for the illness that preceded his death.

The evidence, such as it was, came from the Devices with some curious discrepancies. There are two versions of James Device's comments on Henry Mitton from his examination of 27 April before magistrates Roger Nowell and Nicholas Bannister. The first is included in the evidence for his mother's trial, in which James claims to have 'heard his grandmother say, about a year ago, that his mother, called Elizabeth Device, and others, had killed one Henry Mitton, of the Rough Lee aforesaid, by witchcraft'. He gave revenge as the motive: his grandmother had asked Henry Mitton for a penny, and he had refused, 'thereupon she procured his death'. Despite this pointing to James's grandmother, Elizabeth Southerns, as the instigator of the Mitton murder, it was not included in the material for her trial, and although he refers to 'and others' being involved in the killing, he makes no mention of Alice Nutter. However, in a second version drawn up for Alice's trial, his statement changes to his having heard 'his grandmother say, about a year ago, that his mother, called Elizabeth

Device, and his grandmother, and the wife of Richard Nutter, Alice Nutter, the prisoner, of the Rough Lee aforesaid, had killed one Henry Mitton . . .' The motive remains the same, and his grandmother remains the instigator, but now Alice is brought into the story.

Questioned about the alleged murder, Elizabeth Device gave no details, except to confirm that she and her mother had conspired with Alice Nutter to kill Henry Mitton. Her daughter, Jennet, said nothing about Alice in a statement she made to the court, but gave more damning evidence against her mother. Jennet remembered her mother calling for Ball and that when he asked what she would have him do, her mother told him she wanted him to kill 'one Mitton of the Rough Lee, whereupon the said Ball said he would do it, and so vanished away . . .' Jennet's statement is very like the one she gave regarding her mother's instruction for Ball to kill James Robinson, even down to the detail of how Mitton, like Robinson, had died three weeks after the meeting between witch and familiar. Mitton was laid to rest at St Mary's in Goldshaw Booth in 1610.

When he came to write Alice's story into *Discoverie*, Potts knew that a number of his readers would struggle to understand – as he himself had done, on some level – why she might have become embroiled in Mitton's murder. He had an answer, albeit one he fails to quantify: vengeance. If more was said at Alice's trial, he must have decided against including it in his book, instead declaring: 'The two degrees of persons which chiefly practise witchcraft, are such, as are in great misery and poverty, for such the devil allures to follow him, by promising great riches, and worldly commodity; others, though rich, yet burn in a desperate desire of revenge; he allures them by promises, to get their turn satisfied to their heart's contentment . . .' As an argument put forward to condemn Alice Nutter, it holds as much water as a colander, but it does serve to demonstrate why, perhaps, she was there at all: as an example to the king's subjects that under certain circumstances the devil was able to tempt anyone into his orbit, whether rich or poor, of good standing or less.

*

During Lent 1611, a farmer named John Duckworth, of the Laund, passed away. There was nothing remarkable about his death until James Device later 'confessed' to having used witchcraft to murder him. We know little more than that, except that James was apparently incensed when Duckworth promised him an old shirt but then failed to deliver it.

After a fortnight with no word from Duckworth, James made his way to the Laund. He recalled that he had spoken to the farmer, 'and demanded the said old shirt', but Duckworth refused to give him it. They may have come to blows, for as James walked away from the house, 'the said spirit Dandy appeared' and accused James with something akin to glee, 'Thou didst touch the said Duckworth.' James insisted he did not, but Dandy repeated, 'Yes, thou didst touch him, and therefore I have power of him.' This is an interesting point, for the familiar is declaring that if James had touched him, then he, Dandy, would have control over Duckworth and could override any objection made by James. Realising he was beaten, James later told Nowell that he had then joined with Dandy and 'wished' him to kill John Duckworth. Within a week or two, John Duckworth was dead, his burial recorded in the parish registers of St Mary's.

As far as familiar spirits were concerned, Anne Whittle later claimed to have had her last encounter with Fancie that summer. In her examination before Roger Nowell, she seems only too pleased to be rid of Fancie, whom she blamed for having 'taken most of her sight away'. Not only that, but he had begun to materialise before her at West Close, at 'diverse and sundry times', but always at night and 'in the likeness of a bear', showing his teeth 'as if he meant to bite her'. Anne dated the last time they met precisely as Midsummer's Eve, 23 June, which fell 'upon Thursday'. Fancie turned up at her home and she flatly refused to speak to him. Outraged, Fancie pulled her to the ground, but curiously left her there and never returned.

A week later, trouble came quite literally to the Devices' door. On St Peter's Day, 29 June, Henry Bulcock, a yeoman farmer from Foothouse Gate over in Barley, appeared at Malkin Tower. Bulcock had come to see Alizon, whom he believed to have bewitched one of his children.

He insisted that she should accompany him back to Barley to lift the curse. Alizon must have been alone at Malkin Tower when Henry Bulcock arrived, for had her mother or grandmother been present, they would have stoutly defended her and almost certainly prevented her from agreeing to go with Bulcock. Whether her brother James was there or not is impossible to say but it was he, and he alone, who recounted the incident for the benefit of Roger Nowell. If he had tried to protect Alizon, there is no record of it and he makes no attempt to cast himself in that role, simply telling Nowell that his sister had indeed gone with the furious Bulcock to Barley, where she 'fell down on her knees, and asked the said Bulcock and confessed to him that she had bewitched the said child'.

The grating lack of context, such as Alizon's motive and which child had been bewitched, together with the absence of any statements from accuser or accused is left unexplained. Presumably either Henry Bulcock had no desire to pursue it in court or Alizon was able to convince him that she had undone the bewitching and he was sufficiently relieved to let the matter drop. Why or how it arose during James's questioning is equally uncertain.

Carr Hall was swept away in the post-war desecration of so many of England's grand estates, but even in the last of its many eras was described as 'one of the oldest and most interesting houses in Barrowford district'.[198] At the time of the witch trials, the Carr (later Carr Hall) was still fairly new, built in 1580 on the directions of Henry Towneley. It stood like a rare jewel in the surrounding farmland, with several acres of wooded gardens, and overlooked a large lake at the foot of the lawn. A stone entrance led to the house, which had its own chapel whose uneven walls contained a priest's hiding place.

The Towneleys were the wealthiest of the area's Catholic gentry, owning vast swatches of land and property. The head for many years was John Towneley, who had 'exercised great patronage and influence'.[199] Following the Reformation, he was 'prepared to conform but not to communicate' and, as a result, from 1558 until his death in 1608 most of his time was spent in prison.[200] Towneley Hall in Burnley was the family seat but there were a number of other large estates. The Carr was constructed to give Henry Towneley a home closer to Carr Mill, which he inherited from his father Lawrence but whose lease he passed on in 1569 to four gentlemen, one of whom was Thomas Lister of Gisburn, some seven miles north of Barrowford; Lister will come back into the story shortly.

Henry had been married to Anna Catterall for fifty-one years; their wedding took place in St Mary's Church in Whalley, where the young Elizabeth Southerns had worshipped with her family.[201] They had ten children and several grandchildren, who came and went as they pleased at the Carr. James Device did much the same, but in a far less welcome role, occasionally begging food from the kitchens when he and his mother Elizabeth undertook various forms of casual labour at the Hall. On this particular day, James entered through the back of the house as he always did and made his way into the kitchens where he encountered the mistress of the house, seventy-two-year-old Anna Towneley. The fact that the two of them began chatting highlights how comfortable James – and probably his mother and sisters too – felt at the Carr and in speaking to Anna Towneley, despite the gaping difference between them in social status. And if she were aware of the reputation of her casual workers, then she seems to have paid it no mind. However, at some point their conversation turned; Anna 'charged' James and his mother with stealing peat turves from her for their own use as fuel. If true, then the Devices must have gone on some sort of 'thieving expedition', using a barrow or something similar to ferry the turves away, since it would be difficult to carry home by hand the number of turves needed. It may also be that because the work he and his mother did at the Carr was casual, they had no formal agreement in place regarding payment, and they had taken the turves in lieu of wages.

Whatever the truth, James argued his defence, but Mistress Towneley 'bade him pack the doors', that is, to leave. As James 'went forth of the door' the irate woman 'gave him a knock between the shoulders'.

Her lashing out seems to have been less the result of believing that the Devices had stolen from her and more to do with his reaction. But James knew better than to retaliate at this stage; instead, he returned home and started to fume.

His younger sister, Jennet, later told an avid courtroom that in the wake of this incident, while she was at home with James, she had heard him call for his familiar, a dog named Dandy, 'who thereupon appeared' asking James what he wished him to do. Jennet declared that her brother asked Dandy 'to help him to kill old Mistress Towneley of the Carr, whereunto the said Dandy answered [that James] should have his best help for the doing of the same'. The two then agreed to 'make away the said Mistress Towneley'. James's own account is similar, bar he stated that he had only learnt himself then that the dog wanted to be addressed as Dandy, and that it was he who brought the row to mind. Further, it was Dandy's suggestion that James should 'make a picture of clay, like unto the said Mistress Towneley' and that together they would 'kill or destroy' her. Dandy vanished, but the next morning James did as he was advised, taking some clay to make a clay picture, which he then dried that night by the fire.

The following day, James 'began to crumble the said picture, every day some, for the space of a week' until it was gone. Jennet interjects another scene here, recalling how 'about a week after' Dandy's visit, she too went to the Carr and into the kitchens where she saw the lady of the house 'nothing well', meaning that Anna Towneley appeared extremely poorly. Jennet added that she then realised that James, 'by the help of Dandy, had brought the said Mistress Towneley into the state she then was in'.

There are two noticeable disparities in the statements of brother and sister: James described his familiar as a brown dog, but here both he and Jennet recall Dandy as being black – like the dog who became Alizon's familiar. Furthermore, in his statement James cites his first meeting with Dandy as two or three days prior to the argument with Anna Towneley, while Jennet declared to the court that Dandy had been her brother's familiar for three years previously. There is another discrepancy with timing too: James dates the entire event as having occurred two years previously, when Jennet claims it took place a year before. Anna Towneley may have been ill for some time after the quarrel with James, but the evidence in the parish registers records in stark definition that the seventy-two-year-old Anna, wife of Henry Towneley of the Carr, died on 25 October 1611. How much suspicion fell on James during her languishing and following her death is not clear from the examinations taken by Nowell, or the evidence put forth by Potts. However, the absence of a statement from Henry Towneley strongly implies that if he had made a statement to this effect, it was not sufficient to support the prosecution case, which may be why there is nothing from him in *Discoverie*, only the fact that he travelled to Lancaster in 1612 for the trial.

The ambiguity concerning dates in *Discoverie* makes it difficult to establish a firm timeline of events, particularly with regard to the alleged murders. For instance, Jennet Device provided the names of two brothers whom she said had been killed by her brother, with the first murder taking place shortly after James made his pact with Dandy. Jennet recalled that James had called Dandy to him at home and said that 'he would have him to kill John Hargreaves, of Goldshaw Booth . . . Dandy answered that he would do it'. John Hargreaves, a yeoman farmer, subsequently passed away; the motive behind his 'killing' is never revealed.

Jennet then recalled James summoning Dandy to arrange the killing of John's brother, Blaze (Blazeus) Hargreaves of Higham, to which Dandy had responded that 'he should have his best help, and so vanished away'. Blaze Hargreaves appears in land transactions for Higham Dean involving Alice Nutter's husband's family. He was twice married: two years after the death of his first wife Jenitta in February 1600, he married Isabella Crosley of Padiham. They had been married seven years when Blaze died on 1 March 1609. He was interred at St Leonard's in Padiham. John Hargreaves is harder to pin down: if Jennet remembered incorrectly and John died *after* his brother then the entry in the burial register for John Hargreaves dated January 1612 at St Peter's in Burnley may be the right one.

Presumably Roger Nowell questioned James about the deaths of the two brothers, but Potts includes none of it in *Discoverie*, despite James being charged with their murders. There is very little we can be certain of in relation to the matter: Hargreaves was a very common name in the area, with family 'clusters' around and about the Pendle region, including at Higham, Whitehough and Thorneyholme. Others who shared the surname also appear at a number of junctures within the story.

Some months after the death of Anna Towneley, James Device had a disturbing experience that almost seemed to be a foreshadowing of the horror that would shortly engulf his family.

It was dusk in Pendle, early March 1612, and the last of winter with a nip of frost in the air. James was heading home after work, bone-tired. He later recalled meeting 'a brown dog coming from his grandmother's house, about ten roods from the same'. If this was his own familiar, Dandy, he fails to mention it and the dog did not approach him.

Two or three nights after, again at dusk, and 'about ten roods' from Malkin Tower, he heard a cacophony: 'a great number of children screaking and crying pitifully'. But there were no children to be seen. Another five nights passed and, again at the same hour, but now 'within twenty roods' of his grandmother's house, he heard 'a foul yelling, like unto a great number of cats'.

Finally, 'about three nights after that, about midnight of the same, there came a thing, and lay upon him very heavily about an hour and went then from him out of his chamber window'. James watched it slink out, its form 'coloured black and about the bigness of a hare or cat'.

The extraordinary sequence of events ended there, and no more was said about it between James and his interrogator. Nor did Nowell ask any of James's family if they had seen or heard such a thing. It is left in the midst of the accusations where it remains jarring, out of place, a moment of pure Gothic horror: we feel James's own fear on hearing, during twilight, those invisible children and lost creatures screaming in the shadow of Malkin Tower, before the demonic 'thing' creeps in and sits 'very heavily' on the young man's recumbent form, like Fuseli's *Nightmare*, before vanishing into the darkness.

Part III:
THE KAGE

'See a pin and pick it up,
All the day you'll have good luck.
See a pin and let it lie,
Sure to rue it by and by.'
Old English rhyme, unknown origin.

Chapter Eight

LAME HIM

During those latter days of March 1612, events swept through Pendle like a roaring brast.

Discoverie provides us with three versions of what took place on Wednesday, 18 March 1612: Alizon's confession, the statement of pedlar John Law and his son Abraham's statement. All three are presented as if each individual is speaking in court, but they are in fact transcripts of their interviews with magistrate Roger Nowell in the recent aftermath of events. In each version, what passed between Alizon Device and John Law changes. Thomas Potts does not trouble to draw the reader's attention to any inconsistencies, for he is firmly of the belief that Alizon tried to beg pins from Law, who refused, and she then cursed him, 'a poor, distressed pedlar; how miserably he was tormented, and what punishment he endured for a small offence, by the wicked and damnable practise of this odious witch'.[202]

With the information from the Lancashire parish registers, we now know that in 1612, the 'odious witch' was nineteen years old, her brother James twenty-two, her sister Jennet eleven, and their mother Elizabeth around forty. Alizon, we are told, was heading to Trawden Forest for a day's begging. If she set off early from her home some five miles away, pedlar John Law would have struck out several hours before, living in the region of Halifax, around twenty miles south-east of Colne, where he was headed. He may have broken up his journey by staying somewhere overnight, but he would have been used to long treks, nonetheless. In fact, a large number of pedlars hailed from Scotland and travelled far and wide for their work; around 30,000 Scottish pedlars were living in Poland by 1621. But research conducted by author Charlotte Meredith suggests another possibility: given that pedlars offered credit, and that inventory records show that debts owed to pedlars at the time of their deaths tended to relate to those who lived within a twelve-mile radius, pedlars relied on regular customers near their homes and in the surrounding districts. Unlike some men of the trade, John Law travelled on foot rather than pack horse, and given that he intended to sell his wares at Colne, the main market town in the region and a centre of the woollen industry, he probably lived closer to Colne than Halifax. The weekly markets were originally held in St Bartholomew's churchyard, where the town's wooden pillory stood. Those interested in either buying or browsing would move between stalls and items laid out for sale on the ground, expecting to find a range of goods from clothing to wine, pots and ironware, soap and garden seeds.

Potts, as ever, fails to provide any background for Law, but tells us that he was – or had been, prior to his encounter with Alizon – 'a very able, sufficient, stout man of body and a goodly man of stature'.[203] Thus he was tall, well-built and no doubt physically fit from walking long distances with a pack on his back full of wares to sell. Travelling on foot or by horse was often extremely arduous. The main roads were usually poorly maintained, despite the stipulations of the Highways Act, with potholes a constant concern; the cart tracks and lanes were even worse, frequently inflicting broken legs in animals and humans, and wrecking many a wheeled vehicle. The elements were unavoidable for long, and the threat of robbery and assault of all kinds was ever-present.

Given that Law had an adult son, he was probably about forty to forty-five years old. There were several branches of the Law family in the vicinity of both Halifax and Pendle, the latter at Padiham, Burnley and Wiswell, while others farmed on the Braddyll estates adjacent to Whalley, where Elizabeth Southerns had grown up.

Potts describes John Law as a 'petty chapman'. The trade was hierarchal, with women and men working in the business. There were those who were poorest and hawked their goods in a pack; those who travelled on horseback with their wares; and the better off, who worked from market stalls. Apart from the former, the majority of pedlars sold their wares from a specially made trunk, which they would then open like a portable shop. John Law, despite his age, was clearly living simply, and would have sold items at market and to shops, as well as direct to villagers. Historian Margaret Spufford explains that pedlars were 'responsible for much of the supply of cheap goods to rural areas . . . mainly the materials for sheets, curtains, shirts, shifts and underclothing'.[204] They also offered 'textiles, haberdashery, and ready-made clothing accessories'.[205] Because they travelled in their work and spoke to many different people, pedlars tended to be a useful source of news and gossip. But they were ill-regarded generally in society: shop owners bought from them but worried they would cause trade to decline, and they were listed alongside rogue vagabonds, fortune tellers and the like who were liable to a whipping for their itinerant lifestyle.

It was the nature of the pedlar's job that also brought them under suspicion from Parliament, who believed that some of them were in fact Catholic priests, members of a clandestine network keeping the forbidden faith alive, and using their packs and cases to disperse 'superstitious Trumperies'.[206] The notion was not without foundation: in the 1800s, a pedlar's trunk was discovered hidden in the secret priest's hole at Samlesbury Hall. A pink silk bonnet lay on top of the items within, most of which appeared to be clothing and adornments for selling to fashionable women. On closer inspection, these were found to be vestments and rosary beads, with the remainder of the contents proving that the trunk contained everything a priest might require to say Mass while on the road, including an altar stone and a pewter cup for Holy Communion.[207]

That John Law was in fact a Catholic priest travelling about the region in the guise of a pedlar is therefore a possibility. Whatever the true nature of his existence, we can assume that his daily life involved a good deal of physical exercise and hardship, and that his encounter with Alizon Device changed his world forever.

Before we turn to the events of that day, we should be aware that there are further inconsistencies in the accounts we have, two of which need to be considered here.

Almost all retellings of the encounter refer to only Alizon and John Law as being present. Both Potts and his editor, Judge Bromley, failed to realise that they had left in a curious and extremely telling reference. In his statement, Abraham Law describes 'seeing his said father so tormented with the said Alizon and with one other old woman, whom [John Law] did not know as it seemed'. This is an extremely striking point and one that has almost always been overlooked. Abraham states here that his father was 'tormented' by Alizon and an old woman. We know that Alizon was her grandmother Elizabeth Southerns' closest companion and the two regularly travelled together, with Elizabeth relying on Alizon to be her eyes. Yet this was never mentioned at the trial, and in her statements, Alizon made no reference to anyone else. It seems particularly strange, until we remember that by the time of the trial, Elizabeth Southerns was dead. If her name was raised in court as the potential cause of Law's 'laming', then where might that leave Alizon? Far better to remove her grandmother from the narrative and let the entire fault lie on the young woman's shoulders instead.

Secondly, in her confession, Alizon does not initially state that she was heading into Trawden Forest to spend the day begging; she states that she met John Law at Colne Field, and that after their encounter she then 'went begging in Trawden Forest that day'. But was she heading there originally? And if so, why? Despite its name, the region was not wooded as such, but had little more to offer in terms of possible opportunities to press people for a few coins, encompassing Trawden and two other villages, and several farms and small-holdings. It makes no sense for Alizon to pass the town of Colne, on a bustling market day, to head further away into Trawden, with its scant chances for begging.

Joyce Froome suggests there was a different purpose for Alizon's outing that day. Evidence from a later period reveals that cunning folk were often paid annual retainers by their clients, usually in the spring. One such recorded example from Cornwall describes how a meeting of 'chief persons', including many farmers, was interrupted by a strange man who then took a sum from each man to prevent their farms being troubled by witchcraft in the year ahead. At this point, we might remember Alizon's own father, John Device, who in effect paid just such a retainer annually to Anne Whittle, for the same purpose. There seems no reason to doubt that the practice was not more widespread than has previously been considered, amounting to less protection magic and more protection racket. If Alizon was collecting retainers for her grandmother, which makes even more sense if she were accompanied by Elizabeth Southerns, she might well have preferred Nowell to believe she was simply going begging.

Six miles north-east of Burnley, Colne was then a sizable and thriving hillside town on the edge of the Forest of Pendle. Its population is thought to have doubled between the mid-sixteenth and mid-seventeenth century. A 1554 land survey revealed that the area east of Colne was in an 'indifferent' state of accessibility, and it was here where Alizon said she had met Law 'on the highway, called Colne Field, near unto Colne', which Law confirmed. This area stretched from the edge of the town proper, across to Swanfield and south to Colne Water. Keighley Road now travels west to east, bisecting what was once Colne Field, and to one side is the open, sloping land of Colne cemetery. Most of the roads in the area then would have been little more than cart tracks through the fields; the wider road of Carry Lane is an ancient highway running from Colne to Trawden, where Alizon claimed to have been headed. The steep incline was often busy with drovers, tradesmen and farmers taking cattle to market, who relied on the buttresses against the boundary walls on one side of the road to support horses carrying heavy loads; the wheels of the cart would be backed against a stone to take the weight off the shafts and allow the horse to rest. At the bottom of the road, a bridge passed over Colne Water, and to the right was a well-trodden path used by people heading between Trawden and Colne. Now known as Trawden Flags due to the stones that have been placed there, in those days it was simply a dirt track.

We now know that three people met that day here, or very nearby: Elizabeth Southerns, elderly and partially sighted, but neither frail of spirit nor body; her granddaughter, nineteen-year-old Alizon, thin and poorly dressed; and lastly, petty chapman John Law, strong and tall, in his forties or thereabouts, a crammed 'pack of wares', as he called it, heavy on his back. The two women knew at once that he would be carrying pins. These were not the cheap, steel wire pins we have today, which can be bought in bulk for a few pounds; seventeenth-century pins such as the ones sold by John Law were handmade and quite expensive. Often when people like the Devices wanted or needed pins, they would fashion their own from blackthorn tree thorns: sharp, featherlight and, above all, free.

But the pins offered for sale by pedlars were another class of pin. You may be familiar with the rhyme that opens this part of the story. It was derived from an old English proverb concerning the virtues of thrift, which warned: 'He who will not stoop for a pin will never be worth a pound.' Samuel Pepys wrote the line into his diary in 1668. Either Alizon or her grandmother – or both of them – wanted those pins. A request or demand for pins was made and John Law refused. He may have had any number of reasons for doing so; pedlars bought and sold on credit, as the women would have known – which somewhat supports Alizon's claim that she had asked to buy the pins – and he may have denied her because he didn't trust her to pay at all.

But he may also have either refused to sell or give the women even a single pin knowing that cunning folk and witches set great value on pins. They could be put to any number of uses, such as love magic, causing harm, for protection or healing, to bring good or bad luck, bind a spell, and for divination. One of the commonest uses was for curing warts, the simplest involved using a pin to make the sign of the cross on each wart before discarding the pin. With love magic, on St Agnes' Night (21 January), a young woman eager to know whom she would marry would take a row of pins, saying a Pater Noster (or an Our Father) after she pulled out each pin and stuck it in her sleeve. That night she would dream of her future husband. Love magic was popular yet simultaneously viewed with fear. The law of 1563 dictated that a person using 'sorcery, enchantment, charm or witchcraft to the intent to provoke any person to unlawful love' would be sentenced to a year in gaol and four six-hour sessions in the pillory. Life imprisonment was meted out for a second offence, until 1604 when the punishment was altered to death by hanging.

'Is the heart of wax stuck full of magic needles?' asks Hecate in Thomas Middleton's *The Witch*, written within a few years of the 1612 trials. Perhaps the best-known occult use for pins was in relation to harmful magic, whereby clay pictures were pierced with them. Pins were frequently used in counter-magic, and long-shrivelled animal hearts thrust through with pins have been discovered inside old buildings on several occasions. Similarly, pins are one of the common components found in centuries-old witch bottles, whereby the urine from a cursed person would be contained in a bellarmine jar with items such as nails, hair and salt. There are instances, too, of people who were said to have been either bewitched or possessed vomiting up pins, although pins were sometimes swallowed in the desperate hope that the evil spirit within would be harmed by them.

That there was an argument of some sort between the pedlar and the two women is certain. John Law described Alizon as being 'very earnest with him for pins, but he would give her none, whereupon she seemed to be very angry'. In her confession, Alizon recalled that she had 'demanded of the said pedlar to buy some pins of him' but Law 'sturdily answered . . . that he would not loose his pack'.

The three then made to part; Elizabeth and Alizon apparently towards Trawden, and Law on up the steep incline to Colne, where he hoped to have more success with his wares. In her confession,

Alizon recalled how 'presently, there appeared . . . the black dog'. She recognised it at once as the spirit with whom she had described making her pact some months before yet had not seen since – until it manifested in Colne Field.

'What wouldst thou have me to do unto yonder man?' the black dog asked her, seemingly going unnoticed by the pedlar, who had gone a short distance from them.

'What canst thou do at him?' Alizon replied.

'Lame him,' said the dog.

'Then lame him.'

Law was some 'forty roods' or less from them when he collapsed, 'in great extremity' as he himself phrased it later. Eventually, he managed to get back onto his feet and staggered away. After some hesitation, Alizon followed – either alone, while her grandmother waited nearby, or with Elizabeth. She watched him enter a house 'about the distance [forty roods again] aforesaid'.

Law agreed in his statement that he 'by means got into an alehouse in Colne, near unto the place where he was first bewitched'. His use of the word 'alehouse' rather than 'inn', and Alizon's 'house' are of some significance, given that it seems oddly remiss not to have named the place that he must have regarded, at first, as his sanctuary and whose other inhabitants could surely have provided the prosecution with valuable evidence about his situation. Inns were generally regarded as more respectable than alehouses and were frequented by wealthier clientele who would stay overnight or longer. In contrast, alehouses were private houses opened to the public for the same purposes, but a number of them also sold homemade ale, illegally. The pub signs we see today are due to the law that existed then, requiring both alehouses and inns to display identifying names which, due to widespread illiteracy, were accompanied by descriptive paintings.

If the encounter between Law and the two women did indeed take place on or around Carry Lane, then the nearest alehouse would have been the one located at the top of the incline.[208] Now partly converted into terraced houses, the rest stands in ruins, including the two-storey stable block at the rear.[209] Helped into the alehouse, John Law was given a room and lay in bed 'in great pain, not able to stir either hand or foot'. And then he realised he was not alone: 'He saw a great black dog stand by him, with very fearful, fiery eyes, great teeth, and a terrible countenance, looking him in the face.' The pedlar had failed to notice the dog in Colne Field and was now 'very sore afraid'. His fear heightened when Alizon Device entered the room and stood with the great black dog. She 'looked on him' awhile, then left silently. Law realised the fearsome dog had vanished with her.

In her confession, Alizon appears to agree that she had gone into the alehouse but there is an undeniable ambiguity to her oddly distant phrase about John Law: 'In a house about the distance aforesaid he was lying lame: and so [she] went begging in Trawden Forest.' The brevity of her statement implies that it has been edited, either at source by magistrate Roger Nowell, or afterwards. She may have looked in on him but was too frightened to speak and left swiftly – though not before others had seen her and told John Law who she was: the granddaughter of the notorious Elizabeth Southerns. That he would have been familiar with the name is almost certain, since his travels took him around the neighbourhood and in contact with those who knew of the frequent troubles involving Elizabeth and her family. The notion that he was another of their witchcraft victims would take scarcely an instant to surface and spread.

What did ail John Law? Potts describes him with his head 'drawn awry, his eyes and face deformed, his speech not well to be understood; his thighs and legs stark lame: his arms lame, especially the left side, his hands lame and turned out of their course, his body able to endure no travel'. The general consensus is that the pedlar had a stroke: the sudden loss of use to his limbs that caused him to collapse to the ground at first, the facial paralysis, contorted speech and numbness to the left side of his body especially are all symptoms associated with what is properly termed a transient ischaemic attack, but which Law believed to be Alizon's revenge for having refused her pins. For the next few days, he said afterwards, he was 'tormented both day and night with the said

Alizon Device'. It was a common belief that victims were never safe from a witch who had decided to target them, whether in their own homes – or their own bodies. Victims 'saw' the witch and her familiar inside their own space, where she could materialise at will. Thus, 'one could not flee the witch, or lock her out, or use material means to refix and seal that boundary between self and other'.[210]

In her confession, Alizon recalls that 'about five days' after the confrontation with John Law, the black dog that had lamed him on her instruction appeared again. She was 'going begging in a close near the New Church in Pendle'. The dog said to her, 'stay and speak with me', but whether he was asking or demanding, Alizon refused. It was, she claims, her last encounter with the black dog.

Curiously, her brother recalled that his last meeting with Dandy – his black canine familiar – occurred at the same time. His statement mentions it being 'the Tuesday next before his apprehension', and given that he was arrested on Monday, 30 March, his final sighting of Dandy would have been on Tuesday, 24 March. His sister Alizon last saw her familiar 'about five days' after her ill-fated trip with their grandmother, which would be either Monday, 23 March or the following day.

James's meeting with Dandy was the more dramatic of the two. There is no mention of the location, only that his familiar made one more attempt to persuade him 'to give him his soul absolutely'. When he 'could not prevail' upon James to do so, 'the said spirit departed from him, then giving a most fearful cry and yell, and withal caused a great flash of fire to shew about him'. The 'flash of fire' referred to a bolt of lightning, inferring that James had won that particular battle. Otherwise, when read in conjunction with his sister's account of her familiar's departure, we are left with an unsettling sense that perhaps there were not two black dog familiars after all, but one: Dandy.

If that was the case, and there was only one black dog, then what are we to make of the encounter between John Law and Alizon, which we now know involved Elizabeth Southerns too? Have we, along with the court at Lancaster, been given a reworked version of these events?

John Law failed to spot the black dog in the daylight – albeit given that his back was probably turned – and therefore might this suggest that there was no such black dog in the original encounter? Was it, in fact, Elizabeth Southerns who was presented in those depositions as having harmed the pedlar? When she passed away before her trial, did that then cause someone – most probably Roger Nowell – to edit her out of the encounter as we have already conjectured, and insert the black dog sequence in order to fully implicate Alizon Device, as much for expediency's sake as anything? But whoever reworked that infamous encounter was, ultimately, thwarted by a bit of shoddy editing, which lingers, ghost-like, in the passage to call out the truth.

Despite being under psychic attack and suffering both pain and paralysis, John Law somehow managed to speedily either write or dictate a letter to his son. Abraham Law worked as a clothier in Halifax and recalled that 'upon Saturday . . . being the one and twentieth day of this instant March, he . . . was sent for, by a letter that came from his father'. Three days after the bewitching in Colne Field, John Law implored his son to come to him in Colne, telling him that he lay 'speechless, and had the left side lamed, all save his eye'. Did he, in fact, write to his son or was that someone else's doing? There is an implication of such in the peculiar phrasing of Abraham Law's recollection that he was 'sent for, by a letter that came from his father, that he should come to his father, John Law'. In all probability, the letter was drafted on his father's behalf.

We don't know when Abraham Law left Halifax for Colne, but when he arrived at the alehouse he was relieved to find his father had somewhat 'recovered his speech'. There was still the matter, his father explained, of the ongoing pain, which felt as though he were being 'pricked with knives, elsons and sickles . . . the same hurt [that] was done unto him at Colne Field' after 'Alizon Device had offered to buy some pins of him [but] she had no money to pay for them'. According to Abraham, his father said that he 'gave her some pins' but she had inflicted 'the hurt he had in his lameness . . . by witchcraft'. John Law then confided that he had visions of her, in which 'the said Alizon Device did lie upon him and trouble him'. This was where Abraham stumbled in his statement – or rather, someone else did – recalling that his father was 'so tormented with the said Alizon and with one other old woman, whom [his father] did not know as it seemed'.

Abraham had heard enough. He was well aware that his father would never work again and needed to confront the person, or people, apparently responsible for this calamity. His thoughts in turmoil, he had his horse brought to him from the alehouse stables and set out towards Goldshaw Booth in the shadow of Pendle Hill, to find Alizon Device and her grandmother.

Chapter Nine

PRICKING THUMBS

On Sunday, 29 March, Abraham Law succeeded in finding Alizon Device and brought her to the alehouse for a confrontation with his father. Abraham recalled that 'diverse others' had gathered to watch the young woman whose family were already notorious in the villages below Pendle Hill. The story of how she – and no doubt, her grandmother, who in all probability remained at home – had bewitched the poor pedlar would have spread throughout the region like the proverbial wildfire. No doubt Elizabeth Southerns' name was also mentioned, but the Halifax clothier insisted her granddaughter return with him to Colne.

For Alizon, entering the alehouse under the direction of the grim-faced Abraham Law, and making her way through the hostile crowd, must have been intimidating at best. It was, to all intents and purposes, a trial in miniature, with the pedlar's son acting as judge and jury, and of all those whom she might have expected to be magnanimous to her, John Law was probably the last. Yet, despite being convinced that she was responsible fully or in part for his predicament, the pedlar had made no attempt to reach out to anyone other than his son in the aftermath of his 'laming' – neither the local constable nor the area's justice of the peace. Perhaps he had always intended to leave that to his son, who now pushed Alizon to the front of the crowd and waited for his father to speak, as well as he could.

John Law duly accused Alizon of having 'bewitched him'. And she was terrified, knowing exactly where such an accusation might lead – not only for her, but for her family too. In his statement, Abraham describes Alizon falling to her knees in desperation, pleading with his father for 'forgiveness . . . for the same'. She must have experienced intense, overwhelming relief when John Law 'accordingly did forgive her'. But her relief vanished when Abraham took control of the situation again, displaying none of his father's altruism as he told the entire gathering that he had no intention of letting the matter rest.

The 1612 trials unfold as if they were prised from the mould of the English witch-hunt prototype, whose stages involved the presence of a person (or persons) who was regarded as troublesome by their community; a misfortune that had no obvious explanation and the failure of a social obligation that was angrily spoken about to others; an inkling that the disgruntled neighbour and the misfortune were linked; mounting gossip about that same individual, whose every action now became suspect; an outright declaration that a bewitchment had taken place, followed by a confrontation and a report then to the authorities. Thus, we see how suspicions of witchcraft moved in 'an ever-widening ripple through the village'.[211] Rarely an isolated incident, the rumour of witchcraft grew from an escalation of social tensions, often with a request for some sort of assistance at its heart. Once viewed in this light, the apparently excessive reaction to a relatively small act becomes more logical.

In *Reformation and Resistance in Tudor Lancashire*, Christopher Haigh explains how 'the loss of the assize records for the whole of the reign of Elizabeth and of the quarter sessions rolls for most of the period, makes any discussion of witchcraft accusations difficult, but in view of Lancashire's reputation as a witch-ridden region the problem can hardly be ignored. Between 1562 and 1604, 28 individuals are known to have been accused of witchcraft or similar offences.'[212] In that period, during the late 1590s, Lancashire experienced something of a 'minor witch craze': in 1571, a Whalley schoolmaster and a priest of Harwood who had been accused of sorcery were found to have been aiding recusant clergy; Puritan exorcist John Darrell travelled through the county from 1586 until 1587; the Earl of Derby was believed to have been murdered by (Catholic) witchcraft in 1594; Edmund Hartley was executed for witchcraft and using 'popish charms' in 1597 while 'Alice Brearley, of Castleton, spinster', received a pardon after being accused of killing two men by witchcraft; two women from Rochdale were accused of witchcraft in 1598 and, in that same year, public exorcisms by a group of seminary priests proved huge draws for men, women and children alike. This sudden spurt of witch-related activity coincided with an upsurge in action taken against recusants, since it was widely accepted that 'the use of charms and Catholicism tended to go together'.[213] Even then, in 1590 Puritan ministers grumbling loudly about the dire state of religion in Lancashire found more to say about popery than they did about witchcraft.

Despite the prevalent view of James I of England's reign giving sudden rise to witchcraft persecutions, historian George Lyman Kittredge insists that during the period of James's rule (1603–25) there was 'no more excitement on the subject of witchcraft and no more executions' than there had been during the last twenty-two years of his aunt, Queen Elizabeth.[214] His accession 'was not in any sense the signal for an outburst of prosecution', with the first 'bad year' being that of the Pendle trials, 1612.[215] Nevertheless, the 1604 Act against Conjuration, Witchcraft and Dealing with Evil and Wicked Spirits was one of the first items of legislation passed after he succeeded Elizabeth, altering the definition of witchcraft and extending the death penalty for anyone who used witchcraft not only to kill, but if they had 'wasted, consumed, pined, or lamed' a person. All second offences of witchcraft were now punishable by execution, regardless of whether that might be for finding lost goods, using love magic or any other such acts. New legislation was also brought in for using dead bodies, or parts thereof, in witchcraft, and for the keeping of evil spirits now, as well as conjuring them. The revised laws made it easier to prosecute those suspected of witchcraft but there appears to have been 'no rush to prosecute and execute'.[216] Instead, there appears to have been a steady decline in prosecutions following the 1580s and that continued to be the case until the Civil War.[217]

Although King James had a keen interest in witchcraft, he became increasingly determined to root out those cases he believed to be fraudulent. In 1605, he met with a young Berkshire woman named Anne Gunter, brought to him by her father, Brian. Her alleged possession began following a village football match in which Brian Gunter had attacked two men from the Gregory family who later died from their injuries. As the conflict between the Gunters and the Gregorys intensified, Anne collapsed. Brian Gunter saw an opportunity, and soon his daughter had started to experience fits, her body convulsing and becoming unnaturally heavy. She then began vomiting pins from her mouth, nose, chest and urine. Brian Gunter insisted that two Gregory women should be investigated and was furious when they were found innocent – hence the impromptu visit to the king, who arranged for a delegation to examine the distraught Anne. They found no case to answer and, as a result, proceedings were brought against Brian and Anne Gunter in the Star Chamber. Anne then admitted that she had faked her symptoms on the instructions of her father, who bore such animosity towards the Gregory family that he forced his daughter into a litany of lies and behaviour that included drinking concoctions that made her genuinely poorly. Anne is believed to have married afterwards with a dowry provided by King James himself.

In the midst of the Gunter case, the king and the government began hearing rumours about the conspiracy that led to the arrest of Guy Fawkes on 5 November 1605 as he and his fellow Gunpowder Plotters attempted to destroy the Houses of Parliament. The following year, while James remained paranoid about Catholic subversion, he received a visit from his brother-in-law, King Christian IV of Denmark. Entertainment was provided in the form of Shakespeare's new play, *Macbeth*. Performed at Hampton Court, it was a grand state occasion with all the leading English judiciary in attendance; there is a possibility that Thomas Potts was present but, even if he were not, he would certainly have heard about it afterwards. References were made to the failed, 'tempest-tost' attempt by witches to sink James's ship years before while the three witches with their 'skinny lips' and 'choppy fingers' bore a strong resemblance to those imagined by James in *Daemonologie*. In fact, the Wyrd Sisters might have emerged directly from the pages of the king's book with their poisonous brews, killing of swine, begging, spell casting, sabbath meets on a blasted heath and their familiars – Paddock the toad and a cat named Graymalkin. Historians are still debating to what extent Shakespeare's representation of a Satanic union may have influenced the criminalisation of witchcraft through the lens of political conspiracy. *Macbeth*'s 'secret, black and midnight hags' appear to have been the first witches in English culture to deliberately garble words from the Book of Common Prayer, echoing the widespread belief that witches could not properly formulate the Lord's Prayer.

The fact that Shakespeare's witches were all female likewise reflected how women – particularly those who were post-menopausal or elderly, frequently with a disability and regarded as argumentative – formed the majority of those accused. Scottish witchcraft expert Christina Larner notes: 'The purpose of a witch-hunt was the prising out of dangerous persons who were enemies of God, the state and the people. The fact that these ideological enemies turned out to be 80% female could have added fuel to the misogyny of the age rather than be a direct consequence of it.'[218] Male suspects were often related to women who were charged as witches – as was the case with James Device and John Bulcock. But a woman who was widowed, over the age of fifty, poor or living on the margins, had illegitimate children or was viewed as a 'quarrelsome' disturber of social order often became the focus of suspicion. The overriding view of the Church was that woman – far more than her male counterparts – had a natural propensity for deviation and betrayal: she was a daughter of Eve, after all, whose inability to resist Satan's temptation had brought about the fall of mankind.

The scold, the whore and the witch: these three constructs of woman were perceived as the greatest challenge to the patriarchy, embodying the fear of women's speech, of their sexuality and as the inversion of what a 'good' woman should be.[219] Just how deeply ingrained these concepts were can be seen in the witch trial broadside, replete with female transgressors murmuring corrupt Latin and Pater Nosters while plotting a murder or two.

Punishments for those women who fell into one of these categories can only be described as torture, albeit that English law prohibited the formal use of torture. Most people would nonetheless agree that the unimaginable nightmare of arrest, questioning and being subjected to an invasive physical examination under threat of death amounted to torture in itself. In addition, some of the methods employed to wring a full confession from a suspect certainly amounted to mistreatment; the investigative techniques in place during the 1645 Essex trials comprised relentless questioning, immersing suspects in water and sleep deprivation, with the latter alone producing confusion, delirium and hallucinations.

Two examples of the punishments meted out to those women identified as scolds, whores and witches will suffice, the first being the ducking stool. It is worthwhile explaining that the idea that suspects were declared witches if they survived being thrown into deep water or were innocent if they drowned is mistaken, but based on the procedure of 'swimming' a suspect, which King James referred to as 'their fleeting on the water'.[220] He was much in favour of the procedure, which had regional variations, but generally involved stripping a suspect and tying their hands crosswise to their feet, attaching a rope around their waist and tying a knot in the rope, then pushing the suspect into a pond or lake. Those who sank below or level to the knot were deemed innocent and brought out of the water; those who remained afloat were likewise brought onto land, but in order to then face a trial. The process arose from the theory that since water was the instrument of baptism, it would reject those who had turned their backs on God.

The ducking stool was used in a similar manner (its predecessor in early England was the cucking stool, where 'strumpets and scolds, with bare feet and head' would sit in an open place, subjected to harassment from passers-by).[221] The suspect would be secured on a chair attached to a long pole that was usually operated by the beadle or local constable. Standing on the water's edge, he would then pull and drop the pole repeatedly to fully immerse the chair and its occupant; there were occasions where the suspect was held under the water for such a length of time that it was impossible to survive, while others drowned in the silted mud below many a pool's surface.

In Pendle, Cuckstool Lane is the next turning after Greenhead Lane (where Robert and Christopher Nutter lived) towards Barrowford; at its foot lies Pendle Water, and nearby Quaker's Bridge was where those women known in the locality as scolds were forcibly ducked. Most villages at this time were equipped with a ducking stool and a scold's bridle (also known as a brank). Despite the absence of legislation, the latter was a punishment meted out by the local magistrate on those women who were said to be foul-mouthed, street brawlers or gossipmongers; in Cheshire's town records it is described as 'a bridle for a curste queane'.[222] The iron framework fitted over a woman's head, enclosing it in a cage. Most were furnished with a spike-covered or sharpened plate which fitted inside the victim's mouth, ensuring that she would be horribly maimed if she attempted to shift her tongue even slightly. Lancaster Castle, where the 1612 trials were held, possessed a scold's bridle 'fitted with serrated points, small spiked balls which tore the tongue at the slightest movement'.[223] A town official would then parade the wearer through the streets, pulling a chain attached to the bridle, which caused 'untold agony' to its victim.[224] Crowds hurled abuse and anything they could find to inflict injury, then gathered to give vent fully when she was chained to a pillory, whipping post or market cross. There were many instances of death as a result of blood poisoning due to the scold's bridle.

Unsurprisingly, this state of affairs only served to divide women and pit them against each other, fuelling a view that by 'becoming accomplices of the war against the "witches" and accepting the leadership of men in this regard they could acquire the protection that would save them from the hangman or the stake. It taught them above all to accept the place assigned to them . . .'[225] Actions brought by women against women were many, with accusations ranging from consorting with the devil to slander; a typical case of the latter is that of York's Jane Featherston, who in 1664 subjected Jane Tireman to a spectacular diatribe, shouting that she was a 'whore, arrant whore, damned whore, queen, dissembling queen, liar, witch and bitch'.[226]

Allegations that had been disproven were classed as defamation and heard at the diocesan network of church courts, while witchcraft was prosecuted through the secular quarter sessions and assize courts. Once the suspects became absorbed into the apparatus of the legal system, any agency they might have had vanished into the ether like an erstwhile familiar, for the guards, the gaolers, the magistrates, the juries and the judge were all men. A convenient if reed-thin argument was put forward to answer why the all-powerful witch allowed herself to be captured: at the moment she was apprehended, the witch lost every bit of her supernatural potency, because God was on the side of the state and its sovereign, who naturally stated it as fact in *Daemonologie*.

For those familiar with the case, the first appearance 'proper' of magistrate Roger Nowell in any study of the 1612 trials has a sense of theatrical villainy, as if it should be accompanied by the directive: 'Enter, stage left, Roger Nowell of Read' – followed by loud hissing from an unseen audience. In truth, Nowell was neither pantomime villain nor witchfinder, but a man undoubtedly invested with a sense of his own importance, keen to make productive friendships and almost indivisible from other men of his social standing in his attitudes and beliefs. His key role in the 1612 case would be in conducting the examinations of the suspects, collecting the evidence against them and, as historian and witch trial expert James Sharpe surmises, 'was probably instrumental in coordinating their trials'.[227]

Roger Nowell's ancestors had been landowners in the village of Read, on the medieval road between Whalley and Padiham, since the 1300s. The dissolution of Whalley Abbey proved fortuitous for the family, who bought much of the estate and built Read Hall with its sweeping views of the district on their newly acquired land.

The handsome house was generously proportioned with two large wings projecting either side of the central section. Long windows overlooked grounds laid out with the precision of a garden intended for admiration rather than enjoyment: a sundial stood isolated on a trim lawn that led to perfectly symmetrical flower beds and terraces, with statues framed by clipped yews.

Nowell's father inherited the house due to his brother Thomas – the eldest sibling – having no male heir. He settled there with his wife Florence, and they began a family, with Roger Nowell born around 1558. Theirs was a strictly Protestant household. The Hall had a much-frequented family chapel, and when a descendant converted it into a dining room and caught a cold from sitting in it before the plaster was dry, there were rumours that his forebears had passed judgement on him. Conversely, Nowell's grandfather was 'a very irreligious man, and never attended any public worship' yet his two half-brothers – Nowell's uncles – were among the most eminent divines of their day. One was Alexander Nowell, Dean of St Paul's during Elizabeth I's reign, although she hated him. He was elected Principal of Brasenose College, Oxford in his eighty-ninth year and left lasting legacies in conceiving the catechism and inventing bottled ale.[228] We have already met Alexander's half-brother within these pages: lawyer John Towneley, imprisoned several times for recusancy and sheltering Catholic priests. There were other illustrious relatives whom Nowell would have known personally, including Alexander's nephew, then Bishop of Exeter, and another half-brother, Laurence, who was a zealous Protestant. Their visits to Read, with long discussions about their experiences and beliefs, may well have influenced Nowell's own religious views.

Despite possessing wealth, property, position and a stable family life, Nowell's father was involved in numerous land disputes over the years, which usually concerned villagers digging for stone, slate and turves on various waste ground. The intensity of these disagreements can be seen in the Read Moor confrontation of 1564: Nowell's father and other men were so infuriated by yeomen from Heyhouses digging up turves from land they regarded as non-communal, that they armed themselves with weapons such as swords, daggers, pikes and staves to drive back the farmers. They then destroyed the turves and threw what was left into Sabden Brook. When the case came to court, Alexander Nowell intervened, and the case was resolved in the Nowells' favour, who were granted ownership of Read Moor.

We know that this period was tumultuous in Pendle due to population growth, economic expansion and private ownership, the slow and partial dismantling of the feudal system, and the change in how charity was distributed. As evidenced in disputes such as that of Read Moor, the situation created a severe level of friction, with the 'haves' and the 'have nots' increasingly far apart as wealthier tenants benefitted from further subletting or keeping copyhold land within the family. The Duchy, keen to inflate its own coffers, began taking legal proceedings in 1607 against tenants, on the grounds that copyhold tenancies were invalid, since the land was 'an assart', that is, an area of forest land that had been cleared for agriculture – which was indeed illegal for royal forests. Tenants struggled to plead their case due to a failure to clarify what had been meant by the term 'lease' in the original documents. Those tenants who could afford it agreed to pay twelve years' rent as a penalty, which then allowed them to remain on their land. One historian notes that this 'legal chicanery' may have been a contributing factor to social tension in the area and to 'one of the most notorious witch trials in England'.[229]

When a royally commissioned review was launched into the matter in 1611, one of those heading the enquiry was Sir Ralph Assheton, to whom John Nutter of Greenhead was servant. A very similar settlement was offered to that of 1607, with extra waste land thrown in as an added incentive to those able to pay the settlement. Again, the gentry benefitted while the poorer inhabitants gained nothing, left to stand and watch as the steward's deputies traversed the Forest with demands for payment, and there can be little doubt that some families were evicted in order for their richer neighbours to gain larger plots of land. As magistrate, Roger Nowell would have been lucidly aware that the

Forest was flooded with ill-feeling and anguish at the loss of land held by generations and now surrendered to those whose only concern was feathering their own already generously lined nests.

William Harrison Ainsworth may well have learnt about the 1611 commission during research for his novel, *The Lancashire Witches*, and realised it made for a reasonably plausible plotline. In practice, however, the idea that witch trials were widely implemented as a way of confiscating land from women is not supported by the evidence, as Keith Thomas explains: 'The short-lived 1542 Act ordered the forfeiture of the witch's goods and lands as by felony, but the two subsequent measures of 1563 and 1604 safeguarded the heir's inheritance and the widow's dower, should the accused person be executed. This did not always work in practice, and if there was no heir the property would go to the manorial lord anyway . . . But in England prosecutions can scarcely ever have had a financial motive.'[230]

On 9 May 1581, Roger Nowell married Katherine Morton at St Mary's Church in Whalley. Precisely ten years later – in much the same way that his father had inherited the manor of Read by default from his brother – it passed to Nowell upon his father's death because his elder brother was deceased. Nowell and his wife had a growing brood of children to fill the Hall: five boys and four girls. In 1595, while Katherine was pregnant, their four-year-old son Alexander died, and when the newborn proved to be a boy, they named him in honour of the much-loved son they had lost.

In 1599, another dispute regarding the right to Read Moor was again found in Nowell's favour, but he was accused of wrongfully claiming freehold of six messuages by enclosing the land and adding the holdings to land he legally owned as part of the manor of Read. Such issues rumbled on for a long while, despite Nowell himself following several of his relatives into the law profession, but in the unpaid role of justice of the peace. A prestigious position, the men chosen for its ranks were plucked from prominent local families of sufficient wealth and good standing, loyal to the Crown and adhering to the dictates of the government. They were essential to local government, with new duties and jurisdiction added by central government, increasing the power they wielded. A JP acted individually in their own region and then collectively for the county, within the quarter sessions court. He would find himself dealing with many different infractions: preventing unlawful games or sport, enquiring into neighbourhood disputes and others between employer and apprentice, suppressing rogues and nightwalkers, and committing suspects to prison. He would also conduct preliminary examinations of suspects, victims and witnesses of crime – by himself or in tandem with another magistrate – record depositions and bind over those who were required to appear in court.

The records of the Lancashire Quarter Sessions 1589–1607 reveal some of the cases in which Nowell was involved prior to the witch trial; Nicholas Bannister sometimes worked alongside him, as did Sir Thomas Gerard, both of whom would later be embroiled in the 1612 case. The documents show the punishments meted out, such as the whipping of women for bearing illegitimate children and men imprisoned for failing to pay maintenance. Another entry reveals that a woman named Anne Harrison was to be 'flogged in Preston today and sent to prison as an incorrigible rogue'.[231]

In 1604, Nowell publicly announced his loyalty to the new king by signing the Loyal Address of the Lancashire Gentry, which effectively welcomed James I to his new kingdom. He continued as a magistrate and, in 1610, added another considerable string to his bow when he became High Sheriff of Lancashire. To obtain the high-ranking position, his name would have been on a list of three nominees put forward at a special sitting of high government officials and the Council of the Exchequer. The king then selected a name from the list. Being chosen secured Nowell a letter patent and swore him in as sheriff for a year. But while the shrievalty had achieved 'almost vice-regal status', its responsibilities were decreasing as swiftly as those of the JP rose. Nonetheless, the sheriff supervised elections, contributed to maintaining law and order and helped to ensure the smooth running of both the quarter sessions and assize courts, among other duties. Assisted by his under-sheriffs, he publicised the dates of the various court sessions, served process upon those required to attend, organised the jury, held prisoners in gaol and kept gaol calendars, recording details about those in prison. He was also responsible for organising accommodation for the assize judges and finding entertainment for them. Like the position of magistrate, the role of sheriff was one undertaken primarily to achieve status and further connections.

Status was probably behind the unholy row that broke out in Whalley's St Mary's Church over usage of his family pew, in the same year that Nowell was appointed sheriff. Many people of similar standing had their own seating in church, but 'the Kage' was no ordinary pew. The name was an old one for such structures, albeit that this one was grander. Nine feet square and situated on the south side of the nave, the pew – also known as St Anton's Cage – is imposing and elaborately carved with a number of inscriptions and the family coat of arms. One of Nowell's forebears was responsible for its creation; the first argument about who might sit in it was settled by Sir John Towneley in 1534, with the date carved into the wood. Once Nowell became sheriff, he had the pew enlarged, which he felt was of sufficient importance to be recorded with another inscription: 'Made by Roger Nowell, Esq. 1610.' He was therefore outraged when he discovered that Ralph Assheton of Leaver was using the Kage and he fired off an incensed letter to the Bishop of Chester about it in October 1610.[232] The bickering appears to have been a continuation of the two families squabbling over occupation of the chantry, with Nowell taking grim satisfaction in being able to write directly to the Dean of Sr Paul's – his cousin Alexander Nowell. The Dean then contacted the Archbishop of Canterbury, but the matter festered for years, nonetheless.

By 1612, Nowell was a man of substance in his fifties, extremely well respected, with a solid background in the landed gentry, several very highly regarded relations in the fields of religion, theology and education, and excellent connections to the most important and influential figures in the Blackburn Hundred. He was also a family man who had known the unending grief of losing a child, but his surviving children had made good marriages and were now becoming parents themselves.

At home in Read Hall, as befitting an erudite man in his position, Nowell's library would have been substantial, with several volumes on the subject of witchcraft. *Daemonologie* was the standard text for any magistrate, but the *Malleus Maleficarum* probably stood alongside it on the shelf, and it seems unlikely that he would be without a copy of William Perkins's fairly recently published *Discourse of the Damned Art of Witchcraft*, not least because the author was a colleague and friend of his own relative, Dr William Whittaker. Nowell would certainly have been familiar with the 1604 Witchcraft Act, since his work made that a necessity. But his interest in the subject was more than simply intellectual; it was personal.

Chapter Ten

THE LANCASHIRE SEVEN

Roger Nowell's mother was married twice; she had been widowed a few years prior to marrying his father and had children to her first husband, Laurence Starkie. His family were ancient and wealthy, with several estates to their name, including Huntroyd and Simonstone; the former was their principal seat. Edmund was one of Nowell's brothers from his mother's first marriage; his son Nicholas was thus Nowell's nephew, but close to him in age.

In 1578, Nicholas married Anne Parr, a distant relation to Catherine Parr, last wife of Henry VIII. Anne was the sole heiress of her father's estate at Cleworth in Tyldesley, around ten miles north-west of Manchester. After their marriage, Nicholas and Anne settled at Cleworth Hall, a lovely Tudor home and 'a place of consequence, moated about, constructed upon a stout timber frame with gables and bays, and set on an eminence'.[233] Despite their wealth, the young couple suffered with the loss of four children in infancy. Anne grew increasingly certain that she was cursed and believed her Roman Catholic relations had inflicted such loss upon them in order to prevent her from producing a male heir. She was convinced enough to draw up a will ensuring that her husband and his family would take possession of her lands and wealth, following her death.

In time, Anne realised that her relatives would be thwarted

nonetheless: she and Nicholas had two children who survived, and they were a happy little family until February 1595, when John (aged about eleven) and his sister Anne (aged about nine) fell strangely ill. Anne began twitching, which soon developed into full-blown seizures, while John would suddenly shout and scream, seemingly without reason. Their parents were frantic. Nicholas spent £200, then an enormous sum, on consultations with a doctor to no avail; it seems that most physicians in the early modern period had little interest in children's mental health, regarding them as incapable of reasoning and 'little more than animals'.[234] Nicholas then contacted a Roman Catholic priest to discuss the curse his wife believed had been placed upon them. Then, sometime in 1595, he sought out a cunning man to help – and Edmund Hartley came into their lives.

Hartley's background is obscure, but he may have been recommended to Nicholas Starkie by a relative or family friend. He duly began treating the children on visits to Cleworth Hall, using 'certain popish charms and herbs'. There was some improvement in their condition and, after eighteen months, Hartley informed Nicholas and Anne that while their children were not completely cured, they now no longer required him to visit. He was scarcely out of sight when young John collapsed with some form of haemorrhage. Hartley rushed back and managed to stem the bleeding, but told Nicholas that had he gone some forty roods further, 'no man could have stopped the bleeding'.[235]

Nicholas pleaded with Hartley to remain, and he agreed, after extracting an unwritten contract that ensured he would be paid a vast sum to do so. He tried to convince Nicholas that he needed a place of his own in order to have the requisite distance from his subjects, but even the devoted father felt this to be a step too far and refused. Hartley threatened to make things difficult for the family and both children suffered severe relapses. The madness then spread to three women living at the Hall, one of whom was related to Anne; they began making a terrific noise, barking and howling like dogs. It was 'a strange supernatural and fearful noise . . . the like was never heard'.[236]

Distraught, Nicholas asked Hartley to accompany him on a visit to his father Edmund at Huntroyde Hall. Read Hall was but a short distance away and there is a strong possibility that Roger Nowell was present at the meeting. Whatever occurred, that night Nicholas felt that something supernatural was happening to him. The following day, Hartley told him to walk with him into the woods behind the Hall. Under the tall trees, with only the sound of birdsong breaking the silence, Hartley found an area of clear ground, and with a stick began scraping a circle. He then drew the stick across the soil and leaves again, dividing the circle into four parts and then adding a cross in every section. He then beckoned Nicholas over and told him to walk the circle. His intention is unknown, but it seems unlikely he was attempting to raise a spirit; the circle suggests some form of ritual magic, nonetheless, and inviting Nicholas to walk within it may have been to offer him protection or seeking a resolution. His employer was less enthusiastic, later referring to the circle as 'this wretched dealing of his'.[237]

Nicholas remained keen to discover if there was something more prosaic ailing his son, taking a sample of John's urine to a doctor in Manchester, who found nothing of note. He then called on the mysterious Dr John Dee, astronomer, alchemist, mathematician, astrologer and advisor to Queen Elizabeth I. He had previous experience of demonic possession and had attempted an exorcism on a nurse in his household who afterwards attempted to drown herself before succeeding in cutting her own throat. Dee retreated from the Starkie case immediately, apart from suggesting that Nicholas should work with preachers in prayer and fasting. He then angrily reprimanded Hartley for his handling of the matter, leaving the cunning man fuming with anger.

When the party returned to Cleworth. John screamed that the devil had broken his neck and raged the entire night, hurling his pillows on the bedroom fire. Again, the strange behaviour spread – this time to three other children who lived at the Hall as companions for the Starkie children while receiving an education. These three young girls, together with John and his sister Anne, behaved like a pack of mad dogs, and when they attended church would shout 'filthy and unsavoury' things. Something close to the truth emerged when the girls told Anne Starkie that Hartley would kiss them and that an angel like a dove visited, which they were to follow to heaven through a little hole. One of the young girls had created a gap under her bed where the demon or angel might come to her. Margaret Byrom, Anne's poor relation at the Hall, was also found in an embrace with Hartley in his bedroom and claimed he had asked her to comfort him after being attacked by evil spirits. In the turmoil that followed, Margaret fled to her own home in Salford, but Hartley followed her and refused to leave. The authorities were alerted, and a preacher demanded that Hartley should recite the Lord's Prayer, something that witches were not thought to do easily. Hartley stumbled over his words in his nervousness and was immediately arrested.

A date was set for a confrontation, under observation, between Hartley and Margaret at her home. That morning, shortly before his arrival, as she was sitting by the fireside, Margaret saw 'a great black dog with a monstrous tail and a long chain, open mouth, coming apace towards her'. The creature struck her before transforming into 'a big black cat, staring fearfully at her', and finally 'a mouse, that leapt upon her left knee.'[238] She broke down when Hartley entered and could scarcely speak. Hartley was then taken to Cleworth Hall where all the children became hysterical and were unable to give coherent statements to the local justice of the peace.

In March 1597, Hartley was brought before the Lancaster Assizes, charged with bewitching John and Anne Starkie; another charge of using love magic against Margaret Byrom was dropped, perhaps because she was unwilling to testify. Nicholas Starkie was the only witness to appear in court; his uncle Roger Nowell would have been there to support him. The case was heard before the 1604 Act that brought in stricter punishments for certain infractions and Hartley looked certain to be imprisoned rather than face the gallows. But when Nicholas discussed the circle Hartley had drawn in the woods, the mood in court changed, for the implication was that he had been attempting to raise an evil spirit and the penalty for that was death. As a result, Hartley was condemned to die, despite having declared that no gallows could hang him.

On the day of his execution, before a huge crowd, a ladder had been propped against the gallows on Lancaster Moor. Hartley had to climb the ladder and then wait while the noose was placed about his neck; the ladder would then be kicked away, and he would hang. When the moment came he was asked if he wanted to confess and repent his sins. He refused and then, in a final show of defiance, kicked the ladder away himself. The crowd gasped and then screamed as the rope broke and Hartley crashed to the ground. His previous declaration that no gallows could hang him rung in the minds of many present, but it was evident the Hartley had suffered serious injury. The executioner, however, had a job to do and dragged him backwards, throwing another noose about his neck. On the ladder for a second time, when asked to confess and repent, Hartley did exactly that, 'penitently', choking and spluttering his way through the words.[239] The executioner pulled the ladder away and Hartley swung, the noose holding firm.[240]

Hartley was dead, but the Starkie household was not yet peaceful. A few days after Hartley's execution, Puritan exorcist John Darrell and his assistant George More arrived at Cleworth Hall on the invitation of Nicholas Starkie. The two men spoke to the children, who told them gleefully that Hartley might have hanged but it was not possible to hang the actual devil. Darrell and More told Nicholas that all the children and Margaret Byrom were infested with evil spirits, and that Hartley had told all of them that he could get rid of the devil by kissing them. But rather than view Hartley's actions as sexual abuse, the two exorcists decided that Hartley had kissed his victims in order to 'breathe the devil into their bodies'.[241]

The two men gathered fifty people to Cleworth Hall to say prayers. Then, over a period of forty-eight hours, they performed several exorcisms. The process was excruciating, with Darrell and More shouting the Scripture while the seven at their mercy – six children and Margaret – screamed in terror and experienced severe convulsions. Afterwards, the general consensus was that the demons had been driven out, but for many months the children complained of nightmares in which they were attacked by a black dog, a bear, an ape and other creatures. The two exorcists were also troubled – by the law. In 1598,

John Darrell was tried for performing fake exorcisms in which those who claimed to be possessed had been trained by him to behave in certain ways. As his assistant, George More was likewise tried. Both men were found guilty and imprisoned.

The story of the 'Lancashire Seven' and all that had gone before created shockwaves through the county. The names of those involved were known to most people as a result, while the Starkies were a family left experiencing deep trauma long after the case itself had ended. The influence of Edmund Hartley on John Starkie was profound and would emerge several years after the Pendle trials. By 1612, the family had abandoned Cleworth Hall and were living at Huntroyd, almost neighbours of their relative, Roger Nowell.

In early 1612, Nowell received a missive from the Crown regarding 'the religious question'.[242] As far as the government was concerned, Lancashire was 'a hotbed of seditious intrigue'.[243] In an attempt to stem any budding insurgence, the Crown sent a directive to every justice of the peace within the county, demanding an inventory of all those who refused to take communion in church and to confiscate any weapons from them.

Nowell had other ties to the Crown. He was in a small collective of 'gentlemen of the best calling', all well known to him and including representatives of the Bannister, Shuttleworth, Towneley and Starkie clans. They loaned money to the king when required, on the tacit understanding that they were very unlikely to be reimbursed. Nowell was clearly at the zenith of his success, as he had been for some time, but had he been minded to instigate a witch trial the perfect opportunity would have been a year or two before, when he was sheriff. Abraham Law's complaint against Alizon Device was one which Nowell could not afford to ignore; for all his connections and standing, to brush it aside would have left him at risk of being found in contempt of office.

Two days after Alizon's initial encounter with John Law, and before the pedlar's son approached him, Nowell attended a meeting in Lancaster Castle. All of the county's remaining justices of the peace were present, together with the resident sheriff, Cuthbert Halsall. Their business was mundane: considering applications for alehouse licenses and the like. Nowell's next visit to the castle would be under very different circumstances.[244] In Potts's eyes, Nowell was the perfect man for the task about to befall him: 'A very religious, honest gentleman,' earnest in his duties and thus 'whose fame for this great service to his country shall live after him.' And indeed, Monday, 30 March 1612 proved to be a memorable day for Roger Nowell, one in which he stepped into the history books in a manner he could never have expected.

We cannot be certain of the exact chronology of the day's events – or those of the night before – but in Colne, having made it clear that he intended to take matters further, it seems unthinkable that Abraham Law would have allowed Alizon Device to leave. Given the widespread belief that witches were divested of their powers following capture, it was far wiser to keep her in custody, both to ensure that she could do no further harm and to prevent her from fleeing. In addition, Abraham may have already been in contact with the authorities regarding the matter and an appointment with Roger Nowell for the following day might have already been arranged. There is a strong possibility that Abraham kept Alizon at the alehouse in Colne that evening, under his watchful eye.

We do know that Roger Nowell interviewed both Abraham and John Law the following day. But it is inaccurate to claim, as many do, that after Abraham had insisted that he should take action against Alizon and her family, Nowell then charged off in virulent pursuit of those concerned because he regarded himself as the region's prime witch-hunter and saw an opportunity to make a name for himself as such. In truth, once Nowell had heard the complaint against Alizon, he had no choice but to investigate: witchcraft was a felony, punishable by death, and he was legally bound to take a written statement from victim and complainant before probing the issue further. In addition, the moral and religious universe of that period ensured that those who believed in God were horror-struck at the thought of the eternal damnation that awaited anyone involved in the execution of an innocent person. To that end, no less a person than King James himself had issued a warning to magistrates via his book *Daemonologie* that those who failed to thoroughly investigate suspected cases of witchcraft were themselves acting in such a way as to be errant, morally corrupt and unlawful.

In addition, Nowell would have been aware that John Law might not necessarily survive, and therefore he needed to speak to him as soon as possible. Given that the pedlar was still somewhat incapacitated, that Alizon may have been held at the alehouse, and that Colne was closer to Halifax than Read, it made more sense for Nowell to travel by carriage the approximately ten miles north-east to Colne to conduct the interviews.

Whether it was at the alehouse in Colne, or elsewhere, Nowell conducted the interviews with the two men alone. However, everything they said would have been recorded, and it may be that he had someone assisting him in writing it all down. But there was no compunction then about an independent observer or legal representative sitting in on the interviews – it simply did not work like that then, however appalling that may be for us to comprehend.

Neither statement is particularly lengthy. John Law describes what happened to him in Colne Field, followed by the occult visitations in his bedchamber afterwards; his son explains how he received the letter from his father and recounts everything he had been told before finishing with the previous day's confrontation. But there are crucial differences between the statements, despite their telling of essentially the same story.

In his deposition, Abraham mentions 'an old woman' who 'tormented' his father alongside Alizon, but the older man fails to make any reference to Elizabeth Southerns, plainly the 'old woman'. Abraham also recalled how Alizon's begging for forgiveness had been witnessed by 'diverse others', yet we hear no more about their identity and there are no statements from these people. John Law told Nowell about the black dog that entered his bedchamber, followed by Alizon Device. Abraham recounts that his father had told him about the nightly 'apparitions' of Alizon, and her grandmother, but there is no mention of a black dog as well, despite the fact that this would have been regarded as vital evidence in favour of witchcraft at play.

Yet how did John Law connect a black dog with Alizon? He could never have foreseen that she would tell Nowell her familiar was just such a black dog. There are several possible explanations: that Nowell had already spoken to Alizon, who told him about the black dog, and that Nowell then put the question to Law; or, that by an extraordinary coincidence, Law either dreamt about or hallucinated the dog; or, that an actual black dog just happened to wander into his room; or, that Nowell simply inserted the passage into Law's statement, regarding it as editing evidence rather than falsifying it; or, finally, that Law was indeed visited by Alizon's familiar spirit. Although the former sits more comfortably with a modern and rational understanding of the case, it remains an anomaly.

Once his interviews with John and Abraham Law were complete, Nowell bade them farewell and turned his attention to someone who must have been utterly petrified by now: nineteen-year-old Alizon Device. If the interviews with the complainants had indeed taken place at Colne, afterwards Nowell travelled back to Read either with Alizon or had someone accompany her to follow him there. One person suitable for the task was the Forest of Pendle constable, Henry Hargreaves, whom Nowell is known to have summoned that day. Little is known about Hargreaves personally, other than that in addition to serving as constable, he worked as a yeoman farmer and was married to a local woman.[245] The role of parish constable was unpaid but mandatory and ran for a year from one Michaelmas to the next. Most constables were literate and efficient, responsible for maintaining the king's peace and carrying out the directives of the county bench, as well as apprehending criminal suspects and escorting them to court. On a more local level, Hargreaves was expected to organise some of the community festivities and customs. Known to virtually everyone in his neighbourhood, he would have been aware of any feuds and burgeoning rumours, and in that respect, he cannot have failed to be familiar with the stories circulating for years around the behaviour of the families of Elizabeth Southerns and Anne Whittle.

Likewise, Roger Nowell would have heard of the two families, even in the circles within which he worked and socialised, which included the Towneleys and the Shuttleworths, two of the most prominent dynasties in the Blackburn Hundred. James Device had been suspected of using witchcraft to kill Anna Towneley, a kinswoman of the former family, while Richard Shuttleworth had lost his right-hand man Robert Nutter and his father Christopher in circumstances that implicated Anne Whittle using sorcery. Seemingly acting on his own volition, Nowell decided to haul in members of the two feuding families for questioning on all rumoured matters, perhaps following further consultation with Constable Hargreaves. He turned to the Devices first, instructing to apprehend Elizabeth and James Device, and Elizabeth Southerns. That would have left Jennet, aged eleven, without adult supervision, but perhaps she accompanied her family to Read Hall or remained with her uncle, Christopher Holgate, who lived nearby with his wife and family. Constable Hargreaves may have organised a small group to assist in rounding up the three, particularly if he thought there might be trouble of some kind. He then required a second group, formed entirely of respectable married women, whose task it would be to conduct a very different search: the examination of the suspects' bodies for the telltale mark.

Waiting to assist Nowell in questioning the suspects was fellow magistrate Nicholas Bannister, who was having a memorable year himself, marrying for the second time and turning seventy. His was an ancient and wealthy family, whose ancestral home was the moated manor house of Altham, four miles west of Burnley, where generations of Bannisters had lived for over five hundred years. In 1595, Nicholas Bannister was named by a representative of Queen Elizabeth I as one of the few people who could be trusted to 'spend all the buttons at their doublets to purge Lancashire from idolatry, papistry, seditious seminaries and their favourites'.[246] He was 'a trusted agent of the crown whose remit was to strip local Catholics of a large percentage of their property'.[247] This was a duty he appears to have taken to 'with uncommon gusto'.[248]

Chapter Eleven

A CURSTE QUEANE

The carts carrying the groups of suspects and assistants pulled up in the courtyards to the rear of Read Hall on 30 March. Magistrates themselves could determine whether to question their suspects first and conduct the search for body marks afterwards. Most felt that it was more effective to let the search take precedence, for it immediately put the suspects at a greater disadvantage yet, particularly if any marks were found – which they invariably were – for it emphasised that they were entirely vulnerable and liable to degradation with no recourse to refuse.

The suspects were thus taken into rooms at Read Hall where the searches would be conducted. Potts tells us virtually nothing of what occurred, but we can surmise that Alizon was reunited with her mother and grandmother at this point, and that James Device would have been subject to a similar procedure in another room within the Hall's servants' quarters.

The searches were invasive, humiliating and terrifying. In Scotland, where torture was permitted under law, such searches were often conducted while all manner of brutalities were carried out. Agnes Sampson was forcibly shaved, and a rope tied about her head was pulled gradually tighter until a mark was discovered on her genitals. Torture was prohibited under English law, but the psychological effect of the search was profound. Because the mark was generally believed to be hidden from view, the obvious places to look were in the region of the breasts and genitals, resulting in sexual assault by any standards today. Each look or touch was agony in another sense, for the suspect knew that an old bruise or scar or skin tag – once so innocuous – was now viewed as incontrovertible proof that they had consorted with the devil. A very similar procedure would have been carried out on James, but with men in charge.

Potts tells us nothing of the outcomes of Alizon and her mother being searched. He does, however, recall that Elizabeth Southerns was found to bear 'a mark' on her left side. The women who had searched her showed her a small measure of respect in replacing her clothes carefully to cover her but for the mark. Elizabeth was then led through the corridors of Read Hall to the magistrate, who was the first man to lay eyes and possibly hands on that part of her body since her husband and the father of her son Christopher. Having inspected the mark, during his questioning of Elizabeth's daughter, Nowell asked her about it. Elizabeth Device replied that her mother had had the mark 'the space of forty years'. Since she was then in her forties, her answer was given in defence of her mother, for she was telling Nowell that the mark had been there as long as she could remember and therefore it was nothing sinister.

Once the business of the searches had been dealt with, the magistrates began questioning their suspects individually. The order of the interviews is unknown, but of the four family members brought before them, Nowell and Bannister decided to question only three; for some reason – perhaps because of the shock of being informed that she bore the devil's mark – Elizabeth Southerns was not interviewed that day. Instead, we can probably assume that the magistrates began with their prime suspect: Alizon Device.

Both men were members of their regional justice quorum, which comprised those men who by virtue of their experience were placed in senior positions within the local legal system. The two men were undoubtedly proficient in their work, which made them dangerous for anyone who came before them hoping to either outwit them or prove their innocence. But Nowell and Bannister knew how to build, over a relatively short space of time, a relationship with their suspects, albeit one that was 'brutally unequal', as Lyndal Roper describes it: 'The interrogators shaped the story that the witch confessed, even if they did not consciously believe themselves to be doing so; the witch, though she provided the substance and detail of the material was not free to provide any narrative she liked. Consciously or unconsciously she learned what she had to say.'[249] Precisely how Nowell, especially, convinced his suspects to make statements that acted as virtual stepping stones to the gallows is difficult to grasp; physical torture was prohibited, but there were various forms of psychological coercion that he could employ, especially since the subjects were all members of the same family, and the only one not to have come under suspicion was an eleven-year-old girl who was sister, daughter and granddaughter of those about to be interrogated.

We should remember, too, that the Devices saw themselves as cunning folk and their explanations of meeting with familiars would have been a means of proving themselves to be good cunning folk, who believed they were on the same 'side' as the magistrates – that is, fighting witchcraft. This may explain too why Alizon was eager to denounce Anne Whittle as a witch who had killed her father, John Device, and her good friend, Anne Nutter – among others. Joyce Froome suggests that some of Alizon's claims against Anne Whittle may have come to her through divination; the young woman feared witchcraft while simultaneously believing that she herself had powers that she was not yet completely in control of, but which could be used to expose other witches and their activities.

The examination itself was not unlike today's police procedure of questions and answers, albeit without a solicitor present or a recording being made. The responses nonetheless had to be chronicled and that was the duty of the third person on Nowell's side of the room: a clerk whom the magistrate could trust. This is believed to have been Nowell's relative Margery Whitaker, who had previously acted for him in that capacity. She was therefore aware of the need to produce a coherent piece of writing that read as a flowing statement from which the indictable offences could be drawn. She was not permitted to introduce any other material, but the editing process nonetheless altered what had been said.

It was Margery who inspired Robert Neill to write *Mist Over Pendle*, as he recalled noting that the depositions seemed quite different to the writing in Nowell's 'poor, halting' private letters: 'He had no trick of words, and he could not possibly have written those depositions, with their fine sentences and vivid turns of phrase. Someone else wrote those, someone of intelligence and education, who sat with him, pen in hand, while he questioned the witches.'[250] Our information about Margery is limited, but no doubt she and Alizon exchanged a glance when they met at Read Hall, for Margery was two years Alizon's junior – only seventeen.

We have no way of knowing how long each interview lasted and whether the suspects were questioned more than once that day. We can see that one person's evidence is often influenced by another's, however, and that Nowell would have put questions to an individual after they occurred to him during the interview of another suspect. The interrogator would generally begin by asking how long the suspect had been a witch before moving onto the how, why and when; he would probe into their alleged crimes and invite them to admit to anything more, then bring the examination to a close by asking if they knew of any other witches in their region.

Alizon was the most voluble of the interviewees, perhaps due to being frightened out of her wits by being forced to confront John Law and now, at Read Hall, following a physical examination, she was again pressed to answer all manner of questions by men unlike any with whom she had ever associated. Hence Nowell and Bannister managing to extract from her a number of damning points regarding her grandmother: that she had advised Alizon to let the familiar spirit suck from her; that she had attempted to heal John Nutter's cow but failed; that she had manifested butter and brought about the death of miller Richard Baldwin's daughter, using witchcraft. All these no doubt began as a series of fairly straightforward questions about Alizon's grandmother's work as a cunning woman, such as: 'Has your grandmother ever been called upon to heal a sick animal?', which then led to Alizon telling them about Elizabeth trying to cure John Nutter's unwell cow but without success; rather than recording this tale as the assistance failing, Nowell moulded it into a story of deliberately malicious sorcery.

When the two magistrates then questioned Alizon about the relationship between her family and that of Anne Whittle, she may have regarded it as an opportunity to avenge her father's death, for she provided a stream of pained recollections: how Bessie had broken into their home and stolen their possessions and food; that Anne Whittle had spoiled the drink belonging to John Moore and then bewitched his cattle; that Anne had angered John Nutter's son by charming milk and then killed one of his cows. Finally, she listed those whom she believed to have been murdered by Anne Whittle, beginning with her father, who was killed after failing to pay her annual retainer; her friend Anne Nutter; John Moore's child; and Hugh Moore. She gave the two magistrates the distinct impression that Anne Whittle's favoured method of murder was the use of image magic.

Alizon then described her version of events in Colne Field and its aftermath, which Nowell wrote up as her confession. She may have felt momentarily empowered, for although admitting to keeping a familiar was tantamount to holding a smoking gun, her statements regarding the black dog were enough to send a chill through Roger Nowell. As Alizon described the diabolical hound, Nowell would have been reminded of his nephew Edmund's experiences a few years previously ('Look where Satan is. Look where Beelzebub is. Look where Lucifer is. Look where a great black dog is, with a firebrand in his mouth'). Nowell may well have shuddered at the thought that this was the same black dog that had haunted his family – had it returned to the place where cunning man Edmund Hartley had summoned it? And was Nicholas, living at Huntroyd again, still secretly plagued by it?

Or equally as unsettling, did Nowell fear that Alizon was playing a deviant and unnecessary game by taunting him about the black dog, implying that it was indeed the same hellish hound and was now prepared to defend his mistress by any means?

Why had Alizon confessed to anything when she must have been aware that being remanded on suspicion of witchcraft following one's own words very rarely ended well? In 1584, Reginald Scot answered the question by describing a young woman such as Alizon being 'commonly unlearned, unwarned and unprovided of counsel and friendship [and] void of judgement and discretion. She is daunted by authority, circumvented with guile, compelled by fear, deceived by ignorance and so brought to these absurd confessions.'[251] In the case of the two Pendle families, priding themselves on their cunning skills was a reason in itself. Marion Gibson explains that a cunning woman 'would have her own folk beliefs about witches and magic, often differing from her interrogators' fears. Left to herself, she was more likely to imagine performing healing charms than curses, say she had interacted with ill-defined spirits rather than devils, and invent folkloric stories about bargains with fairies or ghosts instead of formal Satanic worship. But under pressure, her story would come to align with her accusers', to the extent that conviction was plausible.'[252] Confessions also 'clearly reflected real beliefs and experiences', according to Emma Wilby. 'The close links between events described by suspects and those described by victims and accusers cannot all be attributed to interrogational manipulation.'[253]

Overall, Alizon's confession, together with that of her brother and other suspects brought later before Nowell, was largely unambiguous in its references to witchcraft. Nowell must have been relieved, since magistrates could be left wondering how the information they had gathered would work within the context of such an enquiry. For instance, some suspects seemed determined to expose neighbourly conflicts or broken love affairs while being careful not to implicate themselves. We know that many accusations of witchcraft arose from personal feuds, real or imagined slights, and arguments that ended in violence, but some suspects described clashes and disputes in such a way that it left the possibility that witchcraft was involved open to interpretation. The 1612 examinations were replete with decades-long feuding, explosive quarrels and name-calling, but there was no mistaking what lay behind creating wax pictures or telling one's familiar to harm someone.

The only means of avoiding falling into the trap, or having one's words misinterpreted was to say nothing, as Elizabeth Device clearly grasped from the beginning. Her failure to answer questions has led to many commentaries on the case, assuming that she was either unable to understand what was being said or that she was of insufficient intelligence to respond. The fact that she only began cooperating with her interrogators after her children had condemned themselves and each other speaks volumes. Elizabeth's careful responses then, and her refusal to be drawn any further on her initial meeting with Nowell and Bannister, were due to her trying to control the narrative by giving the magistrates as little as possible with which to work.

James Device's examination that day appears to have revolved around his sister being initially blamed for the death of Henry Bulcock's child. There is no mention of the trouble between Alizon and John Law, although Nowell must have expected James to have been aware of it. How the issue arose regarding the Bulcock accusation is left unexplained, unless Nowell or Bannister had heard of the matter and then let James believe that either Bulcock or Alizon had made a statement about another occasion where she had been accused of witchcraft. At first glance, James appears to be denouncing his sister when in fact he is simply stating that Henry Bulcock had indeed accused Alizon, who had confessed to him (Bulcock) and begged his forgiveness. Given that neither Bulcock nor Alizon actually made a statement, we can surmise that Nowell edited James's statement to implicate Alizon. In doing so, he removed all context, and the issue is left drifting without proper clarification.

Nowell and Bannister concluded their work for the time being after speaking to Alizon and her family. The complaint against Alizon regarding John Law was upheld; her family were released but she was kept in custody.[254] By the time James and his mother and grand-mother had arrived home, they must have been in utter turmoil, both exhausted and agitated with what had taken place that day and all they had seen and heard, but above all terrified for themselves and each other, and especially Alizon.

We don't know where Alizon was held; Joyce Froome points out that suspects were supposed to be sent immediately after questioning to the nearest gaol, but in practice that was not always possible and Nowell probably had in mind that he wished to continue questioning Alizon after ruminating over her pronouncements on their first meeting. Most villages had a lock-up where petty criminals would be imprisoned for a few days before being sent for trial or released. In the days before a national system of policing, the lock-up would have been used by the parish constable, in this case Henry Hargreaves. Equally, Alizon may have been kept at Read Hall in a locked room with occasional supervision. But wherever she was held, we can be certain of one thing: alone, formally accused of witchcraft and in utterly unfamiliar surroundings, she would never have known fear quite like it.

Chapter Twelve

FOR THE CARRIAGE OF
THE WITCHES

Anyone taking the Barrowford Road through the village of Fence towards Higham must pass Ashlar House, although they may not notice it standing, sunken yet handsome, with tall chimneys and an uneven roof, below the level of the road. Few old houses are so deceptive; from the roadside it has all the appearance of a charming stone cottage, but its former grandeur is evident when viewed from the original front.

An evocative description of the building is given by a rambler during the 1920s, who approached through 'a long field [which] gently inclines to the turnpike, then follows a rich meadow, with three houses under ash and plane trees'. Nearby 'is another old house with mullioned windows, a gable ridge on which rests a ball and crosse. It has a roof of grey-green slate, that time has beautifully mellowed and toned in delicate tints and washes. There are curious foliations, quaint doorways, deep windowsills, wise inscriptions, old herbs and plants and – I must spend an hour at this Atchelor House some day.'[255] The rambler returned for a second, lingering look:

Bits of floral ornamentation are fairly plain to be seen, though much has been spoiled by weather, limewash and paint. There are indications that this house has been used for religious purposes.

On the gable and nearest Higham is a little ornament, which, seen from the lane, has the appearance of a cross on a globe . . . The different doorposts are made of soft sandstone, and time, wear and tear, have ruined the beauty of their carving. Much of the house is of grit. The window ledges and mullions are massive . . . The doors are true to type, heavy and studded with oaken nails. There are two letters on the mural tablet, NH . . . The house is surrounded with trees; there is a pleasant lawn with a bushy border, and amongst the bushes are a few ornaments which have been taken from some part of the house and placed there . . . The house has a southern aspect, and before Burnley discovered it could weave the outlook from here must have been one of great beauty.[256]

Ashlar, Atchelor and Hachiller are just the three of the names attached to the house over the years; it appears to have been known as The New House until the eighteenth century, after which it was commonly referred to as The Fence House or Hewn Atchelor House. All are thought attributable to the ashlar stones with which it was built – or rebuilt, since one theory holds that it was possibly a timber building originally. In its earliest incarnation it was New House or The Fence, which, like the village nearby, took its name from the fenced enclosure where stags were kept for breeding. It stood between Greenhead Lane, where the Nutters lived in Greenhead Manor, and Foxen Dole Lane, which led to the dwelling place of Anne Whittle and the Redfearns.

Our 1920s rambler was right in his assumption that it was once used for religious purposes; *The Victorian History of the County of Lancaster* states that it was built 'as a Catholic chapel and a dwelling-house for the officiating priest'. The somewhat inscrutable tablet over the door is inscribed: '1594 Richard Greymshe (3) John Box. Fear God. Know thy se. Honour thy Prince N.H.' Despite only ranking as a yeoman, Richard Grimshaw was an extremely wealthy landowner; when he died in his eighties in 1608, he was owed huge sums of money from the important local gentry. Ashlar House then passed from his ownership to James Walmsley of Coldcotes, a man of law, who was related to Sir Thomas Walmsley, Justice in the Court of Common Pleas, and son-in-law of Sir Richard Shuttleworth of Gawthorpe.[257] It was at Gawthorpe Hall in June 1646 where James Walmsley took his last breath; he thus appears to have been part of the same social and working circle as Roger Nowell and his acolytes. This, coupled with the location of his home, explains precisely why he was pleased to allow the local justice of the peace to conduct a second round of interrogations at Ashlar House.[258]

Several people passed through the elegant stone entrance hall of Ashlar House on Thursday, 2 April 1612. Nowell had summoned his suspects: Elizabeth Southerns, Anne Whittle and her daughter Anne Redfearn; and his witnesses, John Nutter, James Robinson and Margaret Crooke. Nowell evidently knew what he wanted to focus on: these last three were related to Anne Whittle's alleged victims Christopher Nutter (father to John and Margaret) and Robert Nutter the younger (their brother), while James Robinson was their grandfather's stepson.

Nowell spoke with his suspects and witnesses alone except for the clerk who recorded everything that was said. It is impossible to know the precise order in which the interrogations ran, but in all probability, he began with Elizabeth Southerns, for whom his opening question was the reliable, 'When did you first become a witch?' She related her initial encounter with Tibb at the stonepit in Goldshaw Booth, after which Nowell led her through the story of her conflict with Richard Baldwin and alleged involvement in his daughter's death.

To her credit, Elizabeth made no attempt to conceal the animosity she felt for Baldwin, nor he for her, with only the dates proving slightly problematic, understandably so. Nowell plainly regarded Tibb's part in the affair as that of an obedient familiar, behaving in a wicked manner whenever he was directed thus. There is another interpretation, which suggests that Elizabeth's telling Tibb, 'Revenge thee either of him, or his', was said with a metaphorical shrug, and that her familiar departed in something of a huff, having realised that it mattered not to her either way what he chose to do. This reading of Elizabeth's interrogation appears to be supported by her mention to Alizon 'presently after her falling out' with Baldwin that she would pray for him 'both still and loud', although Alizon also heard her 'curse the said Baldwin sundry times'.

Joyce Froome has pointed out that Nowell was able to turn Elizabeth's examination into a 'voluntary confession' by some extremely adroit editing – adding the passage about how to kill using clay images immediately after the description of her quarrel with the mill owner, instead of leaving it in its rightful place, where it had been part of the memory of catching Anne Whittle and her daughter moulding clay into various likenesses. Elsewhere, however, his editing was far less sure-footed; he inserted lines from other parts of her statement into sections in order to create something more incriminating, but ended up simply repeating phrases that then made little sense. One such instance concerns Jennet helping her grandmother home after she had attended to the sick cow at Bull Hole Farm, which Nowell also dropped into Elizabeth's visit to Baldwin's house, despite the far greater distance.

While the magistrate plainly knew the witchcraft laws inside out, Elizabeth Southerns did not, and was probably unaware of the danger in which she found herself when describing her wholly illegal interactions with Tibb. If she hoped to be set free after demonstrating what she believed to be examples of refusing to agree to her familiar's attempts to draw her into violence or image magic, she would be chillingly mistaken. Nowell had not quite extracted an outright admission of maleficium from her, but he had enough evidence to convince a jury and was confident of gaining more damning material.

Elizabeth's time with the magistrate was at an end. She was escorted from the room to another part of Ashlar House while Nowell then turned his attention to Anne Whittle. From her 'voluntary confession and examination', we can see that Nowell followed the tried and tested routine of beginning with leading her through how she became involved in witchcraft. Her statement is as straightforward as that of her old adversary Elizabeth Southerns; she described Fancie in some detail, recalling how he invariably made the first approach at their meetings. Again, like Elizabeth, she gave Nowell examples of occasions when she had refused to collaborate with her familiar, such as his asking permission to harm Richard Baldwin's wife and how he had tried to bite her when she would not consent. To that end, she may also have used her familiar as a useful patsy when she felt control of the narrative slipping away – by claiming that the spirit had left her little choice but to go along with certain situations, or attempting to prove that she was of stronger moral stuff by refusing his suggestions even under threat of violence to herself. She described her last encounter with Fancie as a moment of relief, intimating again that she did not actively pursue the strange relationship, despite him being capable of good as well as ill. As far as Roger Nowell was concerned, such a creature could only ever be Satanic, whether it was a shape-shifting boy or a black dog. Anne, like her co-accused, would no doubt have been more reticent to discuss her familiar had she fully grasped that any interaction with spirits was strictly forbidden and that she too had presented Nowell with evidence of her pact with the devil.

Next, they came to the subject of Robert Nutter's death. Nowell was well acquainted with the Nutters of Greenhead; he had been involved in land and property indentures with Robert's parents, Christopher and Ellen Nutter, and could not have failed to hear the rumours surrounding the deaths of father and son. Anne was determined to have her say about Robert Nutter's attempted rape of her daughter, and his threat to have them evicted if he was ever in a position to do so. She was forthright about the charge of murder by witchcraft, declaring that she had called Fancie to her and 'bade him go revenge her of the said Robert Nutter' who then 'lived about a quarter of a year, and then died'. Undoubtedly, her admission was made to protect her daughter from being charged and found guilty of Nutter's death, but her directness about the entire matter appalled Nowell as much as it pleased him to receive her confession. However, she then went on to tell him how she had been approached prior to these events by Elizabeth Nutter, who wanted Robert dead and proposed that she (Anne), and two other women should kill him. This plot, of course, failed to be realised, but if Nowell had not been aware of it prior to Anne's declaration, it must have shocked him, unless the reason for Elizabeth's loathing of her husband's grandson was common knowledge.

Anne further admitted to killing two cows to spite their owners, and to using a charm ('a prayer') to amend spoiled drink. Nowell was later able to extract some information from James Device regarding the clay images of Robert and Christopher Nutter that he had glimpsed Anne and her daughter creating, which was supported by his grandmother's evidence.[259] Curiously, despite Anne Redfearn's presence at Ashlar House, and Nowell's determined efforts to extract damning evidence against her, there does not appear to be any record of her examination, nor 'voluntary confession'. James Robinson was quite clear in his view, stating that Anne Redfearn and Anne Whittle were 'commonly reputed and reported to be witches', and further, that while he had lived at Greenhead Manor, and Robert Nutter had fallen sick, he personally heard him state that 'he verily thought that the said Anne Whittle, alias Chattox, and the said Redfearn's wife, had bewitched him'. But other than his recollection of Anne Whittle spoiling the drink after his wife had employed her to card wool, he had little else to add.

John Nutter confirmed his brother's certainty that he had been 'bewitched by the Chattox' – Anne and her daughter – but he was also surprisingly honest about their father having regarded it as nonsense and telling Robert that he was 'a foolish lad' for believing so. His sister Margaret was slightly more forthcoming, stating that her brother had admitted to a substantial row with Anne Whittle, though not the reason for it. She, again, confirmed that Robert 'did a hundred times at the least say that the said Anne Redfearn and her associates had bewitched him to death'. She displayed the same honesty as her brother John in stating that although their father Christopher 'likewise felt himself to have been bewitched, he had named nobody that should do the same'.

Nowell ended his examinations for the day. If he had then or at a later date demanded to speak with Thomas and Marie Redfearn and Anne Whittle's daughter Bessie, there is no record of any examinations having taken place. All three remained at liberty, despite the evidence against Anne Redfearn being no stronger than it was against her husband, daughter and sister.

Precisely what happened next is a matter of conjecture. Most of Nowell's day had been occupied with taking the confessions and examinations of his suspects, together with statements from his witnesses, who were of course free to leave afterwards. The magistrate knew he had no reason to fear that the witches in his custody might attempt to weave pernicious enchantments about him; he was fully appraised of King James's assertion that the devil revoked a witch's power once she was placed under arrest.

The lateness of the hour might have influenced Nowell's decision regarding whether to send the suspects to Lancaster that day, or if it were better to keep them detained overnight in the cold, vaulted cellars of Ashlar House and make arrangements to transport them onwards the following day. In all probability he opted for the latter. Potts gives us an approximation, stating that Nowell, 'about the second of April last past, committed and sent them away to the Castle at Lancaster, there to remain until the coming of the King's Majesty's Justices of Assize to receive their trial'.[260] The recently transcribed account books of the Shuttleworths of Gawthorpe Hall show that they were responsible for paying towards the costs of transporting their tenants Anne Whittle and Anne Redfearn to prison; the relevant entry reads: 'Paid to the Greave of Pendle a 15th [1/15th of the total cost] for West Close for the carriage of the witches to Lancaster, 13p.'[261]

We know scarcely anything of that journey. Elizabeth Southerns and her granddaughter Alizon were among the other passengers – Potts tells us that much, and there may have been others who had been detained for trial in Lancaster. They were almost certainly shackled or in chains, hauled up brusquely into the cart by guards who were themselves loath to make the journey with all its discomforts and in the company of four malevolent witches; the entry in the Shuttleworth accounts makes it plain that although the women were legally suspects, as far as the people around them were concerned, they were guilty.

The animosity between the four women of the two families would have made for a distressing experience alone, but coupled with the knowledge that their long-standing feud had contributed to the horrifying situation in which they now found themselves must have made the journey virtually unbearable. Particularly for the sensitive Alizon, certain that the woman sitting opposite her was responsible for the death of her peaceable father. Each of them would have been in emotional turmoil, fearful for their families, and terrified of what each hour might bring as they left behind the landscape in which they had dwelled their entire lives.

The route taken has been deliberated many times by those studying the case, with several paths mooted, but the following is widely regarded as the most likely. From Fence, the cart with its sturdy horse in the shafts rumbled away from Higham and through the steep ways of Sabden, with fields undulating on all sides. For the passengers, the long whaleback shape of Pendle Hill changed colour and form as never before, and for the first time they saw what lay beyond the lanes and meadows, the villages and farmsteads that were as familiar to them as their own bodies. It was early April, when the cold fingers of winter might still retain their last grip, and pelting rain was as likely as clear blue skies and the warmth of the spring sun. It was normal practice for prison carts to display their consignment by driving through the busier towns where the shackled individuals might be forced to leave the cart for a few hours to sit in the stocks, to serve as a warning to the townsfolk.

From Clitheroe, with its hilltop thirteenth-century castle keep, the prison cart trundled perilously over Waddington Fell leaving its bleak beauty for the small stone village of Slaidburn.[262] Tradition holds that lodgings were provided for the passengers and their guards in the then 200-year-old inn, The Dog (now The Hark to Bounty), whose upper rooms functioned as the Halmote court for minor disputes in the Forest of Bowland. If true, they began the final stage of their journey the next morning, travelling north-west along the Salt Road and over Salter Fell, through some of the most dramatic scenery in the entire country. The packhorse trail had been used by the Romans, and to transport salt from coast to town, as well as conveying coffins made of Pendle Forest wood from town to coast. Wild and remote then, it remains so now, with eerie silences broken only by the elements, and the animals and birds that inhabit its moorland hills. The cart and its passengers were out in the open, passing through a landscape that imbued its isolation on all who travelled through its 'world of heather and black, peaty pools, where startled grouse will leap from your feet and seagulls scream above you'.[263] Hills stood 'carved in purple against the sky', faraway hills appeared blue, and the grey walls of lonely farmsteads tilted 'crazily to the sky'.[264] The horse struggled valiantly onwards with its cart of huddled, frightened passengers who had to walk at some stages to enable the cart to travel more easily. On towards Littledale, Caton, and a first glimpse of the sea. Finally, they came upon the gentler meadows where the serpentine Crook o'Lune flowed in its green valley that would go on to inspire the nation's greatest writers and artists. But for the women travelling towards Lancaster, its loveliness was soon forgotten as the wheels turned along Quernmore Road.

And now it appeared before them: Lancaster, the county hanging town, with its timber-framed, thatched-roofed houses on the snaking River Lune where the Vikings had once sailed in their longships. The cart moved along the rough surface of Moor Lane, passing a small cluster of timbered houses, and the road dipped before making a final incline known to many as 'Weeping Hill', where the immediate panorama froze the blood.

The castle, 'in all its terrible majesty' came into view: the twin octagonal towers of the gatehouse standing stark against the sky, blackened stone abutting blackened stone. Rising between them was an iron spike bearing something that resembled a misshapen lump of clay. But no strangely thrown pot was skewered there: instead, a human head, impaled to serve as a warning to wrongdoers.

Chapter Thirteen

A WITNESS UNEXPECTED
or
JENNET DEVICE

The 'great assembly' at Malkin Tower 'was not so secret, but some notice of it came to Master Nowell,' writes Thomas Potts. 'They are all confounded, and arrested by God's Justice: brought before Master Nowell and Master Bannister . . .'

News of a sacrilegious Good Friday meeting that had been held on 10 April soon reached Roger Nowell. With the assistance of Constable Hargreaves and his group of volunteers, Nowell acted quickly, searching out and rounding up his suspects like cattle from the verdant hillsides. In Goldshaw Booth, Hargreaves apprehended Elizabeth, James and Jennet Device, and John and Jane Bulcock; scarcely two miles away he found Alice Nutter; then four miles east in Colne, a Katherine Hewitt and an Alice Gray were placed under arrest. The rest, Potts tells us, were 'bound over to appear at the last Assizes' and 'are since that time fled to save themselves'. Elizabeth Southerns' son Christopher Holgate was among them, together with his wife and large family. He was not accused of any form of witchcraft per se, but he had attended this Good Friday meeting and the blood that ran in his veins was the same that coursed under the skin of Old Demdike; it would have been puzzling had Nowell not wanted to speak with him.

But he disappeared, for the time being at least, although he comes back into the story towards its end, several years later. For now, however, Nowell once more arranged to examine his suspects at Ashlar House with Nicholas Bannister in attendance. They made their way to Fence on 27 April, but it is difficult to know precisely what was said, when, or by whom; it is blatantly obvious that the depositions bearing this date are amalgamations from then and the following month when they were again questioned in Lancaster by their gaoler.

These were not easy interrogations for Nowell to conduct; Potts himself was forced to concede that where Elizabeth Device was concerned, 'although Master Nowell was very circumspect, and exceedingly careful in dealing with her, yet she would confess nothing' until her children had been manipulated into giving evidence. Alice Nutter appears to have followed Elizabeth Device's approach and met Nowell's questions with a stoic silence, even apparently when she was confronted with the allegations from James Device and his mother concerning her involvement in Henry Mitton's murder.

Katherine Hewitt and Alice Gray may have responded with the same refusal to speak, for there is not one word of a confession or examination from either woman. They stood jointly accused of murdering one child and plotting to kill another. The evidence against them, such as it was, came largely from James Device, who claimed that at the Good Friday meeting, Katherine and Alice 'did confess . . . that they had killed Foulds' wife's child, called Anne Foulds, of Colne . . .' No further details follow, other than that Elizabeth Device later confirmed that she, too, had heard the conversation. Bearing in mind the capricious spelling of both Christian names and surnames in original documents, the Colne parish registers show that Nicholas Foldes, a man of some means, had buried his young daughter, Anna, on 10 July 1610, at St Bart's, where she had been baptised only seven years before. But what truly lay behind Anna's death will never be known. James further stated: 'And [they] also said that they had then in hanck a child of Michael Hartley of Colne.' The old-fashioned phrase 'in hanck' has several meanings, including to wield power over someone. Elizabeth Device referred to Katherine and Anne having 'gotten hold of another' child but the import of her words has largely been lost. Both Alice Gray and Katherine Hewitt reacted to their indictments with a heartfelt 'not guilty'.

Discoverie is similarly evasive regarding the Bulcocks' alleged crimes, which appear to have materialised in the wake of the Good Friday meeting, when they were charged with practising witchcraft 'in and upon the body of Jennet Deane: so as the body of the said Jennet Deane, by force of the said witchcrafts, wasted and consumed'. James Device provided a little more detail in his examination, claiming that at Malkin Tower he had heard the Bulcocks confess to having bewitched 'at the Newfield Edge in Yorkshire, a woman called Jennet, wife of John Deyne, besides, her reason; and the said woman's name so bewitched, he did not hear them speak of '. According to James and his mother, the Bulcocks had caused Jennet Deyne to become insane, but there was no supporting evidence or further detail supplied. Jane and John Bulcock pleaded not guilty to the other indictments – namely, agreeing that they had consented 'to put the said Master Thomas Lister of Westby to death' and thereafter 'to hanck Master Leonard Lister, when he should come to dwell at the Cowgill, and so put him to death'.

Potts refers to mother and son asserting their innocence despite having earlier admitted the charges against them, for he states that in court the pair 'impudently now at the bar (having formerly confessed) they forswear'. Yet there are no confessions or examinations to this effect in *Discoverie*. Even if they confessed in gaol, by rights they should have been formally examined again by a justice of the peace. In time, John and Jane Bulcock would grow increasingly vociferous in protesting their innocence. Potts describes them in disgust as 'the most desperate wretches (void of all fear or grace) in all this pack', mistaking their dissent for vulgar behaviour, rather than expressions of abject fury born of despair.

Then we come to the Devices, whom Nowell and Bannister were eventually able to pit against each other. Jennet's involvement imbues the case with an even greater repulsion at how the authorities treated their suspects and provokes one of its most enduring, emotional mysteries: why did a child condemn her entire family to their deaths? But Jennet was not culpable at all; the responsibility lay elsewhere, as even a cursory study of the case reveals. Again, it is difficult to determine whether the magistrates called James before them first, or Jennet, for either they framed their questions to him in such a way as to seek her corroboration or they suggested scenarios to Jennet and then confronted James with the broadest brushstrokes of her responses to prompt him into developing matters further. More probably, they questioned James then extracted elements to lay before Jennet, insinuating what they believed was the truth, and then returned to James with his young sister's elaborations for him to confirm or deny.

The indeterminate sequence of the statements made by James makes an accurate assessment of his examination before the magistrates unfeasible. On the surface, it appears that Nowell and Bannister were able to extract a great deal of information from him about the Good Friday meeting especially, incriminating their other suspects – which, on occasion, included his mother, sister and grandmother. Sometimes his story changes, strongly implying that pressure has been brought to bear on him to explain a particular aspect again, or that he has attempted to correct himself.

For instance, James gave two accounts of Henry Mitton's death, declaring in one (dated 27 April) that he had heard his grandmother say that she and his mother 'and the wife of Richard Nutter, Alice Nutter, the prisoner aforesaid, had killed one Henry Mitton, of the Rough Lee aforesaid, by witchcraft. The reason wherefore he was so killed, was for that [James's] grandmother had asked the said Mitton for a penny, and denying her thereof, thereupon she procured his death as aforesaid.' In a second version, dated 27 April again, he declared that he had heard his grandmother say that his mother 'and others, had killed one Henry Mitton of the Rough Lee aforesaid, by witchcraft'. The remainder of the statement is an almost word-for-word rendition of the former account. Elizabeth Device would also name Alice Nutter as having been involved in Mitton's murder, but when her daughter

Jennet gave her account, she said nothing about Alice. The evidence was not included in the documentation Nowell put together for Elizabeth Southerns' trial, despite the fact that she is plainly named as the originator of the murder plot. One obvious explanation is that this evidence was drawn up not at Ashlar House on 27 April after all, but in prison and after Elizabeth Southerns' death, when it would instead form part of the evidence against Alice Nutter and Elizabeth Device. Similarly, the statement James provided regarding his grandmother's urging that he should steal the communion wafer was not included in the evidence against Elizabeth Southerns, but in the papers relevant to James's own trial.

Equally, however, there are instances where he appears to accuse family members quite transparently of murder by witchcraft; he gives a full account of how his mother worked with her familiar, Ball, using image magic to kill John Robinson. But there are other examples of him appearing to implicate his family while simply stating a fact – such as Henry Bulcock accusing his sister Alizon of bewitching his child. James recalled that Alizon had begged Bulcock's forgiveness by falling to her knees and weeping, but nowhere does he explicitly state that she was guilty. How he reacted to the accusations put to him is likewise imbalanced: he confessed to murdering John Duckworth and Anne Towneley – albeit later retracting both confessions – but apparently said nothing about John Hargreaves and Blaze Hargreaves, despite his sister Jennet giving accounts of how he and Dandy had conspired to kill the two men.

Before the magistrates were finished with James, Nowell arranged for Constable Henry Hargreaves to accompany him six miles north to Gisburn. Whether Jennet Preston, who had attended the Good Friday meeting at Malkin Tower, was already in custody there or not, James was brought face-to-face with her for a formal identification. They both knew that the days that lay ahead of them would probably be their last. Jennet was then sent to York prison to await her second witchcraft trial.

James returned with Henry Hargreaves to Pendle. They headed for Goldshaw Booth, striking out through the steeply sloping fields to Malkin Tower, now silent and deserted. James led Hargreaves through the building to the western end. He crouched down and began scrabbling in the earth. After some time, he found what he sought: the human teeth that Anne Whittle – or more probably his grandmother – had taken from the churchyard in the village, and a lump of clay, broken away on one side. Hargreaves, with a slight air of disgust, took the clay and the teeth (which had probably been wrapped in a piece of cloth to keep them safely in one spot), then gestured for James to walk in front of him. Perhaps James took one final look at Malkin Tower as they left, and perhaps he felt a small sense of satisfaction in among the all-pervading fear, knowing that there were some secrets still buried there, in the undisturbed earth.

Most of Jennet Device's evidence in *Discoverie* is presented as if she were speaking in court, but sections of it are taken from the examination Nowell and Bannister very carefully made at Ashlar House on 27 April. It was not entirely unusual for children to testify in England's witch-hunts, but it was much less common than on the Continent, where children often gave evidence after having been rounded up as part of a substantial group and regarded as suspects. Being kept apart from their families rendered them extremely vulnerable, but if they somehow found reserves of strength and attempted to refuse the courts in any way, they were threatened and sometimes beaten into compliance.

When children appeared in English witch trials, it was usually as victims of witchcraft; those who gave evidence tended to have been tutored or manipulated into doing so. In his study *Children Against Witches*, Ronald Seth asserts that this was the case with Jennet Device, who was treated as a pawn in a deadly game. A child like Jennet could be motivated by a variety of reasons: fear, obviously, but also because they were susceptible generally or specifically to some form of bribery, or enjoyed the sudden attention in a world where their views were often dismissed; some saw an opportunity to make life more interesting, while others were spurred on by a need for revenge and took pleasure in reversing the social order by turning adults into scapegoats. But the prime factor seems to have been simply a need for attention. The majority of child accusers were female, and therefore enjoyed a previously unknown sense of importance and influence at a social and legal level after being the most invisible members of society, not grasping that every word made them more vulnerable than ever.

Another study opines: 'The English witch trials in which children appeared were a blueprint for what later happened in New England. Most of the shocking events associated with the Salem girls, and the subsequent trials and executions, were essentially duplicates of English trials. In fact, it is highly likely that the bewitched girls in Salem learned what they knew about bewitchment from the infamous trials of their English predecessors.'[265] England's earliest known witch trial, at Chelmsford in 1566, featured the testimony of twelve-year-old Agnes Brown, which led to the conviction and execution of Agnes Waterhouse. We now know that Jennet was eleven rather than twelve when she gave evidence in 1612 and probably appeared younger due to the effects of poverty. Today, there is no lower age limit restriction on children giving evidence in criminal court proceedings. Competency is based upon understanding rather than age. Nonetheless, children under fourteen can only give unsworn evidence; courts decide on an individual basis whether older children should take the oath, and special measures are in place for the welfare of all children giving evidence. But in the sixteenth and seventeenth century, children under the age of fourteen were viewed as unreliable witnesses, despite a number of exceptions in witch trials. James I then stated his opinion in *Daemonolgie*: 'Children, women and liars can be witnesses over high treason against God.'

Nonetheless, as Potts knew very well, the king would not take kindly to being made to look a fool. The clerk therefore introduced her as a witness more or less sent by divine intervention: 'It pleased God to raise up a young maid, Jennet Device, [Elizabeth's] own daughter, about the age of nine years (a witness unexpected) to discover all their practises, meetings, consultations, murders, charms, and villainies.' He added that theirs were the kind of intrigues that 'as reverend and learned judge of this kingdom speaks, of the greatest treason that ever was . . .' and that 'when these things shall be related to posterity, they will be reputed [reputable] matters . . .'[266] Potts astutely made the connection between Pendle and the Gunpowder Plot by asserting that Jennet's evidence was as reliable as the pronouncements of Sir Edward Coke, the king's attorney general, when he had spoken at Guy Fawkes' trial six years before. It was an especially shrewd remark given that a gunpowder plot discussed at a witches' sabbath would likewise be raised at the Lancaster Assizes.

Jennet's examination laid out what she knew – or claimed to know – of the Good Friday meeting and her family's magical charms. She also recalled in some detail how her mother had asked for Ball's help to kill Henry Mitton and the Robinson brothers of Barley. In a very similar fashion, she described how Dandy had assisted her brother with his 'best help' to murder John Hargreaves of Goldshaw Booth, Blaze Hargreaves of Higham and Anna Towneley, whom she had seen shortly before her death and realised her poor state was the doing of James and Dandy.

Once Nowell and Bannister had sufficient evidence from Jennet, they then called her mother in again. Confronted with the damning content of her children's depositions, Elizabeth's iron resolve cracked, and she essentially confirmed everything her son and daughter had said in regard to the accusations made against her.

The two magistrates brought their day to a close. They then had to decide, if they had not already, what to do with their prisoners. With Jennet as his prize witness, Nowell would not have been willing to risk contaminating her evidence, which would need to be repeated in court, by allowing her to go back to her mother and brothers. In any case, whether Jennet's relationships with her mother, siblings and grandmother had been positive or not – and there is no reason to assume they were not loving and supportive – she must have been experiencing intense emotional upheaval and perhaps even felt fearful of her mother and James, now painted as monsters by her new circle of adults, and themselves having confessed to murders in which the devil or his demons had provided assistance.

Roger Nowell knew that he had to build on any uncertainty Jennet felt, especially with regard to her own future. He also needed to keep up a certain level of pressure, kindness and sternness as he continued to prepare her for court. Although there was a large measure of self-interest in his actions, Nowell was a man of his time and circumstances, and regarded those who had attended the Good Friday meeting as wicked fools who for all their own culpability, had found themselves at the mercy of the most powerful demonic entity in existence. The war against good and evil raged, and people such as the Devices were casualties of that war. Perhaps he had ideas about saving Jennet from the devil's clutches – he was a deeply religious man after all.

Thus, in all probability he kept all his prisoners bar one – Jennet – in the cellars at Ashlar House again, or at the very least, separate from her. In order to keep building her trust and ensure that she would not collapse in court and renege on all she had said, he more than likely took her home with him, to Read. It was not a world Jennet recognised, but it was one that Nowell knew would impress her beyond anything she had experienced. His own family and staff were no doubt told exactly how to behave towards the young maid who was going to assist him in the biggest case of his life – one which would make his name. But Nowell's true feelings towards Jennet are chillingly plain in how he phrased her responses, for although she was his witness, throughout all her statements, the magistrate employed the phrase 'she confesseth' – just as if she, too, were a witch.

Within a day or so of the final examinations at Fence, seven more persons accused of witchcraft were sent shackled from Pendle to Lancaster: Elizabeth and James Device, Alice Nutter, Katherine Hewitt, John and Jane Bulcock, and Alice Gray. Those headed for Lancaster would have followed the same route as the women before them, enduring the same endless hours of bumping along rough tracks through town and fell in a cart with the able-bodied trudging on foot before reaching Lancaster.

Chapter Fourteen

MALICE OF HEARTS
or
JENNET PRESTON

Across the border in Yorkshire, a storm of considerable might was gathering in Gisburn.

Today, following the boundary changes of 1974, Gisburn is once more part of Lancashire, but in the seventeenth century it was a village in the Craven district of Yorkshire's West Riding. Set back from the River Ribble's meandering steep banks, Gisburn's prosperity was partly due to the principal Skipton to Clitheroe road passing through its centre. Most of the handsome houses now standing were built after the time of Jennet Preston but the Church of St Mary the Virgin is believed to date from the twelfth century, and in 1285 the abbot of nearby Sawley Abbey accused Gisburn's vicar of thieving game from the abbey warren.

Retinens vestigia famae – 'following in the footsteps of our fame' is the Lister family motto. Lords of the Manor for hundreds of years, the Listers held the title of Lord Ribblesdale. Arnoldsbiggin became the family seat after 1520 and was a substantial country house. One of their kinsmen – and great uncle to this case's Thomas Lister the elder – was Cardinal William Allen, who helped to disseminate the Catholic Mission among Lancashire's gentry. Allen then escaped to

France for a second time, establishing the English College at Douai in 1570. He both assisted with the planned invasion of England by Catholic Spain and encouraged his fellow Englishmen to lend their support. But the failure of the Spanish Armada campaign secured Protestant rule in England and gave Elizabeth I an air of invincibility while Allen died debt-ridden in Rome six years later. In his study of Jennet Preston's case, Jonathan Lumby suggests that when Thomas Lister the younger (hereafter Thomas Lister) conformed to the established church, he experienced the guilt and Puritan passion of an uneasy convert. This may have played some part in his pursuit of Jennet Preston for witchcraft, but the beginnings of the story are uncertain. The Lister family history sheds only a little light on its origins, but more than was known previously.

Thomas Lister grew up at Westby Hall, about three-quarters of a mile south-west of Gisburn; the present Westby Hall Farm stands near to the now demolished family seat, Arnoldsbiggin. An early eighteenth-century painting depicts Westby Hall falling into ruins, but it had evidently been a beautiful home, with avenues of trees and two large ponds in elegant pleasure-grounds. Although the Hall stood in Yorkshire, the southern boundaries of the Listers' lands encroached upon the Forest of Pendle. Thomas Lister the elder was married to Jane Greenacres, daughter of one of the first two MPs for Clitheroe and she bore Thomas several children.

How Jennet Preston came into their lives is unknown. The Gisburn parish registers have an entry for Jennet Balderston and William Preston's wedding on 10 May 1587. Jennet was around twenty-two years old when she married, and her husband twenty-three, yet Potts refers to him as 'Old Preston' at the Lancaster Assizes when he would have been only forty-eight – but grief and stress would have taken their toll.

Although it has been suggested that Jennet knew Thomas Lister the elder in the capacity of a servant, Potts himself tells us that she had 'free access to his house, kind respect and entertainment', which is scarcely the description of someone working below stairs. The two were of the same age and probably knew each other from childhood, remaining close after Jennet's marriage and motherhood, when she and her family lived near the Listers.

However, there is a strong possibility that Jennet's parents were in the Listers' employ, for the last will and testament of an earlier Thomas Lister of Arnoldsbiggin, who died in 1542, dictates that an amount of money was to be left to 'Nicholas Balderstone' while 'Agnes Balderstone was to be gifted a 'stirk' (a bullock or heifer)', and immediately afterwards the text reads, 'to all my other servants, one sheep each . . .'[267] The association may have been long-standing, given that another Lister ancestor of the previous century also bequeathed money 'to the boys of Richard Balderstone of Middop'.[268] This Richard Balderstone and his son John were either given or sold land in Middop by William Lister, according to documents in the Lancashire Archives.[269] Even more intriguingly, an indenture dated 28 October 1612 outlines the leasing of a messuage and tenement and another parcel of land, all in Yorkshire, to 'Richard Preston, son of William Preston, of Arnoldsbiggin in Yorkshire, husbandmen, for 3,000 years.'[270] This would appear to refer to Jennet's husband and son, who were living at Arnoldsbiggin, the family seat of the Listers.

From all this we can fairly safely assume that Jennet's parents and their family before them had worked for the Listers very many years, and that she and her husband William lived with their children at Arnoldsbiggin and were therefore neighbours of Thomas Lister the elder, whom Jennet had in all probability known her entire life and enjoyed his friendship and was on good terms with his wife (otherwise she would not have been welcomed into their family home). But everything was about to change.

On 29 January 1607, sixteen-year-old Thomas Lister married Jane Heber, then aged twenty-one. The Hebers were another wealthy landowning family, with property in Skipton, Wakefield and a number of other areas in Yorkshire. Jane's father, Thomas Heber, was a justice of the peace in the West Riding (a path his son-in-law was shortly to follow), and until the turn of the century they had lived at their estate and manor, Stainton Hall near Gargrave, just north-west of Skipton. Thomas Heber and his wife Elinor and children then settled at Marton, around five miles east of Gisburn. Jane was the eldest child of Thomas and Elinor, but not their heir; her brother Thomas would inherit. Nonetheless, she would have been in possession of a substantial dowry, with her parents eager to facilitate the marriage. The Listers had increased their wealth and importance through marriage and had strong links with the Bannisters of Park Hill and the Towneleys of Carr Hall. Both families would have been delighted with the marriage of Thomas and Jane, which took place at St Michael's Church in Bracewell, almost exactly halfway between Gisburn and Marton. Representatives of all the leading gentry families would be present and there is a strong possibility that Roger Nowell and his wife would have been among the congregation.

But at some point during either the ceremony or the protracted celebrations that followed, the bridegroom's father collapsed. He was placed in a bedchamber at the hall or manor house in Bracewell where the wedding dinner and dancing should have lasted into the early hours, and his condition deteriorated. In his delirium, he apparently began shouting: 'Jennet Preston is near – she is in this house – look where she is, take hold of her! For God's sake, shut the doors! Take her – she cannot escape away! Look about for her and lay hold on her!'

Two people later gave evidence that they had heard the ailing man crying out these words: Anne Robinson, who had been in the Listers' employ for a substantial length of time, and Thomas Lister. Potts makes one of his not infrequent slips by stating that 'in the end Anne Robinson and others were both examined' about the shouting; clearly 'both examined' refers to two people, rather than a number, although he mentions Lister the elder crying out 'unto them that stood about him . . . [he] cried very often in his great pains, to them that came to visit him during his sickness'. The dying man had more to say, and according to Potts, his son and servant gave evidence that 'he cried out in great extremity, Jennet Preston lies heavy upon me, Preston's wife lies heavy upon me; help me, help me: and so departed, crying out against her'.

Historian Malcolm Gaskill points out: 'Crucially the last words of any person in extremis had strong evidentiary statue in law on the assumption that those about to be judged by God were unlikely to lie.'[271] In a contemporary account, *A Guide to Grand-Jury Men*, Richard Bernard advised caution when assessing such statements, which came to be known as 'spectral evidence':

> Because of the strong imagination of such as suspect themselves to be bewitched, which will make them think verily that they see strange apparitions; and for fear will dream of the suspected, and so may cry out and talk to him or her in their fearful dreams, the fantasy being oppressed. And if the disease called the [Night] Mare, happens to such a one, then their sweating, their moving, and struggling, with an imagination of one creeping upon them, from the feet, to their breast, (they awaking in fear and trembling) will make them say and swear too, that they are bewitched.'[272]

The idea that a witch could appear at will, materialising before her victim while she herself remained at a distance was a common one. Michael Dalton included spectral evidence in his list of observations of witches in *The Country Justice*: 'Their Apparition to the sick Party in his Fits.'[273] A sensible explanation for such an occurrence was provided by Samuel Wesley in the late seventeenth-century journal, the *Athenaean Mercury*, warning that the effect could be the result of 'vapours from crude and undigested concoctions, heat of blood, as after hard drinking, and several other natural ways; but sometimes 'tis really effected by witches, which first gave the name to the common oppression in sleep called the night-mare: History is full of such instances.'[274]

Apparitions such as that apparently experienced by Thomas Lister the elder tapped into the fear that if a witch set her sights on you, then you could do almost nothing to break the spell. The idea that the witch was in total control, able to manipulate a person to do as she wished, coursing through their body like an unstoppable virus, created real fear among people. The attacked person was never safe, for the witch could simply materialise at any time or place – or send her familiar if she preferred. The only means of salvation was to draw blood from the witch, since that was believed to prevent her from doing more harm.

The encounter as related by Anne Robinson and Thomas Lister is more ghostly than demonic. And indeed, King James himself was not convinced by such tales, which may be why neither Potts nor Nowell began busily building the occurrence – likely to have been an instance of sleep paralysis or fever caused by his life ebbing away – into something more significant. But assuming that Lister did cry out in such a fashion, why was Jennet Preston on his mind?

In his otherwise excellent book about the case, Jonathan Lumby posits a theory that Jennet was the elder Thomas's mistress, and that his widow and son were pained and horrified when her name was the last on his lips. Lumby suggests that in order to save face, they then clutched at rumours that he had been bewitched, which ended with Lister pursuing Jennet all the way to the gallows. Lumby's theory is built upon the concept (already established by the sixteenth century) that some accusations of witchcraft emerged when a person who felt himself to be a victim recalled an act of unkindness or lack of charity, thereby having given the witch reason to hold a grudge against him.

However, there are several reasons to doubt Lumby's proposition. In the first place, we only have the evidence of Thomas Lister and a loyal family servant that the dying man mentioned Jennet. The servant, Anne Robinson, may have been related to, or otherwise named as, 'Agnes Robinson of Gisburn' to whom Lister the son bequeathed a cottage seven years after Jennet's trial – perhaps as a demonstration of gratitude for a particular task? Lumby also suggests that Nowell later supplied Lister with 'proof' that Jennet had attended the Good Friday meeting at the home of the Devices where she had discussed plotting to murder him and his uncle – and thereby gave Lister the impetus to pursue her more fervently through the courts. But there is no evidence that Nowell did so, or why he might have been motivated to provide Lister with such claims. It is also worth considering why, if the dying man were calling for his lover, he would have referred to her as 'Preston's wife'. We might expect him to forego decorum in his delirium and wail for his 'Jennet', rather than as another man's wife.

There is, of course, a similar instance in this case: when John Law lay depleted in the alehouse in Colne, he believed that Alizon and her familiar had visited him and claimed afterwards to have been 'tormented both day and night' with her. His son Abraham confirmed this, adding that his father had used the same phrase in relation to Alizon as Lister the elder with Jennet, namely that she 'did lie upon him and trouble him'.[275] But there is no suggestion that John Law and Alizon Device were in a relationship.

Returning to Jennet Preston, it seems implausible that the bereaved son who was hellbent on murderous revenge would wait five entire years to instigate proceedings – and in the meantime, according to witnesses, show Jennet the same warmth and kindness as his father before him. Furthermore, there is ample evidence that Jennet's husband was distraught to see his wife and the mother of his children accused in court; he attended not only her hearings, but the trials in Lancaster too, actively gathering supporters to challenge what was said in court and making sure that anyone within earshot knew that Jennet was innocent of all charges. Their marriage was clearly a strong one and to suggest that Jennet betrayed her husband unintentionally adds further insult to her memory – and to that of the faithful William.

There is an alternative explanation, and one that again has a precedent in this case: that at some stage, Lister the younger made unwanted sexual advances towards Jennet or her daughter and sought to retaliate when he was rejected – just as Robert Nutter had done with Anne Redfearn, bringing Anne Whittle's wrath upon him, followed by rumours of witchcraft. But as James Crossley mused in his footnotes to the reprint of *Discoverie*: 'Whether superstition or malice prompted [Jennet's] prosecution, on the part of Mr Lister, it is difficult to say. Some grudge he entertained, or cause of offence he had taken up against this Jennet Preston, might be her death warrant in those days . . .' We simply do not know.

*

Thomas Lister the elder died on 6 February 1607, still in the bed-chamber in Bracewell, having never sufficiently recovered to be brought home. He was thirty-eight years old. His return to Gisburn from his son's wedding was not how anyone had imagined it would be prior to the nuptials.

At Westby Hall, the elder Lister was laid out to be wrapped in his winding-sheet, a long length of linen from the family home which would either be swathed about the body or tied in knots at both ends and sewn up along the middle to cocoon the corpse. As people filed into the house to pay their respects to the dead man, his son and the ever-present Anne Robinson were there, and witnessed a most unusual scene.

Jennet Preston approached the body of her old friend and lightly lay her fingertips upon him. Although Potts tells us that 'many other' people who had been present 'were further examined and deposed' to describe what followed, not a single word of these exists in *Discoverie*. Anne Robinson and Thomas Lister nonetheless declared that when Jennet touched the corpse it 'bled fresh blood presently, in the presence of all . . . which hath ever been held a great argument to induce a jury to hold him guilty that shall be accused of murder, and hath seldom or never, failed in the trial'.

Along with spectral evidence, the notion that a corpse might bleed at the killer's touch was commonly held to be true. Even the well-known sceptic Reginald Scot viewed reports of such an occurrence as 'credible'.[276] In 1593, Shakespeare had written the phenomenon into *Richard III*, depicting the king's dead body beginning to bleed in the presence of the Duke of Gloucester. A few years later, King James declared in *Daemonologie*: 'If the dead carcass be at any time thereafter handled by the murderer, it will gush out blood, as if the blood were crying to heaven for revenge of the murderer, God having appointed that secret, supernatural sign, for trial of that secret, unnatural crime . . .'[277] *The Country Justice* supported the idea, listing 'bleeding of the dead body in his presence' as grounds to bring a suspect to court.[278]

Had Lister somehow manipulated Jennet into touching his father's corpse in order to test whether she was responsible for his death? Possibly, although she might have done so spontaneously. But perhaps Lister was genuinely beginning to feel unnerved, especially if rumours were circulating about his father's death and about the fact that he had just wed a woman of good standing, with a substantial dowry, and his father's passing so soon after his wedding day had swelled their coffers substantially, as he then inherited the whole estate. And then, almost a year to the day after his father's death, Lister's mother passed away. Following the loss of both parents – Lister himself was still only seventeen in 1608 – a period of ill fortune commenced, in which he suffered a 'great loss in his goods and cattle'. But it seems he did not yet blame Jennet, for as Potts tells it, Lister continued to extend 'favour and goodness' towards her, until 'her execrable ingratitude' led her to openly practise 'much mischief' against him. 'These things in time did beget suspicion,' intoned Potts, 'and at the Assizes and general gaol delivery held at the Castle of York in Lent last past, before my Lord Bromley, she was indicted and arraigned for the murder of a child of one Dodgsons . . .'

The accusation seems to emerge from nowhere; precisely how the unknown Dodgsons might have been connected to the Listers and Jennet remains unexplained, with Potts failing to provide any sort of clarification. The Dodgson name was prevalent around Gisburn, and especially in the adjacent villages of Paythorne, Newsholme and Bolton-by-Bowland. The parish registers for the latter reveal a potential pointer, recording that a boy named Thomas Dodgson ('the son of Edward Dodgson') had been baptised on 10 September 1610 but died seven months later and was buried in Bolton-by-Bowland on 19 April 1611.[279] How the child's death might have been related to Jennet is a poignant enigma, but almost a year later, in March 1612, she was arrested, examined and sent for trial.

William the Conqueror built York Castle between the rivers Ouse and Foss in 1068, but it was destroyed the following year by his opposers. When they retreated, the castle was rebuilt, with mottes on either side of the Ouse. In 1190, waves of anti-Semitic riots broke out in the city, following suspicion that had been provoked towards Jews and Muslims by the Crusades. The Jewish population of York sought sanctuary at the castle, where the constable sheltered them from a mob intent on murder or enforced baptism. When the constable was called away, the terrified Jews inside the castle refused him entry. The king's troops joined the encircling mob outside the castle walls, and those within realised they had no hope of survival in the city; a rabbi instructed all the fathers to kill their wives and children, and then themselves. Those who were left set the castle timbers alight; despite a promise from the mob leader, the few who attempted to escape were set upon and killed.

The castle was rebuilt but Richard III had it dismantled with ambitions to construct a superior fortification, but by 1535 it lay in ruins. Two years later, during the Pilgrimage of Grace, Robert Aske was hanged from the summit of the tower. Gaoler Robert Redhead was accused of demolishing further sections of the castle towards the end of the sixteenth century, but some repairs were made around 1608. Within the collapsing courtyard walls was a cluster of old houses linked by passageways and makeshift access points. Prisoners were given rooms within these buildings, apart from those who were locked in the dungeons below for reasons of increased security. It was common practice to lease out prisons to private management, with inmates forced to pay for their keep, giving rise to a relentless cycle whereby those who could not afford the fees were kept in prison, increasing their debt. Gaolers were corrupted by the system, offering a number of privileges in return for money.

Jennet Preston entered the crumbling, lice-infested buildings after being driven by cart with other prisoners, shackled for the sixty-mile journey east from Gisburn. She may have been thrown into a solitary room or in a communal area within what passed for the female prison. Even the keeper was appalled by the conditions, petitioning the Priory Council about its ruinous, insanitary state, while warders were much vexed by inmates escaping by crashing through the crumbling walls.

On 6 April 1612, Jennet Preston was brought before the Lent Assizes, indicted and arraigned with causing death by witchcraft of Dodgson's child. Potts is our sole source for her trial, and he dispenses with it in no more than a single sentence: 'By the favour and merciful consideration of the jury thereof [she was] acquitted.' Although her second trial will be our focus, there are two matters of importance to note: Edward Bromley presided as judge, in his first Lancashire witchcraft trial. Four months later, he would take his seat at the Lancaster Assizes. The prosecuting magistrate stating the case against Jennet is believed to be the man who would thus reprise the role in July: Thomas Heber, the father-in-law of Thomas Lister.

Jennet walked free from court and returned to Gisburn, and into the arms of her husband and children. If, as James Device claimed, she believed that it was Lister who had 'borne malice unto her, and had thought to have her put away at the late Assizes at York', it was either a brave or foolish – or both – decision that she made to then attend the Good Friday meeting at Malkin Tower only a day or so later. For both she and Lister now detested and feared each other, and were locked in a vendetta where there could be only one victor.

Chapter Fifteen

UPON A WITCH-FREQUENTED GREEN

or

KATHERINE HEWITT

and

JANE AND JOHN BULCOCK

By any standards, Elizabeth Device's life had not been easy. But the weeks leading up to Easter 1612 were the most difficult she had ever endured – thus far. Her mother and daughter were now imprisoned in Lancaster, whose reputation made her fear for their survival even before they faced trial, while a thick cloud of suspicion hung over Elizabeth herself and her two other children. All the rumours of the past few years had been gathered up like flowers in a deadly bouquet and presented to the magistrates, who had picked them out, bit by bit, until their poison blighted everything.

Bur Elizabeth had never been one to accept that she was beaten, and neither was she prepared to simply wait to let events take their course and potentially destroy her family. She called on those whom she could trust and would be willing to help her, asking them to join her for a Good Friday dinner at Malkin Tower, where she and her son and young daughter were now living. We know from the statements the three of them made that they had taken over Elizabeth's mother's home, but the reason behind it remains something of a mystery. Perhaps it gave Elizabeth comfort to be there – or perhaps her mother had asked her to protect the place, not merely out of sentiment or even in the hope that she might one day return home, but for other, unknowable intentions.

After daylight gate on Maundy Thursday – the eve of Good Friday – James Device brought home what would become the main dish in the dinner his mother had planned. His sister Jennet recalled that he arrived carrying 'a wether of Christopher Swyers of Barley' and killed it within sight of her. James agreed in part with her statement, but later told Nowell and Bannister that he 'stole' a wether from 'John Robinson of Barley', brought it to Malkin Tower 'and there killed it . . .' James was a strong young man, but to have carried a live sheep from Barley was not an easy task, and begs the question of why he waited until arriving home to slaughter it. He adds a detail that Jennet omits: that he had stolen the sheep from the family in neighbouring Barley whose taunting of his mother ended in her being accused of murdering two of their relatives – brothers James and John Robinson.

Everything we know about the Good Friday meeting on 10 April originates from the evidence that would be given by Elizabeth, James and Jennet in their examinations at the end of the month before Nowell and Bannister. That Good Friday was already a date of some significance for the Devices is evident from references to it and the Last Supper and crucifixion throughout their family charm. The Catholic ceremonies in observance of Good Friday were forbidden by law, but it was a public holiday even in modern Protestant England, and a day of deep mourning for Christ's followers. There has been some speculation that the meeting at Malkin Tower, which took place during those hours when the religious remember the crucifixion, was in fact a Catholic mass, and that a priest was in attendance for a formal service, although there is no evidence for such.

As far as Thomas Potts and his ilk were concerned, the meeting was something else entirely: an abomination of the true meaning of the day and an inversion of its holy rituals. 'A great assembly of all the most dangerous, wicked and damnable witches in the county, far and near,' he writes in *Discoverie*, adding, 'upon Good Friday they met, according to solemn appointment, solemnized this great festival day according to their former order, with great cheer, merry company, and much conference'. In another passage he describes it in similarly sacrilegious terms: 'A solemn meeting at Malkin Tower of the Grand Witches of the counties of Lancaster and York, being yet unsuspected and untaken.' In his eyes, 'these hellish and devilish band of witches, (the like whereof hath not been heard of)' were making their way to Malkin Tower to mock Christianity's Holy Week by participating in that essential constituent of Continental demonology: the Satanic sabbath.

As the witch trials overseas persisted, the perception of the devil-worshipping sabbath evolved into a distinctive 'combined religious service and business meeting followed by a debauch of feasting, dancing and wild lust'.[280] The devil himself would invariably be present in one of his many fiendish forms or as a man or a 'huge, demonic goat' as old and new disciples appeared to pay homage to him and to confirm or seal their pact (often by kissing his buttocks), thereby renouncing their Christian faith.[281] Each witch would be assigned a demonic familiar and there would often be a wild orgy before the witches departed on poles, chairs or some other form of seating that had been smeared with an ointment to imbue them with the power of flight.

In his 1929 study of witchcraft, George Lyman Kittredge observes that 'in no single recorded witch trial during the reign of Elizabeth is there the slightest trace of the Witches' Sabbath'.[282] Matters were somewhat different in Scotland, where accusations and trials of witchcraft tended to follow the Continental example more closely; the North Berwick trials famously include scenes of devil-worship in a church, with witches dancing down the aisle while the devil watches on approvingly from the pulpit, but it was not until the 1612 trials in Lancaster that the witches' sabbath arose in evidence. Hence the lack of reference to demonic assemblies in the Witchcraft Acts of 1542,

1563 and 1604. Curiously, the idea of the witches' sabbath then disappears from view until 1634, when it forms part of the second Pendle case. Thereafter, once Matthew Hopkins and John Sterne began their witch-hunts, it becomes an element of the trials and achieves 'a more or less permanent status' due to Hopkins, an erudite man, believing in it 'devoutly'.[283]

The meeting at Malkin Tower was a far tamer affair than the debauchery that was said to be taking place on the Continent: no orgies, wild dancing or drinking – perhaps unsurprisingly, the devil did not trouble to put in an appearance either. The first recorded witches' sabbath in English legal history was instead simply a gathering of relatives, friends and neighbours over a meal to discuss what they might do to assist those in prison.[284] Collating the evidence, such as it was, from hosts Elizabeth, James and Jennet, it seems that everyone had arrived by late morning to share the meal at noon: a considerable repast, given their undeniably humble circumstances, with beef, bacon and mutton roasted on a spit.

There are discrepancies in the accounts provided by brother and sister regarding who attended the gathering. Jennet later stated in court that her mother had told her that all of them were witches; she recalled 'about twenty persons, whereof only two were men' but only knew six by name: 'the wife of Hugh Hargreaves Under Pendle, Christopher Howgate of Pendle, uncle to this Examinate, and Elizabeth his wife, and Dick Miles, his wife of the Rough-Lee; Christopher Jackes of Thornyholme, and his wife.'

James recalled 'a number of persons' and included himself in stating that 'three were men . . . and the rest women'. He then provided Nowell and Bannister with the names of those he knew: 'the wife of Hugh Hargreaves of Barley; the wife of Christopher Bulcock, of the Moss End, and John her son; the mother of Miles Nutter; Elizabeth, the wife of Christopher Hargreaves, of Thornyholme; Christopher Howgate, and Elizabeth, his wife; Alice Gray of Colne, and one Mould-heeles' wife, of the same: and this Examinate, and his mother'.

Elizabeth, who had called the meeting, later told Nowell and

Bannister that the group consisted of all witches, confirming that she 'doth verily think them to be witches'. She related the same names as those her son had listed, adding that there were also 'two women of Burnley Parish, whose names the wife of Richard Nutter doth know. And there was likewise there one Anne Crouckshey of Marsden.'

Potts duly compiled a list of 'Witches at the Great Assembly and Feast at Malking Tower' from the depositions, curiously adding another name – Grace Hay of Padiham – to those mentioned by Jennet, James and Elizabeth. He declared that more had attended and were bound over to appear at the Lancaster Assizes but had 'since that time fled to save themselves'. Working from Potts's list and the names provided by Elizabeth, James and Jennet, there appears to have been around eighteen people in all present (apart from those whom Potts mentions but fails to name):

- Elizabeth Device.
- James Device.
- Jennet Device.
- Christopher Holgate (Elizabeth Southerns' son, half-brother to Elizabeth Device and uncle to James, Alizon and Jennet) of Pendle.[285]
- Elizabeth Holgate, wife of Christopher Holgate.
- Christopher Hargreaves (also called Christopher Jackes) of Thorneyholme.
- Elizabeth Hargreaves, wife of Christopher Hargreaves.
- Jennet Hargreaves, wife of Hugh Hargreaves of Under Pendle.[286]
- Jane Bulcock.
- John Bulcock.
- Alice Nutter.
- Alice Gray of Colne.
- Katherine Hewyt of Colne, alias 'Mould-heeles'.[287]
- Anne Crouckshey of Marsden.[288]
- Jennet Preston from Gisburn.
- Grace Hey of Padiham.

- Two women from Burnley; Elizabeth Device stated afterwards that Alice Nutter ('the wife of Richard Nutter') knew their names.

Looking briefly at the more unfamiliar names, it is immediately apparent that Jennet Hargreaves of Under Pendle in Barley and married couple Christopher and Elizabeth Hargreaves all shared the same surname as Constable Henry Hargreaves; none of the three were prosecuted.

Alice Gray of Colne appears in both the Pendle and Samlesbury trials. Probably a family friend of the Devices, she would shortly stand accused of committing crimes with Katherine Hewitt, also of Colne, where Gray/Grey was an uncommon surname. There is just one entry in the parish records for the relevant period: in the burial register, an Alice Gray was laid to rest at St Bartholomew's in Colne on 29 April 1613. Given that 'our' Alice survived the Lancaster trials, it is a strong possibility that the entry is the correct one, and that she died eight months later.

Anne Crouckshey of Marsden appears to have been related to the Cronckshaws of West Close, a long-established landowning family who were Anne Whittle's neighbours. One of the Cronckshaws – a woman named Jennet – would eventually be accused of witchcraft in the second Pendle case. It may be that the Devices and Anne Whittle's friends had agreed to set aside any differences in order to work out how to assist their loved ones in Lancaster gaol.

Likewise, Grace Hey of Padiham also had family who were long-term residents of West Close. There may have been a further family association between Grace and Lawrence Hey, who would later stand charged with witchcraft at the Samlesbury trial.

It has been suggested that the 'two women from Burnley' were those who had been involved with Anne Whittle in the Robert Nutter murder plot. However, since they were both said to be dead by the time of Anne's examination on 2 April 1612, they were clearly not the same individuals.

While these attendees remain obscure, there is a little more to discover about Katherine Hewitt and Jane and John Bulcock. There are hints of a tenuous and convoluted family association between Elizabeth Southerns and Katherine Hewitt, whose surname has many variations. The evidence against Katherine appears to have been provided by the Device family but is thinner than moorland mist.

The small but vibrant market town of Colne was built on coal with much of its trade being in cloth, woollen and worsted goods. According to James Device, Katherine was the wife of John Hewitt, 'alias Mould-heeles, of Colne, in the county of Lancaster, clothier'. The Clitheroe Court Rolls reveal that this was in all probability John Hewitt, who was related to the wealthier landowning Blakeys, who were also clothiers – and recusants. The punishing fines they accrued for remaining true to Catholicism proved to be their downfall. A Colne historian notes: 'Little is known of Katherine Hewitt, but the circumstances of her husband being a clothier would seem to warrant the inference that she was of higher rank than many of her companions in misfortune.'[289]

Clothiers needed a steady supply of water for their work, and the Hewitts lived in one of the cottages that had been recently and illegally built on Waterside. Many clothiers' wives worked alongside their husbands to keep the costs of running a business low; anyone passing the Hewitts' cottage would have heard the unmistakable 'thud of the treadles and the clack of the shuttle'.[290] By referring to 'the said witch, called Katherine Hewitt, alias Mould-heeles', James Device inadvertently provides us with a little insight into another money-saving method used by clothiers. 'Mould-heels' was Katherine's husband's moniker, and while 'heels' was a common suffix, the first part is believed to refer to the mould that grew on handloom warps when a liberal amount of animal fat had been applied to 'bulk out' the cloth, suggesting that John Hewitt may have had a reputation for being less than scrupulous with the fabric he sold.[291]

The last of the gathering were John and Jane Bulcock, mother and son, who lived at Moss End Farm. There were several branches of Bulcocks, including at Ravensholme, Whitehough and

Foothouse Gate, with Christopher and Jane cropping up repeatedly as Christian names. The Whitehough Bulcocks are thought to be the nucleus, and the home they created just east of Barley in the Pendle Water valley still stands: Whitehough Grange – originally Whitehough House – bears an inscription on the south porch: 'This house was built by Christopher Bulcock and Jennet his wife 1593.' They were perhaps the most affluent of the Bulcocks, having supplemented their income with the business of weaving.

A theory holds that the other branches of the family were each headed by sons of Whitehough Christopher. While there may be some truth to this, Elizabeth Device's comment to Roger Nowell hints that the Moss End Bulcocks hailed from further afield: 'The said Bulcock's wife doth know of some witches to be about Padiham and Burnley.' Although the exact details are – again – unknown, the Jane Bulcock who was hanged as a witch gave birth in Padiham to the son who would die alongside her; John was baptised on 30 June 1592 at St Leonard's Church with his father listed as 'Christopher Bulcocke'. We now have an explanation for how Jane might 'know of some witches' in Padiham, at least.

The family relocated to Goldshaw Booth, settling at Moss End Farm, probably around the turn of the seventeenth century.[292] The farm of that name, which stands today at the head of Sabden Brook valley, is a later building, either eighteenth or early nineteenth century, when it was known as Moss Nook. The original Moss End is thought to have stood closer to the site of Spenbrook Mill, in the same area. Nevertheless, their nearest neighbours were the Nutters of Bull Hole Farm and Elizabeth Southerns of Malkin Tower. They were not, in any sense, persons 'of the lowest class' as James Crossley phrased it in his annotations to Potts's *Discoverie*, but yeoman farmers with good local connections. When Christopher Bulcock died in April 1617, he left a will, and if he was also related to the Whitehough Bulcocks, then the family were prospering – until the investigation into witchcraft caught up with them.

*

Both James and Jennet Device specifically placed Jane and John Bulcock at the Good Friday meeting, but Elizabeth's recollections are oddly phrased. She refers to 'at the said meeting at Malkin-Tower, as aforesaid, Katherine Hewyt and John Bulcock, with all the rest then there, gave their consents . . .' but does not say that his mother was present, only that she 'doth verily think, that the said Bulcock's wife doth know of some witches to be about Padiham and Burnley'. Jennet, in contrast, remembered where Jane had sat, and that John had turned the spit. Both she and James further claimed to recall the conversations that had passed between the Bulcocks and others. Nowell's editing may have been at fault, causing the jarring references and even the disparity in those named as present or not.

Most of those present at the meal were from the immediate vicinity, although Jennet Preston had travelled from Gisburn, around eight miles north of Goldshaw Booth. When the Devices were later questioned by Nowell and Bannister about the purpose of the meeting, their responses were unexpected and somewhat disparate, although they all agreed on one aspect: their intention to 'christen' Alizon's familiar. This is curious for several reasons, not least because this implies that the ceremony had been arranged beforehand and could only refer to the black dog. Yet there is no tradition within the witch trials whereby a familiar was given a name; in the initial encounter, or very soon afterwards, the familiar would state its name – a powerful magic in itself. There are no other instances within the 1612 trials of a familiar being named in a formal ceremony, although had any occurred, they would indeed have appeared to mock the baptism of infants. Only during the North Berwick trials did something similar take place, when Agnes Sampson confessed to having taken a cat 'and christened it, and afterwards bound to each part of that cat, the chiefest parts of a dead man, and several joints of his body', thereafter casting it into the sea in order to create magic.[293] Nowell might have remembered reading the passage and enquired if anything similar was planned at the Malkin meet, but if so, then it resulted in a particularly inexplicable passage. Nevertheless, following the publication of *Discoverie* and its references to the familiar-naming ceremony, legal guidelines were drawn up stating that this was an aspect of witches' gatherings and one that magistrates should seek out.

James Device later told Nowell that the naming ceremony was deferred due to his sister's absence. However, one woman had brought her familiar along: Jennet Preston, who according to James, 'had a Spirit with her like unto a white foal, with a black-spot in the forehead'.[294] It was Jennet Preston, too, who apparently raised one of two other subjects that were discussed at the meeting. James related how she had requested help in 'the killing of Master Lister of Westby, because (as she then said) he had borne malice unto her, and had thought to have put her away at the last Assises at Yorke, but could not'. James claimed not to know Jennet's name, referring to her instead as 'the woman dwelling in Gisburn parish' whom he heard say that 'her power was not strong enough to do it herself, being now less than before time it had been'. He returned – or was returned – to the subject on further occasions, stating that he had heard all those present at Malkin Tower 'give their consents to put the said Thomas Lister of Westby to death'.

James then gave a third, fuller account of Jennet Preston's request, which was yet more incriminating: 'And after Master Lister should be made away by witchcraft, then all the said witches gave their consents to join all together, to hanck [kill or bind by spells] Master Leonard Lister, when he should come to the dwell at the Cow-gill, and so put him to death.' Leonard Lister was the brother of Thomas Lister the elder. He lived with his wife Anne and three young children in Cowgill Farm, some three miles from Gisburn. Whether he had helped fuel his nephew's determination to bring about Jennet's ruin is unknown, but not impossible.

Nowell was aware of Jennet Preston and her recent acquittal in York; now he would be able to present his colleague Thomas Heber with explicit evidence of her intentions towards not only the younger Lister but his uncle as well. This no doubt made sense to Nowell, but it seems extremely unlikely that Jennet (however fearful she may have been of Lister) made the suggestion in all seriousness. It was courageous of her to attend the meeting, given her recent acquittal, but if anyone could give them an idea of what their loved ones were facing, it was Jennet. Nonetheless, Elizabeth Device concurred that their group had agreed to the 'killing of Master Lister of Westby' and 'the said Master Leonard Lister'.

But Elizabeth vehemently denied that the third and final purpose of their gathering was as outlined by her son: 'For the delivery of his said grandmother . . . said sister Alizon . . . said Anne Chattox, and her daughter Redfearn; killing the gaoler at Lancaster; and before the next Assises to blow up the castle there: and to that end the aforesaid prisoners might by that time make an escape, and get away.' Jennet Device, in contrast, agreed with her brother. There can be no doubt that the imprisonment of their family was the main reason for the gathering, and the subject to which every conversation that day returned, and it isn't beyond the bounds of possibility that someone declared, in a spontaneous but fierce outburst, that they ought to kill the gaoler, blow up the castle and free all the prisoners. It was an utterly impractical suggestion in all seriousness, far beyond their capabilities. But if it was indeed said, even in a throwaway moment of anger, Nowell could scarcely have wished for anything more sensational. The Gunpowder Plot of 1605 had been stymied, but it had caused seismic shockwaves, nonetheless, leaving the Crown, government and gentry utterly paranoid about potentially lethal Catholic insurgency. The fact that two of the conspirators had been captured while making their way to Lancashire, where they had planned another uprising, only increased the sense of paranoia. For Roger Nowell, playing even a small role in uncovering a nest of traitorous witches hellbent on blowing up one of the country's most formidable fortresses was the opportunity of a lifetime for any magistrate.

James Device had one last revelation about the events of Good Friday 1612. He later described how, when the meeting ended, they all agreed to meet on the same day the following year at Jennet Preston's house, where she 'promised to make them a great feast'. This very much reads as if the Good Friday meetings were an annual event, with each member of the group taking turns to host. James added that 'if they had occasion to meet in the meantime, then should warning be given to meet up on Romleys Moor'.[295] And then, James said, 'All the said Witches went out of the said house in their own shapes and likenesses; and they all, by that time they were forth of the doors, were got on horseback, like unto foals, some of one colour, and some of another; and Preston's wife was the last: and when she got on horseback, they all presently vanished . . .' This last was Jennet Preston's familiar, which James had already mentioned as being 'like unto a white foal, with a black-spot in the forehead'.[296] His odd manner of describing the group's leaving – that they 'went out of the said house in their own shapes and likenesses', reads as if he is about to suggest that they then shape-shifted, but lost his confidence in the telling of his story. Unless, of course, Nowell's occasionally uneven editing was to blame, for ultimately the group simply appear to leave Malkin Tower and journey home on horseback.

Thus ended the witches' sabbath in Pendle, on a note as muted and ordinary as the events of the gathering itself. Two days later, on Easter Sunday, a cautionary notice was read out from every pulpit in Lancashire declaring that non-communicants had twenty days to amend their ways or face prosecutions. One of the signatories was Roger Nowell.[297]

Chapter Sixteen

ONE FOR SORROW

'Cease, cease to mourn, all tears are vain & void,
He's fled, not dead, dissolved, not destroy'd.
In Heaven his soul doth rest, his body here
Sleeps in this dust, and his fame everywhere
Triumphs. The town, the country, farther forth,
Speaks of a man so kind, so courteous,
So free, and every way, magnanimous.
That story told at large here do you see
Epitomis'd in brief, Covell was he.'[298]

The memorial plaque in Lancaster Priory, which stands slightly back from the castle as if attempting to distance itself from its history, gleams like gold in the bright sun of a winter's day. The plaque that accompanies has the same rich hue, but its surface is badly worn and dented. Originally fixed to the floor of the chancel, where its subject is buried, the engraving is effaced to leave only the ghostly outlines of the engraved figure in his alderman boots, breeches and fur-edged cloak with voluminous sleeves and a wide Elizabethan ruff. The hands are joined in beatific prayer, but the face above them is no more.

The story told 'at large' on the commemorative plaque is a typically florid account of a man known to all his fellow townsfolk in some capacity – an intensely ambitious, formidable man who was a divisive character in Lancaster, where he held various positions of power and influence. Some saw him as John Taylor the 'water poet' did, when they met in 1618: 'kind Mr Covell'; while others viewed him in the same light as did Henry Burton, Puritan minister of London, describing him as a 'beastly man'.[299] Burton's depiction is an appropriate introduction, given that his impression of Covell was as a prisoner meeting his gaoler.

Burton was incarcerated for thirteen weeks in 1637 at Lancaster, where he was received into gaol on his arrival by Covell, who was sitting in an old chair that had belonged to John of Gaunt and, after berating him, took him to 'a vast desolate room within the iron gate of the Common Gaol, where none had laine for almost twenty years, where there was nothing but bare, cold walls, and those with wide and ruinous clefts to let in the cold winds; and windows, having iron bars outward, and wooden bars in the midst . . . The door also of the room was open below, so as when the cold North, or North-east wind did blow, it filled it both with cold and smoke.'[300] Burton could not walk about the room because of the dangerous uneven, thick floorboards. He suffered terrible colic due to the cold and thought he was going to die; even then, Covell would not help him, no matter how he pleaded. At the end of his sentence, he declared his thanks to God that he was leaving and 'the keeper Covell, being vexed at this, said, but you are here yet'.[301] Afterwards, Burton shuddered at the memory of Covell, who had stood by while he had had his ears cropped, and declared: 'He intended to make an end of me.'[302]

Thomas Covell was certainly no ordinary gaoler. Elsewhere described as a man whose 'principal talent' seems to have consisted of 'tenacity of place', he served as magistrate, coroner, mayor, innkeeper and gaoler.[303] Born in 1561, Covell was thirty when he achieved his first public position, as Keeper of Lancaster Castle, a position he held until his death. Gaols during this period and throughout the seventeenth century were 'notoriously decrepit', as J. S. Cockburn writes, in *A History of English Assizes, 1558–1714*.[304] Commonly unfit to keep prisoners at all sheltered from the vagaries of the weather, they were without exception overcrowded and insanitary, resulting in suspects attempting to flee or commit suicide. Gaolers 'might accelerate either eventuality by allowing prisoners to escape, or by indulging the extortions and vicious maltreatment traditionally associated with their office. Northern gaolers in this period were a law unto themselves' and 'brought their quota of corruption to assize trials.'[305]

Prison conditions were largely dictated by the outlook of the gaoler, who invariably exploited his position by offering to make life easier for his subjects – depending how much they could afford to slip him. He could provide better food and water, bedclothes, pass messages in and out of prison, and even agree to try rigging the jury or helping a prisoner escape. Whether they fulfilled their promises was another matter. Although it was well known that prisons operated on the basis of bribery, gaolers nonetheless had to keep up appearances, for those found to be running rackets were liable for prosecution. Gaolers who were involved in compiling lists of prisoners to be sent for trial might omit the names of those who were wealthier, in order to extract more money from them by ensuring their protracted incarceration. Covell himself must have been physically fit, for prison conditions were often so dire and infectious that even someone able to come and go at will was at risk of illness and disease.

Two years into the role of keeper of the castle, Covell was made a county coroner, another position he would hold until his death. The Chancellor of the Duchy of Lancaster made the appointment from those men who were responsible for various local administrative tasks. It was an unpaid role but provided him with several powers, influence and further opportunities for extortion. As a coroner, Covell investigated suspicious deaths and enjoyed semi-magisterial authority, including the right to take depositions, to detain persons suspected of murder and to bind over witnesses and suspects at assizes or quarter sessions. Covell was undoubtedly literate; one of his roles was to inspect inquest reports, which were then sent to the King's Bench. Towards the end of the century, Covell entered the Corporation of Lancaster, finding another role for himself in the town's municipal government body that managed public services and local administration.

During Covell's early years as keeper of the castle, there were several instances of what one local historian refers to as 'interesting but ghastly chapters', the latter of which directly affected Roger Nowell's family, the Starkies: 'It may be assumed that [Covell] was present when Edward Kelly, the seer and associate of Dr Dee, had his ears cut off. In his official capacity, Covell would give up to the Sheriff the reputed conjuror, Edmund Hartlay, who was executed in 1597 for witchcraft alleged to have been practised by him on the family of Nicholas Starkie at Cleworth . . . this being the first execution for witchcraft in Lancashire of which there appears to be any record.'[306]

In some respects, however, Covell was viewed as too lenient with his prisoners. In 1598, the Bishop of Chester, Dr Richard Vaughan, complained to a friend: 'I hear that the prison at Lancaster is very ill kept; that the recusants there have liberty to go when and whither at they list; to hunt, to hawk, and go to the horse races at their pleasure; which notorious abuse of law and justice should speedily be reformed.'[307] Temporarily at least, Covell might have been distracted from his work, for on 14 August 1599, he married Dorothy Watson. Their daughter Elizabeth was born two years later. At the turn of the new century, Covell tried his hand at an altogether different form of employment: he was granted a licence to operate as an alehouse keeper. Lancaster had several public houses, one of which was The George, run by his brother Edmund, with whom he was on affectionate terms.

In July 1600, Covell handed two Roman Catholic priests over to the sheriff: Edward Thwing and Robert Nutter, a distant relation of Alice Nutter's husband, Richard. An account of their imprisonment and execution recalls that they were 'laid upon a hurdle at the castle gates and drawn through the streets of the old town to the Tyburn-shaped gallows on the Moor, there to be hanged, [disembowelled] and quartered, their dismembered remains being afterwards exposed on the Gateway Tower at Lancaster, or on church towers in other parts of the county'.[308] The same fate befell two more priests under Covell's care in March 1601: Thurstan Hunt and Robert Middleton, and Laurence Bailey, in September 1604.[309] The following year, having been elected mayor, Covell presented prisoner Anne Waters to the sheriff for execution; she and her lover had conspired to kill her husband, but he had fled, leaving Anne to be arrested after a neighbour dreamed about the murder and even led a constable to the grave. Anne's fate, as a woman found guilty of murdering her husband and therefore convicted of petty treason, was to be burnt to death.

Lancaster appears in its earliest cartographical form in John Speed's *The Theatre of the Empire of Great Britaine*, as surveyed in 1607. Home to around 1,500 citizens, the map depicts a small town whose castle sits above a cluster of narrow streets, with ships dotted on the serpentine river like toy boats. Parts of the original fortress have survived, including the soaring square mass of the keep. Over eight hundred years old and appropriately known as the Lungess ('heavily built') Tower, apertures in the thick walls used 'by the bowmen of old' can still be seen today.[310] The court rooms, where trials had been held since 1210, were housed south-west of the keep on the first floor of the medieval hall.

Before the end of the Middle Ages, lodging towers were built on either side of the gatehouse. The Dungeon Tower was demolished in the early nineteenth century and replaced by the Female Penitentiary, but the Well Tower has survived, and it is here where tradition states the suspects from Pendle were incarcerated. Dr Colin Penny, curator at Lancaster Castle, explains: 'We don't know for certain that the witches were held in the Well Tower; they are just as likely if not more so to have been imprisoned in the old dungeon tower that was demolished.'[311] Nevertheless, the existent structure reveals the conditions in which they would have been held for the last few months of their lives. The rectangular tower stands right of the gatehouse, the mellow stone of its tall, commanding exterior walls deepening in parts and very different to the adjacent structures; recent dendrochronology of its timbers showed that work began on the building after 1256 and the upper floors were repaired after 1378. The Well and Dungeon Towers each had large windows overlooking the wide courtyard, with fireplaces, privies and window seats, and probably provided accommodation for visiting dignitaries and their staff. Most of the windows were bricked up at a later date.

Padlocked steel gates now guard the arched entrance to the Well Tower. In the past, a heavy wooden door would have blocked access – and escape. Behind it, however, immediately to the left, is a chasm leading to an old tunnel; the lichen-covered well that gives the tower its name is far deeper underground, reached only by a corridor from the security guards' room today. Rain from the castle roof was channelled into the well, providing cool, safe water for those trapped inside when the building was under siege.

Steps, the stones uneven and worn, lead down under a low roof into darkness some twenty-five feet below. To the right is a doorway, its lintel low, the gaol door now gone but the fastenings still visible in the stone. Inside is the dungeon. The vaulted, wattle-and-daub roof rises to a height of seven feet; the walls are about five feet high, ice-cold to the touch. Large blocks of stone create an even floor, some twenty feet by twelve feet. In the centre, fastened solidly to the floor, is a heavy iron ring six inches wide, where prisoners would be chained. In the absence of artificial light, it is a chamber of darkness in every sense, lacking air, and with an overpowering despair still lingering. Victorian writer Cross Fleury described it aptly as 'a veritable inferno of gloom, that sort almost capable of being cut with a knife. There is not a ray of light. Death in her angrier form has reigned here.'[312] Both the Dungeon Tower and the Well Tower 'seem to have been abodes of special suffering and horror, their underground rooms having little or no light or ventilation'.[313] It was said that 'so appalling was the stench from the closely-packed prisoners, the warder on opening the doors in the morning had to leave them for some time ajar before he could enter'.[314]

Small wonder that this place was regarded 'from earliest times as a hellhole'.[315] Or that, cramped together with no sanitation, the stench of bodily waste, unimaginable psychological pressure, terror of mistreatment, little hope of avoiding the executioner, and only damp, impenetrable darkness, 'family loyalties broke down . . . fear in the face of judicial action combined with years of poverty and rejection by the community left the families weak and vulnerable to outside attack'.[316]

Thomas Covell felt nothing but repulsion towards those from Pendle; he knew, of course, that the story waiting to be told at the assizes involved a plot to murder him and destroy the place that he regarded as his dominion. Although torture was illegal, violence and maltreatment were rife in gaol, where the keeper held the keys to the prisoners' well-being and could mete out viciousness without fear of recourse. Something particularly terrible happened to James Device during his incarceration; a physically fit young labourer, who could carry a stolen sheep over hills quite easily, appeared in court 'so insensible, weak, and unable in all things, as he could neither speak, hear, or stand, but was held up when he was brought to the place of his arraignment'. Apart from an evident psychological breakdown, James had been subjected to vicious brutality, and Potts's phrasing that Covell took 'very great pains' to extract information from him during their meetings is as telling as it is disturbing.

Given James's severe physical and emotional deterioration, there is good reason to suppose that author Joyce Froome's suggestion that Elizabeth Device's appearance might equally have been the result of mistreatment at the hands of Covell or his assistants. Potts had tried to equate Elizabeth's damaged eye with moral deformity, branding it a 'preposterous mark in nature' and assumed – having only encountered the suspects in court – that she had appeared thus 'from birth', but there is nothing other than his remark to confirm it, and Froome rightly points out that this may have been the result of a fractured eye socket, caused by a violent blow to the eye.

There was much else to fear in prison, not least outbreaks of typhus, or gaol fever, as it was more commonly known. An outbreak of the disease among prisoners at the summer assizes in Oxford in 1577 raged through the courtroom and into the town, killing two judges, the sheriff and almost four hundred more.

Whether an infection was to blame or the daily deprivations, humiliations and torment of incarceration in the dark belly of the town, between Good Friday and mid-May, 'firebrand' Elizabeth Device passed away, her spirit broken, her life snuffed out, plunging her family into even deeper darkness. When Thomas Potts sat down to write *Discoverie*, he was determined to reveal her as a woman suffused with evil intent, 'the devil's agent' in her hometown. But he achieved precisely the opposite, for Elizabeth Southerns emerges from his pages as a fearless matriarch whose life ended in poverty and despair but had proven rich and rewarding in many ways. A cunning woman in the best sense, she understood her world as others never could, for all their material wealth, and remained active and sought after by those in need until the last months of a long and worthy life. There were those who hated and feared her, but she held onto the love and respect of her family beyond death, as her granddaughter Alizon would demonstrate with a flash of uncharacteristic defiance in court. Her name remains known, and even in the pre-war days of the 1930s, when newspaper columnists writing about the trial were often scathing, one journalist reminded his readers: "That Mother Demdike lifted her family from being mere beggars to a spiritual dominance over twenty-four square miles of North-East Lancashire proves great strength of character.'[317]

Elizabeth Southerns died an innocent woman. Her death before the assizes leaves the mystery of where she was buried. Her son, Christopher Holgate, was the only close relative beyond the confines of the prison other than her granddaughter, Jennet, but even if family were permitted to claim her body, Christopher was in no position to do so. Having died without being convicted of any crime, Elizabeth may have been buried on the outskirts of the castle, or in the grounds of the adjoining priory, which holds thousands of unmarked graves.

Elizabeth's daughter, granddaughter, Alizon and grandson James had all witnessed her passing and grieved together in the cell below ground, perhaps taking some comfort from a swifter end to the suffering she had endured. Her old friend Anne Whittle must have experienced a maelstrom of emotions. She was perilously near to breaking point herself; Potts's description of her is as 'a very old, withered, spent and decrepit creature, her sight almost gone' and admits that anyone gazing upon 'this poor creature, in respect of her great contrition and repentance' would be moved to pity, before he reminds us of 'her hellish practises'. It is impossible to know whether Anne was in reasonably good health before her incarceration, but the fact that she survived would suggest this was the case and that her appearance in court was, like that of Elizabeth and James Device, the result of a relentless lack of mercy.

On 19 May, Anne Whittle had some small respite from the dungeon when she was interviewed by Thomas Covell, who almost certainly examined all of the prisoners at some point. In an unknown location within the castle, she was confronted by questions from Covell and two other men: William Sandes, then Mayor of Lancaster, and James Anderton, Justice of the Peace. With Elizabeth Southerns no longer living, Anne clearly saw an opportunity to attribute as much incriminating material as possible to her, knowing that it could have no further impact as far as Elizabeth was concerned. Her intentions are obvious: she told Covell, Anderton and Sandes that she had become a witch 'through the great persuasions' of Elizabeth around 1598, but previously she had discussed having been approached to arrange the murder by witchcraft of Robert Nutter – who died in 1593. She stated that his death was due to his being 'bewitched by [me], the said Demdike, and Widow Loomeshaw (late of Burnley) now deceased', thus implicating no one at liberty to be charged, other than herself. She then told the three men that Elizabeth had admitted murdering Richard Assheton of Downham in 1597. The Asshetons owned substantial tracts of land, including the manor of Downham and areas of West Close; they were related to the Towneleys, the Listers, the Starkies, Roger Nowell and Sir Thomas Gerard. However, Covell and his cohorts were unimpressed with this last offering and left it in the evidence virtually as an aside. But Anne was desperate to save her daughter from the gallows and clutched at the idea of appearing cooperative – even to the extent of confessing to killing Robert Nutter – in the vain hope that they would release her daughter.

Covell duly delivered Anne Whittle back to the dungeon cell and brought out James Device. Precisely how much of James's statements were made that day can no longer be ascertained, or what sort of state he was in while being examined. The section of his evidence which Potts dates to 19 May is brief; James was adamant that he had never given his soul to the spirit Dandy, and had in fact vanquished him, sending him away with 'a most fearful cry and yell' and 'a great flash of fire'. But the three listening men viewed James's story as incriminating nonetheless – in their eyes, it was superb evidence that he had consulted with spirits, and they returned him to the dungeon quite satisfied with the information they had managed to extract.

Of the other detainees, Jane and John Bulcock must have given formal confessions during their incarceration, since there are none credited to Nowell's presence in *Discoverie*, but Potts refers to their protesting in court and retracting their previous admittances. Any and all retractions would have caused Covell considerable embarrassment and frustration, particularly if these were made following confessions to Nowell, who would be angered and concerned at the prospect of neatly tied-up evidence beginning to unravel. There may have been an implicit agreement between the two men that Nowell would shuffle the evidence about as he saw fit, knowing that Bannister would turn a blind eye if necessary.

A few weeks later, in mid-July, the doors to the acrid underground chamber were unbolted and footsteps sounded on the stone stairs. Their prison was expanding, in number only, as two more women suspected of witchcraft entered their cell.

Chapter Seventeen

THE WITCH IN THE WOODPILE
and
THE WINDLE WITCH
or
MARGARET PEARSON AND ISOBEL ROBEY

It was the strangest of sights and a matter of public record, yet no one claimed to have seen it. On a midsummer's night in the Lancashire town of Padiham, an unbridled mare galloped madly, two figures clinging to her mane and tail. One rider was a woman in her early fifties, gleeful and wild, hair streaming in the night breeze. The other appeared to be a man, exultant as his companion, but his legs where they pressed against the mare's sweating flanks were not human: he was part goat, coarse-haired and strong-smelling, and his feet were cloven.

The woman was a witch named Margaret Pearson. The other, her familiar.

They had stolen the mare earlier that evening, making good use of the shadows to enter Dodgson's land. The stone stables were ventilated by loopholes, allowing Margaret and her companion to magically slip inside through the arrow-slit gaps and into a stall. Purloining a horse for mischief was common game among witches; the mare they chose was unable to resist as they leapt upon her.

The crash of the stable door failed to wake the nearby household. Margaret urged her ride through the yard, on and on, along the street that wound up from the marketplace, past church and mill and meadow, all by the milky light of the moon. A narrow, winding lane brought them onto a sudden sweep of moorland and the great hill where the first glimmer of daybreak, a pale seep of summer light, brought their exertions to an end. The horse, with her wind-tangled mane, was returned to the stable, while the two figures fled.

John Dodgson discovered his poor mare lying dead in her stall shortly afterwards, exhaustion writ upon her. He knew at once that she had been 'hag-ridden', and whose witchery was to blame – again.[318]

That was the tale that brought Margaret Pearson before the authorities in July 1612. Unusually, it was the third time she had faced charges of witchcraft. A small detail gleaned from the old parish registers gives some insight into how she reached such a dreadful predicament.

Margaret was born a Bowker.[319] Most of the Padiham Bowkers came from nearby Newchurch-in-Pendle or Croston, further afield in the vicinity of Preston. Padiham offered opportunity and a close-knit community; its markets had begun to rival those of Burnley, some three miles east and better established. North and east of Padiham were the two great estates: Huntroyde, home of the Starkie family, and the Shuttleworth's Gawthorpe.

Beyond the indelible imprint of the industrial revolution, Padiham as it was in Margaret's time is still discernible, with steep streets, winding lanes and cobbled snickets following the ghostly contours of the past. A few shops and an alehouse or two existed even then, while markets and fairs were held on land south of St Leonard's Church, where Margaret married Edward Pearson on 7 August 1581.[320]

A small detail in *Discoverie* reveals that Margaret and her husband were involved in Padiham's thriving textile business, probably as clothworkers, buying and preparing wool for sale.[321] They would have owned a spinning wheel or two, and possibly a loom, and may have owned sheep to produce their own wool.

It was Anne Whittle, in her courtroom testimony, who claimed that this ordinary life was not all it seemed, for Margaret Pearson 'is a very evil woman, and confessed to [me] that she is a witch and hath a spirit which came to her the first time in likeness of a man, and cloven-footed'. In the absence of further detail regarding Margaret's compact with the devil, Potts states nimbly: 'How long she hath been a witch, the devil and she know best.' He declared there was 'little inferior in her wicked and malicious course of life to any that hath gone before her. A very dangerous witch of long continuance, generally suspected and feared in all parts of the country, and of all good people near her, and not without great cause. For, whosoever gave her any just occasion of offence, she tormented with great misery, or cut off their children, goods, or friends.'

Reiterating that 'this wicked and ungodly witch revenged her fury upon goods, so that everyone near her sustained great loss', Potts then affirms that 'this is the third time she is come to receive her trial; one time for murder by witchcraft; another time for bewitching a neighbour; now for goods'. He reveals nothing of the second charge, and recounts little more about the third, referring to Anne Whittle's testimony that Margaret had told her how 'she bewitched unto death one Childers' wife, and her daughter . . .'[322]

Again, the parish registers are useful in uncovering information relating to this alleged double murder. Thomas Childers, son of a Padiham constable, and his wife Elizabeth had several children who survived into adulthood. Like the Pearsons, they worked in Padiham's textile industry and enjoyed the patronage of local gentry such as Dean Nowell and Sir John Towneley, whose families feature prominently in the wider story.[323] Childers' wife, Elizabeth, died towards the end of the sixteenth century; their daughter, Alicia, passed away in August 1601, at the age of twenty-five.[324] Unfortunately, there are no extant records to establish when or why Margaret was tried for their murders, but it is a fact that accusations of witchcraft could be brought before the courts many years after the offences were said to have occurred. Margaret was plainly found not guilty, indicating that someone may have spoken in her defence, or that the evidence against her was weak, or shown to be manufactured – or a combination of these.

A second 'not guilty' verdict was returned in the matter of Margaret bewitching a neighbour. But it seems likely that Margaret had made a grudgeful enemy, while the repeated attempts to peg her as a witch hint that she was known about Padiham as a cunning woman. The Pendle case demonstrates how, if a remedy failed or was used to harm instead of heal, relations between client and cunning person could sour, swiftly and very dangerously. Potts of course, was at pains to persuade his reader that Margaret was a witch of seething malevolence. He regarded the failed charges as supporting evidence in that respect and set out how Margaret had 'wickedly, maliciously and voluntarily' killed the stolen horse. Working animals were valuable commodities, and a little delving into the ownership of the deceased mare uncovers a potentially significant element in her case.

The horse belonged to John Dodgson, who was married to Anna Childers; her mother and sister were said to have been murdered by witchcraft – at the hands of Margaret Pearson. That all Margaret's 'victims' were so closely related may be nothing more than coincidence, but many witchcraft trials emerged from the tangled webs of personal vendettas, and it isn't beyond the realms of possibility that there was an element of revenge bringing Margaret repeatedly before court.

Prior to her third trial, Margaret was summoned again before the local justice of the peace: Nicholas Bannister. The exact circumstances that led to Margaret's third indictment are unknown, but Potts asserts that Bannister had at his disposal 'accusations, depositions and particular examinations' against Margaret that were 'infinite and able to fill a large volume'. None of this paperwork has survived. The only contemporary reference to her trial apart from *Discoverie* is an entry in the meticulously kept household accounts of Gawthorpe Hall, which record that in July 1612, the Shuttleworths paid a fee for the conveyance of Margaret Pearson to prison: 'The constable of Padiham, for a xv*th* towards the carriage of Pierson, his wife to Lancaster, iiij*d*.'[325]

Nicholas Bannister welcomed further evidence to support his case. Less than a fortnight before Margaret was due to stand trial for killing Dodgson's mare and unspecified 'diverse other wild and odious practises', Jennet Booth provided him with a sworn statement. She lived with her husband James and their young child in Padiham, where she worked for the Pearsons as a wool carder.[326] One Friday in July, shortly before Margaret was transferred to prison, Jennet arrived at work and settled her baby before fetching a quantity of oiled wool and a pair of wooden paddles to begin carding. After a while, she asked Margaret if she might have a little milk for her child. Margaret obliged, bringing some in a pan, ready to warm on the fire. Noticing how the flames had dwindled, Jennet broke up some kindling and set them on the coals with the pan. With the milk heated, Jennet removed the pan and saw 'a toad, or a thing very like a toad', which seemed to come 'out of the fire, together with the said pan, and under the bottom of the same'.[327] Margaret appeared again, approaching the hearth with a pair of coal tongs. Jennet watched her deftly pick up the toad, 'or a thing very like a toad', and carry it outside. What she did with the creature afterwards, 'this examinate knows not', Bannister solemnly recorded.[328]

The unexpected visitor in the woodpile was circumstantial evidence of witchcraft. The humble toad was firmly established in the minds of the public and judiciary alike as 'a common companion to the witch and the sorcerer. A familiar of long renown, its abilities to blight fields, transport witches, suckle at the devil's mark and play the impish demon, sowing chaos, like salt, into the wounds of Christendom, are something to marvel at.'[329] Belief in the toad's mystical qualities reached far back into antiquity: Pliny the Elder informed readers in first-century Rome that a toad in the room could impose silence on those present, adding that a bone from a toad's left side would protect against dog attacks and one from its right had the power to prevent water boiling. Alchemists were rumoured to have concocted a powder that induced 'fantastic visions' from a wine and salt solution containing live toads.[330]

Amulets of toad parts were worn by sufferers of the plague, who believed that the affliction would pass from their deadly buboes to the warty skin of the toad. Similarly medicinal charms were in use until the nineteenth century, with 'toad doctors' selling silken bags containing the head or legs that had been cut from a live toad as a cure for rheumatism or scrofula, a skin condition known as 'the king's evil'.[331] Toad remedies endured in many forms, such as placing a live toad on the back of the neck to stem a nose bleed. Childhood bed-wetting was thought to be preventable by tying a live toad between the legs in the belief that when the infant began to urinate, the toad would croak in protest, waking the child and halting the flow.[332]

But there was a darker view of the toad's magical properties. A thirteenth-century manuscript depicting the devil's coat of arms shows three toads, and in his papal bull of 1233, Pope Gregory IX informed bishops that those who attended the secret meetings of heretics would encounter the devil himself in many forms, often as a toad. The toad came to be widely regarded as the personification of the devil.

Witches were believed to use toads in a variety of ways. The prized antidote to the medicinal properties of the toad was in its toxins: when threatened, a toad will spurt milky drops of venom from the glands behind its eyes and occasionally from its skin. Witches were said to use the 'swelter'd venom' of toad saliva mixed with the sap of the sow-thistle and paint the concoction on their bodies in the form of crooked crosses to render themselves invisible.[333] A well-nourished toad could be 'milked' to produce a substance necessary for flying ointment, useful for magical transportation.

Shakespeare discovered such tales when he researched witchcraft for *Macbeth*. In the opening scene, one of the witches is called by her familiar, a toad named Paddock. A second toad, hiding under a stone, is thrown into their cooking pot to provide them with poison. Shakespeare habitually employs the toad as an ill omen of warty mysticality, but in *Macbeth* we find the prevailing popular view of the toad: witch familiar and cauldron classic.[334]

The evidence put forward for Margaret's trial had precedent, for toads hop with increasing frequency through witch trials, whether on the Continent, where the witches of Labourd confessed in 1609 to baptising toads and dressing them in red or black velvet with bells at their necks and feet, or in England. Three of the best-known examples occurred within a decade of each other. At the St Osyth trials of 1582, Ursula Kempe's young son testified that his mother had four familiars, including a black toad named Pigin; in 1589, a toad belonging to Joan Upney of Dagenham obediently killed a neighbour's wife; and two years later, at the North Berwick trials, Agnes Sampson was accused of attempting to shipwreck King James's vessel, with melting a toad forming part of the plot. Ursula, Joan and Agnes were all executed. Although there was a perfectly reasonable explanation for the toad in Margaret Pearson's home, Jennet Booth implied that it had magically survived the fire and was therefore most probably Margaret's familiar, able to change form whenever it wished – but it could not save its mistress from the dungeons of Lancaster Castle.

Windle lies within the township of St Helens, some ten miles north-west of Warrington. In 1612 it was a gently bucolic landscape where there had been a few rumours of witchcraft emanating from Rainford, Crank and Billinge, all within a few miles to the north-east. Two women from St Helens are said to have been examined at the Chapel in 1602 and then sent for trial at the Lancaster Assizes, but it was mostly cunning folk who were known in the region.

Ten years later there was another case, and on 12 July 1612, the investigation began. Thomas Gerard was in charge of the case; his was an illustrious family fond of using the same Christian names repeatedly within a single generation, and prone to the habit of referring to each other and their associates as 'cousin' – a common practice of its time but causing confusion ever afterwards. The Gerards were lords of the manor of Windle, and wealthy landowners in general, with large estates in Lancashire and Staffordshire. Thomas's father, Sir Gilbert, owned land and property in Pendle and was about as well connected as a gentleman could hope to be. He was attorney general for twenty years during Queen Elizabeth's reign, six times an MP (in four different constituencies), vice-chancellor of the Duchy of Lancaster and Master of the Rolls, making him the second most senior judge in the kingdom. He managed to avoid scandal, but not suspicion: his wife was a staunch Catholic all her life, and there were mutterings about him, not least because his cousin's son was John Gerard, a Jesuit priest who had escaped prosecution for complicity in the Gunpowder Plot by fleeing to France. Sir Thomas Walsingham, courtier to Queen Elizabeth, sniped that Sir Gilbert was 'a protestant in London and a papist in Lancashire'.

When Sir Gilbert died in 1593, his eldest son Thomas inherited the family estate. He had been just twenty years old when he became MP for Lancaster; his brother-in-law, Sir Richard Molyneux had been High Sheriff of Lancashire. Another sister married Sir Richard Houghton who, like Molyneux, had been her father's ward; Houghton, too, was Sheriff of Lancashire, in 1598, and lived increasingly beyond his means at Houghton Tower, six miles east of Blackburn. In 1611, Thomas showed his loyalty to King James by being one of the first to purchase a baronetcy for £1,000. The king was delighted by the gesture and returned the fee in recognition of the Gerards' services to his mother, Mary, Queen of Scots, and visited Thomas at his home.

Thus, Thomas Gerard moved in powerful, interlocking circles in which the same names appear again and again. Whether he deliberately used the prosecution of a local woman to achieve a place of even greater prominence for himself, alongside several of his close friends at the Lancaster Assizes of 1612, is impossible to know – but it certainly did his reputation no harm.

The evidence against Isabel Robey was thinner than parchment.

Her background is largely lost to us, although Robey/Roby was a common enough surname in the area at the time, with several in Windle, Billinge and Rainford. We get a sense of a mature woman from *Discoverie*, and if so, then one of the two entries for a William Roby in the relevant burial registers, for April 1574 and March 1584 respectively, may refer to her husband. Despite the dearth of information, it seems that – as was so often the case – Isabel's troubles began within a family setting. Isabel herself seems to have been a woman who spoke her mind, but whether she truly said everything that was attributed to her is another matter.

The first of Thomas Gerard's witnesses was the husband of Isabel's goddaughter. Peter Chaddock related how he had heard talk before his marriage that Isabel was 'not pleased' by the match, whereupon he called Isabel a witch and said that he didn't care for her either. A couple of days later, he felt 'sore pained' in his bones, and having made an appointment to meet a Master John Hawarden at Peasley Cross, on the far side of St Helens, he asked his friend Thomas Lyon if he would go with him. On their return, both men experienced pains, but this passed quickly.

Chaddock then recalled that despite his wife and Isabel being on good terms generally, about four years ago, the two women argued while Isabel was visiting them. His wife stormed out of the house, followed by Isabel, who was clearly 'not well pleased'. The following day, while Chaddock and his wife were busy with hay-making, he felt 'a pain and a starkness' about his neck 'which grieved him very sore'. Surprisingly, Chaddock admitted that he had sought assistance from a cunning man named James, a glover who lived in Windle, and asked him to pray for him. Chaddock again recovered but at the same time was plagued by a terrible thirst and fever, and although he had drink with which to slake his thirst, something prevented him from taking a draught. James the Glover visited him and Chaddock told him of his desperation, saying, 'I would to God that I could drink.' James advised him to take the drink and will himself to swallow it 'In the name of the Father, the Son, and the Holy Ghost,' then say, 'The devil and witches are not able to prevail against God and his word.' Chaddock did as he was bade and drank every drop and felt much better for some while.

But on Lady Day (25 March) 1611, he felt the same nagging pain ('warch') in every bone and limb and still suffered with it, even as he spoke to Gerard. He was certain it was caused 'by means of the said

Isabel Robey'. Although Gerard does not appear to have examined Thomas Lyon, who had experienced similar pains, he did speak to Lyon's wife, Margaret, who was well acquainted with Isabel. During a visit that Isabel had made to the Lyons' home, they spoke about Peter Chaddock's malady, and Isabel declared that he 'should never mend until he asks for my forgiveness. But I know that he will never do.' Margaret asked why she said such a thing, when Peter was 'a true Christian, and would ask all the world forgiveness?' Isabel shook her head, replying, 'That is all one, for he will never ask me forgiveness, therefore he shall never mend.' Afterwards, Margaret spoke to Isabel's goddaughter who said that her husband had spoken to another cunning man named Halseworths and was now satisfied that 'Isabel Robey was no witch' but then added, 'I think that my husband will never mend until he has asked her forgiveness, that's my opinion.' He then said that when he needed to ask Isabel's forgiveness, he would, but he didn't see any reason to do so.

Margaret Lyon told Gerard that she believed Chaddock was putting on a front, for his wife had told her privately that Isabel 'had done him much hurt', and that he was afraid of meeting her, and when he did, in the lane, he had turned back rather than face her. Chaddock evidently changed his mind towards Isabel's culpability between then and speaking to Gerard, whose third witness was a woman named Jane Wilkinson. As was so often the case in witchcraft accusations, she had refused an entreaty from Isabel for a little milk. When they met again afterwards, Jane experienced a sudden urge to vomit and could hardly stay on her feet. The following day, while she was travelling to Warrington, she felt an invisible hand 'pinch' her thigh, 'with four fingers and a thumb twice together' and vomited again. She made the return journey on horseback and recovered slowly.

The final witness, Margaret Parre, probably saved the day for Gerard. Without her testimony, it is difficult to see how he could have hoped to successfully prosecute Isabel. But Margaret recounted how Isabel had come to her house and Margaret asked how Peter Chaddock was faring. Isabel answered that she knew not, for she did not visit him.

Margaret then enquired after Jane Wilkinson, whom she suspected of having been bewitched. Isabel then suddenly blurted out, 'I have bewitched her too.' Margeret's response was surely aimed at staying any thoughts Isabel might entertain regarding cursing her, for she declared that she knew she could bless herself from all witches and defy them. To which Isabel replied, 'Would you defy me?'

Potts tells us that Isabel was charged with having 'practised, exercised and used her devilish and wicked arts called Witchcrafts, Enchantments, Charms and Sorceries'. Who had instigated proceedings against her is not recorded, but Gerard was pleased enough with the material he had and arranged for Isabel to be sent on to Lancaster.

The stage was now largely set for England's most notorious witch trial.

Part IV:

PARLIAMENT OF
ROOKS

'As to the Story now to tell
The Truth I will Declare,
It was the Witches' Children small
That they did not Beware;
For God into these Infants' Hearts
Did pour the Light of Reason,
And all against their Mothers spoke
Of Witchcraft and of Treason . . .'
A Newe Ballad of the Life and Deaths of Three Witches
Arrayned and Executed at Chelmsford 5 July 1589.

Chapter Eighteen

CITY OF SCAFFOLDS

Henry II had begun the practice of judges travelling through England on recognised circuits in 1166. The court system thus took to the road, enabling royal justice and the laws of central government to be dispensed throughout the country at a series of assizes rather than all in Westminster. The system remained in place until 1971. By 1550 England was divided for judicial purposes into six circuits – Home, Midland, Norfolk, Northern, Oxford and Western – with two judges allocated to each circuit. The assizes were twice yearly, Lent and summer, and although the criminal cases attracted the most attention, the courts also dealt with other matters, such as civil actions. The Northern Circuit was regarded as the least desirable on account of the wild, vast tracts of land that had to be traversed to reach its towns; occasionally the judges had to travel by horseback due to the roads being unfit for carriages. Those assigned to the Northern Circuit were known as the Red Judges, working in areas so lawless that armed escorts were provided.

On the morning of 27 July 1612, 'a great many poor, distressed people' waited in the cells of York Castle for the assizes to decide their fates.[335] The place was in an execrable state of decay; its prisoners had to rely on 'the charity of well-disposed persons', otherwise they had scarcely 'a bit of bread or a drop of drink' except that which they were 'compelled to buy of the keepers of the prison' for extortionate sums.[336]

That summer, Jennet Preston found herself once more incarcerated at York Castle, having walked free – or so it had seemed – only two months earlier. One hundred and seventeen cases of charming, sorcery and witchcraft were brought before the church courts in York between 1567 and 1640: most revolved around telling fortunes through divination, finding lost property and removing charms. The more serious cases were heard at the assizes, such as the charge Jennet found herself facing: 'that she feloniously had practised, used, and exercised, diverse wicked and devilish arts, called Witchcrafts, Enchantments, Charms, and Sorceries, in and upon one Thomas Lister of Westby in Craven, in the County of York Esquire, and by force of the same Witchcraft, feloniously the said Thomas Lister had killed'. Her plea of not guilty was recorded.

Hearing Jennet's case was Sir James Altham of Oxhey Place in Hertfordshire. In his late fifties, Altham was Essex born but of Yorkshire stock, and the son of a former sheriff of London and Essex. Educated at Cambridge alongside his brothers, his legal career began in 1575. Having served briefly as an MP in Sussex, in 1595 he was put forward for the post of Recorder of London and described by the Lord Mayor as 'very well thought of for his honesty and skill in law, both throughout the whole City and elsewhere', who felt that 'her most excellent Majesty . . . will take very good liking of him'.[337] Altham failed to achieve the post – twice – but was knighted and made Baron of the Exchequer in 1607.

That year he presided over his first witchcraft case. Blanche Worman, of Moulsham in Chelmsford, was accused of murdering three men and three women over a period of four years. Following a guilty verdict, Altham sentenced her to death, and she was hanged on the gallows at Rainsford Lane in Chelmsford on 23 March 1607. Altham was appointed to the Northern Circuit that same year. His occasional difference with the king aside, he was an avowed upholder of the Protestant Church and regarded as 'a good, learned and discreet judge, of great estimation for his wisdom, gravity, affability and order'.[338] In 1611, Altham was consulted by the

Lord Chancellor Ellesmere on two cases of heresy. Both men were burnt to death as a result – the last such cases in England. Three months after the second immolation, Altham returned to the Northern Circuit and took his seat in the court at York Castle.

As Jennet Preston glanced about the room, she no doubt recognised her prosecutor: forty-five-year-old magistrate Thomas Heber – Thomas Lister's father-in-law. This unorthodox and certainly unethical state of affairs could not have gone unnoticed by their contemporaries and colleagues, yet nothing was said about the need for impartiality in law. Jennet must surely have known but was in no position to challenge Lister and Heber. But William Preston, her husband, was present and Potts records that he protested vigorously in court – if not specifically about the relationship between prosecutor and pursuant, then about the crookedness of the case generally. But presumably he waited until after the verdict and asked those – and there was quite a crowd – who had accompanied him to support his wife to do the same. Potts, naturally, regarded Heber as the 'best instructed of any man of all the particular points of evidence against her'. There is a distinct whiff of irony in that expression.

The jury was sworn in, having been selected by the sheriffs (York habitually had two until regulations altered in 1835): William Watter, a saddler in his 'regular' profession, and Thomas Agar, a tanner. Both men later served as Lord Mayors of York. Their duties dispensed, proceedings now began in earnest, with the first witness, Lister's loyal servant, Anne Robinson, telling the court how she had been present at the elder Lister's deathbed, when he had wailed 'in great extremity' that Jennet 'laid heavy' upon him before he 'departed, crying out against her'. Heber then led her on to a discussion about the elder Lister being laid out after death. Prompted, Anne declared that when Jennet touched the corpse, it 'bled fresh blood'. Thomas Lister's evidence more or less echoed everything that had been said by Anne.

Jennet's visit to Malkin Tower was brought up, and the jury were told that the next three witnesses would not appear in court, but their depositions had been received to be read out at the York Assizes. Jennet could not contest what was said by James, Elizabeth and eleven-year-old Jennet Device; she simply had to listen. If Nowell was in court that day in York – perhaps with his fellow justice Nicholas Bannister – he must surely have been convinced that not allowing Jennet to give her evidence in person had been the correct decision: he simply could not risk 'spooking' her in that first appearance in court whether because she was intimidated by the whole experience or to prevent her from fully grasping that her words might result in an execution. Her statement, and that of her mother, added little but supported part of James's more substantial evidence, which concerned the Good Friday meeting and Jennet's arrival with a spirit 'like unto a white foal, with a black spot in the forehead'. The court listened to his account of Jennet successfully convincing her fellow Good Friday diners to assist her in the murders of Thomas Lister the younger and Uncle Leonard and how she had offered to make them a meal at her house the year after.

James had lastly identified Jennet in a face-to-face meeting in the presence of Constable Henry Hargreaves, who was himself interviewed on 5 May by Nowell, Bannister and Robert Holden. The three justices of the peace took a statement from him regarding Anne Whittle's declaration that she knew Jennet Preston and would have expected her to be at the Malkin Tower meeting, adding further that she regarded Jennet as 'an ill [wicked] woman, and had done Master Lister of Westby great hurt'. But it was unclear whether she was referring to the elder or younger Lister. Nowell's choice of assistants when taking Hargreaves' statement is interesting, for yet again there was a close familial relationship between the two men: Holden lived at Holden Hall in Haslingden with his wife, Alice Bannister – daughter of his colleague Nicholas Bannister. The interconnecting nature of all these relationships resembles the endless ripples that appear when a stone is thrown into water.

All evidence dispensed with, Judge Altham directed his thoughts towards the jury, instructing them 'to observe the particular circumstances; first, Master Lister in his great extremity, to complain he saw her, and requested them that were by him to lay hold on her, after he cried out that she lay heavy upon him, even at the time of his death'. Secondly, he told the jury, that 'of more consequence than all the rest', was the testimony that Lister's corpse had begun to bleed when Jennet touched him'. He accepted that without question, along with the remainder of the evidence, making it plain that the jury could convict Jennet on everything they had heard that day.

Despite Altham's decisive summing up, the gentlemen of the jury spent 'most part of the day' deliberating what they had heard – an unusually lengthy period in that era, plainly suggesting that they were not nearly so convinced by the evidence, or Altham's direction. But eventually they filed back into court, where Jennet's husband was sitting tensely among his wife's supporters, finding it difficult to keep his emotions under control but praying desperately that his wife and the mother of his children would be granted her liberty once more.

But this time it was not to be. The jury delivered their verdict of guilty, and as the court erupted, Judge Altham turned towards Jennet, solemnly declaring that she would be hanged for her offence.

'And so, the court arose,' wrote Potts, reminding his readers, 'Forget not the blood that cries out unto God for revenge, bring it not upon your own heads . . . I would always entreat you to remember, that it is as great a crime (as *Salomon* sayeth, *Prov.* 17) to condemn the innocent, as to let the guilty escape free. Look not upon things strangely alleged, but judiciously consider what is justly proved against them.' It was the only occasion throughout *Discoverie* when he quoted directly from the Bible and its placement was quite deliberate, for it mirrored precisely how King James had also reminded his readers in the closing pages of *Daemonologie* that judges should be mindful of whom they convicted: 'For it is as great a crime (as Salomon sayeth) to condemn the innocent, as to let the guilty escape free.'[339]

'City of Scaffolds', they used to call York. The city makes many legitimate historical claims, but few are so grim as owning the most gallows within its boundaries. The first clear records of executions in York date back to the thirteenth century, and it is said that the first operational gallows stood near the north bank of the Ouse, at St Mary's Abbey within the city walls. Another stood at St Leonard's Hospital, once the largest of its kind in medieval northern England; a third within the precincts of York Minster, which also had its own prison, and at Tyburn, on the boggy boundary adjacent to the road leading south to London. At least four more gallows have been recorded, but the one at Tyburn remains the most infamous, and it was certainly the most industrious, much to the consternation of visitors, who would often be confronted by the sight of limp bodies left hanging from the ropes.

The Tyburn site came into use after a dispute arose with the monks of St Mary's Abbey. In 1379, the city's aldermen decided to construct a proper, working gallows to serve York and selected a spot on the Knavesmire. A gibbet post was already in situ, on which the bodies of executed felons would be left in chains to serve as a warning, but which often became the site of revelry. When convicted killer Tom Otter was gibbeted in 1806, people picnicked around the body, which was left hanging until it blew down almost fifty years later; before then, a bird built its nest in a cavity in his jaw, sparking the rhyme: 'Nine tongues within one head,/The tenth went out to seek some bread,/To feed the living in the dead.'[340] Gibbeting in England came to an end in 1834.

The new gallows for York was built opposite the access to York Moor, an ancient common, now called Little Hob Moor, and fixed into place on 7 March 1379, just under two miles from the castle. Three legs supported the timber triangle, and it was known as both 'the three-legged mare' and 'the thieves' gallows' until it became York Tyburn after the gallows at Marble Arch in London. For over four hundred years, those condemned to hang would be executed there, leaving the remaining gallows in other parts of the city to rot. The first hanging occurred shortly after its construction in 1379 and the last in 1801 – and in both cases the condemned man was a soldier convicted of rape.[341] Less than ten years before Jennet Preston was executed there, the area was also used to house plague victims in makeshift huts on Hob Moor. People would leave food for them near the plague stone, which still bears the depression where coins were left in water or vinegar as payment, hoping the liquid would destroy the disease.

Hangmen later became infamous in their own right, but at this time they were referred to simply as 'the Common Hangman' or 'the Executioner'. Most had permanent positions in a particular town or city and would carry out other punishments dictated by the court: beheading, pressing to death, drawing and quartering, burning, branding, mutilating, whipping and pillorying. Hangmen usually earned a small wage and commission for each individual he punished or executed. Then there were bonuses: collections were sometimes taken on the hangman's behalf, and he could cut the noose into sections for selling on to the public. He was allowed to keep the clothing of those whom he executed, either for himself or to sell, which led to some condemned prisoners kicking off their shoes into the crowd to deny him a sale. When Sir Thomas More dressed for his execution in 1535, he put on his finest silk robes until the Lieutenant of the Tower of London advised him to change into something more simple and less expensive; More did as he was advised.

Often, hangmen were figures of derision, particularly those who mishandled an execution, which might lead to furious beatings from the public. It was sometimes difficult to find men 'of good character' to take the position, which led to felons and drunkards carrying out the task. Hangmen in York tended to be pardoned criminals. But for others, the role was one they enjoyed, largely for its notoriety. Playing up to the festival atmosphere of public executions, with chapbook sellers and street vendors hawking their wares noisily, a professional hangman recognised the spectacle of the event and often behaved much like a theatrical villain or the main act at a show which, in effect, they were. At the original Tyburn in London, stands were constructed to give the spectators somewhere to sit while tenants in the houses overlooking the gallows could earn a tidy sum charging visitors for the privilege of watching from a window. Later, special 'execution' trains were laid on to carry those from farther afield into the city; these would be heaving with people chatting excitedly about the day ahead. The two-mile journey from Newgate Gaol to Tyburn could take up to three hours due to the press of crowds.

For those condemned to die in York, wooden sledges and hurdles were used to convey them along the journey, occasionally travelling with their own coffins. If several were to be executed, they travelled by cart, guarded by a sheriff, officers and as many as thirty dragoons on either side. Boisterous crowds would accompany them through the streets over Ouse Bridge, up along Micklegate and on towards the Knavesmire where a vast throng would likewise be waiting, often drinking and carousing, then jostling to get the best view from the top of the slope. The hanging of large groups was a particular draw: in 1600 a multiple hanging of smugglers and killers attracted around six thousand spectators. Unsurprisingly, there were scenes of uproar along the route. In 1649, a couple who were to be executed together for murder departed the castle in a cart at 7.30 a.m. but struggled to pass along Castlegate because the throng was so deep: 'Nothing could be seen but a forest of hats, and in the Pavement the people had to form a passage for the cart to pass through, the crowd pulling off their hats as the solemn cavalcade passed by. In turning to Fossgate, the street was one mass of human beings. One woman had her leg broken in the crowd, and a young man had his thigh broken; both were removed to a doctor.'[342]

On 30 April 1649, another twenty-one people, most of whom were condemned for 'rebellion' left the castle for the Knavesmire. Among them was thirty-two-year-old Isabella Billington; she and her husband were convicted of crucifying her mother at the town of Pocklington, east of York, on 5 January. They were said to have killed a cock and a calf as a 'burnt offering'. Imprisoned at York Castle, they were found guilty of witchcraft and sentenced to death at the Lent Assizes. Isabella's husband did not hang with her, but fourteen men and six women were listed to die alongside her, and a huge crowd gathered near the gaol to follow. An account of the journey and execution provides a chilling insight into Jennet Preston's last moments on earth:

On entering Castlegate, that street appeared one mass of human beings, and the solemn procession was stopped for some time before it could proceed, the people were so closely jammed together. The whole of the twenty-one culprits joined as one voice in singing psalms from this street to the gallows. They were stopped several times in Micklegate by reason of the great number of spectators that thronged the road to the Tyburn . . . they arrived at the place of execution at ten minutes past ten o'clock . . . All seemed firm but resigned to their fate, and after being engaged for a short time in devotional exercises, they all gave themselves up to the hands of the executioner, and in about five minutes, twenty-one lifeless corpses were hanging suspended between earth and heaven. It was a most awful scene – a terrible day, and thousands witnessed the dreadful spectacle.[343]

Executed as a witch, Isabella was both hanged and then her body burnt, as was the case with most of those who died on the scaffold.[344] Some were handed to surgeons in York and Hull for dissection and to be anatomised, though a surprising number were buried in churchyards and a rare few were returned to their relatives for private funerals. Some felons were hung, drawn and quartered, while others were also decapitated; their severed heads were then impaled on a spike atop Micklegate Bar to serve as an example to all.

For a time, people were encouraged to attend executions, in part because the authorities felt that it would act as a deterrent. In 1731, the first annual horse races were held on the Knavesmire, deliberately timed in August to coincide with the assizes and attendant hangings; crowds could thus observe the executions and then stroll across the grass to enjoy the races, which subsequently became part of the society calendar. But there were strong objections to such behaviour, and from 1802 felons were hanged at the new drop at the assize courts. Seven years later, on 20 March 1809, Mary Bateman, known as 'the Yorkshire Witch', was executed there after being convicted of murder by poisoning. Her corpse was displayed in public, where thousands paid to gaze upon it while strips of her skin were sold as charms to protect from evil. The proceeds were given to charity. Three years later, the Knavesmire gallows was finally dismantled.[345]

But the Tyburn tree was still standing on 29 July 1612. Two days after being sentenced to death, Jennet Preston was led out to the execution cart in the shadow of York Castle. There would have been crowds, no doubt, eager to catch a glimpse of another Yorkshire witch who carried the added frisson of being associated with a pack of witches from Pendle.

The rattling cart followed a well-trodden route through the city streets, where all was clamour, frenzy and confusion, until the buildings grew less, and the roads widened. The first sight of Hob Moor caused a frantic mutter of prayer to burst out from those sitting with Jennet inside the cart. The wheels slowed and turned towards the path where the crowd gathered, baying, on a telling rise.

Today, the site of Jennet Preston's execution on York's Knavesmire has forgotten her. People still gather there in their thousands, but only to watch horses thundering across unseen graves.

'Tyburn' is inscribed on a low, squat block of grey stone sitting like an afterthought on the rise. An information board recounts the tale, but there is no mention of Jennet. There is of Dick Turpin, whom the information board describes without a trace of irony as 'not famous in his lifetime' or until his 'legend was created by Harrison Ainsworth in his novel *Rookwood*, published in 1834, almost a hundred years after Turpin's death'.

The same Ainsworth who penned *The Lancashire Witches*.

But still no mention of Jennet.

Chapter Nineteen

WICKED PERSUASIONS

James Altham was extremely glad to be leaving York. After Jennet Preston's trial, he met up with his younger colleague Edward Bromley, then in his early forties. Shropshire-born, Bromley came from a family whose backgrounds were in law; his father had been chief justice for Chester and treasurer for the Inner Temple, while his uncle was ex-Lord Chancellor Thomas Bromley, who had presided over the trial of Mary, Queen of Scots. Edward Bromley had been appointed surveyor on lands in the southern area of the Duchy of Lancaster in 1607 and was thus familiar with the county prior to being assigned to the Northern Circuit in 1610. More mild-mannered than his colleague Altham, he was dismissively referred to as 'an obscure lawyer of the Inner Temple' on being made a Baron of the Exchequer in 1610.[346] Aware of such views, he hoped to progress to one of the better regarded Southern Circuits but needed to win the king's favour to realistically stand a chance. His Puritanical nature is evidenced by his signature on the 1617 petition for the banning of all Sunday sports in Lancashire that was delivered to the king by northern reformers.

The Red Judges travelled by carriage, heading north to Durham, with the two men having much to discuss. Bromley had never sentenced anyone to death for the crime of witchcraft and may have been somewhat apprehensive of the task that waited for them on the last sitting of the circuit. Altham, whose severity was known even to the king, had been taken aback by events in York. Bromley listened as his colleague spoke of having been in the eye of the hurricane surrounding the execution of the woman that he himself had recently acquitted of witchcraft. The trial had ended chaotically as the condemned woman's husband shouted about the terrible miscarriage of justice taking place.

Afterwards, Altham learnt that William Preston and his family and friends had vowed to spread the word about Jennet's wrongful execution. No doubt they would be planning on making another scene at Lancaster, and causing great embarrassment to the Listers, who had suffered so much already. Those were Altham's views; he simply could not understand the outcry over a woman who had been given enough chances, especially when, just a week before he sentenced her to death, five people had been executed for witchcraft in Northampton. Altham rumbled on as loudly as the wheels of their carriage. From Durham they travelled to Newcastle and then west to Carlisle and Kendal, before the final twenty-five mile journey south to Lancaster, where Thomas Covell was already well prepared for their arrival.

It was a considerable undertaking, particularly in Lancashire, with its lavish tradition of the Sheriff's Table, where the JPs would dine in grand style with the high sheriff and occasionally the judges, ostensibly to discuss any issues in the county that needed airing. The records of the Sheriff's Table in August 1612 have been misplaced, but those for Lent that year show that Roger Nowell was in attendance.[347] Twenty years later, when Thomas Covell is thought to have been steward at the castle, he secured a contract to provide all the food and refreshments for the judges and their entourages at the assizes.[348] He was also to supply most of the tableware and items such as wine, sugar and venison. His brother Edmund was running The George during the 1630s, on the upper end, south side of Market Street, and given Covell's excessively shrewd business acumen, in all likelihood the two brothers had some agreement regarding supplies, which benefitted them both.

Sir Cuthbert Halsall was Sheriff of Lancaster from March 1612 through to March 1613. 'Bad Sir Cuthbert' as he was later known, was an English politician from a very old Lancashire family whose already substantial estate increased with his marriage. He was knighted by the Earl of Essex at Dublin in 1599, having served alongside him in the military in Ireland. He had held the office of sheriff previously, in 1601, but was removed under suspicion of Catholicism. Ever ambitious, he conformed and was able to pursue his career again until his life fell hopelessly into ruins following his addiction to gambling. Before then, in 1612, it was his duty to handpick the jury for the trial from local men of good standing, with responsibilities to their community, such as constables or coroners. A jury could consist of thirteen men and as many as twenty-three. There is a theory that – particularly given his dubious character – he 'rigged' the jury to assure a beneficial outcome for those who saw an opportunity to curry favour with the king and advance their own reputations.

On Sunday, 16 August 1612, Judges Bromley and Altham arrived in Lancaster. It was a far more muted greeting than in York, but nonetheless, there were officials and worthies to meet and welcome them. Bromley and Altham were joined that day by Thomas Covell, who presented them with the gaol calendar containing the list of prisoners for the assizes; there would have been far more names than the list included in *Discoverie*, which only shows those accused of witchcraft. A decision had been made – possibly in the light of events in York – that Bromley would preside over the criminal cases, including the witchcraft indictments. The judges were then shown to their lodgings, close to Castle Hill.

The Lancaster Assizes began on Monday, 17 August, but it was not until the following day that the group from Pendle and those associated with them were brought up to be arraigned. Clad in their scarlet robes, Bromley and Altham attended a church service with the sheriff and his entourage. The chaplain delivered a lengthy sermon, after which crowds began to convene in and around the castle, for the opening of the assizes and the first batch of prisoners to be arraigned.

In the dungeons far below, the prisoners were brought to their feet.

The Devices, Anne Whittle and her daughter, the Bulcocks, Alice Nutter, Katherine Hewitt, Alice Gray, Margaret Pearson and Isobel Robey all moved forward with their fellow prisoners. Months of mistreatment, physical and psychological trauma and the knowledge that their lives might end on the gallows must have rendered them in an unimaginably disturbed state. Out from the belly of the castle, through the open courtyard with its stark sunlight and draughts of clearer air, they were led into the medieval hall. On the ground floor were the stables, where the clip of hooves against wood sounded.[349]

And then they waited.

The judges habitually made a grand entrance, despite the huge majority of courtrooms being housed in ancient buildings that were all but collapsing. Judges frequently complained about the potential danger to life, along with the lack of comfort. Although the old courtroom at Lancaster was small in comparison to more modern counterparts in the castle, it was adequate. Where possible, the judges liked to be sat on a raised bench with county magnates. The rest of the congregation would usually be arranged about a table in order of ranking, with the jury box behind and the prisoners' dock a few feet away.

When everyone was in place, the court crier asked for silence to allow the clerk to read out the commission.

Thomas Potts got to his feet.

As the clerk of court, he headed a small team that was responsible for the administration of the circuit, its smooth operation, various clerical tasks such as drafting indictments and producing examinations and witness statements in court when needed. A sound working knowledge of the law was vital; some clerks were barristers until they assumed office, when they were prohibited from practising on their circuit. Thomas Potts had sufficient legal training to be efficient, but neither a university education, nor – contrary to claims elsewhere – was he listed among any of the Inns of Court. But he was, nonetheless, an extremely well-placed and well-connected clerk.

His was a sought-after position, with a good income, despite expenses – including stationery – and plenty of scope for improved prospects, although 'most clerks probably contented themselves with the modest gentility and opportunities conferred by their office'.[350] *A History of the English Assizes* explains the role more fully:

> By the mid 17th century the clerk of assize had emerged as a virtually full-time administrative official, responsible for the coordination of a compact and highly professional administrative department. He had also developed a certain self-conscious dignity and subtly effective methods of reminding provincial officials of the prerequisites of his office. As an outgoing Northumberland undersheriff warned his successor in 1661, it was wise to accommodate the assize clerk with a venison pasty and a 'pottle' of wine during the assizes and to make sure that the clerk was paid his fee for the gaol calendar.

Once Thomas Potts was seated again, Sir Cuthbert Halsall rose to return the writs of assize and *nisi prius* ('unless before' – cases which might take priority) together with a calendar containing the names of the justices of the peace, mayors of corporations, coroners, constables and bailiffs, etc. All those entered were obliged to attend and any absences would be noted. Officials then handed in their records.

Historian and witch trials expert Marion Gibson explains how Potts tries to dazzle us with pomp and circumstance and the heroizing of the judges. The latter, especially, prompts him to omit sections of process that we now would want to know. Thus, he recreates Judge Bromley's entry into the hall and the issuing of his proclamation, then omits the convoluted but intrinsic procedures of submitting the indictments to the grand jury. These indictments – the charges against each prisoner – were written mainly in a distinctive form of Latin. The jury had to decide whether there was a case to answer, marking them either 'ignoramous' ('we do not know' – no further action), or 'prima facie' and therefore 'billa vera' ('a true bill').[351] This also necessitated the hearing of evidence from witnesses and the reading of suspects' examinations. The jury at Lancaster decided each indictment was a true bill.

The suspects were thus brought up a flight of stone stairs to an open door and a cacophony of voices. Below the vaulted ceiling, in a space that seemed too small for the jurymen and judges, quite apart from the number of spectators, the prisoners lined up. Light slanted into the room from the arched window; among the cramped benches and tables they could see Roger Nowell, his stern-faced coterie and the fearful faces of family and friends.

The translated indictments were read out for each person to enter their plea. Anyone remaining mute would be regarded as having confessed; those who stayed silent on charges of felony were until 1772 pressed to death. Those who replied 'not guilty' were asked how they wished to be tried and gave the standard response: that they would put themselves on God and their country. Prisoners were arraigned until there were enough for a jury to try. Much like today's trials, statements would be read out and witnesses examined; unlike today's trials, there was no defence council. The judge was expected to be impartial and preside over a fair trial whose outcome was for the jury to decide – although judges could and did overrule their verdicts.

Again, Gibson is our guide in explaining how *Discoverie* distorts our understanding of what took place. Potts presents each person's indictment with the material pertaining to their charges, giving the impression that each suspect was afforded individual consideration. But courts were frantically overworked; cases tried on the Home Circuit, for instance, on average took no more than twenty minutes to be heard – and that included time for a jury to consider their verdict. Judges often processed as many as fifty cases in one day. Those who pleaded guilty saved the court time; they were set aside until sentencing.

Alizon Device attempted to enter a guilty plea, but the judge insisted on hearing all the evidence against her, nonetheless. If Bromley had intended to create a dramatic set piece, he could not have wished for it to be more effective.

Unbeknown to Alizon, pedlar John Law was waiting with his son

Abraham in the Moot Hall assembly place. Thomas Gerard asked to present him as Alizon was about to answer her indictment. Potts tells us that 'the pedlar, deformed by her witchcraft, and transformed beyond the course of nature', hobbled into the court and Alizon 'saw it was in vain to deny it, or stand upon her justification. She humbly upon her knees at the Bar, with weeping tears, prayed the court to hear her.' Bromley instructed her to step forward, away from the other prisoners, and stand in the centre of the room. There, again, she fell to her knees and 'humbly asked forgiveness for her offence'. Law told the assembled court that he had 'continued lame, not able to travel or take pains' ever since she had bewitched him (despite plainly having made his way to Lancaster and into the hearing), before bursting into tears himself. He then turned to Alizon, sobbing, 'This thou knowest to be too true.' She then 'humbly acknowledged the same, and cried out to God to forgive her; and upon her knees with weeping tears, humbly prayed him to forgive her that wicked offence; which he very freely and voluntarily did'. Law's acceptance of her apology alarmed Roger Nowell, who scrambled to his feet, worried that the jury might be so moved by this display of forgiveness that they, too, might pardon Alizon. He asked the court to 'respect that this fact of witchcraft was more eminent and apparent than the rest' and to demonstrate that, he had Abraham Law's examination read out, giving full vent to how Alizon's cursing had destroyed the pedlar, whose body was 'able to endure no travel, and thus remains at this present time'. Again, despite Law standing before them.

At this point, Alizon was asked whether she could use her powers to 'help the poor pedlar [return] to his former strength and health'. Alizon replied that she could not, and when the request was put to the other witchcraft suspects, they likewise demurred. But Alizon then did something quite extraordinary: in a courageous show of defiance, she told the court that if her grandmother, Elizabeth Southerns, had lived, then she 'could and would have helped him out of that great misery'. Other voices joined hers, and for a moment the court was forced to reflect upon Elizabeth's death in the underground cell.

Then Bromley returned them to the present, and Alizon's predicament. She now 'humbly acknowledged the indictment against her to be true'. She thus pleaded guilty, confirming that she 'justly deserved death' for that and 'many other' offences, 'whereupon she was carried away, until she should come to the Bar to receive her judgement of death'.

Before proceedings continued, Judge Bromley turned to those wealthy gentleman who had observed the 'lamentable spectacle' and asked if they were willing to make some contribution to Law's 'relief and maintenance'. Thomas Gerard and Sir Richard Houghton were among those who agreed to do so – in another highly unusual turn of events. Bromley thanked them and turned back to the matters in hand.

Few trials were without their moments of intense emotion. Most were 'nasty, brutish, and essentially short'. They could be extremely chaotic, filled with clamour, with judges struggling to get to their seats through a hot press of bodies. If fights broke out, it was often the judge who had to try to restore order by pulling the brawlers apart. In one courtroom a gun went off; in another the floor collapsed under the weight of so many people present and, at Hereford in 1588, a man was murdered in front of the judge. Most of the time, the people on trial could scarcely hear or understand what was being said about them and 'against this colourful background Crown pleas were conducted at top speed, a full day's business beginning, even in winter, at seven o'clock in the morning and continuing, by candlelight, as late as eleven at night'.[352] Amid the grotesquely carnival-like atmosphere, adjournments would be announced with trumpets. The sheriff's men with their halberds in their hands, followed by under-sheriffs holding their white wands, would then accompany the judge as he swept out of the room for respite at his lodgings.

But on the morning of 18 August, once the pleas had been fully entered, the jury were sworn in, and the cases were then put before them. Potts, naturally, discards this information and habitually presents evidence as if each prisoner were speaking in court, but most of what was heard came from the examinations that had been made previously – in some cases, several months before. Potts occasionally slips up in his presentation, and we grasp that the prisoner's words are being read. But sometimes it is impossible to decide which parts of the statements are spoken, after they had been expertly written up by Roger Nowell. He, like all other examining magistrates, was responsible for editing the interviews that he had conducted, shaping each examination into something salient, concise and coherent. Then came the painstaking process of extracting passages relevant to the charges against each individual, cross-referencing them and creating a new set of documents for each defendant. At the end of the process, Nowell had been left with a vast collection of papers containing much repetition but with a logical form, nevertheless. After he had delivered the material to the assizes, the clerk – Thomas Potts – had then organised it once more for the prosecution. The vast majority of those passages in *Discoverie* that are presented as if spoken in court, had in fact gone through a rigorous editing process.

Anne Whittle had no interest in saving herself. Remarkably, despite all she had endured, she remained utterly focused on attempting to convince judge and jury that her daughter, Anne Redfearn, had had no involvement in Robert Nutter's death. She managed this convincingly, with Potts grudgingly admitting that she 'was never found to vary, but always to agree in one, and the self-same thing'. Elsewhere he tells us that she was unintelligible in court, but at the same time, lucid and to the point. There would certainly have been issues with communication, however: many more dialects existed then, varying from region to region, even from village to village, and there was a distinct north-south divide. The suspects would have spoken a form of dialect that no longer exists and probably sounded incomprehensible to anyone from London. But certainly Nowell and other local landowners would have had sufficient contact with people deemed their 'inferiors' to grasp what was being said.

Anne Whittle very nearly succeeded in saving her daughter from the scaffold. Even Thomas Potts was forced to admit that the case for

Anne Redfearn having murdered Robert Nutter was 'not very pregnant against her'.[353] He tells us that 'upon Tuesday night', nonetheless to his surprise, 'by the favour and merciful consideration of the jury . . . she was acquitted and found not guilty'. For Anne's husband and daughter, and other family and friends who were all sat tensely awaiting the verdict, the news was greeted ecstatically. Anne Whittle was no doubt overwhelmed that her daughter was saved. But for Roger Nowell, the acquittal at the end of the day was a punch to the stomach, and a reminder that for all his efforts, guilty verdicts were not a given.

Sometimes, they required a little manipulation.

Our focus is on those individuals known well to each other from the Pendle area, together with Margaret Pearson and Isabel Robey. They all stood charged with murder by witchcraft, except for Isabel, and John and Jane Bulcock: none of them were accused, or would be convicted, of taking a life. But in the midst of their trials came another: that of the Samlesbury witches.

Chapter Twenty

THE AXE LAID TO
THE TREE

Around thirteen miles south-west of Pendle Hill is the old Catholic village of Samlesbury. On its outskirts stands the magnificent Samlesbury Hall, once the home of the Southworth family. In his *History of Whalley*, Whitaker observes: 'There is about the house a profusion and bulk of oak that must almost have laid prostrate a forest to erect it.'[354] The original Lower Hall, north of the village and on the bend of the River Ribble, was destroyed in 1322 during a Scottish raid led by Robert the Bruce. It was rebuilt, probably as a dower house to Samlesbury Hall – then the Upper Hall – which remained in the ownership of the Southworths until it was sold in 1789.

The Samlesbury case is much darker than that of Pendle. In some respects, it bears little resemblance to other witch trials of the age. The Sowerbutts are the Devices of the story, but they were neither desperately poor nor wealthy, and the same is true of most of those involved in the case, apart from the Southworths. There were no long-held and heartfelt festering resentments, no gradual escalation of accusations, and no refusals of charity. The accusations, when they came, were sudden and explosive, and like the tail-end of a firework, then revealed both undercurrents of family tension, since the allegations were made by a young girl, accusing her aunt and grandmother of unimaginable horrors, and further, outright dislike from an elderly man towards his grandson's young wife. But these served as a smokescreen for something on a much larger and more abhorrent scale – if, that is, the truth really was revealed in the outcome of the case at Lancaster Assizes.

Where the Pendle case is more relatable in its origins, and was as mundane in some senses as it was fantastical in others – all quarrelling neighbours, umbrages both real and imagined, and often the result of clashing social classes – elements within the Samlesbury indictments reflect more closely the demonic crimes laid out by the *Malleus Maleficarum*: the purposeful murder of infants, witches with vampiric tendencies, supernatural flight, coven gatherings and sexual abandon. When the smokescreen dispersed after the chaos of the courtroom suddenly seemed to lay bare reality, the story was revealed to be one of vengeful popery. Or at least, our erstwhile narrator Thomas Potts presents it as such, with his permanent quest to promote the tenets of Church and Crown, as Deborah Lea explains in *Witchcraft, Possession and Confessional Tension in Early Modern Lancashire*:

> Potts's account tackles popular superstitions and illustrates the fate awaiting those who persist in pursuing their erroneous ways. With Samlesbury we are encountering another of the problems which were perceived as plaguing Lancashire, Catholic missionaries. Here their deceptive and dangerous nature is displayed as three innocent women are persecuted, a young girl corrupted. It is only by analysing the Pendle and Samlesbury trials side by side that we appreciate how significant a publication Potts's pamphlet was. This was not merely a titillating tale of supernatural curiosities in the provinces. It was a parable designed to accord with a monarch's policies and illustrate that the path to salvation and security lay only with the established church.[355]

The Southworths were one of Lancashire's leading recusant families. Their name and location appeared on Lord Burghley's 1590 map of the county's 'subversive Catholic elements', commissioned due to the paranoia that another Gunpowder Plot might be in the offing.[356] Most of the Southworths remained true to their faith, despite paying out a fortune in fines, and the repeated arrest of the family's head, Sir John, who was involved in the plot to oust Queen Elizabeth from her throne and replace her with Mary, her Roman Catholic sister. Sir John 'rendered himself conspicuous by his violent opposition to the reformed faith' and was 'held in high esteem by those involved in papal intrigue' – and thus loathed among many Protestants.[357]

Married to Sir Richard Assheton's daughter, Mary – whose brother Anne Whittle claimed had been murdered by Elizabeth Southerns – Sir John was sent to London for questioning by Dean Nowell – Roger Nowell's great uncle. He spent a brief period overseas but shortly after his return he was arrested for harbouring a Jesuit priest at Samlesbury Hall and was imprisoned at Manchester's New Fleet Gaol. He was released and then re-arrested and imprisoned twice: 'His downfall almost came as a result of the impossibly large sum of fines he had to pay as a result of his recusancy, which had been brought in as part of the 1581 Act. In order to save his estates, he attended a Protestant church from time to time.'[358]

Nevertheless, in 1586 Sir John and his family, together with more than thirty servants, were reported to the authorities for, among other offences of a religious nature, holding daily masses at the lodge in Samlesbury Park. The fact that the Southworths appeared on Lord Burghley's 1590 map confirms that they remained under suspicion until November 1592, when the local justice of the peace headed a dawn raid on Samlesbury Hall. Although no priests were found sequestered about the place, the authorities discovered a secret vault over the dining chamber containing brass candlesticks 'of the fashion used in the time of superstition' (pre-Reformation).[359] Three years later, Sir John Southworth passed away, aged sixty-nine.

He and his wife had ten children, three of whom died young. Thomas, the eldest surviving son, endured a spell in gaol after hiding a Catholic priest at his lodge in Samlesbury Park, but following his marriage to Rosamund Lister – of the Westby Listers – he converted to Protestantism in common with several of his in-laws. There were rumours that his father would disinherit him, but these proved groundless. Thomas and Rosamund's son John married Jane, the illegitimate but publicly acknowledged daughter of Sir Richard Sherburne of Stonyhurst, and the Lower Hall became their home. In the years preceding his death, Sir John had taken a great dislike to Jane after learning that she had renounced her Catholicism. He refused to pass the Lower Hall lest they should meet.

Jane's husband died in 1612. She continued to live at the Lower Hall with their nine young children and appears to have been on good terms with her father-in-law, Thomas. But in April of that year, the daughter of one of the Southworths' tenants came forward with an extraordinary story involving Jane and several others.

Grace Sowerbutts was fourteen years old and lived with her mother, after whom she was named, and father, Thomas, who had built their home, Yew Tree Farm, which abutted onto a green which later became Sowerbutts Green. The family had already lived in the area for some time; in 1556, a John Sowerbutts (presumably Grace's grandfather) was charged at the manor court with 'lodging beggars and strangers' and was fined alongside Thomas Walmsley for 'making a tussle or hobbleshove' (fighting).[360] In addition to being the Southworths' tenants, the Sowerbutts were part of their Catholic circle. But there was some trouble in the family; a couple of years before the witchcraft accusations, one of Grace's siblings – her younger brother, Thomas – had been labelled 'delinquent' and the family had had their estate sequestered as a result.

Exactly when and how Grace's story was reported to the local magistrate is unknown, but from *Discoverie*, it seems that her initial examinations were held in Blackburn just after 15 April.[361] Her statements pass to us through the usual editorial process effected by the examining magistrate and then by Thomas Potts; the former just happened to be Robert Holden, of Holden Hall in Haslingden. Holden was married to Alice, daughter of his colleague Nicholas Bannister; we recall that the two men, together with Roger Nowell, were responsible for interviewing Constable Hargreaves on 5 May 1612 about Jennet Preston. Incidentally, the Holdens were Catholic, but Robert seems to have been determined to prove that he could be loyal to the Crown and made an outward show of conformity.

Grace informed Holden that for 'some years now' she had been 'haunted and vexed' by four women: her grandmother Jennet Bierley, Aunt Ellen Bierley, Jane Southworth and another, Old Doewife, of whom she said no more, except that on one occasion the four women had violently drawn her by the hair 'and laid her on the top of a hay mow, in the said Henry Bierley's barn'. Henry was Grace's uncle, married to Ellen, and ran an alehouse at their small farm, Birleys, near Turner Green. This story, like so many of Grace's tales, seems to have petered out after she was brought to the barn.

The other incidents she described were fairly recent and did not involve Jane Southworth either. In the first, she recalled meeting her grandmother near Yew Tree Farm; Jennet initially appeared to her granddaughter 'in her own likeness', but afterwards 'in the likeness of a black dog'. As Grace climbed over a stile, her grandmother pushed her but did her no harm. Grace then visited her aunt's home again where nothing untoward happened. However, when she was collected by her father, she told him that the women had mistreated her 'both then and at sundry times before that'. She had said nothing earlier because she simply 'could not speak thereof, though she desired so to do'.

Grace then told Holden about a peculiar encounter with her grandmother on Saturday, 4 April of that year. She had gone out to meet her mother, who had been in Preston, and would be returning on the ferry across the River Ribble. Hugh Walshman operated the boat, which had been in operation since 1379 and finally stopped running in 1826. He lived near the ferry on the Samlesbury side. Not far off, at the Two Bridges, Grace met her grandmother again, who appeared first as a woman and 'in the likeness of a black dog, with two legs'. The dog sidled up to walk alongside her. When they neared a pool, the dog tried to persuade Grace to drown herself, telling her it was 'a fair and an easy death'. At this moment of danger, 'there came one to her in a white sheet' who carried her to safety. Both the 'white thing' – presumably an angel – and the black dog departed.

But two or three fields further along, the black dog materialised again. It carried Grace into a nearby barn owned by ferryman Hugh Walshman and laid her on the floor. After covering her with straw, the dog lay on top of her for an indeterminate length of time, with Grace trapped below, 'her speech and senses . . . taken from her'.[362] Grace subsequently learnt that she had been 'out to it' until Monday night, 6 April. She was found by friends, who carried her into the ferryman's house to recover. Incidentally, the Walshmans were related to the Sowerbutts family, but the wives of both Hugh and Thomas (the elder of the two Walshmans) attended mass at the Lodge in Samlesbury Park.

Grace told Holden that events had continued the following day, Tuesday. During the early evening, she was collected from the ferryman's house by her parents and taken home. The next time she was out walking, she encountered her grandmother and aunt, but 'they did nothing unto her', as Holden recorded. 'Neither did she ever see them since.'

Grace then began relating for Holden the incidents that had caused her so much distress. One evening her grandmother Jennet had insisted that Grace should accompany her and Grace's aunt Ellen to Thomas Walshman's home. 'Coming thither in the night, when all the household was abed', Jennet nonetheless managed to gain access to the house. While Grace and her aunt Ellen remained inside, her grandmother 'went into the chamber where the said Walshman and his wife lay, and from thence brought a little child'. Grace told Holden how her grandmother had then made her sit by the fire with the child on her knee. Holden records what happened next: '[Jennet] did thrust a nail into the navel of the said child: and afterwards did take a [quill] pen and put it in at the said place, and did suck there a good space, and afterwards laid the child in bed again.' The women then walked Grace home. To Holden, Grace confirmed that the child's parents remained unaware of all that had occurred, 'and the said child did not cry when it was hurt'. But Grace knew that 'the said child did thenceforth languish, and not long after died'.

Grace's tales of horror – throughout which she seems to have expressed not a flicker of emotion – continued. On the evening after the burial of the Walshman child, Grace accompanied her grandmother and aunt once more at their insistence, to the graveyard at Samlesbury Church, where they disinterred the infant's body. 'Jennet did carry it out of the churchyard in her arms,' Holden duly wrote, 'and carried it home to her own house, and having it there did boil some thereof in a pot . . .' A bizarrely homely scene of cannibalism follows, with the two older women eating parts of the infant's body while both Grace and her cousin (likewise named Grace) politely refused. Afterwards, Jennet and Ellen boiled the child's bones in a pot 'and with the fat that came out of the said bones, they said they would anoint themselves, that thereby they might sometimes change themselves into other shapes'. They agreed that they should re-bury the bones in their rightful place the following night.

Unsurprisingly, the genteel Holden had heard enough at this point and brought Grace's testimony to a close. Her stories were utterly fantastical but tapped into standard tales of witchcraft in European demonology from the fifteenth century onwards. The *Malleus Maleficarum* relates how witches would kill children in their cribs or steal them from their parents, or after a traditional burial, 'secretly take them from their graves, and cook them in a cauldron, until the whole flesh comes away from the bones to make a soup which may easily be drunk.'[363] As an educated man and magistrate, Robert Holden should have had some idea that this was standard European fare.

He then called in Thomas Walshman, whose feelings at being told his child was believed to have been killed, disinterred, dismembered and eaten can scarcely be imagined. He confirmed that he and his wife had lost a one-year-old child at Lent 1611. The child had languished for two or three weeks prior to death and was buried at Samlesbury Church. Walshman appears to have said nothing condemnatory towards the Bierleys, merely confirming the incident in the barn, when Grace had been found and that after she had been brought into the house 'she did not speak, but lay as if she had been dead'.[364]

Holden examined Grace again. She returned to her final encounter with her grandmother and aunt on Tuesday 7 April, (the day after she had regained consciousness in the barn), providing fresh detail. Immediately after meeting the two women, she had fallen down 'and after that was not able to speak, or go [move] till the Friday following'.[365] During this time, as she lay at home, the two women had looked in on her but left her alone and she was certain that 'neither did she ever see them since'.[366]

None of Grace's tales had included Jane Southworth. Perhaps prompted by the magistrate, Grace related how, in late 1611, she would meet her grandmother Jennet and aunt Ellen together with Jane Southworth at Red Bank on the north side of the Ribble for two Thursday and Sunday nights in a row. In *The Famous Witches of Samlesbury*, Glen Clayton points out that the Red Bank was the 'wooded escarpment of Red Scar, around the northern bank of the Ribble's Horse Shoe Bend . . . the river is very deep around the bend and the steep bluff of Red Scar rises precipitously from the river – there is no room for a picnic, dancing or any other activity'.[367]

But to return to Grace's story: they had been carried across the water by 'four black things' that stood upright 'yet not like men in the face'. At Red Bank, there was a feast of strange food, which the three older women ate but Grace dared not for 'she never saw such meat'. After they had eaten, all four danced 'with one of the black things' and had intercourse with them. Grace was specific about this, stating that 'the black thing that was with her, did abuse her body'.

Philip C. Almond, in *The Lancashire Witches: A Chronicle of Death and Sorcery on Pendle Hill*, suggests that the experiences Grace claimed to have had implies either demonic possession or an obsession with such, particularly given her age. The majority of demoniacs in early modern England were adolescents: around two thirds were female children or adolescents and around one fifth were boys or adolescent males. Typical symptoms include being rendered completely immobile and unable to speak. Grace's evidence incorporated several of the features of demonological interpretations of witchcraft and the battle between good and evil for her body and soul, particularly the scene of the black dog urging her to commit suicide before she was rescued by a figure in a 'white sheet'. There are no accurate figures for demonic possession in this period but a reading of contemporary English literature featuring such indicates that around a hundred people experienced the phenomenon between 1550–1700.

On 15 April, Holden examined William Alker of Samlesbury, a servant of the Southworth family. He related Sir John's dislike of Jane, his grandson's wife, and how the old man had avoided meeting her. However, Alker claimed this was due to Sir John's belief that Jane would 'bewitch' him.[368] It was around this time that Jane Southworth, Jennet Bierley and Ellen Bierley were dispatched to Lancaster Castle Gaol where they were imprisoned with the Pendle suspects.

Holden was called in briefly on Jennet Preston's case before he returned to examine Grace again. Revisiting the subject of the Red Bank witches' sabbath, he asked how the women had crossed the river again afterwards. Grace replied that 'the same black things that carried them thither' brought them back, and indeed that there were 'diverse other women' at the Red Bank feast, 'some old, some young' whom she believed must dwell on the north side of the Ribble, since they had not crossed the water. But these women were like statues, for they neither ate nor danced, but simply 'looked on'.

Holden pressed her for more information regarding Jane Southworth, of whom she had said little. Grace obligingly provided him with a series of encounters that she claimed had taken place ten days after her initial examination with the magistrate at Blackburn; some of her recollections post-date Jane and her co-accused arriving in Lancaster Castle, but Holden does not appear to have made anything out of the discrepancies.

In the first incident, Grace had been away for some time at an uncle's house in Houghton and had only recently returned home to Yew Tree Farm. Seemingly out of nowhere, Holden records, Jane Southworth appeared 'and did carry her into the loft and there did lay her upon the floor, where she was shortly found by her father and brought down, and laid in a bed'. Once more, she 'had her speech and senses taken from her'. She came 'somewhat to herself', but then 'Widow Southworth came again . . . to her bedside, and took her out of bed. Grace recalled that Jane had then threatened her, telling her that she had done her no harm before compared to what she was about to do. But this appears to have amounted to nothing more sinister than Jane carrying her to a high haystack and leaving her there, 'some three or four yards high from the earth'. During an extensive search, Grace was found by a neighbour's wife, who put her to bed, 'where she remained speechless and senseless as before [for] the space of two or three days'.

One week later, Jane Southworth appeared again at Yew Tree Farm. Again, the tedious business of carrying Grace away from her home ensued, but this time Jane laid Grace 'in a ditch near to the house upon her face, and left her there, where she was found shortly after, and laid upon a bed, but had not her senses again of a day and a night, or thereabouts'. The last incident had taken place only the Tuesday before the present examination, when Jane yet again turned up at Yew Tree Farm, 'took her and carried her into the barn, and thrust her head amongst a company of boards that were there standing'. Grace was found once more and put to bed, where she 'remained in her old fit until Thursday evening, when she came to her senses'. Grace's testimony before Holden ended there.

The magistrate sought witnesses but was sorely disappointed. On 7 August, he examined John Singleton, keeper of Samlesbury park and another Southworth family retainer, who merely confirmed William Alker's recollection that fear and dislike of Jane had prompted Sir John to avoid the Lower Hall. Singleton added that Sir John had regarded his grandson's wife 'an evil woman, and a witch: and he said that he was sorry for her husband, that was his kinsman, for he thought she would kill him'.[369] However, both Singleton and Alker appear to have perjured themselves, since Sir John died in 1595, and his grandson is not thought to have married Jane until two or three years later.

Their first child was born in 1599 and the Lower Hall became their home around ten years after Sir John's death. But no one appears to have flagged up these inconsistencies – or if they did, then someone quickly quashed them to ensure that Jane would probably hang.

The case of the Samlesbury witches was heard at Lancaster Assizes on Wednesday, 19 August 1612 before Edward Bromley, who knew the Southworths personally. Potts's presentation of the case is disjointed and confused. He lists seven people as having been committed to prison from Samlesbury on witchcraft charges: John Ramsden, Elizabeth Astley, Isabel Sidegraves, Lawrence Hay, Jennet Bierley, Ellen Bierley and Jane Southworth. He adds Alice Gray to this group, despite her inclusion among the Pendle suspects, as Katherine Hewitt's co-accused in the murder of the Foldes child. Not unreasonably, this has led to speculation that the group (apart from the three women who were then tried at Lancaster Assize) were in some way connected to the Pendle group rather than Samlesbury.

But one of them at least can now be said to be more firmly affiliated with the Samlesbury case. Elizabeth Astley hailed from Osbaldeston, a village less than two and a half miles north-east of Samlesbury Hall. Grace Sowerbutts had relatives living in Osbaldeston. Elizabeth's role in the case remains a mystery but years later, as an impoverished widow, she requested financial assistance on at least two occasions and was recommended, having 'lost her sight and afterwards the use of her limbs' while still retaining her 'loving spirit'. Unfortunately, the outcome is not recorded. As to the other names: an 'Isabel Sidegreaves' was buried in Lancaster Priory just one year after the trials and a John Ramsden can be found in the Padiham registers, marrying in January 1607/8. Ramsden, Sidegraves, Astley, Gray and Hay were all declared not guilty. But we hear no more of them, other than Judge Bromley's address, in which he clearly regards their acquittal as suspect, warning, 'Presume no further of your innocence than you have just cause, for although it pleased God out of his mercy to spare you at this time, yet without question there are amongst you, that are as deep in this action as any of them that are condemned to die for their offences.' His words also clearly relate far more to the suspects from Pendle rather than Samlesbury. Lastly, Bromley instructed them – at least according to *Discoverie*: 'Pray unto God you fall not again . . . the judgment of the court is: you shall all enter recognizances with good sufficient sureties, to appear at the next Assizes at Lancaster, and in the meantime to be of the good behaviour.'

Jennet Bierley, Ellen Bierley and Jane Southworth pleaded not guilty to the charges of having feloniously practised, exercised and used 'witchcrafts, enchantments, charms, and sorceries, in and upon one Grace Sowerbutts'. Their alleged victim was present in court, but again which parts of her speeches were read and which were spoken remains a point of conjecture. Like Bromley, Potts spends a good deal of his narrative lambasting Grace's testimony with all the suspicion he might equally have extended towards Jennet Device.

The case quickly fell apart under the scrutiny of the court. Potts recounts how, 'after he had heard all the evidence at large against the prisoners for the King's Majesty, demanded of them what answer they could make. They humbly upon their knees with weeping tears, desired him for God's cause to examine Grace Sowerbutts, who set her on, or by whose means this accusation came against them.'

Grace said nothing, but her face told all. The witnesses standing behind her 'began to quarrel and accuse one another'. Bromley shouted for order before instructing Grace to step forward. She tried to avoid his questions, and the jeers of the rest of court, but finally blurted out that she had been 'put to a Master to learn'.

Bromley then demanded 'to discover this damnable practise', who had put Grace 'to accuse these poor women, and bring their lives in danger, and thereby to deliver the innocent'. He advised that 'if a Priest or Jesuit had a hand in one end of it, there would appear to be knavery, and practise [trickery] in the other end of it'. He demanded Grace's father, Thomas Sowerbutts, should tell them 'what Master taught [your] daughter' but the yeoman insisted he did not know. As for Grace, Potts notes, 'The wench had nothing to say.'

But the women she had accused began shouting that it was Thompson, a seminary priest, who was to blame. Thompson had 'instructed and taught her this accusation against them, because they were once obstinate Papists, and now came to Church'. This caused further furore, Potts relates: 'Still this fire increased more and more, and one witness accusing another, all things were laid open at large.'

Bromley adjourned the case. He wanted the three accused women, and Grace, to be examined independently and away from the noisy courtroom. The two men instructed to carry out the interviews were the Puritan clergyman William Leigh, rector of Standish, and Edward Chisnal; both were justices of the peace. Leigh, a key player in Stuart patriotic Protestantism, had marked the first anniversary in 1606 of the Gunpowder Plot with a work titled *Great Britain's Great Deliverance, from the Great Danger of Popish Powder*. He had tutored King James's son, Prince Henry, and that year, 1612, praised the king under whose rule 'the flowers flourish and the kingdoms are united, religion prospereth and superstition withereth'.[370]

The three women were naturally desperate to make themselves heard. Jennet Bierley, Grace's grandmother, told the magistrates that Thompson was the alias of Christopher Southworth, son of Sir John, and a seminary priest. She believed that her granddaughter had been brought to the priest at John Singleton's home – the Southworth family retainer who had given evidence to Holden – after Grace had first 'been in her fit' and that it had been the suggestion of Grace's mother 'that she should be brought unto her master', Christopher Southworth, for assistance. He had then grasped the chance to tutor the young girl in her accusations. Jennet held the priest solely responsible for the fact that her granddaughter had accused her of witchcraft and that he had done so because she herself attended church. Ellen Bierley agreed with Jennet, adding that she had seen 'Master Thompson, alias Southworth' some six to eight weeks before her committal to gaol, and that she was certain that his motivation was that she, too, attended church. Jane Southworth said the same, but gave a little more detail, including that she had had 'conference' with the priest about six weeks before her imprisonment, in a place called Barn Hey Lane, 'where and when she challenged him for slandering her to a witch'. He replied that he had heard she *was* a witch from her own mother and aunt. But Jane remained convinced he had accused her of his own volition, and that because she 'would not be dissuaded from the church'.

Leigh and Chisnel then examined Grace, who admitted that 'Master Thompson, alias Southworth' had indeed persuaded, counselled and advised her in her lies. She confessed that 'she never did know, or saw any devils, nor any other visions, as formerly by her hath been alleged and informed'. Nor had she been 'thrown or cast upon' any hay but had gone 'upon the mow' herself.

The two magistrates presented their findings to Bromley, who immediately ordered the jury to find Jennet Bierley, Ellen Bierley and Jane Southworth innocent. Grace broke down and when Bromley asked her if she ever went to church, she said that she did not, adding fervently that from then on, however, she would absolutely attend, 'and that very willingly'.

Although the Samlesbury women were acquitted, they received no apology, nor any acknowledgement of what they had endured. Instead, Bromley repeated his directive to the other five found not guilty, telling them that 'with good, sufficient sureties', they were to appear at the next assizes at Lancaster, and in the meantime to be of good behaviour, finishing again: 'All I can say to you, Jennet Bierley, Ellen Bierley, Jane Southworth, is that God hath delivered you beyond expectation. I pray God you may use this mercy and favour well; and take heed you fall not hereafter. And so, the court doth order you shall be delivered.'

The case ended there. But the fate of the man whose shadow fell across the court – in Potts's words, 'the bloody butcher', Christopher Southworth – remains a mystery. Much influenced by his father, Sir Christopher, he had studied at the English College in Rome and trained for the priesthood at Douai. In 1587, he had been imprisoned at Wisbech Castle and is almost certainly the priest named 'Southworth' who arrived at Westminster in December 1598 to be kept a close prisoner. But by 1600 he had escaped and was heading back to

Lancaster. He then only reappears with substance during the 1612 trials. His motivations seem much less clear to us – that he should go to such extreme lengths to invent evidence – but it served the assize court well to demonstrate that this might be true.

All those involved in the Samlesbury case would have been forced to face each other again, for they all lived within fairly close proximity. Ten years later, in early 1623, the 'malignant spotted fever', thought to be typhus, which had killed many, came to Samlesbury. Over forty inhabitants died of the disease, including Thomas Sowerbutts, Grace's father, her brother John and her aunt Ellen's husband John. Grace therefore became a wealthy woman, having inherited a large sum from her father, which in his will he states was that 'which I owe her'. The story behind those words has unfortunately been lost to us. Jane Southworth continued to live at the Lower Hall until one of her children died of the fever. She appears to have then left the immediate area and remarried. The Lower Hall was demolished shortly thereafter, due to its propensity for flooding.

Samlesbury Hall fell into disrepair after there was no one left to occupy it at the turn of the twentieth century. A building firm from Blackburn bought it in 1924, intending to knock it down and use the materials for new housing until the Ancient Monuments Society began a campaign to raise funds to save it. They purchased the Hall in 1925 but it was almost another fifty years before it opened to the public, in July 1974. One of the most beautiful houses in the north, it serves a wide variety of uses including exhibition spaces and as a wedding venue. The eerie priest hole above the dining room can be seen, while the room adjacent to it is – naturally – said to be haunted.

In Potts's handling, the Samlesbury case served as a useful chunk of anti-Catholic propaganda while simultaneously aiming to silence accusations that Bromley was a relentless persecutor of women and children. No one, Potts believed, would now suggest that Bromley had failed to act impartially when faced with his first cases of witchcraft. Bromley himself was no doubt satisfied that the case served a Protestant purpose and showed him to be a zealous investigator of truth. Such was the intention of *Discoverie*, at least. It was the perfect sister to the Pendle case in all these respects, for it showed how the prosecution 'contrasted witches who really populated English forests and courtrooms to the excessively voracious and licentious spectres of legends and lies'. For while the Pendle witches were 'never so cruel nor barbarous' as their Samlesbury counterparts, it was precisely this, the 'moderated brutality that qualified their "otherness", making them believable, terrifying, and therefore, all the more worthy of a severe punishment.'[371]

Chapter Twenty-One

DOLLS OF CLAY

Following the overturning of the case against the Samlesbury accused the court returned to the matter of Anne Redfearn's acquittal. What had passed between Nowell and his fellow magistrates and judges the previous evening will forever remain lost, but a strategy had been devised to place Anne Redfearn on another charge: that eighteen years before, she 'feloniously had practised, exercised, and used her devilish and wicked arts, called witchcrafts, enchantments, charms, and sorceries, in and upon one Christopher Nutter' and that 'by force of the same witchcrafts, feloniously did kill and murder' him. The announcement of this new charge would have sent shockwaves around the court, not least in its effect upon Anne Whittle, who had expected to go to her death taking the one comfort that she had saved her daughter from the same fate. For those who were superstitious – and they all were, to some extent – it must have seemed as if Robert Nutter was pursuing her from the grave.

Anne Redfearn, naturally, pleaded not guilty. Her calamitous predicament begs the question of whether the jury was now changed; if Bad Sir Cuthbert had indeed intended to rig the jury, his attempt had failed miserably. Perhaps another jury was sworn in, one that was assured of being more sympathetic to the prosecution, even though events would show that they could not be relied upon either, since Alice

Gray – Katherine Hewitt's co-accused in the accusations against her – was also acquitted. But Potts does not tell us anything of her time in court. Nor does he tell us – although he has no need – that judicial interference was the one and perhaps only certainty in criminal trials.

The evidence that Anne Redfearn had murdered Christopher Nutter was simply a rehash of that concerning his son's death and amounted to her having assisted in making clay pictures and John Nutter's testimony that his father, Christopher Nutter, was certain he had been bewitched but did not volunteer a name. Potts assures us that 'many witnesses' were examined in court 'viva voce', and that they had charged Anne with 'many strange practises, and declared the death of the parties, all in such sort, and about the time in the examinations formerly mentioned'. He continues: 'All men that knew her affirmed, she was more dangerous than her mother, for she made all or most of the pictures of clay, that were made or found at any time.' The 'many witnesses' remain conveniently unnamed, but inevitably Anne was found guilty and knew that she would now die alongside her mother.

In a trial replete with high drama and intense emotion, perhaps the most shocking – and certainly the most important in terms of its influence on legal process afterwards – was when Nowell presented his star witness: Jennet Device.

The evidence against Elizabeth Device had followed that of Anne Whittle, and preceded her son James, who despite being scarcely able to stand, nonetheless was able to state now that he was innocent of all charges. But Elizabeth was about to be confronted by her youngest child in court. However cruel Potts is in his description of Elizabeth, we can be more or less assured that his opinion represented those standing in condemnation of her: 'Barbarous and inhuman monster, beyond example, so far from sensible understanding of thy own misery, as to bring thy own natural children into mischief and bondage; and thyself to be a witness upon the gallows, to see thy own children, by the devilish instructions hatched up in villainy and witchcraft, to suffer with thee, even in the beginning of their time, a shameful and untimely death.' Elizabeth entered court having watched her much-loved mother die in utter squalor, and in the knowledge that she and two of her children would – bar some completely unexpected and wholly unlikely supernatural intervention – die on the gallows, leaving her youngest at the mercy of the world. That Elizabeth found the strength to stand before, and defy, those who would condemn them all is a remarkable testimony to her.

Jennet was brought into court by Roger Nowell, who had no doubt spent a great deal of time and effort on preparing her for the expected confrontation. Jennet's family – her mother, sister and brother – must have been utterly aghast when she followed the magistrate into the room.

Looking far younger and smaller than her eleven years, Jennet was about to give evidence when Elizabeth began screaming. Potts tries to convince us that her distress and fury were directed at her own daughter: 'Her mother, according to her accustomed manner, outrageously cursing, cried out against the child in such fearful manner, as all the court did not a little wonder at her.' But Elizabeth Device's 'outrageous cursing' was directed towards the magistrate rather than her daughter – it simply serves Potts's purposes far better to imply that the focus of her anger was Jennet.

Unsurprisingly, Jennet herself broke down when she realised the depth of her mother's despair. All Nowell's careful tutoring was about to go to waste: 'With weeping tears she cried out unto my Lord the Judge, and told him she was not able to speak in the presence of her mother.' Bromley directed the guards to remove Elizabeth Device, who was thus unceremoniously hauled from the courtroom, while Nowell spoke to Jennet quietly, encouraging her to remember what she had been taught. Once order had returned, and all those present were more settled if not entirely silent, Bromley instructed Nowell to set Jennet upon the table before him so that she might deliver her evidence to him, rather than face the crowd – and her siblings, who remained in the same room: 'My mother is a witch, and that this I know to be true . . .'

There had been previous instances in England, and wherever witch trials were held, whereby children gave evidence, often against their own parents. Agnes Waterhouse had been sentenced to death in 1566 after the twelve-year-old Agnes Brown had accused her elder namesake of possessing a black dog familiar, among others; Agnes was also alleged to have caused illness, killed livestock and used witchcraft to bring about the death of her husband. Curiously, among those present at Agnes Waterhouse's second examination was Sir Gilbert Gerard, then the Queen's Attorney – who also happened to be the father of Thomas Gerard, the magistrate in charge of Isabel Robey's prosecution. Writer Peter Haining speculates: 'What these four men [including Gilbert Gerard] deliberated and decided was to serve as a precedent for many later witchcraft trials.'[372]

There were other instances of child witnesses. In Maldon, Essex, Elleine Smith's thirteen-year-old son had supplied evidence that his mother kept three familiars, two in bottles, one in a pack of wool; when their home was searched, the bottles were found but the familiars had vanished and Elleine was hanged in April 1579. During the 1582 St Osyth trial of sixteen women, the eight-year-old son of Ursula Kemp gave evidence against her; his mother was subsequently executed. In 1596, fourteen-year-old Thomas Darling had been instrumental in bringing about Alice Gooderidge's imprisonment on charges of witchcraft; she died before her trial.[373]

But these testimonies, and especially that of Jennet, have baffled us ever since. Jennet is often portrayed as a spiteful child, with some unknown grudge against her mother – perhaps due to being illegitimate – but this is to forget that the entire experience was utterly terrifying and foreign to her. Essentially, people in positions of great power had informed her that she was related to monsters – Satan's agents on earth. If Jennet spoke out against them, then she was not only saving herself, but her family too, for they were at the mercy of the devil and eternal damnation unless she could make them admit their crimes and repent. Equally, Jennet may well have been warned – as other children in such trials were also warned – that if she refused to support the indictments against her mother and siblings then she, too, might be accused of being a witch. As Joanna Kucinski explains in *Representations of Witches in Popular Literature in England, 1566–1645*:

> The most common form these accusations took was to have a child implicate his or her mother in the practice of witchcraft . . . The testimony of young children against their mothers was a common and integral element of popular pamphlets throughout the period . . . This evidence was undoubtedly coaxed or coerced from bewildered and frightened children by magistrates through leading questions and possibly threats . . . most pamphlet writers chose to incorporate the evidence given by the witches' children in some detail. Such evidence is most likely included in order to suggest that the witches' acts were so terrible that they turned even the witches' own children against them, disrupting the normal ties of blood.[374]

The most well-known instance of evidence given by children in witch trials is that of Salem, where in 1692 nineteen people were executed – despite the children retracting their stories. Here too:

> . . . was an emotionally charged community, with accounts of witchcraft commonplace. Nearly everyone in 17th century Salem believed in the power of witches . . . The adults who interrogated the circle girls used eclectic interviewing techniques. On the one hand, parents and other powerful adults actively encouraged and shaped their children's "recollections" by encouraging them to elaborate their statements, always providing leading questions and positive attention for answers congruent with the charge of witchcraft. Sometimes the children were locked in jail cells for days while they were relentlessly interviewed.[375]

We have no way of genuinely knowing what techniques Nowell might have tried to extract Jennet's loyalty to him, whether after years of deprivation, her life was 'thrillingly transformed by the legal spotlight', lending her a completely unfamiliar sense of power and the undivided attention of adults.[376]

Whatever Jennet might have felt, by the time she was led into Lancaster Castle, she was a deeply traumatised child. In later years, she may have been haunted by her part, however much it was due to fear and coercion, in her family's death. One of the Salem girls offered a public explanation fourteen years after the infamous trial; her words may speak for the vast majority of those who were children at the time of their testimony, for Ann Putnam recalls being 'made an instrument for the accusing of several persons of a grievous crime, whereby their lives were taken away from them, whom now I have just grounds and good reason to believe they were innocent persons; and that it was a great delusion of Satan that deceived me in that sad time'.[377] She said what she had done was 'not out of anger, malice or ill-will to any person, for I had no such thing against them, but what I did was done ignorantly'.[378]

The court erupted again during Jennet's testimony when Bromley apparently decided to test her veracity regarding those persons said to have been present at the Good Friday meeting, with particular attention to Alice Nutter, whose trial Potts introduces by paraphrasing lines from King James's *Daemonologie*:

> The two degrees of persons which chiefly practise witchcraft, are such, as are in great misery and poverty, for such the devil allures to follow him, by promising great riches, and worldly commodity. Others, though rich, yet burn in a desperate desire of revenge; he allures them by promises, to get their turn satisfied to their heart's contentment . . . But to attempt this woman in that sort, the devil had small meanes: for it is certain she was a rich woman; had a great estate, and children of good hope: in the common opinion of the world, of good temper, free from envy or malice.

Alice, of course, was neither in want of riches nor motivated by a desire for revenge. The charge against her – the murder by witchcraft of

Henry Mitton, due to his having slighted Elizabeth Southerns when she asked him for a penny – was almost as nonsensical to Thomas Potts as it is to us today. His short account of her trial betrays his utter bafflement as to how she became accused of being embroiled in 'murder, and many other wild and damnable practises'. Alice pleaded not guilty and, as far as we know from *Discoverie*, then maintained her silence. Despite claims to the contrary, her family were almost certainly there to support her, since Potts states that even her own children could not move her to either confess 'or declare anything' right up until the end. He ends his account: 'And here I leave her, until she come to her execution, where you shall hear she died very impenitent.' Her silence proved deafening.

Following the reading of Jennet's list of Malkin Tower attendees, Bromley had her removed from the courtroom and 'away into the Upper Hall'. He then instructed Thomas Covell to line up his prisoners, but between each witchcraft suspect was placed 'another prisoner, and some other strange women amongst them, so as no man could judge the one from the other'. Jennet was then brought back into court and set on the table once more. Potts recounts that Bromley 'took great pains to examine her of every particular point. What women were at Malkin Tower upon Good Friday? How she knew them? What were the names of any of them? And how she knew them to be such as she named?' Bromley then asked Jennet if she recognised any of them among those in court. Jennet replied that she did, 'whereupon in the presence of this great audience, in open court, she went and took Alice Nutter, this prisoner, by the hand, and accused her to be one, and told her in what place she sat at the feast at Malkin Tower, at the great assembly of the witches, and who sat next her, what conference they had, and all the rest of their proceedings at large'.

Finally, Bromley asked her if she knew or could see 'Johan a Style' – the generative name used in the legal profession when referring to an invented or unknown person. Jennet shook her head. No, she knew no such woman to have been there, nor had she ever heard her name. Bromley warned her that 'this could be no forged or false accusation, but the very Act of God to discover her' and that it would 'save her [Johan's] life'. But Jennet said nothing; she did not know anyone of that name.

The prosecution thus appeared vindicated: every word from the child's mouth must be true. Jennet further pointed out John and Jane Bulcock as having attended the Good Friday meet; again 'she went and took Jane Bulcock by the hand, accused her to be one'. She then turned to John Bulcock, whom she said had turned the spit there, and described something of their conversation. This led to the Bulcocks 'swearing they were never at the great assembly at Malkin Tower . . . crying out in very violent and outrageous manner'.

Bromley barked at the Bulcocks to pipe down, so that Jennet might take up her story again. She then 'told his Lordship, there was a woman that came out of Craven to that Great Feast at Malkin Tower, but she could not find her out amongst all those women'. Potts then adds a triumphant aside: 'What a singular note was this of a child, amongst many to miss her, that before that time was hanged for her offence, which she would never confess or declare at her death?' Jennet's words caused uproar; Jennet Preston's husband was in court, with his family and friends, and began shouting furiously that the child was lying and that his wife had died an innocent, persecuted woman. Potts, of course, used this opportunity to insert into his text the accompanying, and false, explanation that Jennet's supporters now regretted their anger towards the Listers and Judge Altham, and that 'Old Preston, her husband [was] fully satisfied his wife had justice, and was worthy of death.' But as Potts well knew, nothing could have been further from the truth.

When Potts presents Bromley's summing up to the jury it is in fact his amalgamation of the judge's comments throughout proceedings. Potts offers this up as if it were Bromley's grand address to the jury, but until the late eighteenth century, most judges did not sum up evidence as such: it would have been regarded as wasting time. Bromley simply reminded the jury to consider their own consciences and act according to God. Those prisoners found guilty would have the word *cul(pabilis)* written above their name on the indictment. Those declared not guilty were *non cul(pabilis)*.

Nor would the verdicts of life and death have been delivered individually, with observations made about each prisoner. Although Potts attempts to persuade us otherwise, he writes: 'Whereupon Master Covell was commanded by the court in the afternoon to bring forth all the prisoners that stood convicted, to receive their judgment of Life and Death.' At this, a 'pitiful clamour' broke out in court as prisoners and their families cried out to the judge to be merciful when passing sentence.[379]

It was late afternoon, 19 August 1612. In the small, crowded courtroom, a palpable tension began to build as gaoler Thomas Covell marshalled his prisoners into reasonably orderly lines. But before Judge Bromley spoke the tension snapped and a great ripple of shouts, weeping, jeering and pleading broke out. He asked them to be quiet, but to no avail, for the cacophony mounted; he asked again and still the din rose; finally, he shouted across the courtroom in an irritated boom that anyone unable to remain quiet for whatsoever reason would be removed. The clamour abated to a few whispers, sniffs and shuffles on the wooden seating.

Thomas Potts got to his feet again, holding a piece of paper bearing an inky list of names. He glanced at Bromley, but the judge was looking elsewhere: at the petrified faces staring back at him. It seemed to him as if they were behind a veil, for in the pale sunlight, dust motes whirled endlessly. Thomas Potts then read the names aloud, pausing between each one:

'Anne Whittle. Elizabeth Device. James Device. Anne Redfearn. Alice Nutter. John Bulcock. Jane Bulcock. Alizon Device. Isabel Robey.'

When Potts sat down, Judge Bromley addressed the prisoners. Not the grand, eloquent speech of *Discoverie*, but a speech of sorts which ended with the solemn intonation of that most final of endings:

'You shall all go from hence to the Castle, from whence you came; from thence you shall be carried to the place of execution for this county, where your bodies shall be hanged until you be dead. For your comfort in this world I shall commend a learned and worthy preacher to instruct you, and prepare you, for another world. All I can do for you is to pray for your repentance in this world, for the satisfaction of many, and forgiveness in the next world, for saving of your souls. And God grant you may make good use of the time you have in this world, to his glory and your own comfort.

'And God have mercy upon your souls.'

Chapter Twenty-Two

PLACE OF SKULLS

Margaret Pearson did not hang. She alone of the eleven persons found guilty was permitted to live. Although Potts tells us that 'diverse witnesses' had spoken out against Margaret in open court and left 'no question' of her guilt in killing Dodgson's mare, the indictment was not of a capital nature. It may have helped her case somewhat further that the magistrate who had led the investigation into her case was not in court at any stage of proceedings. Nicholas Bannister had been unwell for some time and drew up his will the week before the assizes. He took his last breath on 20 August 1612 – one day after Margaret's conviction – and was laid to rest in Altham's church.

After sentencing the ten to death, Judge Bromley turned to Margaret and told her, 'The judgment of the court against you is this: that you shall stand upon the pillory in open market, at Clitheroe, Padiham, Whalley, and Lancaster, on four market days, with a paper upon your head, in great letters declaring your offence. There you shall confess your offence. After, you are to remain in prison for one year without bail, and then bound with good sureties, to be of good behaviour.'

Numerous commentaries on the case have echoed the words of James Crossley in his *Discoverie* footnotes: 'This Padiham witch fared better than her neighbours, being sentenced only to the pillory.' But there was no such 'only' about it.

Pillories are often confused with the stocks, a quite different punishment. The pillory was a wooden, cross-like structure with holes for the standing prisoner's hands and head; the stocks were seated. Most were designed to hold one person, but some held several at once. Some multiple pillories were raised above the ground with braces stretching out in the manner of a carriage wheel, leaving each prisoner looking at the other.

Pillories first appeared during King Edward's reign in the late thirteenth to early fourteenth century, when they were colloquially known as 'stretch necks' or 'catch necks'. Every town had its pillory: 'Perhaps no engine of punishment was more generally employed. Where there was a market, a pillory might be seen, for the local authorities, neglecting to keep it ready for immediate use as occasion might require, ran the risk of forfeiting the right of holding a market. Lords of Manors, in addition to having the right of a pillory, usually had a ducking-stool and gallows.'[380] Some pillories were combined with a whipping-post and stocks, and the prisoner would usually bear his or her offence on a white paper on their heads. When Robert Ockham was convicted of perjury in 1543, he and two other criminals were made to sit on horseback, facing backwards, with the telltale papers on their heads, and rode about Windsor, Newbury and Reading to stand in the pillory of each town. Other crimes that usually merited a stint in the pillory were adulterers, forgers, cutpurses and liars.

In 1552, a man found guilty of fraud was confined to the pillory at Cheapside, and had his ears nailed to it. When his time was finished, he was unable to rise until one of the beadles used a penknife to slit his ears upwards in order to free him. Having one or both ears nailed to the wood was a common punishment; the ears would be left on the pillory afterwards to warn that crime did not pay. Other pillory prisoners had their noses slit, or their faces branded with hot irons. When Lady Jane Grey briefly became queen, a man who had spoken ill of her had his ears nailed to the pillory and then cut clean off.

The 'mitre of paper' became a more regular fixture as time wore on.[381] In Canterbury's Market Place pillory in 1524, a man was made to wear a paper on which was written: 'This is a false, perjured and forsworn man.'[382] When his sentence ended, he was thrown out of town still wearing the paper mitre. Not everyone could read by any means, but the hat exposed them even more to ridicule and humiliation. Standing for hours in the pillory would cause insufferable pain in the back and legs, while the prisoner was also completely vulnerable to being attacked in any number of ways. Rocks, mud, faeces, rotting meat – all were common missiles from the mob. There were many deaths caused in the pillory, either by heavy things being thrown, or punches.

This was especially true on market days when people travelled far and wide to reach a certain town either to buy or sell. In 1711, eight women who were pilloried in Ireland for witchcraft were viciously beaten by a crowd; one had an eye struck out. Occasionally guards would gather, ostensibly to keep the prisoner from being badly harmed, but too often becoming a referee. An incident in the pillory at Charing Cross saw a man attacked by a large crowd hurling 'small shot, such as rotten eggs, filth and dirt from the street, which was followed up by dead cats, rats, etc., which had been collected in the vicinity'.[383] A group of Newgate prisoners in the pillory were similarly 'poured upon' from all sides: 'blood, garbage, and ordure from the slaughter-house, diversified with dead cats, turnips, potatoes, addled eggs and other missiles to the last moment'.[384] At Seven Dials, in 1731, a police informant was pelted to death in the pillory.

Those convicted of witchcraft were usually made to stand in the pillory for six hours at once, followed by three months in gaol, and then the process was repeated until all sentences had been served. This caused some inconvenience and expense to the local authorities who were instructed by the courts to transport the convicted witch to various towns. However, the larger the area covered, the more notoriety the prisoner gained, alerting locals to a witch in their town, which in turn made it difficult for a person convicted of witchcraft to move elsewhere in the hope of starting afresh. The pillory continued as a punishment until it was fully abolished in 1837.

In 1612, the prospect of getting safely close to one of the notorious

Lancaster witches was a huge draw. Margaret was set on the pillory in Lancaster, Clitheroe, Whalley and Padiham with the white mitre on her head condemning her as a witch who had killed a mare. She could not sit in silence, even if that was her preference; the terms of her sentence dictated that she had to state her offence loudly, and that she would be in the pillory for six hours at a time on market days, whatever the weather, and regardless of what was being pitched at her. She was then transported back to gaol for three months before her next stint in the pillory.

We don't know what became of Margaret Pearson – whether she survived all her long and excruciating hours in the pillory and her prison terms. Perhaps her husband, family and friends were there to support and protect her when she returned to her home town of Padiham, to serve another part of her sentence there. The pillory and stocks stood, together with the Market Cross, on the Market Place. All are now gone. But if you look carefully, you will find the brown plaque on the side of an ancient house near St Leonard's Church, at the junction of Church Street and Moor Lane, which reads in part: 'The stocks and pillory were hereabouts and Margaret Pearson stood here in 1612 to confess her sins of bewitching a horse . . .'[385]

Justice was meted out swiftly in seventeenth-century England. Until 1830, those who had been condemned to death at the Lancaster Assizes would be hanged the following day, unless that happened to be a Sunday. Executions did not take place within the castle grounds until the turn of the nineteenth century, but thereafter continued publicly until March 1895. Following the passing of the Private Execution Act, a hidden spot left of the steps to the new courtrooms became known as Hanging Corner. But until executions were switched to the castle, Lancaster Moor was 'a notorious marginal landscape in medieval and post-medieval England'.[386]

It is impossible to imagine how those prisoners condemned to death at the 1612 Summer Assizes must have felt as they were taken back to the chamber underground for their last night on earth.

They passed the hours in darkness, knowing that death crept closer with every passing breath, every movement and whisper. But nothing could now be done. Their course was set; the compass pointing in a direction that no one wanted to travel, marked on a map of its time with a tiny stick figure hanging limply from 'the fatal tree'.

The man who plotted their journey had promised them a guide, a 'learned and worthy preacher' to help them prepare for death. This spiritual counsellor was silently tasked with bringing about the prisoners' final confessions, for he was 'duty-bound to persuade the prisoner to atone'.[387] These undertakings almost certainly fell to Puritan preacher William Leigh, who had been present in court and would be regarded as an infinitely suitable man for both missions. Around sixty years of age, Leigh was the extremely popular pastor at Standish Hall where he received a great number of requests to conduct funeral sermons, being regarded as 'a sincere professor of true religion, a powerful opponent of heresy, and a most eloquent preacher'.[388] James Crossley, editor of the 1845 edition of *Discoverie*, suggested that with regard to the Pendle executions, it might be that 'amongst [Leigh's] papers or correspondence, if they should happen to have been preserved, some account may eventually be found of the sad closing scene of these melancholy victims of superstition'.

Although that precise account has not been found, another does indeed exist – and for the very next Lancaster Assizes, Lent 1613. Published as *The Dampe of Death: Beaten Back with the Glorious Light and Life of Jesus Christ*, Leigh introduced his sermon by recalling how he had 'preached unto those poor delinquents then ready to die by the doom of justice' at the castle. He sensed himself 'sharply censured of some, that I preached too much mercy, and too little judgement, and that like an unskilful Samaritan, I poured into the sore of those wounded souls and broken hearts over much oil and too little vinegar'.[389] He vowed that nothing 'shall ever make me cruel against the penitent' before addressing the condemned prisoners: 'And such you are, whose salt tears this day, do well express your sorrowful hearts, who having been humbled at the bar of God's justice, why should you not appeal to the bar of his mercy . . . for when is need if not now? When the fear of death is before your face, when the horror of your sins cry vengeance against your souls, when your best friends fail you and this whole world forsakes you, when Satan winnows you like wheat . . .'[390]

Supposing the prisoners' most pressing thought to be: 'Oh, but life is sweet, and death is fearful, how may I be prepared for that hour?' he declared: 'There is no privilege against the grave, there is no pity against the grave, and there is no pleading with the grave . . . [Death is] the laying away of a heavy burden, the lighting from a mad and furious horse, a deliverance from a ruinous house, and house of clay: the end of all griefs, the escape of all dangers, the destroyer of all evils.' He reassured those in his care that they would meet with God, 'and be at peace in a joy ever after', reiterating, 'heaviness may endure for a night but joy commeth in the morning'.[391]

But it was not joy that came in on the morning of Thursday, 20 August 1612 within the precincts of the castle; it was gaoler Thomas Covell. Assisted by guards, he brought them up from the pitch-black chamber and into the courtyard, where a long cart stood empty but for the horse standing patiently in the shafts. Groups of men circled like stern-faced suitors at a silent ball: Sir Cuthbert Halsall in his capacity of sheriff, the chaplain, the hangman, and several pikemen with their steel-tipped poles of ash and glinting armour to keep any overzealous spectators from clambering aboard the execution cart for a closer look. Covell's assistants removed the prisoners' heavy shackles but pinioned their hands tightly in front to enable prayer. As the prisoners were heaved into the cart, few of them grasped that the benches on which they sat were their own coffins.

At an officious shout from the back of the courtyard, the cart gave a jolt as the horse moved forward, towards the gatehouse. On the other side were the crowds. Thousands and thousands of them. An average crowd might number around 10,000, but here were ten witches to hang – thus the numbers were swollen further. They lined the castle slopes to watch the horse bring out the hangman's quarry. There were many from Pendle in the crowd, who had walked all through the night to reach Lancaster in time for the hanging. Two hundred and fifty years later, it was reported that a huge number of people had spent the night traipsing the road to watch a murderer from Colne hang; when they learnt he had committed suicide in his cell the previous evening, their rage was palpable.

The journey was slowed by the crowds, who ran in front of the cart and surrounded it until the guards forced them back. It was a long while before they reached the bottom of Moor Lane, where another multitude lined both sides of the street.[392] The road began to climb, Moor Lane into Moor Gate. Then a slight turn, the unsprung cart creaking and straining on the last stage of its journey.

The great sweep of the moor lay before them now. There the gallows stood on barren, hollowed-out land overlooking the now distant castle gaol, ribbon of sea, and Lake District fells. The usually barren ground teemed with spectators, who greeted the sight of the cart with a deafening roar. In among the crowd were street hawkers, shouting about their wares: the murder ballads and trial pamphlets that told the story whose ending was imminent.

The horse dragged the cart underneath the gallows beam. There was movement in the cart as the hangman jostled the prisoners to their feet, looping a noose around each of the ten. But the end was not yet begun: while the prisoners stood, some weeping, some defiant, some utterly lost, the King's Commission was read, then a proclamation that anyone who was not appointed to take part in what was about to happen should stand back. The crowd was usually close; the hangman warned again for them to stand back. The chaplain, the sheriff, the hangman and his assistant remained standing with the prisoners. Most prisoners, especially those who – like the ten – were not hardened criminals would react to the sight of the gallows with 'convulsive shaking and audible distress'.[393] Some were paralysed with terror; some fainted.

A study of executions from this period observes how the panic of those about to be hanged 'started to complicate the executioner's course of action. Few prisoners could avoid producing a sharp adrenalin rise, sweating profusely, making it more difficult for the hangman to handle condemned bodies. Historically a hormonal trigger known as classic "fight or flight mechanism" stimulated some criminals to try to resist execution, others felt compelled to escape, and the remainder were rigid with trepidation . . .'[394] Few were those who did not experience an 'awful sense of anticipation caused by an acute stress response'.[395] The terror produced 'a physical showcase of slippages – in blood, sweat and tears, as well as urine, excreta and semen'.[396]

The chaplain stepped forward, addressing the prisoners but including the crowd in an all-important stage of the proceedings. For above all, those about to hang were encouraged to demonstrate courage, to show a latent morality, and to make 'a good end', thus ensuring that they were 'launched into eternity in a contrite and penitent frame of mind'.[397] The pamphlets that would be sold afterwards required a 'last dying confession' from the prisoner: 'Such speeches, far from being used as the occasion to hurl a final defiance at an unkind world, were usually marked by an acceptance of the justice and deservedness of the sentence which was about to be carried out, a warning to those present to avoid a similar fate and a confession not only of the crime which had brought about retribution, but also of a career of past sinfulness . . . Most accounts suggest that prisoners were generally willing to assist in this process.'[398]

But the ten from Pendle were not like others in that respect. When the chaplain brought the religious service to an end ('the beautiful prayers for the dead'), he asked those standing with the nooses about their neck if they understood the meaning of atonement? Were they willing to repent? Would they now publicly confess their sins? Did they wish to address the crowd? As convicted witches, their pleading for forgiveness would demonstrate beautifully the triumph of good over evil, of the devil being vanquished by the power invested in the Church, the state and the courts.

We don't know how every member of the ten reacted. But we do know that John and Jane Bulcock were not willing to play the gallows game. Potts tells us that they persisted in 'crying out in a very violent and outrageous manner, even to the gallows' – that is, they shouted their innocence loudly at every opportunity until the chaplain addressed them, when 'they died impenitent for anything we know, because they died silent in the particulars'. They stood silent. They refused to say a word of contrition. Much to the shock of Roger Nowell and his ilk, Alice Nutter behaved in the same manner. Potts relates in disgust: 'Here I leave her, until she come to her execution, where you shall hear she died very impenitent; insomuch as her own children were never able to move her to confess any particular offence, or declare anything, even in *Articulo Mortis* [point of death]: which was a very fearful thing to all that were present, who knew she was guilty.'

No doubt Alice's family were present, together with the friends and family of the rest. It seems quite possible that the ten from Pendle had, in effect, taken a vow of silence on the eve of their execution, for although Potts singles out these three as an example of dying 'impenitent', had the rest made heartfelt speeches, or indeed begged forgiveness, he would surely have included those words in *Discoverie*. In that case, there would have been a sense of profound shock among the normally bawdy crowds, for everyone knew that if you didn't repent at the end, then the devil would be waiting on the other side.

'Until I see in glory, what I feel in grace. And when, even in an instant and less than a thought, I shall pass from the bowels of this earth, to the bosom of my Christ, whither God bring both you and us, for his son's sake. To whom be glory, power and praises, both now and ever, amen. *Amen.*'[399]

The ritual ended with the chaplain's intonation; the hangman was quick; the horse, feeling the whip on its back, pulled forward; and the cart rolled away from the gallows, leaving the ten swinging by their necks.

Executioners were not medically trained, leading to misplacing the knot of the noose behind the ear, where it might slip, or at the front of the throat. The victim would be strangled, their skin stretching under their body weight and the neck dislocating rather than breaking. Most passed out but were still breathing. If the neck still failed to break and the rope continued to tighten, the heart would still send blood to the brain, but it had nowhere to go because of the restriction caused by the rope. This caused haemorrhaging, with the eyes protruding and the face turning purple and then black. In hot weather, when prisoners would perspire even more than normal, sometimes the noose would slip from a sweating neck. On one occasion, two men at Newgate Gaol waiting to hang found their ropes burning under the 'heated friction' that then caused the ropes to snap.

The long drop method was designed to be humane; it broke the neck, if carried out correctly, resulting in a quick death. But the ten hanged that day, 20 August 1612, were victims of the short drop. The noose would tighten about the neck slowly due to the weight of the victim's body, a far slower and more painful process. Death could take three minutes or more; the prisoner would move convulsively, even though they were not necessarily conscious – such was 'the Tyburn jig'. Those watching would see the victims' faces swell, their tongues protrude, and the eyes start to bulge and redden as a scarlet froth issued from their lips and nostrils. The struggles would lessen. The crowd would fall quiet, all of their senses affected by what they were witnessing.

The last moments on the scaffold from the viewpoint of a hanged individual were later described by the 'half-hanged' housebreaker John Smith, who was executed at Tyburn in December 1705. Seven minutes into his hanging, a reprieve arrived, and he was cut down, revived and regained consciousness. Following an examination, a report stated that: 'When he was turned off, he for some time was sensible of very great pain, occasioned by the weight of his body, and felt his spirits in a strange commotion, violently pressing upwards. That having forced their way to his head, he as it were saw a great blaze, a glaring light, which seemed to go out his eyes with a flash, and then he lost all sense of pain.'[400]

When the crowds had dispersed, the bodies were left hanging from the gallows for up to an hour to ensure that life was extinct. Official pronouncements regarding death would have been made by both the Lancaster coroner, Thomas Covell, and the prison surgeon.

What happened to the bodies afterwards is unknown. They may have been set on fire and the ashes scattered; the rough coffins may have been thrown into a pit and burnt or buried; or the bodies could have been disposed of in the quarry area. There is also a possibility that they were buried nearer to the castle; after the execution of Lawrence Britliffe, his friends declared that they had ensured he had a decent internment in the place appointed for executed criminals near the castle. There were certainly many others buried there, laid to rest vertically rather than horizontally to make better use of the space. But most felons were buried or burnt near the site of their execution.

One theory, long-held, suggests the ten from Pendle were buried in the old Quaker burial ground, close to the intriguingly named Golgotha area of the city, opposite today's Williamson Park, which stands on what was once Lancaster Moor and the quarries. In the Bible, Golgotha means 'Place of the Skull' and refers to the site of Jesus's crucifixion, outside the old walls of Jerusalem. Lancaster's Golgotha still retains a sense of antiquity; the oldest of its ten charming cottages dates from 1685 and may have been built for the quarry workers. By the 1880s, it was a place largely of women, with twenty of the twenty-two houses occupied by laundresses. To the west of the cottages is a small door in a tall wall, overgrown and boarded up, easy to miss. But it is here where local folklore holds that those who were executed on Gallows Hill were buried, before the land was purchased in the mid-1600s by the Quakers. Its setting might not be coincidental, since a few early Quaker burial sites 'bear nominal association with gallows and gibbets through place-names inherited from prior land use. This suggests that a pattern of land acquisition relating to prior morbid use may be drawn.'[401] The cemetery closed in 1955, when it was 'handed over to the town as open space'.[402]

The other possibility is that the ten executed prisoners were buried at Lancaster Priory – perhaps near to Elizabeth Southerns. There is a common misconception that convicted witches could not be laid to rest in consecrated ground, but there are several records of people condemned as witches being buried in churchyards. The accounts of

St Andrew's Church in Newcastle-upon-Tyne record in 1649: 'Paid at Mrs Watson's when the justices sat to examine the witches, 3s 4d, paid for a grave for a witch, 6d, paid for trying the witches, £1 5s.' This is thought to refer to the burial of no less than sixteen witches, while three women hanged as witches at the 1656 Michaelmas Assizes were buried in the corner of the churchyard at St Mary-on-the-Hill in Chester. Similarly, in St Anne's churchyard in the pretty little village of Woodplumpton, not far from Samlesbury, a boulder lies among the Gothic headstones, marked with a plaque. It reads: 'The Witch's Grave. Beneath this stone lie the remains of Meg Shelton, alleged Witch of Woodplumpton, buried in 1705.' Meg's real name was Margery Hilton, and although she is believed to have been murdered by a villager, rather than judicially hanged, her 'witch's grave' is in a singularly prominent position near the path and marked for visitors to find. There are also reputed to be instances where executed criminals were interred in churchyards in deliberate ignorance of their incumbents.

There is one other factor that suggests the idea of the burial of the Pendle ten at Lancaster Priory is not completely without foundation: when Isabella Rigby was hanged for witchcraft on Lancaster Moor, records show that she was subsequently buried in the priory graveyard, in 1666. Perhaps the ten who hanged on 20 August 1612 were granted quieter graves than we know.

EPILOGUE

The heart of legal London must have seemed a singularly appropriate place for the writing of *The Wonderfull Discoverie of Witches in the Countie of Lancaster*. The events of that summer in the north of England were still fresh in the mind of Thomas Potts when he began writing his account in the autumn of 1612, in rooms on Chancery Lane. It was not the quietest spot to write a book, with activity never ceasing around the Inns of Court and of Chancery, but no matter: with the documents he had retained from the case piled up beside his desk, Potts was inspired enough to complete his work quickly.

London was not his usual home; although the assumption has always been that he was born there, evidence suggests that he was a Yorkshireman. He dedicates *Discoverie* to the couple who raised and educated him, Sir Thomas Knyvet and his wife Lady Elizabeth, presenting them with 'their first fruits of my learning . . . who nourished then both me and them, when there was scarce any being to me or them'. Knyvet had more strings to his bow than an entire orchestra, having been part of the royal court since Elizabeth's reign, he was variously Gentleman of the Privy Chamber, Keeper of the Palace, a Justice of the Peace in Westminster, Member of Parliament and further. He is best described as someone for whom 'life ran smoothly . . . consistently high in Royal favour, his career was rather as a courtier than as a politician'.[403]

Knyvet's greatest moment came when 'a little before the stroke of twelve on a cold November night', he and his attendants left Knyvet's home – on the site of what is now 10 Downing Street – and headed for the Houses of Parliament.[404] His search of the cellars brought him face to face with Guido Fawkes, and the stores of gunpowder laid by the conspirators; in Fawkes's pockets he found slow-matches and tinder and placed him under arrest. Knyvet had been knighted at the Tower in 1604, but his apprehension of Fawkes assured his place in the king's favour. He and his wife were guardians to the king's daughter, Mary, and responsible for her education. King James referred to him as 'one of whose ancient fidelity both the late Queen and our now Sovereign have had large proof'.[405] His life was not without controversy, but he was assured of his place in the king's loyalties and was made Baron of Escrick in York in 1607, after which he rose to even greater prominence as a member of the Council of Queen Anne and a Warden of the Mint, present at almost all state functions. Knvyet was also a major landowner in the areas around York, holding the manors of Wheldrake, Wigginton and Escrick at various times.

Our humble clerk of court, Mr Thomas Potts, was thus raised in a household of considerable distinction. He was to all intents and purposes Knvyet's protégé. Later, living primarily at Skipwith Woods, some four miles south of Escrick, on the outskirts of York, Potts served as Deputy Surveyor under Royal Commission to Queen Anne, both before and after the Lancaster trials of 1612. While his family life remains unknown, the facts could not state more clearly where his religious and political sensitivities had begun. He acknowledges Knyvet's influence in this regard, stating that his 'grave and reverent counsel reduced my wavering and wandering thoughts to a more quiet harbour of repose'. But it is also plain to see where his thoughts might have wandered now, while writing *Discoverie*, with regard to the alleged 1612 gunpowder plot, his loyalty to the king, his views on witchcraft and demonology, and much else besides. Hence James Crossley's observation in his annotations to Potts's book: 'It must be admitted that the writer has chosen his patron very felicitously. Who so fit to have the book dedicated to him as one who had acted so conspicuous a part on the memorable occasion at Westminster?

The blowing up of Lancaster Castle and good Mr. Covell, by the conclave of witches at Malkin Tower, was no discreditable imitation of the grand metropolitan drama on provincial boards.'[406]

Nonetheless, however apposite the case may have been in this respect, there is no truth in the idea that Potts was somehow behind the allegations. As ever, that notion seems to have arisen from William Harrison Ainsworth's *The Lancashire Witches*, where we meet the character 'Thomas Potts' in Lancashire on legal business, and who hears rumours from Pendle and seizes his chance to make more of it, musing: 'If I can unearth a pack of witches, I shall gain much credit from my honourable good lords the judges of assize . . . besides pleasing the king himself, who is sure to hear of it and reward my praiseworthy zeal.'[407] But as witch trials historian George Lyman Kittredge points out: 'Potts had nothing to do with getting up the evidence or fomenting the prosecution.'[408]

The impetus to publish an account of the trials came from judges Altham and Bromley – not Potts, nor Knyvet. Potts is transparent about his commission from the outset, and it is clear that the primary motivation was to quell criticism of the judges and judicial process generally, and to present Bromley and Altham as honourable upholders of the law of the land. The three men were certain of the book's success and had little doubt that it would advance their prospects yet further, for they were supremely confident of the king's views and undoubtedly had found in Pendle a case that encapsulated his beliefs. Potts tells us as much in his sole reference to the king's book within the pages of *Discoverie*, declaring: 'What hath the King's Majesty written and published in his *Daemonologie*, by way of premonition and prevention, which hath not here by the first or last been executed, put in practise or discovered?'[409] Sections of *Discoverie* can be read as Potts paraphrasing *Daemonologie* – and in some instances, very closely, such as the passages relating to the case of Alice Nutter. With good reason, in his history of witchcraft, Wallace Notestein refers to the Pendle trials as 'the most remarkable event of the sort in James's reign' and 'clearly the outcome of his writings and policy'.[410]

When Robert Neill came to write his bestseller, *Mist Over Pendle*, he dedicated it to Thomas Potts's 'dusty memory', while simultaneously describing him as 'a zealous lawyer who had not one grain of common sense. He believed everything, sifted nothing, and gave no connecting links. He merely printed the depositions sent in by Roger Nowell, and added summaries of the evidence given in court.' Neill was mistaken: Potts made a very careful inspection of the material he had to hand, working it into a narrative with a purposefulness that few authors could claim. Hence his use of some original material – at a time when most witch trial pamphlets had little interest in reproducing such accurate legal detail.

One greater mystery remains: the authorship of the account of Jennet Preston's trial. Like the main body of the narrative, the case was included to defend both Altham as the judge and the Lister family, for in Gisburn there had been enormous anger from the local community, who believed that Thomas Lister the younger had pursued her relentlessly without reason. Above all, the book was meant to serve as a rejoinder to Jennet's loyal and grieving husband, William Preston, as the text itself addresses directly, extraordinarily, to 'you that were husband to this Jennet Preston; her friends and kinsfolks, who have not been sparing to devise so scandalous a slander out of the malice of your hearts, as that she was maliciously prosecuted by Master Lister and others; her life unjustly taken away by practise; and that (even at the gallows where she died impenitent and void of all fear or grace) she died an innocent woman, because she would confess nothing'. The author demands: 'I suffer you not to wander any further, but with this short discourse oppose your idle conceits able to seduce others . . .' It was a risk, indeed, to bring such accusations as William Preston and his supporters had made into the public arena at large, but it was clearly a risk the author felt worth taking, and in his own lifetime it appears to have had the desired effect.

But was Thomas Potts the author of both works published under the title of *Discoverie*? The fifteen-page pamphlet *Jennet Preston* refers to the Lancaster trial that followed it, and bears a date of 1612, unlike the remainder of *Discoverie*, which is dated 1613. No copy of the fifteen-page pamphlet *Jennet Preston* exists independently, and nor was it registered in *The Stationers' Register*, in which publishers could register their claim to print a written work. The only copy that exists is the one contained within *Discoverie*. There is a curious line that certainly hints Potts might not have been *Jennet Preston*'s author, for as witch trial documents expert Marion Gibson has pointed out, the text refers to Potts' book, 'wherein I find such apparent matter . . .' as if indicating the hand of a different author. It may be, as Philip Almond claims in his study of the 1612 trials, that Potts substantially edited and enlarged an earlier work by a different author, on the understanding that both works would be published jointly, after he had completed *Discoverie*.

Four years after the publication of his book, Thomas Potts died a wealthy man but intestate, on Christmas Day 1616, and was buried at St Helen's Church in Skipwith. His patron, Sir Thomas Knyvet, died six years later at Stanwell, where there is an impressive monument to him in the chancel of the parish church, and a school established in his name.

But it is, somewhat reluctantly, fair to say that – as Robert Neill states in his dedication of *Mist Over Pendle* – to Thomas Potts 'whom we owe it all'.[411]

What became of Jennet Device following the executions of her entire family is often misinterpreted; almost invariably, claims are made that she was among those women imprisoned in Lancaster Castle during another apparent outbreak of witchcraft in Pendle during 1634. The latter accusations were made by a ten-year-old boy, Edmund Robinson, who had heard tales of the previous case from his neighbours and invented a similar story to account for his being too late home to help bring in the cows.

Evidence regarding Jennet – or indeed her uncle Christopher Holgate and other family members – is non-existent after the end of the Lancaster Assizes. But when a 'Jennet Device' is named among those imprisoned at Lancaster as a result of Edmund's tall tales, it naturally strikes many as a terrible irony that she should find herself in the same predicament as her grandmother, mother and siblings twenty years before. Thomas Covell was still in charge at the time of the second round of accusations; he remained so until his death in 1639.

But the two Jennets are not the same. The Jennet imprisoned in Lancaster during 1634, and doomed to remain there until she could afford to settle the fees for her keep after the truth about Edmund's story was revealed, was not the Jennet of 1612. The Jennet Device at Lancaster in 1634 was also recorded as 'uxor' to William Device – the wife of a man bearing that surname. This is clarified in another contemporary document discussing the later trials.[412]

After the 1612 trials, eleven-year-old Jennet returned to Pendle. What happened to her during the next twenty years is unknown; she may have been allowed to remain with Roger Nowell and his family, although that seems unlikely. She may have been taken in by her uncle, Christopher, wherever he ended up – although not Malkin Tower, which was destroyed in the wake of the trials; or perhaps she was taken in by her father, whom we know was a man named Seller, living nearby. But however neatly and unpleasantly ironic it may be to believe that she was the victim of someone else's witchcraft tales, on the balance of probabilities, it is the death of our 'witness unexpected' that we find recorded in the parish registers of Newchurch-in-Pendle, where the entry for St Mary's reads: *Jenet Seller alias Devis, buried on 22 December 1635.*

Whatever the full truth of events that swept through the region in 1612, it died with Jennet and remains forever locked within the hauntingly beautiful landscape surrounding Pendle Hill. But there is one last, lingering hint that might just resolve the mystery of where her family home, Malkin Tower, stood. Its whereabouts have been debated for centuries, but perhaps the truth was hidden in plain sight all along.

Many sites have been mooted as the possible location of Malkin Tower. There is a Malkin Tower Farm in Blacko, some three or four miles east of Newchurch-in-Pendle; another location, Mancknowles Ing, has also been suggested, and in 2011, an old cottage was unearthed near Black Moss reservoir in Barley, which caused great excitement among the world's press as the potential home of 'Mother Demdike'. But the cottage was of a much later date and the presence of the skeleton of a poor cat found in its walls, said to be protection from witchcraft, negates rather than supports the theory, regardless.

Malkin Tower is said to have stood 'on the declivity of Pendle'. Blacko is not on the slopes of Pendle and nor is it near the main sites of interest throughout the story of the 1612 trials. Both Elizabeth Southerns and Anne Whittle visited Bull Hole Farm regularly – and that would have been a much longer trek for the partially sighted Elizabeth had she lived over in hilly Blacko. We remember, too, that Elizabeth stated that she first met her familiar, Tibb, 'near to a stone pit in Goldshaw Booth' when she was returning home from a day's begging. This was Faugh's Delph, on Well Head Road. She also instructed James to attend Newchurch communion service in order to purloin bread to give to Tibb, who would be waiting for it. Tibb then tackled James at the same stone pit on his way home. And even more infamously, the human remains discovered by Constable Hargreaves at Malkin Tower had been stolen from St Mary's churchyard.

It was common at the time of the trials to demolish empty buildings and reuse the materials to build a new structure. There was certainly no one likely to object to the demolition of Malkin Tower and its 'melancholy associations'. Curiously, however, there is a reference to the Rev. Richard James, scholar and mutual friend of Shakespeare and Ben Jonson. Rev. James stated that when visiting relatives at Heywood Hall in 1636, he 'visited Pendle and Malkin Tower five times'. Immediately afterwards, he penned his celebrated poem, *Iter Lancastrense*, which was republished by the Chetham Society in 1846 and contains the lines: 'I long to climb up Pendle; Pendle stands,/Round cop, surveying all ye wild moorlands, /And Malkin Tower, a little cottage, where/ Report makes captive witches meet to swear/Their homage to the devil . . .'

Thus, Malkin Tower was in fact still existent in 1636. Saddlers Farm, on Well Head Road in Newchurch-in-Pendle, was rebuilt around

1660. *Rural Houses of the Lancashire Pennines* states that it is 'a two-cell house of two storeys with TIE 1714 over doorway of single-story porch . . .' Saddlers Farm has long been regarded as the site of Malkin Tower by many scholars, including local historian Dr John Laycock of nearby Sabden, and William Mitchell, who lectured extensively about the case in the mid-twentieth century.

Dr Laycock, in 1900, wrote:

In the year 1828 four fields are described in Capper's Farm as "Bogard Holes" and in Sadler's Farm three fields bear the name "Malkin", giving an area of 10 acres in all. This seems a much more probable place that the somewhat distant Blacko, and is far more central . . . Malkin Tower is stated to have stood on the declivity of Pendle, but one could hardly call a place on the other side of Roughlee to be on the slopes of Pendle. I don't think Potts, however, mentions that it was on the declivity of Pendle, but simply states that it was in the Forest of Pendle.

Clifford Moorhouse, another local author, takes up a frustrating aspect to this story:

In a survey of Goldshaw Booth taken in the year 1828, four fields are described in Saddler's Farm, three fields bear the name 'Malkin', giving an area of 10 acres in all. The mention of these three fields as Malkin, is questioned by some recent writers because they do not appear on the deeds, but knowing the thoroughness with which he dealt with his subjects, I do not doubt the authenticity of his statements.

However, Moorhouse – who is writing in the late 1980s – goes on to tell us:

The owner of Saddlers Farm, Mrs Rose Warburton, lives in Sabden and has kindly allowed several people to examine the deeds of that farm. She has told me that the enclosure or croft near the farm is called Kiln Yard. I, along with Mr Wiseman [*author's friend*] examined this area and found near to the farm buildings, stones which formerly formed a wall and could have been part of a building. Unfortunately, most of the area where the building had been was covered by a hen cabin. What we would have liked to investigate further or dug out was signs of burnt stones.[413]

There is a similar story from the 1930s, where a local farmer told reporter James Anderton for his piece about rambles about Pendle: 'Meadow Top [an adjacent farm] was rebuilt and roofed with thatch in 1604 and rebuilt in 1734. In the south-east corner of the garden is the site of two ancient cottages, one of which was the home of Mother Demdike before she went to Malkin Tower.' This is a curious statement, but of interest, nonetheless. It should also be borne in mind that four other key farms stand within the immediate area: Tynedale, Bull Hole, Moss End and Lower Well Head.

An application for renovation of Saddlers was in recent years lodged with the local council. The architects involved submitted an enquiry to the Lancashire Historic Environment Record to determine if any entry was present for the site. An entry exists but contains little substantial detail. However, the architects noted that the farmhouse is 'a good example of a small, early 18th century yeoman farmhouse, with a date of 1714 present over the principal entrance, suggesting this is the year of the house's construction. The identity of the initials has not been elucidated. The history of the building isn't well documented.' They consulted various records but admit that their research was not exhaustive.

The farm first appears as 'Sadlers' on the OS map of 1848, where the building outline appears to be T-shaped, suggesting that only the house and porch were extant. A larger building, presumed to be a barn, is shown to the south-west. The architects state that Saddlers itself, in the form of the datestone, provides evidence of settlement on the site then in the form of residential and agricultural uses. Regarding the datestone, they state:

'The farmhouse can firmly be dated to 1714 as evidenced by the existing datestone, however, this is relatively common amongst farmhouses of the 17th and 18th centuries. The historical association of the patron of these buildings is manifested within the date stones, however their identity has not been elucidated. The construction of the farmhouse places it within the category of between 1540 and 1750, prior to when much of the nation's agricultural buildings were constructed.'

The common datestone on domestic and agricultural buildings in some areas of the north-west consist of three initials in a triangle over the date – as we find at Saddlers. The upper initial usually represents the surname, with the two lower letters giving the initials of the husband and wife. The date usually represents the building of the structure but can also confirm an important event such as marriage, moving into the property, while retaining the initials of the builders of the original building on that spot.

'I/T E' reads the datestone above the old door at Saddlers Farm in Newchurch-in-Pendle, a few minutes' walk from St Mary's Church where a 'Jennet Seller alias Device' lies buried, and along from the wild well of Faugh's Quarry. Three initials above the datestone: husband and wife, who built earlier on this site, whose home was destroyed but perhaps partially used to rebuild Saddlers and whose names were commemorated by those who followed them:

Ingham
Thomas Elizabeth
1714.

'*Crucifixus hoc signum vitam Etername. Amen.*'

GLOSSARY

A few key terms regarding the business of the land are listed below:

Booth:
Originally referred to the cowkeepers' dwellings in the vaccaries, 'booth' later defined each hamlet in the Forest of Pendle.

Canon Law:
The law of the church.

Copyhold:
A form of land ownership similar to leasehold. The Lord of the Manor held the title deeds of the property and residents were obliged to provide him with services in exchange for certain privileges. The exact terms of a tenancy, which could vary from manor to manor, were set out in the manorial roll, a copy of which was given to the tenants, hence the term 'copyholders'.

Greave:
An official elected by the inhabitants of the booths and tasked with running the community.

Honour:
An area of land comprising a number of manors and estates under the administration of an overlord, to whom the lords of the manors would defer.

Laund:
Taken from the Old French, it referred to a glade or pasture. Within the Forest of Pendle, a laund was an enclosure for deer.

Manor:
This referred to the land linked to a major house, owned by the lord of the manor, who had various rights

over the land and his tenants.

Messuage:	A house, its outbuildings, yard and garden.
Vaccary:	A cattle farm.
Waste:	The uncultivated land found beyond the boundary of a settlement.

AUTHOR'S NOTE
and
CHRONOLOGY

For readers unfamiliar with the period covered in the bulk of this book I have tried to make the text as accessible as possible without over-simplifying matters. With this in mind, I'd like to highlight the following:

In this book, each year begins on 1 January, but until 1752 the Julian calendar was used in British Isles and 25 March was the first day of the new year (until 1600 in Scotland).

I have taken the liberty of modernising the spelling and punctuation of quotations and titles. Where single names are spelled differently in the original texts, I have used the same spelling throughout for convenience and clarity.

During the time of the witch trials, England's monarchy reigned as follows:

1509–47:	Henry VIII
1547–53:	Edward VI
1553–58:	Mary Tudor
1558–1603:	Elizabeth I
1603–25:	James I (James VI in Scotland); married to Anne of Denmark who died in 1619

Finally, a list of important dates relating to this case:

PRE-1612

1530s–early 1940s	The Reformation takes place.
1542	First Witchcraft Act passed in England.
1562	Stricter Witchcraft Act passed during Queen Elizabeth's rule.
1583	Father John Nutter is executed.
1584	Publication of Reginald Scot's *The Discoverie of Witchcraft*.
1587, 15 May	Jennet Balderston marries William Preston at Gisburn Church.
1588	Spanish Armada.
1592	Elizabeth Southerns first encounters her familiar, Tibb.
1592	Thomas Lister the younger born.
1595, Candlemas, 2 Feb	Robert Nutter dies, believing he has been bewitched by Anne Whittle and her daughter Anne Redfearn.
1595	The Starkie household is bewitched.
1595, Maudlintide, 22 July	Christopher Nutter dies, believing he has been bewitched.
1595, 3 November	Sir John Southworth dies.
1597, March	Edmund Hartley hanged for bewitching the Starkies.
1597	First publication of *Daemonologie* by James VI of Scotland.
1597	Richard Assheton dies; Elizabeth Southerns later blamed.

1598	A dog-like spirit takes blood from Elizabeth Southerns, leaving her 'stark mad' for eight weeks.
1598	Anne Whittle gives her soul to Fancie, her familiar, 'a thing like a Christian man'.
1600	Anne Whittle steals eight teeth from three skulls in Newchurch cemetery.
1600, 26 July	Father Robert Nutter is executed at Lancaster.
1601	Bessie Whittle, Anne's daughter, steals from the Devices.
1601	John Device dies after failing to pay Anne Whittle.
1603	*Daemonologie* is reprinted in the same year that James IV of Scotland becomes King James I of England.
1604	A new Witchcraft Act comes into force, superceeding that of 1563.
1605	The Gunpowder Plot takes place.
1606	Hugh Moore of Pendle dies, believing himself bewitched by Anne Whittle.
1607	John Nutter's son argues with Anne Whittle and when his cow dies thereafter, she is blamed.
1607, early February	Thomas Lister the younger marries Jane Heber.
1607, 8 February	Burial at Gisburn of Thomas Lister the elder.
1608	William Perkins publishes *A Discourse On the Damned Art of Witchcraft*.
1608	John Robinson, alias Sawyer, dies after Elizabeth Device fashions a clay picture of him.
1608, 20 February	Jane Lister, widow of Thomas Lister the elder, dies.
1609	Elizabeth and James Device become witches, according to Jennet Device.

1610	Roger Nowell serves as High Sheriff of Lancashire for a year.
1610, Lent	John Duckworth dies after a row with James Device.
1610, Maundy Thursday	James Device attends communion at Newchurch, disobeying his grandmother's request for the bread.
1610, Easter Monday:	James encounters his familiar spirit and becomes a witch.
1610	James rows with Anna Towneley of Carr Hall; she dies within a fortnight.
1610	James spots the Redfearns making clay pictures.
1610	Anne Whittle is accused of bewitching John Moore's ale. His son John dies six months later.
1610	Anne Nutter dies after Anne Whittle accused her of laughing at her.
1610	Richard Baldwin of Wheathead Mill rows with Elizabeth Southerns and his young daughter falls ill.
1610	Elizabeth Southerns magically changes milk into butter.
1610	Alizon meets a black dog in John Robinson's close in Roughlee.
1610, summer	Fancie comes to Anne Whittle 'like a bear'.
1610, September	Thomas Dodgson, son of Edward of Bolton by Bowland is baptised.
1611, 6 April	Little Thomas Dodgson dies and is buried on this date.
1611	Richard Baldwin's daughter dies.
1611	Thomas Walshamn's one-year-old child dies after an illness lasting about two weeks.
1611, St Peter's Day	On 29 June, Henry Bulcock claims Alizon Device has bewitched his child.

1612

4 January	William, infant son of Thomas Lister, is buried at Gisburn.
18 March	Alizon encounters John Law, the pedlar.
21 March	Abraham Law receives word that his father is ill.
23 March	Alizon encounters a black dog in Newchurch.
27 March	James Device sees a brown dog come from Malkin Tower.
29 March	Abraham Law takes Alizon to see his father in Colne; she confesses to having bewitched him.
30 March	Roger Nowell examines Alizon and Abraham at his home in Read, along with Elizabeth and James Device. He detains Alizon but releases her mother and brother. Elizabeth Southerns is found to bear a damning mark.
2 April	A supernatural black cat lies on James. On this same date Roger Nowell examines Elizabeth Southerns, Anne Whittle, Anne Redfearn, John Nutter, Margaret Crooke and James Robinson, all at Ashlar House in Fence.
4 April	Nowell sends Elizabeth Southerns, Anne Whittle, Anne Redfearn and Alizon Device to Lancaster Gaol.
6 April	Jennet Preston is tried in York for the murder of Dodgson's child.
9 April	On Maundy Thursday, James Device steals a sheep from John Robinson of Barley.
10 April	Good Friday: the meeting at Malkin Tower.
15 April	Robert Holden hears evidence about the Samlesbury case.
21 April	James is visited by his familiar for the final time.

27 April	Roger Nowell and Nicholas Bannister examine Elizabeth, James and Jennet Device at Fence.
5 May	Nowell, Bannister and Robert Holden take a statement from Constable Henry Hargreaves.
7 May (c.)	Grace Sowerbutts again examined by Robert Holden.
May	Elizabeth Southerns dies in Lancaster Gaol.
19 May	Mayor William Sandes, James Anderton and Thomas Covell examine Anne Whittle and James Device in Lancaster.
12 July	Sir Thomas Gerard examines the witnesses in the case against Isobel Robey.
27 July	Jennet Preston is tried for a second time in York and found guilty.
29 July	Jennet Preston is executed on York's Knavesmire.
7 August	Robert Holden examines John Singleton and probably Grace Sowerbutts about the Samlesbury allegations.
9 August	Jennet Booth gives evidence against Margaret Pearson to Nicholas Bannister.
15 August	Nicholas Bannister makes his will; he passes away five days later.
16 August	Judges Bromley and Altham arrive in Lancaster from Kendal.
17 August	The Assizes open in Lancaster.
18 August	James and Elizabeth Device, along with Anne Whittle, are tried and found guilty; Anne Redfearn is tried for the murder of Robert Nutter and cleared but faces a further trial.
19 August	Anne Redfearn is tried for the murder of Christopher Nutter and found guilty.

The trial of the Samlesbury Witches is heard and adjourned, with Grace Sowerbutts admitting deceit.

Alice Nutter and Katherine Hewitt are tried and found guilty.

The Samlesbury witches are acquitted.

John and Jane Bulcock, Alizon Device, Margaret Pearson and Isobel Robey are tried and found guilty.

The following are sentenced to death: Anne Whittle, Elizabeth and James Device, Anne Redfearn, Alice Nutter, Katherine Hewitt, John and Jane Bulcock, Alizon Device and Isobel Robey.

Margaret Pearson is sentenced to being pilloried and imprisoned.

20 August	Those found guilty are publicly executed on Lancaster Moor.
1612	*The Arraignment and Trial of Jennet Preston* is published, with Potts declaring his reason for writing it: 'I think it necessary not to let the memorie of her life and death die with her.'
1613	*The Wonderfull Discoverie of Witches* is published by Thomas Potts.

POST-1612

1616	Christmas Day: Trial chronicler Thomas Potts passes away.
1617	Trial judge James Altham dies.
1618	Michael Dalton's legal handbook Country Justice is published, with advice based on observations of the 1612 trials.
1619	Thomas Lister the younger dies.

1623	Roger Nowell dies; his son inherits Read Hall.
1626	Trial judge Sir Edward Bromley dies.
1633	Second Pendle witch trial takes place.
1634	*The Late Lancashire Witches*, by Heywood and Brome is performed for the first time. More plays and other fictions based on the case follow.
1635	Death of Jennet Device; she is buried in Newchurch.
1639	Lancaster Castle gaoler, Thomas Covell, dies and is buried in Lancaster Priory.
1677	John Webster's critical study, *The Displaying of Supposed Witchcraft* is published, condemning the trials.
1685	Alice Molland, hanged in Exeter, is thought to be the last woman executed for witchcraft in England.
1736	Parliament passes a new Act repealing the laws against witchcraft but imposing fines and imprisonment on those claiming to possess magical powers.
1810	Sir Walter Scott includes Potts' book in his collection of *Scarce and Valuable Tracts*.
1837	Two youths in Lancashire are certified insane after setting fire to barns to ensure they were rid of the witches.
1845	James Crossley of the Manchester Chetham Society publishes Potts' book in a new, annotated edition.
1848	After a suggestion from his friend James Crossley, the celebrated novelist William Harrison Ainsworth writes *The Lancashire Witches*. It appears in serialised form initially, then as a book in 1849. It becomes a huge success.

1944, May	Helen Duncan imprisoned under the 1735 Witchcraft Act. It is not an offence to produce spirits of the dead, only to pretend to do so, and Helen is convicted of this, although attempts are later made to pardon her.
1944, September	The last person to be convicted under the 1735 Witchcraft Act is Jane Rebecca Yorke of London. Like Helen Duncan she is convicted of pretending to produce spirits, but due to her age she is fined rather than imprisoned.
1951	*Mist Over Pendle*, Robert Neill's fictional account of the witch trials is published to great acclaim.
1951	Repeal of 1736 Witchcraft Act; replaced by Fraudulent Mediums Act (itself replaced in 2008).
1976	*The Witches of Pendle*, a television film about the trials, airs twice on BBC Two.
1987	*Lucifer Over Lancashire*, a documentary about modern-day Pendle and the impact of the trials, is broadcast on BBC Two.
1987	Plans for a Pendle Witches theme park proposed and rejected.
2001	To mark the fiftieth anniversary of the repeal of the Witchcraft Act, a number of events take place related to the Pendle trials.
2011	Discovery of a 'witch's cottage' at Lower Black Moss.
2012	The 400th anniversary of the trials is commemorated with several events, including the display of '1612' on Pendle Hill, the Lancashire Witches Walk featuring iron tercet way markers, and the unveiling of a statue of Alice Nutter in Roughlee.

2019	Publication of Stacey Halls' best-selling novel *The Familiars*, featuring the Pendle witches.
2022	Pendle Hill named the UK's most haunted location.
2023	Following the failure of previous attempts, a new campaign is launched to pardon the Pendle witches and reaches the requisite 10,000 signatures to ensure it is debated in Parliament.
2024	A sculpture of Dandy, James Device's black dog familiar, becomes a permanent feature in Clitheroe.

ACKNOWLEDGEMENTS

This was not a book I ever expected to write. For the past fifteen years, I've been writing 'conventional' true crime, and I thought it unlikely that any publisher would be willing to take a risk on a book from me about the Pendle witches. But during a discussion with Justine Taylor, editor of my last book about poisoner Graham Young, I said how much I would love to write about the trials and she responded, 'I'd publish it.' So, my first acknowledgement has to be to Justine, particularly since neither of us knew then that I was slipping into a mental health crisis. I was unable to think straight, let alone write, and my original submission date for the manuscript became a distant memory. But Justine never gave up on me or the book, and her faith helped immeasurably as I began to recover. I will forever be grateful to Justine, and to Robert Smith, who has proven to be both the best literary agent any writer could hope to be represented by, and a true friend too.

Throughout my research and writing, I was acutely aware that I was standing on the shoulders of giants: those dedicated professors, historians and archivists who have spent years making ancient documents decipherable and available to the wider public. In this case, their number includes those largely unsung heroes of the literary world: the local historians. I doubt anyone has researched the subject of the Pendle witches and their environment more thoroughly than John A. Clayton, whose books are listed in the *Bibliography*, along with other treasures by Gladys Whitaker, Kathleen Eyre, Mary Brigg, Jacqueline Davitt, John A. Laycock, Jenny Palmer, John Hope, Clifford Moorhouse, Glenn Clayton and Clifford Byrne. I am as grateful to them as I am to experts such as Diane Purkiss, Marion Gibson, Christina Larner, Emma Wilby, James A. Sharpe, Owen Davies, Julian Goodare, Ronald Hutton and Malcolm Gaskill for bringing the period of the witch trials to life.

My research took me into a number of archives, museums and libraries, and I give thanks to the staff of the following institutions: the Lancashire Record Office in Preston, the Hull History Centre, the National Archives, Burnley Central Library, Nelson Library, York Explore Library, the Lancashire University Library, the Pendle Heritage Centre in Barrowford, the Judges Lodgings Museum (former home of Thomas Covell), Gawthorpe Hall, the Ryedale Folk Museum, Clitheroe Castle Museum, Blackburn Museum and Art Gallery, Towneley Hall in Burnley, the Cottage Museum in Lancaster, the Harris Museum in Preston, Houghton Tower, Lancaster City Museum, and Samlesbury Hall. I'd also like to thank especially Neil Adams of the Borthwick Institute in York for his expert guidance, and Fiona Callaghan, assistant archivist at the British Museum, for pointing me in the direction of Thomas Potts' original *Discoverie*.

Gratitude aplenty to Gary and Anne who work at Lancaster Castle, Martin for giving me access to the Well Tower, and to Debbie Garritty of the Duchy of Lancaster for granting permission. Colin Penny, Museum Manager at Lancaster Castle, was the first person I spoke to about the case after returning to work; I thank him for his kindness, patience and expertise, and for showing me around areas of the Castle that are otherwise off limits. I was also fortunate to attend Colin's presentation at Gawthorpe Hall about the witch trials and Cuthbert Halsall, and look forward to his forthcoming book on the subject.

Since my first visit to Pendle in 2012, I have stayed there more times than I can remember. Each time I am struck anew by the beauty of the landscape and the warm welcome offered by its residents.

For hospitality and good company, I want to thank especially Veronica and Jeremy, who run the Hen House and Rooster's Rest holiday cottages in Barley, likewise Kerry and David at One Tree Under Pendle, as well as the staff at Ribblesdale Park in Gisburn, at Greendales in Downham, at the Assheton Arms in Downham, at the Bay Horse in Roughlee, at the Pendle Inn and Barley Mow in Barley, and also Maureen Stopforth, proprietor of that well-known institution *Witches Galore* in Newchurch-in-Pendle.

Above all, I want to thank my friends and family for their support, love and understanding. I could neither have written this book nor got through these past eighteen months without my partner Lee and his daughter Rosie, my son River and his partner Erin, Ali Dunnell, Tina Barrott, and Tricia, Faith and Catherine Room (and many thanks for accompanying me to Pendle, Cathy). I have to single out the uniquely gifted Sharon Moore, for opening my eyes to the fact that real magic – of the sort understood by the cunning folk and seers of the past – does indeed exist in this world and is waiting to be discovered by all of us.

My last debt of gratitude is to my familiars, Bear and Reggie, our two beloved rescue cats, who are my constant companions and brought me such comfort while I was writing. They were also at my side when I learned during the latter stages of this book, that my great-grandmother, Rosina, had been imprisoned in Wakefield Gaol during 1904, with her criminal status recorded in the prison register as 'rogue vagabond – fortune-telling.'

I wish I had known her. Failing that, I dedicate this book to her, Rosina Lee.

BIBLIOGRAPHY

BOOKS:

Abbott, Geoffrey, *Lords of the Scaffold: A History of the Executioner* (Palgrave Macmillan, 1991)

Abram, William Alexander, *A History of the Township of Billington, In the Paish of Blackburn, Co. Lancaster: Its Ancient Families, Lords, and Freeholders; With an Account of the Parochial Chapel and Chapelry of Langho, Part I* (The Historic Society of Lancashire and Cheshire, 1873)

Adam, Isabel, *Witch-Hunt: The Great Scottish Witch Trials of 1697* (Macmillan, 1978)

Almond, Philip C., *The Lancashire Witches: A Chronicle of Sorcery and Death on Pendle Hill* (I.B. Tauris & Co., 2012)

Almond, Philip C., *Demonic Possession and Exorcism in Early Modern England: Contemporary Texts and Their Cultural Contexts* (Cambridge: Cambridge University Press, 2004)

Ames, Joseph, *Typographical Antiquities: Being an Historical Account of Printing in England* (London: Printed for W. Faden, 1749)

Andrews, William, *Old-Time Punishments* (London: Corner House, 1975)

Apps, Lara and Gow, Andrew, *Male Witches in Early Modern Europe* (Manchester University Press, 2003)

Arnovick, Leslie K., *Written Reliquaries: The Resonance of Orality in Medieval English Texts* (John Benjamins Publishing Company, 2006)

Ash, Russell, et al., *Reader's Digest Folklore, Myths and Legends of Britain* (Reader's Digest Association, 1977)

Axon, Ernest, *Bygone Lancashire* (Wakefield: S. R. Publishers, 1971)

Bailey, Brian, *Hellholes: An Account of History's Most Notorious Prisons* (Orion, 1995)

Baker, Emerson W., *A Storm of Witchcraft: The Salem Trials and the American Experience* (Oxford: Oxford University Press, 2016)

Baker, Margaret, *Folklore and Customs of Rural England* (David & Charles, 1974)

Baker, Margaret, *Discovering the Folklore of Plants* (Shire Publications, 1969)

Baker, Margaret, *Folklore and Customs of Love and Marriage* (Shire Publications, 1974)

Barstow, Anne Llewellyn, *Witchcraze: A New History of the European Witch Hunts* (Bravo Ltd., 1995)

Bennett, Walter, *The Pendle Witches* (The County Borough of Burnley, Libraries and Arts Committee, 1957)

Bennett, Walter, *The History of Burnley I & II* (Burnley Corporation, 1969)

Bentley, Phyllis, *Colne Valley Cloth: From the Earliest Times to the Present Day* (Huddersfield: The Huddersfield and District Woollen Export Group, 1947)

Bernard, Richard, *A Guide to Grand-Jury Men, Divided into Two Bookes* (London: Felix Kingston, 1627)

Billington, Richard Newman, *St Peter's, Lancaster* (Sands & Co, 1910)

Blakey, Jesse, *The Annals and Stories of Barrowford* (Blakeys, 1929)

Borman, Tracy, *Witches: James I and the English Witch Hunts* (Vintage, 2014)

Bourke, Angela, *The Burning of Bridget Cleary: A True Story* (Pimlico, 2006)

Bradshaw, Suzanne, *The People's Park: A History of Williamson Park Lancaster* (Palatine Books, 2022)

Bridges, Todd Andrew, *The 400th Anniversary of the Lancashire Witch Trials: Commemoration and its Meaning in 2012* (University of Essex, 2016)

Brigg, Mary, *The People of Pendle I: The Early History of the Forest of Pendle* (Pendle Heritage Centre, 1989)

Briggs, K. M, *Pale Hecate's Team* (New York: Humanities Press, 1962)

Brinley, John, *A Discovery of the Impostures of Witches and Astrologers* (London: John Wright, 1680)

Burford, E.J. and Shulman, Sandra, *Of Bridles and Burnings: The Punishment of Women* (Robert Hale, 1992)

Burton, Henry, *A Narration of the Life of Mr Henry Burton* (London: John Bothwell, 1643)

Callow, John, *Embracing the Darkness: A Cultural History of Witchcraft* (I. B. Tauris & Co. Ltd, 2018)

Callow, John, *The Last Witches of England: A Tragedy of Sorcery and Superstition* (Bloomsbury Academic, 2023)

Champness, John, *Lancaster Castle, A Brief History* (Preston: Lancaster County Books, 1993)

Carr, James, *Annals and Stories of Colne and Neighbourhood* (John Heywood, Manchester, 1878)

Carr, William, *The Dialect of Craven, in the West Rising of the County of York* (London: Wm. Crofts, 1828)

Carver, Stephen, *The Author Who Outsold Dickens: The Life and Work of W.H. Ainsworth* (Pen & Sword History, 2020)

Catlow, Richard, *The Pendle Witches* (Hendon Publishing Co. Ltd, 2002)

Cawthorne, Nigel, *Witches: History of a Persecution* (Chartwell Books, 2006)

Ceci, Stephen J. and Bruck, Maggie, *Jeopardy in the Courtroom: A Scientific Analysis of Children's Testimony* (Washington: American Psychological Association, 1995)

Chollet, Mona, *In Defence of Witches: Why Women Are Still On Trial* (Picador, 2023)

Clayton, Glen, *The Famous Witches of Samlesbury* (Glen Clayton, 2012)

Clayton, Glen, *Saint John Southworth of Samlesbury: His Life and Times* (Glen Clayton, 2017)

Clayton, John A., *The Pendle Witch Fourth Centenary Handbook: History and Archaeology in Fact and Fiction* (Barrowford Press, 2012)

Clayton, John A., *The Lancashire Witch Conspiracy: A History of Pendle Forest and the Pendle Witch Trials* (Barrowford Press, 2007)

Clayton, John A., *Valley of the Drawn Sword: The Early History of Burnley, Pendle and West Craven* (Barrowford Press, 2012)

Clayton, John A., *The Other Pendle Witches* (Barrowford Press, 2012)

Clayton, John A., *A Pendle Witch and the Dean of Chester 1536–1612* (Barrowford Press, 2024)

Cleghorn, Elinor, *Unwell Women* (Weidenfield & Nicholson, 2021)

Cobban, Jenny Lee, *The Lure of the Lancashire Witches* (Palatine Books, 2011)

Cockburn, J. S., *A History of English Assizes 1558 – 1714* (Cambridge University Press, 1972)

Collins, Herbert C., *The Roof of Lancaster* (London: J. M. Dent & Sons, 1951)

Conroy, Michael P., *The Shuttleworths of Gawthorpe* (Bury: The Lancashire Family History and Heraldry Society, 1999)

Cornwell, John, *Earth to Earth: The True Story of the Lives and Violent Deaths of a Devon Farming Family* (Penguin, 1984)

Creager, Angela and Jordan, Wiliam, *The Animal/Human Boundary: Historical Perspectives* (University of Rochester Press, 2002)

Croston, James, *A History of the Ancient Hall of Samlesbury in Lancashire* (Whittingham & Wilkins at the Chiswick Press, 1871)

Dalton, Michael, *The Country Justice: Containing the Practice of the Justices of the Peace, Out of their Sessions* (London: William Rawlins and Samuel Roycroft, 1690)

Davies, Owen, *Popular Magic: Cunning Folk in English History* (Hambledon Continuum, 2007)

Davitt, Jacqueline, *Pendle and the Ribble Valley: Murder and Crime* (The History Press, 2007)

Davitt, Jacqueline, *Witches and Ghosts of Pendle and the Ribble Valley* (The History Press, 2006)

DeGraaff, Robert, *The Book of the Toad: A Natural and Magical History of Toad-Human Relations* (Inner Traditions, 1991)

Dell, Christopher, *The Occult, Witchcraft & Magic: An Illustrated History* (Thames & Hudson, 2016)

DeRosa, Robin, *The Making of Salem: The Witch Trials in History, Fiction and Tourism* (McFarland & Co., 2009)

Dolan, Frances, *Dangerous Familiars: Representations of Domestic Crime in England, 1550-1700* (Cornell University Press, 1994)

Dolan, Frances, *True Relations: Reading, Literature and Evidence in Seventeenth Century England* (University of Pennsylvania Press, 2013)

Douglas, Arthur, *The Fate of the Lancashire Witches* (Countryside, 1979)

Easlea, Brian, *Witch-Hunting, Magic and the New Philosophy: An Introduction to the Debates of the Scientific Revolution 1450-1750* (Humanities Press Inc., 1980)

Eaton, Robert, *A History of Samlesbury in the Hundred of Blackburn, County of Lancaster* (J. Dickinson & Sons Ltd., 1936)

Eaton, Robert, *The Illustrated Guide to the Ancient Hall of Samlesbury* (J. Dickinson & Sons Ltd., 1947)

Eidinow, Esther, *Envy, Poison, and Death: Women on Trial in Classical Athens* (Oxford: Oxford University Press, 2016)

Entwistle, Simon, *Ghostly Tales of the Unexpected* (CreateSpace Independent Publishing Platform, 2014)

Ekwall, Eilert, *The Place Names of Lancashire* (Longmans Green & Co., 1922)

Ernest, A., *Bygone Lancashire* (Simpkin, Marshall, Hamilton, Kent & Co., 1892)

L'Estrange-Ewan, C., *Witch Hunting and Witch Trials: The Indictments for Witchcraft from the Records of the 1373 Assizes Held from the Home Court 1559-1736* (Routledge, 2015)

Eyre, Kathleen, *Witchcraft in Lancashire* (Dalesman Publishing Co., Ltd., 1974)

Eyre, Kathleen, *Lancashire Legends* (Dalesman Publishing Co., Ltd., 1992)

Fairfax, Edward, *The Fewston Witches 1621-1623: A Yorkshire Coven* (PWCA Books and Pamphlets, 2022)

Fairfax, Edward, *Daemonologia: A Discourse on Witchcraft* (Frederick Muller Ltd., 1971)

Farrer, William and Brownbill, J., *The Victoria History of the County of Lancaster, Vol.6* (Constable & Company Ltd, 1911)

Farrer, William, *The Court Rolls of the Honor of Clitheroe in the County of Lancaster Vol.1* (Emmott & Co., 1897)

Farrer, William (ed.), *The Registers of the Parish Church of Burnley in the County of Lancaster: Christenings, Weddings and Burials 1562 to 1653* (Aldine Press, 1899)

Federici, Silva, *Witches, Witch-Hunting, and Women* (PM Press, 2018)

Few, Janet, *Coffers, Clysters, Comfrey and Coifs: The Lives of Our Seventeenth Century Ancestors*, (The Family History Partnership, 2012)

Fleury, Cross, *Time-Honoured Lancaster* (Lancaster: Eaton & Bulfield, 1891)

Foster, Donald with Banton, Tobian (eds.), *Women's Works Vol 3: 1605–1625* (New York: Wicked Good Books, 2013).

Forsyth, J. S., *Demonologia or Natural Knowledge Revealed* (London: John Bumpus, 1827)

Froome, Joyce, *Wicked Enchantments: A History of the Pendle Witches and Their Magic* (Palatine Books, 2010)

Fuller, Basil and Cornes, John, *No 10 Downing Street* (Greenberg Publishers, 1936)

Gage, Matilda Joslyn, *Woman, Church and State* (C.H. Kerr & Co., 1893)

Gaskill, Malcolm, *The Ruin of All Witches: Life and Death in the New World* (Penguin, 2022)

Gaskill, Malcolm, *Witchfinders: A Seventeenth Century English Tragedy* (John Murray, 2006)

Gibson, Marion, *Witchcraft and Society in England and America 1550-1750* (Cornell University Press, 2003)

Gibson, Marion, *Witchcraft: A History in Thirteen Trials* (Simon & Schuster, 2023)

Gibson, Marion, *The Witches of St Osyth: Persecution, Betrayal and Murder in Elizabethan England* (Cambridge University Press, 2022)

Gibson, Marion, *Early Modern Witches: Witchcraft cases in Contemporary Writing* (Routledge, 2000)

Gibson, Marion, *Reading Witchcraft: Stories of Early English Witches* (Routledge, 1999)

Gleason, J. H., *The Justices of the Peace in England 1558 – 1640* (Oxford University Press, 1979)

Goodare, Julian (ed.), *The Scottish Witch Hunt in Context* (Manchester University Press, 2002)

Goodare, Julian, *The European Witch-Hunt* (Routledge, 2010)

Goodier, Christine, *1612: The Lancashire Witch Trials* (Palatine Books, 2011)

Grosart, Rev. Alexander B., *The Spending of the Money of Robert Nowell* (Manchester: printed for private circulation by C. E. Simms, 1877)

Haigh, Christopher, *Reformation and Resistance in Tudor Lancashire* (Cambridge University Press, 1975)

Haining, Peter (ed.), *The Witchcraft Papers* (Robert Hale & Co., 1974)

Hall, Spencer T., *Pendle Hill and Its Surroundings* (Landy Publishing, 1995)

Harland, John and Wilkinson, Thomas Turner, *Lancashire Folk-Lore* (Frederick Warne & Co., 1882)

Harrington, Joel F., *The Faithful Executioner: Life and Death in the Sixteenth Century* (Vintage, 2014)

Harrison, G. B., *King James the First: Daemonologie* (1597), (New York: Barnes and Noble, 1966)

Harland, John (ed.), *The House and Farm Accounts of the Shuttleworths of Gawthorpe Hall in the County of Lancaster, September 1582-October 1621* (Chetham Society, 1856)

Hasted, Rachel, *The Pendle Witch-Trial 1612* (Lancashire County Books, 1993)

Haynes, Alan, *The Gunpowder Plot* (The History Press, 2016)

Heygate, Richard and Carr-Gomm, Philip, *The Book of English Magic* (Hodder Paperbacks, 2010)

Hilton, John Anthony, *Catholic Lancashire: from Reformation to Renewal, 1559–1991* (Phillimore: Chichester, 1994)

Hodge, Alistair, *A Short History of Samlesbury* (Carnegie Publishing Ltd, 1986)

Holding, David, *The Pendle Witch Trials of 1612* (DH Publications, 1996)

Holdsworth, Bruce, *Witches Chronicle* (Pennine Printing Services Ltd., 1984)

Hole, Christina, *English Folklore* (B.T. Batsford, 1940)

Hole, Christina, *A Dictionary of British Folk Customs* (Helicon, 1995)

Hole, Christina, *Witchcraft in Britain* (Flamingo, 1979)

Hole, Christina, *English Home Life 1500 to 1800* (B.T. Batsford, 1949)

Holland, Nick, *The Real Guy Fawkes* (Pen & Sword History, 2017)

Holmes, Ronald, *Witchcraft in British History* (The Book Service Ltd., 1974)

Hurren, E. T., *Dissecting the Criminal Corpse: Staging Post-Execution Punishment in Early Modern England* (Palgrave Macmillan, 2016)

Hutton, Ronald, *The Witch: A History of Fear from Ancient Times to the Present* (Yale University Press, 2018)

Janes, Derek, *Lancaster* (Dalesman Books, 1980)

Keighley, Jack, *Walks in Lancashire Witch Country: An Illustrated Guide to 30 Short Circular Walks On and Around Pendle Hill* (Cicerone Press, 2012)

Kirby, J. W., *The Manor and Borough of Leeds 1425-1662: An Edition of Documents, Publications of the Thoresby Society, Vol LVII. No.27* (The Thoresby Society, 1983)

Kittredge, George Lyman, *Witchcraft in Old and New England* (Atheneum, 1972)

Knipe, William, *Tyburn Tales: The Criminal Chronology of York Castle* (London: The History Press, 2010)

Kramer, Heinrich, *Malleus Maleficarum* (London: John Rodker, 1928)

Larner, Christina, *Enemies of God: The Witch-Hunt in Scotland* (Chatto & Windus, 1981)

Larner, Christina, *Witchcraft and Religion: The Politics of Popular Belief* (Blackwell, 1985)

Larner, Christina, Hyde-Lee, Christopher, and McLachlan, Hugh V., *A Source Book of Scottish Witchcraft* (The Grimsay Press, 2005)

Larrington, Carolyne, *The Feminist Companion to Mythology* (Pandora Press, 1992)

Laycock, John A. and Wilson, Amy, *The Registers of the Parish Church of Padiham in the County of Lancaster, Christenings, Burials and Weddings 1573-1653* (Strowger & Son at the Clarence Press, 1903)

Laurence, Anne, *Women in England 1500-1760* (Weidenfeld & Nicholson, 2005)

Lee, Alastair, *Pendle: Landscape of History and Home* (Frances Lincoln, 2009)

L'Estrange Ewen, C., *Witch Hunting and Witch Trials: The Indictments for Witchcraft from the Records of the 1373 Assizes Held from the Home Court 1559-1736* (London: Routledge, 1929)

Levin, Carole, *Dreaming the English Renaissance: Politics and Desire in Court and Culture* (Palgrave, 2008)

Licence, Amy, *Woodsmoke and Sage: The Five Senses 1485-1603: How the Tudors Experienced the World* (London: The History Press, 2021)

Lipscomb, Suzannah, *A History of Magic, Witchcraft and the Occult* (Dorling Kindersley, 2020)

Lofthouse, Jessica, *Lancashire's Fair Face* (Robert Hale Ltd., 1976)

Lowe, Norman, *The Lancashire Textile Industry in the Sixteenth Century* (Manchester University Press, 1972)

Lowe, Norman, *The Lancashire Textile Industry in the Seventeenth Century: Vol. 20* (Manchester University Press, 1986)

Lumby, Jonathan, *The Lancashire Witch Craze: Jennet Preston and the Lancashire Witches, 1612* (Lancaster: Carnegie Publishing Ltd., 2007)

Lyttelton Lyster Denny, Henry, *Memorials of an Ancient House: A History of the Family of Lister or Lyster* (Edinburgh: Ballantyne, Hanson & Co., 1913)

Macfarlane, Alan, *Witchcraft in Tudor and Stuart England* (Routledge, 1999)

Mackay, C. and Mackay, L., *How to Find Witches on Pendle Hill: A History and Select Walks of the Area of Pendle Hill* (Independently Published, 2019)

March, Henry Colley, *East Lancashire Nomenclature and Rochdale Names* (London: Simpkin & Co., 1880)

Matusiak, John, *James I: Scotland's King of England* (The History Press, 2018)

McClain, Lisa, *Lest We Be Damned: Practical Innovation and Lived Experience Among Catholics in Protestant England, 1559-1642* (Routledge, 2004)

McKechnie, Sam and Portelli, Alexandrine, *The Magpie and the Wardrobe: A Curiosity of Folklore, Magic and Spells* (Pavilion Books, 2015)

Mendelson, Sara and Crawford, Patricia, *Women in Early Modern England, 1550-1720* (Oxford: Clarendon, 1998)

Mercer, A. D., *The Wicked Shall Decay: Charms, Spells & Witchcraft of Old Britain* (Three Hands Press, 2018)

Meredith, Charlotte, *My Mother is a Witch and This I Know to be True: The Voices of Pendle* (Motte and Bailey Publishing, 2023)

Merrifield, Ralph, *The Archaeology of Ritual and Magic* (Batsford, 1987)

Midelfort, H. C. Erik, 'Social History and Biblical Exegesis: Community. Family, and Witchcraft in Sixteenth-Century Germany', in David C. Steinmetz (ed.), *The Bible in the Sixteenth Century* (Durham and London: Duke University Press, 1990)

Mitchell, W. R., *The Lancashire Witches* (Dalesman Publishing Co., Ltd., 1984)

Mitchell, W. R., *Exploring The Lancashire Witch Country* (Dalesman Publishing Co., Ltd., 1978)

Mitchell, W. R., *Lancashire Witch Country* (Dalesman Publishing Co., Ltd., 1974)

Moorhouse, Clifford, Sabden: The Birth of a Lancashire Village (Clifford Moorhouse, 1975)

Moorhouse, Clifford, Sabden: The Forgotten Valley (Clifford Moorhouse, 1978)

Morrison, Blake, *A Discoverie of Witches* (Smith/Doorstep, 2012)

Newall, Venetia (ed.), *The Witch Figure* (Routledge & Kegan Paul, 1973)

Nichols, John, *The Progresses, Processions and Magnificent Festivities of King James the First* (London: J. B. Nichols, 1828)

Notestein, Wallace, *A History of Witchcraft in England from 1558 to 1718* (The American Historical Association, 1911)

Ormerod, Rev. T., *Calderdale* (Lupton Bros., 1906)

Quintrell, B. W. (ed.), *Proceedings of the Lancashire Justices of the Peace at the Sheriff's Table During Assize Week, 1578-1694* (The Record Society of Lancashire and Cheshire, 1981)

Page, Sophie, *Spellbound: Magic, Ritual and Witchcraft* (Ashmolean Museum Publications, 2018)

Palmer, Jenny, *Witches, Quaker and Non-Conformists* (Nu-Age Print and Copy, 2022)

Palmer, Jenny, *Whipps, Watsons and Bulcocks: A Pendle Family History 1560 – 1960* (Nu-Age Print and Copy, 2016)

Parnell, Edward, *Ghostland: In Search of a Haunted Country* (William Collins, 2019)

Peach, Howard, *Curious Tales of Old East Yorkshire* (Sigma Press, 2010)

Pearson, Sarah, *Rural Houses of the Lancashire Pennines 1560 – 1760* (HMSO, 1985)

Peele, Edgar and Southern, Pat, *Trials of the Lancashire Witches: A Study of Seventeenth Century Witchcraft* (David & Charles, 1969)

Penny, Colin and Kemp, Graham, *A History of Lancaster Castle* (Palatine Books, 2022)

Peters, Christine, *Women in Early Modern Britain 1450 – 1640* (Palgrave, 2003)

Pickering, Andrew and Pickering, David, *Witch-Hunting in England* (Amberley Publishing, 2010)

Plowden, Alison, *Tudor Women: Queens and Commoners* (The History Press, 2002)

Pollitt, Irene, *The Lancashire Witches: Condensed and Translated* (Veevers & Hensman Ltd, 1964)

Poole, Robert (ed.), *The Lancashire Witches: Histories and Stories* (Manchester University Press, 2003)

Porteus, Thomas Cruddas, *A History of the Parish of Standish* (J. Starr & Sons Ltd, 1927)

Potts, Thomas and Crossley, James (ed.), *Discoverie of Witches in the County of Lancaster* (Manchester: The Chetham Society, 1845)

Prest, W. R. (ed.), *The Diary of Sir Richard Hutton, 1614–39* (London: Selden Society, 1991)

Purkiss, Diane, *The Witch in History: Early Modern and Twentieth Century Interpretations* (Routledge, 1996)

Rackham, Oliver, *The History of the Countryside: The Classic History of Britain's Landscape, Flora and Fauna* (Weidenfeld & Nicholson, 2020)

Reay, Barry, *Popular Culture in Seventeenth Century England* (London: St Martin's Press, 1985)

Raine, James (ed.), *Depositions from the Castle of York, Relating to Offenses Committed in the Northern Counties in the Seventeenth Century* (HardPress Publishing, 2014)

Ramirez, Janina, *Femina: A New History of the Middle Ages Through the Women Written Out of It* (W.H. Allen, 2023)

Rennison, Eileen, *Yorkshire Witches* (Amberley Publishing, 2012)

Richardson, R. C., *Puritanism in North-West England: A Regional Study of the Diocese of Chester to 1642* (Manchester University Press, 2022)

Roach, Marilynne, *Six Women of Salem: The Untold Story of the Accused and Their Accusers in the Salem Witch Trials* (Da Capo Press, 2013)

Roper, Lyndal, *Witch Craze: Terror and Fantasy in Baroque Germany* (New Haven and London: Yale University Press, 2004)

Rosen, Barbara, *Witchcraft* (New York: Taplinger, 1972)

Rouse, A. L., *The Elizabethan Renaissance: The Cultural Achievement* (Chicago: Ivan R. Dee, 2000)

Russell, Jeffrey B., *A History of Witchcraft: Sorcerers, Heretics & Pagans* (Thames & Hudson, 2024)

Sailor, Dan, *The County Hanging Town: Trials, Executions and Imprisonment at Lancaster Castle* (Challenge, 1994)

Schiff, Stacy, *The Witches: Salem, 1692, A History* (Weidenfeld & Nicholson, 2016)

Scot, Reginald, *The Discoverie of Witchcraft* (London: Elliot Stock, 1886)

Seth, Ronald, *Children Against Witches* (Robert Hale Ltd., 1969)

Sharpe, J. A, *A Fiery and Furious People: A History of Violence in England* (Random House Books, 2016)

Sharpe, J. A., *Instruments of Darkness: Witchcraft in Early Modern England* (University of Pennsylvania Press, 1997)

Sharpe, J. A., *Witchcraft in Early Modern England* (Routledge, 2019)

Sharpe, J. A., *Crime in Early Modern England 1550–1750* (Routledge, 1998)

Shaw, Allyson, *Ashes & Stones: A Scottish Journey in Search of Witches & Witness* (Sceptre, 2023)

Shaw, Claire, *Women of York* (Destinworld Publishing Ltd., 2021)

Simpson, Jacqueline and Westwood, Jennifer, *The Lore of the Land: A Guide to England's Legends, from Spring-Heeled Jack to the Witches of Warboys* (Penguin, 2005)

Sinclair, George, *Satan's Invisible World Discovered: Or a Choice Collection of Modern Relations* (London: James Clarke, 1814)

Skal, David J., *Death Makes a Holiday: A Cultural History of Halloween* (Bloomsbury: New York, 2003)

Smith, Victoria, *Hags: The Demonisation of Middle-Aged Women* (Fleet, 2024)

Spee von Langenfeld, Freidrich and Hellyer, Marcus, *Cautio Criminalis, or a Book on Witch Trials* (University of Virgina Press, 2003)

Spicer, Henry, *The Witch-Wife: A Tale of Malkin Tower; A Drama in Five Acts* (Thomas Bosworth, 1849)

Spufford, Margaret, *The Great Reclothing of Rural England: Petty Chapman and their Wares in the Seventeenth Century* (London: Hambledon Press, 1984)

Steinmetz, David C. (ed.), *The Bible in the Sixteenth Century* (Durham and London: Duke University Press, 1990)

Sterling, Jane, *Famous Northern Crimes, Trials and Criminals* (G.W. & A. Hesketh, 1982)

Strevens, Summer, *Burned at the Stake: The Life and Death of Mary Channing* (Pen & Sword, 2017)

Summers, Rachel, *By the Pricking Needle: The Malleus Maleficarum and Cautio Criminalis: Abridged and Modernised* (Independently published, 2018)

Summers, Montague, *The History of Witchcraft and Demonology* (Obscure Press, 2022)

Taylor-Taswell, Stephen Taylor, *Whalley Church and Abbey* (Blackburn, The Times, 1905)

Thomas, Keith, *Religion and the Decline of Magic* (New York: Charles Scribner's Sons, 1971)

Tigar, Clement, *Forty Martyrs of England and Wales* (Stella Maris, 1961)

Twyford, A.W. and Griffiths, Arthur, *Records of York Castle: Fortress, Courthouse and Prison* (Gale, Making of Modern Law, 2010)

Veerapen, Steven, *The Wisest Fool: The Lavish Life of James VI and I* (Birlinn Ltd, 2023)

Waters, Thomas, *Cursed Britain: A History of Witchcraft and Black Magic in Modern Times* (Yale University Press, 2020)

Whitaker, Thomas Dunham, *An History of the Original Parish of Whalley, and Honor of Clitheroe* (Nichols, Son and Bentley, 1818)

Whitaker, Thomas Dunham, *The History and Antiquities of the Deanery of Craven in the County of York* (Joseph Dodgson, 1878)

White, John, *A Defence of the Way to the True Church* (London: Felix Kyngston for William Barret, 1624)

Wilby, Emma, *Cunning Folk and Familiar Spirits: Shamanistic Visionary Traditions in Early Modern British Witchcraft and Magic Sussex* (Sussex Academic Press, 2005)

Wilby, Emma, *The Visions of Isobel Gowdie: Magic, Shamanism and Witchcraft in Seventeenth Century Scotland* (Liverpool University Press, 2010)

Williams, Ann, *The Witches of Pendle: The Magic and the Myths* (Coach House Press, 2019)

Willmoth, Frances, *Sir Jonas Moore: Practical Mathematics and Restoration Science* (Woodbridge: Boydell Press, 1993)

Winsham, Willow, *Accused: British Witches Throughout History* (Pen & Sword Books, 2022)

Winsham, Willow, *England's Witchcraft Trials* (Pen & Sword Books, 2018)

Winterbottom, Vera, *The Devil in Lancashire* (Manchester: The Cloister Press, 1963)

Wray, Michael, *The Witches of North Yorkshire* (East Coast Books, 2001)

Wright, Thomas, *Narratives of Sorcery and Magic from the Most Authentic Sources* (Redfield, 1852

BOOKLETS, PAPERS, ARTICLES AND ONLINE MEDIA

Anonymous, *The Famous History of the Lancashire Witches*, Chapbook (app. 1780): https://books.google.co.uk/ books?id=vY7Jar3yktoC&printsec=frontcover&source=gbs_ge_ summary_r&cad=0#v=onepage&q&f=false

Baratta, Luca, 'Lancashire: A Land of Witches in Shakespeare's Time', *Journal of Early Modern Studies 2* (March 2013): https://www.researchgate.net/publication/307651576_Lancashire_a_Land_of_ Witches_in_Shakespeare%27s_Time

Barrowclough, David, *The Malkin Tower, A Seventeenth Century Witches' Coven Discovered? The Archaeological and Historical Evidence behind the British Witch Trials of 1612 Considered* (2012): https://www.academia.edu/10316559/The_Malkin_Tower_A_Seventeenth_ Century_Witches_Coven_Discovered_The_Archaeological_and_Historical_ Evidence_Behind_the_British_Witch_Trials_of_1612_Considered

Blundell, John D., *The Pendle Witches: A Trial in 17th Century Lancashire Exhibition at Towneley Hall Art Gallery and Museums, Burnley, 19 May – 30 September 1972*, Exhibition Guide (Towneley Hall Art Gallery and Museums, 1972)

Bonzol, Judith, 'The Medical Diagnosis of Demonic Possession in an Early Modern English Community', *Parergon*, Volume 26, Number 1 (2009)

Borough of Pendle, *On the Trail of the Father of Time in Pendle, Lancashire: The Jonas Moore Trail in the Foothills of Pendle Hill*, Tourism Guide (undated)

Bowd, S., 'John Dee and the Seven in Lancashire: Possession, Exorcism and Apocalypse in England', *Northern History*, Vol. 47, No.2 (2010): https://www.pure.ed.ac.uk/ws/portalfiles/portal/10662281/John_Dee_and_The_Seven_In_Lancashire.pdf

Bradshaw, Suzanne, *They Walked These Floors: A History of the Forgotten Keepers of the Judges' Lodgings* (Friends of Lancaster Judges' Lodgings, 2021), available to read at Burnley Library

Brennan, Michael G., *The Book of Hours of the Braddyll Family of Whalley Abbey* (University of Leeds, Brotherton MS. 15, 1997): https://www.hslc.org.uk/wp-content/uploads/2017/05/146-2-Brennan.pdf

Brigg, Mary, *The Forest of Pendle in the Seventeenth Century* from *The Historic Society of Lancashire and Cheshire, 1961* (1961)

Brigg, Mary, 'The Forest of Pendle in the Seventeenth Century, Part Two' from *The Historic Society of Lancashire and Cheshire, 1963* (1963)

Brown, James, 'Margaret Alcock's Evil Eye: Witchcraft Defamations in Early Modern England', 31 October 2016, Inner Lives: Emotions, Identity, and the Supernatural 1300-1900 blog: https://innerlivesblog.wordpress.com/2016/10/31/margaret-alcocks-evil-eye-witchcraft-defamation-suits-in-early-modern-england/

Byrne, C. H., *The Pendle Witches: A New Look* (1980) typescript only, available to read at Burnley Library

Byrne, Clifford, *Newchurch-in-Pendle: Folklore, Fact, Fancy, Traditions and Information* (Marsden Antiquarians, 1982)

Cameron, Debbie, *Language: A Feminist Guide* 'What Are Words Worth? Thoughts on the Pardoning of Witches', 16 January 2022: https://debuk.wordpress.com/2022/01/16/what-are-words-worth-thoughts-on-the-pardoning-of-witches/

Champness, John, 'Lancaster Castle: The Rebuilding of the County Gaol and Courts', *Contrebis* 2019, Vol. 37, Lancaster Archaeological and Historical Society (2019): https://lahs.archaeologyuk.org/Contrebis/Champness%20Castle%2018C%20C.pdf

Colne Neighbourhood Plan: Non-Designated Heritage Assets (2020):
https://colnetowncouncil.org.uk/ctc/wp-content/uploads/2020/01/Colne-Local-
Heritage-List-InfoImages-2020-01_DRAFT.pdf

Cox, Edward W., 'Lancaster Castle', 5 November 1895 in *Transactions of the
Historic Society of Lancashire and Cheshire*, vol. 48, p95-122 (1896)
https://www.hslc.org.uk/wp-content/uploads/2017/06/48-5-Cox.pdf

Darrel, John, *A True Narration of the Strange and Grievous Vexation by the Devil of
Seven Persons in Lancashire and William Somers of Nottingham, 1600*:
https://quod.lib.umich.edu/e/eebo/A19860.0001.001/1:3?rgn=div1;view=fulltext

Davies, Owen, 'The Nightmare Experience, Sleep Paralysis, and Witchcraft
Accusations', in *Folklore* 114 (2003)

Davies, Simon Francis, 'Witchcraft and the Book Trade in Early Modern
England', thesis, University of Sussex (2013):
https://sussex.figshare.com/articles/thesis/Witchcraft_and_the_book_trade_in_
early_modern_England/23394920

Dee, Katherine, 'Witchcraft is Not Gen Z's New Religion', *The Spectator*,
29 October 2022:
https://thespectator.com/topic/witchcraft-not-gen-z-new-religion/

The Enquiring Eye: Journal of the Museum of Witchcraft and Magic, Issue 2 (2018):
https://www.academia.edu/99653831/The_Enquiring_Eye_Journal_of_Museum_
of_Witchcraft_and_Magic_Issue_2_

Ermacora, Davide, *Embedded Pins and Migratory Needles: A Historical Folklore
Perspective – Part 1, Contemporary Legend,* Series 3, vol. 8 (2018), download from
Indiana University:
https://www.iu.edu/index.html

Ermacora, Davide, *Embedded Pins and Migratory Needles: A Historical Folklore
Perspective – Part 2, Contemporary Legend,* Series 3, vol. 9 (2019), download from
Indiana University
https://www.iu.edu/index.html

Farrow, Thomas J, *Gallows and Golgotha: Morbid Conventions in the Inherited
Place-names of Seventeenth Century Quaker Burial Grounds* (Liverpool: Liverpool
University Press, June 2021)

Francisconi, Tsea M., *Witch Pamphlets* (2021), *Graduate Student Theses,
Dissertations and Professional Papers*, University of Montana (2021), download from
University of Montana:
https://scholarworks.umt.edu/etd/11850/

Gaskill, M., 'Reporting Murder: Fiction in the Archives in Early Modern England', *Social History*, 23 (1), 1-30 (1998), p. 25: https://doi.org/10.1080/03071029808568018

Gardiner, Karen, 'Witch Hunt Tourism is Lucrative; It Also Obscures a Tragic History', *National Geographic* (23 October 2020): https://www.nationalgeographic.com/travel/article/a-better-way-to-commemorate-the-witch-hunts

Gerrard, Sue, *Isabel Robey: The Windle Witch* (Charles North Publishing, 2011)

Golgotha, 'Lancaster' in *Lancaster Civic Vision Guide 93:* Lancaster Civic Vision: https://www.lancastercivicsociety.uk/wp-content/uploads/2022/07/93-Golgotha-2022.pdf

Gottschall, Anna Edith, 'The Pater Noster and the Laity in England c.700-1560', thesis, University of Birmingham (2014), download from University of Birmingham: https://etheses.bham.ac.uk/id/eprint/6535/

Harley, David, 'Historians as Demonologists: The Myth of the Midwife-Witch', *Social History of Medicine*, Vol. 3, Issue 1 (April 1990)

Hasted, Rachel, 'The New Myth of the Witch', *Trouble and Strife: A Radical Feminist Magazine*, Issue 2, Spring 1984, (Manchester: Amazon Press, 1984)

Herman, Eleanor, 'A Brief History of Calling Women Witches', *Literary Hub* website (19 September 2022)

Hickey, Roy S., 'Radical Religion and the Background to the Development of the Quaker Movement in the area of Pendle, the Ribble Valley, Craven, Westmoreland and the Yorkshire Dales, c1570 to 1652', thesis, University of Manchester, (2020)

Hirsh, John C., 'Credulity and Belief: The Role of Postconditions in the Late Medieval Charm', in *Preternature: Critical and Historical Studies on the Preternatural*, Volume I, Number I, 2012: https://muse.jhu.edu/article/470477

Historical Commission on Historical Monuments, *York Castle* (The Campfield Press, 1973)

Historical maps online: the National Library of Scotland: https://maps.nls.uk

Historical Lancashire maps online: Lancashire County Council Heritage Mapping: https://experience.arcgis.com/experience/07bf8178a1a3485ea148b46939415a5c

Hoggard, Brian, *The Archaeology of Counter-Witchcraft and Popular Magic* in *Beyond The Witch Trials*, Manchester Hive (30 July 2018)

Hope, John, *In Pendle's Shadow: The Newchurch Story* (William Pownall & Sons Ltd., c.1994)

The Journal of Antiquities: Ancient Sites in Great Britain and Southern Ireland: https://thejournalofantiquities.com/about/

Kennerley, Eija, *Thomas Covell of Lancaster, Esquire* (Lancaster City Museums, 1989)

Kucinski, Joanna J., *Representations of Witches in Popular Literature in England, 1566–1645* (Sweet Briar: Sweet Briar College, 1998)

Lancaster Castle History: *The Castle Studies Group Journal* No.26 (2005-6): http://www.castlestudiesgroup.org.uk/CSGJournal2012-13X6-LancasterRev1.pdf

Lancaster University Map Resources: historical maps of Lancashire: https://lancaster.libguides.com/maps/historicmaps#s-lg-box-11473656

Laycock, Dr J. A., *Sabden Before the Year 1600; A Lecture – Pendle Forest Witches;* Reprinted from the *Burnley Express and Clitheroe Division Advertiser*, October 26 to November 23, 1898 (Marshall Branch Library, 1898)

Lea, Deborah, 'Witchcraft, Possession and Confessional Tension in Early Modern Lancashire', thesis, University of Liverpool (May 2011) https://livrepository.liverpool.ac.uk/3174065/1/539498.pdf

Leeds Libraries, *On Some Pre-1841 Sources of Leeds People,* The Secret Library: Leeds Libraries Heritage blog (29 September 2017): https://secretlibraryleeds.net/2017/09/29/on-some-pre-1841-sources-of-leeds-people/

Leigh, William, *The Dampe of Death: Beaten Back with the Glorious Light and Life of Jesus Christ*, sermon preached at Lancaster Assizes (Thomas Creede for Arthur Johnson, 1613): https://quod.lib.umich.edu/e/eebo2/A72540.0001.001?view=toc

Marsh, Mark, *Isabel Robey* (June 2002): *http://sthelens-connect.net/sitefiles/isabel_robey.pdf*

Martin, Lisa A., 'Children, Adolescents, and English Witchcraft', thesis, University of North Texas (December 2005): https://digital.library.unt.edu/ark:/67531/metadc4952/m2/1/high_res_d/thesis.pdf

Mattison, Alyxandra, 'The Execution and Burial of Criminals in Early Medieval England c.850-1150: An Examination of Changes in Judicial Punishment across the Norman Conquest', thesis, University of Sheffield (2016): https://etheses.whiterose.ac.uk/17173/#:~:text=Abstract,so%2Dcalled%20'execution%20cemeteries'

McDonald, S. W., 'The Devil's Mark and the Witch-Prickers of Scotland', *Journal of the Royal Society of Medicine*, Volume 90 (September 1997): https://journals.sagepub.com/doi/pdf/10.1177/014107689709000914

More, George, *A True Discourse Concerning the Certain Possession and Dispossession of Seven Persons in One Family in Lancashire* (1600): https://quod.lib.umich.edu/e/eebo2/B07953.0001.001/1:2?rgn=div1;view=fulltext

Morton, Ian, 'The Tale of Mr Toad', *Countrylife* (2 December 2017): https://www.countrylife.co.uk/nature/tale-mr-toad-medieval-instrument-torture-wind-willows-170689

Motzkau, Johanna, 'Children As Witnesses' in Cook, Daniel T (ed.), *The SAGE Encyclopedia of Children and Childhood Studies* (SAGE, 2019)

Museum of Witchcraft and Magic, Boscastle, 'Betwixt and Between: Isobel Gowdie, The Witch of Auldearn', exhibition 1 April – 31 October 2019: https://museumofwitchcraftandmagic.co.uk/exhibitions/betwixt-and-between-isobel-gowdie-the-witch-of-auldearn-2/

Nelson, Jessica Dr., *An Examination of Witches in the 17th Century*, The National Archives blog (8 April 2021): https://blog.nationalarchives.gov.uk/an-examination-of-witches-in-the-17th-century/#note-53687-2

Nims, Dave, *The Life and Times of William and Dinah Nutter: Prairie Pioneers*, Nims Leistiko blog (October 2013): http://www.nims-leistiko.info/nims-leistiko/NutterStory.htm#WM

Old Fields of History blog by Stephen Oldfield: http://oldfieldsofhistory.blogspot.com/2014/09/the-lancashire-witches-1612.html

Parsons, Naomi H., *Going to East Road: A History of Lancaster Workhouse* (2022): https://drive.google.com/file/d/1qvl8hjNCv1H7A2m40Id-yXzHEPg3tz1S/view?pli=1

Paul, K. J., and Greenhalgh, J., *A Curse on Pendle* (Lancashire Education Resources Unit, 1983)

Peacock, Mabel, *Executed Criminals and Folk Medicine*, Folklore 7:3, 268-283 (1896): https://www.tandfonline.com/doi/abs/10.1080/0015587X.1896.9720365

Pendle Heritage Centre, *A Bannister Family History*, guide book (Heritage Trust for the North West, 2006)

Pendle Hill Partnership, *The Hunt for Malkin Tower: A Compendium of Research and Reports* (2019): https://www.pendlehillproject.com

Pendle 'Witch Trial Trail): local history and area guide run by Charlie Clutterbuck: https://sites.google.com/site/pendlewitchtrail/home?authuser=0

Nate Picowicz, 'Who Was Cotton Mather?', *Tabletalk* magazine, 25 October 2019.

Pilkington, Lee, *Gawthorpe Hall and Witches in Lancashire (Part One)*, Gawthorpe Hall – Lancashire County Council: Stories from Lancashire Museums (2024): lancashiremuseumsstories.wordpress.com/2024/04/19/gawthorpe-hall-and-witches-in-lancashire-part-one/

Poole, Robert (ed.), *The Lancashire Witches Walk* (Green Close Studios Ltd, CreateSpace Independent Publishing Platform, 2013)

Purkiss, Diane, 'Charming Witches: The "Old Religion" and the Pendle Trial' in *Preternature*, vol. 3, issue 1: 'Capturing Witches' (The Pennsylvania State University Press, 2014)

The Queen's Survey of Scholes Manor 1611 in *The Barwicker*, No.55, Barwick in Elmet Historical Society (September 1999): http://www.barwickinelmethistoricalsociety.com/publns.html#contents

Read, Ailsa, 'The Re-envisaging of the Pendle Witches', doctoral thesis, University of Huddersfield (2020): http://eprints.hud.ac.uk/id/eprint/35337/1/FINAL%20THESIS%20-%20 AILSA%20READ.pdf

Selwood, Dominic, 'Alice Nutter: A Witch – or a Secret Catholic?' in *Catholic Herald* (4 October 2018): https://catholicherald.co.uk/alice-nutter-a-witch-or-a-secret-catholic/

Serpell, James, *Guardian Spirits or Demonic Pets: The Concept of the Witch's Familiar in Early Modern England 1530-1712* in Creager, Angela and Jordan, William, *The Animal/Human Boundary: Historical Perspectives* (University of Rochester Press, 2002)

Shannon, William D., *From Lancaster's Tyburn to Sugar House: Richard Kuerden's Map of Lancaster in 1685*, *Contrebis* 2020, Vol. 38, Lancaster Archaeological and Historical Society (2020): https://lahs.archaeologyuk.org/Contrebis/shannonkuerden.pdf

Smith, Moira, 'The Flying Phallus and the Laughing Inquisitor: Penis Theft in the Malleus Maleficarum', *The Journal of Folklore Research* Vol. 39, Issue 1, Indiana University Press (2002): https://go.gale.com/ps/i. https://go.gale.com/ps/i.do?p=LitRC&u=googlescholar &id=GALE %7CA87146072&v=2.1&it=r&sid=googleScholar&asid=772719f2

Smith, Victoria, *The Hypocrisy of Witch Lit: The Novels are an Empty Substitute for Action*, UnHerd (13 January 2023): https://unherd.com/2023/01/the-hypocrisy-of-witchlit/?=refinnar

Spooner, Catherine, *Lucifer Over Lancashire* in *Hellebore* zine, No.3, The Malefice Issue, Samhain 2020

StitchWitch, *Pick It Up*, Making of Magic: Stories of Stitching, Weaving, Knitting and Knotting blog (16 September 2019): https://makingofmagic.wordpress.com/about/

Studders, Stephanie, *Stories from the Museum Floor: Visitor Team at Manchester Museum: Familiar Spirits (part three): Poisonous Pinching Toads* (9 November 2018): https://storiesfromthemuseumfloor.wordpress.com/2018/11/09/familiar-spirits-part-three-poisonous-pinching-toads/#:~:text=Toads%20were%20not%20well%20liked,and%20use%20to%20kill%20people.

Sunderland Peacock and Associates Ltd., Saddlers Farm: Heritage Appraisal, pdf (2021)

Thornton-Bryar, Ian & Sparshatt, John, *The Lancashire Witches Walk Guide* (Postmark Books, 2013)

Tonge, Mildred, *The Lancashire Witches: 1612 and 1634 in The Historic Society of Lancashire and Cheshire* (1931): https://www.hslc.org.uk/wp-content/uploads/2017/06/83-7-Tonge.pdf

Van Fleet, Grace D., 'From What They Wrote Came Fire: An Analysis of the Malleus Maleficarum and Its Impact', Master's paper submitted to the Faculty of the School of Information and Library Science of the University of North Carolina, April 2022

E. C. Vansittart, 'The White Pater Noster', in *The Antiquary: A Magazine Devoted to the Past*, Vol. XL., January-December 1904 (London: Elliot Stock, 1904), online edition: https://archive.org/stream/antiquary40slsniala/antiquary40slsniala_djvu.txt

Wade, Peter, 'Lancaster's Lost Observatory', paper in the *Journal of the British Astronomical Association*, vol. 102, no.3, p.160-162 (1992)

Walton, Jean, *Pendle Forest Folk* (Crastre Press, 2010)

Whichelow, Alice, *A Book of Magical Charms: MS. E Mus.243*, Archives and Manuscripts at the Bodleian Library, Bodleian Library Blog (27 April 2020): https://blogs.bodleian.ox.ac.uk/archivesandmanuscripts/tag/magic/

White, Andrew, *Lancaster Castle in the Middle Ages, Contrebis* 2019, Vol. 37, Lancaster Archaeological and Historical Society (2019): https://lahs.archaeologyuk.org/Contrebis/White%20Castle%20E.pdf

Whitaker, Gladys, *Roughlee Hall: Fact and Fiction* (Marsden Antiquarians, 1983)

Wilkinson, D. J, *Performance and Motivation Amongst the Justices of the Peace in Early Stuart Lancashire in Transactions of the Historic Society of Lancashire and*

Cheshire (1989):
https://www.hslc.org.uk/wp-content/uploads/138-3-Wilkinson.pdf

Wilkinson, D. J, *The Commission of the Peace in Lancashire 1603–1642 in Transactions of the Historic Society of Lancashire and Cheshire* (1983):
https://www.hslc.org.uk/wp-content/uploads/2017/05/132-5-Wilkinson.pdf

Woods, Mike, *The Search for Malkin Tower: An Archaeological Witch Hunt in Preternature*, Capturing Witches, Volume 3, Issue 1 (2014):
https://www.forestofbowland.com/files/uploads/pdfs/_FINAL_Complete%20Malkin%20Tower%20Report.pdf

Wormwood, E. H., *Toad Lore: The Natterjack at the Edges of Occult History (26 April 2023), The Mit Press Reader* Blog:
https://thereader.mitpress.mit.edu/toad-lore-the-natterjack-at-the-edges-of-occult-history/

FICTION:

Ainsworth, William Harrison, *The Lancashire Witches* (Granada, 1980)

Halls, Stacey, *The Familiars* (Zaffre, 2019)

King, Sarah L., *The Gisburn Witch* (CreateSpace Independent Publishing Platform, 2015)

King, Sarah L., *A Woman Named Sellers* (CreateSpace Independent Publishing Platform, 2016)

Michael, Livi, *Malkin Child* (Independently published, 2019)

Middleton, Christine, *The Witch and Her Soul* (Palatine Books, 2012)

Mulholland, Kate, *A Cry of Innocence: A Novel of the Pendle Witches* (Devereux Publishing, 1990)

Neill, Robert, *Mist Over Pendle* (London: Arrow, 2011)

Perkins, Karen, *Murder By Witchcraft: A Pendle Witch Short Story* (LionheART Publishing House, 2021)

Perkins, Karen, *Divided By Witchcraft: Inspired by the True Story of the Samlesbury Witches* (LionheART Publishing House, 2019)

Ralphs, Camille, *Malkin: Poems about the Pendle Witch Trials* (Emma Press, 2015)

Sharratt, Mary, *Daughters of the Witching Hill* (Houghton Mifflin, 2010)

Winterson, Jeanette, *The Daylight Gate* (London: The Grove Press, 2013)

FILM:

The Lancashire Witches, Kenneth Prior, amateur film, North-West Film Archives, 1939

The Witches of Pendle, BBC Production, drama, BBC2, 1976

Lucifer Over Lancashire, Open Space, documentary, BBC2, 1987

The Pendle Witch Child, Wingspan Productions, documentary, BBC4, 2011

Most Haunted: Live at Pendle Hill, Antix Productions, paranormal reality entertainment, Living TV, 2019

Digging Up Britain's Past: Witches (Series One Episode 6), Elephant House Studios/Channel 5 Television, documentary, Channel 5, 2019

The Haunted Hunts at Pendle Hill, Fourth Dimension, paranormal reality entertainment, Amazon Prime, 2020

PODCASTS:

The Newcastle Witches 1649-50, Candle & Bell Productions, presented by Maria Caruana Galizia and Cairlin Bramwell, 2023: https://candleandbell.com/newcastle-witches-podcast

Witch Hunt: The History of Scotland's Witch Hunts, produced by BBC Radio Scotland, presented by Susan Morrison and Louise Yeoman, 2019: https://www.bbc.co.uk/programmes/p07rn38z

Witches of Scotland, produced by Madison Mitchell, presented by Claire Mitchell Q.C., and Zoe Venditozzi, 2020-2024: https://www.witchesofscotland.com/podcast

Betwixt the Sheets: The History of Sex, Scandal & Society, Episode 160: *History of the Witch*, produced by History Hit, presented by Kate Lister, 31 October 2023: https://shows.acast.com/betwixt-the-sheets/episodes/history-of-the-witch

NOTES

INTRODUCTION

1 *Misty* ran for two years until it merged with *Tammy*, at which point I gave up on it.

2 Wilf Prigmore, *The Tale of Little Wytching*, *Misty* comic, issue 72, page 12.

3 Ibid.

4 The universal depiction of witches wearing black hats and riding broomsticks is often mistakenly attributed to the medieval alewives of Europe, who ran the brewery industry before men took over. The alewife wore a tall hat and propped an alestick outside her home to let people know she was selling beer. However, the association of witches with broomsticks originated from the belief that witches rubbed flying ointment into household objects to carry them to sabbath meetings – and the broomstick was the easiest item to draw. The earliest sketches of witches riding broomsticks date from the 1450s; in Victorian times, when women rode horses side-saddle to maintain their decorum, witches were depicted in the same fashion upon broomsticks. The tall black hat is thought to have several sources: the rural dress of seventeenth-century working-class women; the conical hats that heretics were often made to wear for their execution; and the pointed hats associated with alchemists and magicians.

5 Dan Brown, *The Da Vinci Code* (London: Transworld Publishers, 2004), p 132. The source of the quotes within the character's text do not relate to the *Malleus*.

6 Wallace Notestein, *A History of Witchcraft in England from 1558 to 1718* (Washington: The American Historical Association, 1911), p. 130.

7 Stacy Schiff, *The Witches: Salem 1692 – A History* (Little Brown, 2015), p. 285.

8 Nate Pickowicz, 'Who Was Cotton Mather?', *Tabletalk* magazine, 25 October 2019.

9 'Witches: No Pardon from Straw', *Lancashire Telegraph*, 29 October 1998.

10 Ibid.

A SHORT HISTORY OF WITCHES

11 John Callow, *Embracing the Darkness: A Cultural History of Witchcraft* (I. B. Tauris & Co. Ltd, 2018), p. 13

12 Deborah Lea, 'Witchcraft, Possession and Confessional Tension in Early Modern Lancashire', thesis, University of Liverpool, May 2011, p. 40.

13 Emerson W. Baker, *A Storm of Witchcraft: The Salem Trials and the American Experience* (OUP, 2016), pp. 258–9.

14 Alan Macfarlane, *Witchcraft in Tudor and Stuart England* (Routledge & Kegan Paul, 1970), p. 140.

15 Ibid.

16 Silvia Federici, *Witches, Witch-Hunting, and Women* (PM Press, Oakland, 2018), p. 26.

17 Hammurabi, 'The Code of Hammurabi', *Everand* website: https://www.everand.com/book/318444400/The-Code-of-Hammurabi

18 H. C. Erik Midelfort, 'Social History and Biblical Exegesis: Community. Family, and Witchcraft in Sixteenth-Century Germany', in David C. Steinmetz (ed.), *The Bible in the Sixteenth Century* (Durham and London: Duke University Press, 1990), p. 13.

19 Ibid

20 Ibid, pp. 13–14.

21 Esther Eidinow, *Envy, Poison, and Death: Women on Trial in Classical Athens* (Oxford: Oxford University Press, 2016), p 11.

22 Eleanor Herman, 'A Brief History of Calling Women Witches', *Literary Hub* website, 19 September 2022: https://lithub.com/a-brief-history-of-calling-women-witches

23 Grace D. Van Fleet, 'From What They Wrote Came Fire: An Analysis of the Malleus Maleficarum and Its Impact', Master's paper submitted to the Faculty of the School of Information and Library Science of the University of North Carolina, April 2022, p 21.

24 Kramer, Heinrich, *Malleus Maleficarum* (London: John Rodker, 1928), p 47.

25 Ibid, p 107.

26 Ibid, p 121.

27 Ibid, p 121.

28 Ibid, p 119.

29 Diane Purkiss, *The Witch in History* (London: Routledge, 1996), p. 8.

30 Keith Thomas, *Religion and the Decline of Magic* (New York: Charles Scribner's Sons, 1971) p. 440.

31 Portal Editor, 'Martin Luther – Reformation Movement and Witch Burning', *Alaturka* website, 29 July 2018: https://www.alaturka.info/en/culture/religion/4529-martin-luther-reformation-movement-and-witch-burning

32 H. C. Erik Midelfort, 'Social History and Biblical Exegesis: Community. Family, and Witchcraft in Sixteenth-Century Germany', in David C. Steinmetz (ed.), *The Bible in the Sixteenth Century* (Durham and London: Duke University Press, 1990), p. 17.

33 Keith Thomas, *Religion and the Decline of Magic* (New York: Charles Scribner's Sons, 1971), pp. 455–6.

34 J. S. Cockburn, *A History of English Assizes, 1558–1714* (Cambridge: Cambridge University Press, 1972), p. 98.

35 James Sharpe, 'Introduction' in Robert Poole (ed.), *The Lancashire Witches: Histories and Stories* (Manchester: Manchester University Press, 2002), p. 3.

36 Simon Davis, 'Witchcraft and the Book Trade in Early Modern England', thesis (University of Sussex, 2018), p. 110

37 Ibid, p. 131

38 Anon, *Newes from Scotland, Declaring the Damnable Life and Death of Doctor Fian* (London, 1591), p. 14. The original text can be found in the book itself; I have changed into modern English.

39 Keith Thomas, *Religion and the Decline of Magic* (New York: Charles Scribner's Sons, 1971), pp. 455–6.

40 Ibid, p. 455.

CHAPTER ONE: FIREBRAND *or* ELIZABETH SOUTHERNS

41 Daniel Defoe, 'Letter X: Lancashire, Westmorland and Cumberland', *Vision of Britain* website, undated, https://www.visionofbritain.org.uk/travellers/Defoe/34

42 'Visionary George Fox 1624-1691', *Pendle Radicals* website, undated: https://www.pendleradicals.org.uk/pendle-radicals/george-fox/

43 Herbert C. Collins, *The Roof of Lancashire* (London: J. M. Dent & Sons, 1951), p. 134.

44 Thomas Potts, *Discoverie of Witches in the County of Lancaster* (Manchester: The Chetham Society, 1845), p141. The *Internet Archive* website: https://archive.org/details/pottsdiscoveryw01pottgoog/page/n9/mode/2up?q=condition

45 John A. Clayton, *The Pendle Witch Fourth Centenary Handbook* (Barrowford: Barrowford Press, 2011) p. 182.

46 George Blackburn (1515–1548) and Elina Nuk (1520–1559) married around 1538.

47 Clayton states that the Clitheroe Court Rolls and land and property surrenders held at the Preston Records Office show numerous records relating to the extended Blackburn family who were tenant farmers of the Braddyll estate at Billington, on the outskirts of Whalley. Two of the principal tenants were William Blackburn (of Billington) and George Blackburn (of Dinckley). The Elizabeth Blackburn baptised at Whalley in 1541 and her children carry exactly the same Christian names as the children of brothers William and George Blackburn. This baptism could well be confirmation of the folklore that Demdike was a daughter of the Blackburn family from Whalley; instead of Elizabeth Blackburn coming to Barrowford and giving birth to Elizabeth Southern we see her giving birth to Elizabeth Device (the child's later surname by marriage). This Elizabeth Blackburn moved to Pendle Forest from Whalley and would have been around seventy when she died in 1612. Thus, the available recorded evidence appears to reinforce local rumours that were passed to Ainsworth.

48 The background of Elizabeth Southerns prior to motherhood is fairly straightforward to my understanding, apart from one issue. Her daughter with Thomas Ingham – Elizabeth Ingham – is shown marrying John Device in 1590 in the parish registers of Newchurch-in-Pendle. There are two baptisms for 'Elizabeth Ingham' in the family area of Whalley around the correct time, but neither was fathered by Thomas Ingham: one was born to Johannis Ingham in 1566, and a second to George Ingham in 1567. The reader is asked to bear in mind the difficulties with the information we have to work from, which have already been described. I hope that someone with far better genealogy skills than mine will be inspired to create a series of definitive family trees for those who were executed at Lancaster in 1612. To date, John Clayton and Thomas Broad have completed the most credible and ongoing compelling research in this respect.

49 William Alexander Abram, *A History of the Township of Billington, In the Paish of Blackburn, Co. Lancaster: Its Ancient Families, Lords, and Freeholders; With an Account of the Parochial Chapel and Chapelry of Langho, Part I*, 1873, The Historic Society of Lancashire and Cheshire website:
https://www.hslc.org.uk/wp-content/uploads/2017/07/25-6-Abram.pdf

50 Vera Winterbottom, *The Devil in Lancashire* (Manchester: The Cloister Press, 1963), p. 12.

51 One source claimed that Abbot Paslew was hanged on a grassy knoll in Holehouses on the Billington side of the Calder, about a quarter of a mile from Whalley Abbey. A damaged slab, reputed to be Abbot Paslew's gravestone, can be seen against the wall in the north aisle of St Mary and All Saints Church. There are numerous tales of ghostly monks and disembodied chanting in and around Whalley.

52 Thomas Dunham Whitaker, *An History of the Original Parish of Whalley, and Honor of Clitheroe*, (Nichols, Son and Bentley, 1818), p. 184.

53 Whalley parish register 1538–1601. In all probability this was the Thomas Ingham who was baptised on 23 September 1544 in Whalley, son of Thomas Ingham (1515–1573) and Agnes Thorne (1516–1566). There is another entry, however, for a marriage between Elisabeth Blackburn and Thomas Jagham (which Ancestry picked up as Ingham) in Whalley on 25 July 1563, but I can find no further exact details.

54 Thomas Dunham Whitaker, *An History of the Original Parish of Whalley, and Honor of Clitheroe* (Nichols, Son and Bentley, 1818), p. 184.

55 Ibid, p. 184.

56 The legal process involved four parties – steward, auditor, receiver and their clerks – attending the manor courts to deal with the necessary paperwork. When complete, the pages of parchment were stitched together and rolled up, referred to thereafter as the 'court rolls'.

57 Silvia Federici, *Witches, Witch-Hunting, and Women* (PM Press, Oakland, 2018), p. 9.

58 Amy Licence, *Woodsmoke and Sage: The Five Senses 1485-1603: How the Tudors Experienced the World* (London: The History Press, 2021), p. 344.

59 Ibid, p. 88.

60 Herbert C. Collins, *The Roof of Lancashire* (London: J. M. Dent & Sons, 1951), p. 134.

61 John Hope, *In Pendle's Shadow: The Newchurch Story* (William Pownall & Sons Ltd., c.1994), p. 22.

62 Clifford Byrne, *Newchurch-in-Pendle: Folklore, Fact, Fancy, Legends, Traditions and Information* (Marsdens Antiquarians, 1982), p. 18.

63 John Hope, *In Pendle's Shadow: The Newchurch Story* (William Pownall & Sons Ltd., c.1994), p. 12.

64 Clayton suggests various other explanations and the reader is referred to his works for further information in this regard.

65 Joyce Froome, *Wicked Enchantments: A History of the Pendle Witches and Their Magic* (Lancaster: Palatine Books, 2010), p. 3.

66 The Holgate family had been tenants in their own right since 1513, when Henry Hartley of Pendle surrendered a farm (possibly Mancknowles Ing), of twenty-two acres in Barley, delivered to him by Richard Holgate. There was also a land transaction involving the Holgates in 1524 when John, Richard and Robert Bulcock, along with Thomas Varley, surrendered a farm and other buildings in Hay Booth (one of the farming divisions of Barley) to the use of the same Richard Holgate. Here, as elsewhere, surety for his tenancy was provided by John Smith and Miles Nutter (Alice Nutter's father-in-law), the wealthiest men in Roughlee. As late as the end of the nineteenth century, Holgates were running Barley Green Mill while others who were merchants, a banker and a solicitor from the Burnley district were in possession of Under Pendle Farm in Barley and had probably been tenants there for a long period. Clayton speculates that Under Pendle might have been the farm where Christopher Holgate lived while his mother occupied Malkin Tower. In the 1570s, a predecessor of Roger Nowell left provision in his will for the distribution of woollen cloth to the poorer people of Whalley and Pendle. Among those named as receiving the benefice was an Elizabeth Holgate, which might possibly refer to Demdike.

67 Clayton must be credited with discovering the entries for the family in the Newchurch-in-Pendle parish registers. The surname 'Denis' refers to Elizabeth Device and her husband and children. There are five entries for 'Denis' and one 'Dennis'. It was an extremely rare surname in the area, occurring nowhere else within the whole of the Forest of Pendle over the 180-year period covered by the early registers. As we know, at the time of the trials, church officials habitually recorded names phonetically in a jumble of Latin and English. Those writing at a later date frequently wrote the letter 'N' to resemble 'V'. Thus 'Denis' is 'Devis', which when modernised becomes 'Davis/Davies'. These records confirm that Elizabeth's maiden name was Ingham, helping us reconstruct the family history. During the period with which we are concerned, Newchurch-in-Pendle (then Goldshaw Booth) was served by one incumbent, Thomas Varley, from 1567 to 1607; he would have known the Devices well, and others caught up in the

witchcraft accusations. His name can be seen carved into the wall of St Mary's, overlooking the Nutter family tomb, which is often mistakenly referred to as 'the witch's grave'.

68 Keith Thomas, *Religion and the Decline of Magic* (New York: Charles Scribner's Sons, 1971), p. 5.

69 Amy Licence, *Woodsmoke and Sage: The Five Senses 1485-1603: How the Tudors Experienced the World* (London: The History Press, 2021), pp. 327–8.

70 Macfarlane, *Witchcraft in Tudor and Stuart England*, p.126.

71 Barry Reay, *Popular Culture in Seventeenth Century England* (London: St Martin's Press, 1985), p. 113.

72 Macfarlane, *Witchcraft in Tudor and Stuart England*, p. 126.

73 Keith Thomas, *Religion and the Decline of Magic* (New York: Charles Scribner's Sons, 1971), p. 257.

74 Perkins, cited in A. L. Rouse, *The Elizabethan Renaissance: The Cultural Achievement* (Chicago: Ivan R. Dee, 2000), p. 302.

75 John Brinley, *A Discovery of the Impostures of Witches and Astrologers* (London: John Wright, 1680), p. 4.

76 Ibid, p. 45.

CHAPTER TWO: THE HEART, ILL EYE, ILL TONGUE *or* ANNE WHITTLE

77 Potts, *Discoverie*, p.124.

78 Clitheroe Court Roll 45; see also Farrer, William and Brownbill, J (eds.), *A History of Lancashire, Volume VI* (London: 1911), p.516. The latter notes: 'John Nutter of the Bull Hole occurs several times in the witch trials. Another John Nutter, of this district, became Dean of Chester and has been noticed as rector of Sefton and of Aughton. He died in 1602. Richard Nutter of the hall in Sabden was in 1671 the surviving trustee of Christopher Bulcock of Barley.'

79 Ibid, p.516.

80 Information largely drawn from Ancestry.co.uk. Clayton also believes the Brown marriage is the most likely explanation.

81 In *The Lancashire Parish Register Society: Vol. 154: The Indexes and Registers of Newchurch-in-Pendle, 1574-1754* (Manchester: Lancashire Parish Register Society, 2002); Whittle appears as 'Whyttle'. Her granddaughter Jennet appears to have married John Hartley (1552–?) and had a child, Anne Hartley.

82 Henry Colley March, *East Lancashire Nomenclature and Rochdale Names* (London: Simpkin & Co., 1880), p. 238.

83 James Anderton, letter, *The Nelson Leader*, 11 March 1932.

84 Clayton considers the possibility that 'Chattox' was a corruption of the surname Chadwick in light of genealogical information contained in Rev. Alexander B. Grosart's *The Spending of the Money of Robert Nowell* (Manchester: printed for private circulation by C. E. Simms, 1877). The reader is referred to both Clayton and Grosart for further information, but if there is any validity in the suggestion, then in all likelihood, 'Old Chattox' was related to the magistrate who pursued her case, Roger Nowell.

85 'An Act Against Witchcraft', '1604: 1 James c.12: An Act against Conjuration, Witchcraft, and Dealing with Evil and Wicked Spirits', transcript, the National Archives (Catalogue Ref: C 65/181), National Archives website:

https://www.nationalarchives.gov.uk/education/resources/early-modern-witch-trials/an-act-against-witchcraft/#:~:text=Michael%20the%20Archangell%20next%20coming,%2C%20out%20of%20his%2C%20her%2C

86 Michael Dalton, *The Country Justice: Containing the Practice of the Justices of the Peace, Out of their Sessions* (London: William Rawlins and Samuel Roycroft, 1690), p. 384.

87 James A. Serpell, *Guardian Spirits or Demonic Pets: The Concept of the Witch's Familiar in Early Modern England, 1530–1712*, in Creager, Angela, and Jordan, William (eds.), *The Animal/Human Boundary: Historical Perspectives* (University of Rochester Press, 2002), p. 159.

88 Ibid.

89 Vera Winterbottom, *The Devil in Lancashire* (Manchester: The Cloister Press, 1963), p. 35.

90 Emma Wilby, *Cunning Folk and Familiar Spirits: Shamanistic Visionary Traditions in Early Modern British Witchcraft and Magic* (Eastbourne: Sussex Academic Press, 2005), p. 81.

91 Ibid, p. 47.

92 Ibid.

93 James A. Serpell, *Guardian Spirits or Demonic Pets: The Concept of the Witch's Familiar in Early Modern England, 1530–1712*, in Creager, Angela, and Jordan, William (eds.), *The Animal/Human Boundary: Historical Perspectives* (University of Rochester Press, 2002), p. 178.

94 Keith Thomas, *Religion and the Decline of Magic* (New York: Charles Scribner's Sons, 1971), pp. 445–6.

95 Michael Dalton, *The Country Justice: Containing the Practice of the Justices of the Peace, Out of their Sessions* (London: William Rawlins and Samuel Roycroft, 1690), p. 384.

96 G. B. Harrison, *King James the First: Daemonologie* (1597), (New York: Barnes and Noble, 1966), p. 33.

97 L'Estrange Ewen, *Witch Hunting and Witch Trials: The Indictments for Witchcraft from the Records of the 1373 Assizes Held from the Home Court 1559-1736* (London: Routledge, 1929), p. 62.

98 James A. Serpell, *Guardian Spirits or Demonic Pets: The Concept of the Witch's Familiar in Early Modern England, 1530–1712*, in Creager, Angela, and Jordan, William (eds.), *The Animal/Human Boundary: Historical Perspectives* (University of Rochester Press, 2002), p. 178.

99 Marion Gibson, *Reading Witchcraft: Stories of Early English Witches* (London: Routledge, 1999), p. 1.

100 Emma Wilby, *Cunning Folk*, p. 7.

101 James A. Serpell, *Guardian Spirits or Demonic Pets: The Concept of the Witch's Familiar in Early Modern England, 1530–1712*, in Creager, Angela, and Jordan, William (eds.), *The Animal/Human Boundary: Historical Perspectives* (University of Rochester Press, 2002), pp. 179–80.

102 Emma Wilby, *Cunning Folk*, pp. 8–10.

CHAPTER THREE: THAT FRIDAY SPELL *or* ELIZABETH DEVICE

103 See *The Lancashire Parish Register Society: Vol. 154: The Indexes and Registers of Newchurch-in-Pendle, 1574-1754* (Manchester: Lancashire Parish Register Society, 2002). John Device was probably older than his wife Elizabeth; it may be that, according to Clayton's reading of the 1633 Pendle witch trials, he already had a son named William Device, who was then described as half-brother to Jennet Device. Due to Christopher's marriage to Isabell, when his sister was accused of killing John and James Robinson of Barley, the two men were almost certainly related to him through his wife. John Robinson taunted Elizabeth about having an illegitimate child, which sounds like a family rumour that might have erupted during a row. The Robinsons were also related to miller Richard Baldwin of Wheathead, having pledged the dower for one of the Baldwin women. The Robinsons and Baldwins seem to have been on the same social scale and probably shared the same Puritan sensibilities.

104 In *The Lancashire Parish Register Society: Vol. 154: The Indexes and Registers of Newchurch-in-Pendle, 1574-1754* (Manchester: Lancashire Parish Register Society, 2002), James appears as 'Jacobus Denis'. Christopher and Elizabeth gave their children the same names. The registers show the Devices celebrated the baptisms of Alicea (Alizon Device) in 1593 and Jenneta (Jennet Device) in 1600, while the Holgate children appear in the same registers as Alicea (Alizon) Holgate, baptised in 1590, and Jenneta (Jennet), baptised in 1594 and buried the following year. There are other Holgate children recorded: Anna Holgate, baptised in 1592; Henry Holgate, baptised and buried in 1596; Maria Holgate (recorded as daughter of Christopher of Pendle, baptised in Padiham) in 1600; George Holgate, baptised in 1604; Henry Holgate, baptised in 1607; Christopher Holgate baptised in 1609 and buried the following year, 1610; and their last child to be baptised, Jennet Holgate, in 1611. The registers also show that an Isobel Holgate was buried in 1636, which may well be Christopher's wife and mother of his children.

105 In *The Lancashire Parish Register Society: Vol. 154: The Indexes and Registers of Newchurch-in-Pendle, 1574-1754* (Manchester: Lancashire Parish Register Society, 2002), Alizon appears as 'Alicea Denis'.

106 Explanation from the *Encyclopaedia Britannica*. The average length could vary from 9ft to 28ft (2.743 to 8.534 metres). 'Rod' derives from the Old English *rodd* and is similar to the Old Norse *rudda* (club), and the Dutch *rood*. This latter referred to a land area of 40 square rods, equal to one-quarter acre, or 10,890 square feet (1,012 square metres).

107 Potts, *Discoverie*, p. 146.

108 Ibid, p. 107.

109 Froome, *Wicked Enchantments*, p. 1.

110 Thomas, *Decline*, p. 42.

111 Diane Purkiss, 'Charming Witches: The "Old Religion" and the Pendle Trial' in *Preternature*, vol. 3, issue 1: 'Capturing Witches' (The Pennsylvania State University Press, 2014), Kindle Edition, loc. 520.

112 Ibid.

113 *Evilspeak* is the title of a 1981 film about a student of Latin who conjures spells after discovering a long-dead priest's belongings.

114 Purkiss, 'Charming Witches', Kindle edition, loc. 568.

115 For more discussion regarding this charm and others see also Joyce Froome, *Wicked Enchantments* (Palatine Books, 2010), Barbara Rosen, *Witchcraft* (New York: Taplinger, 1972); Jonathan Lumby, *The Lancashire Witch Craze* (Lancaster: Carnegie Publishing Ltd, 1999); K. M. Briggs, *Pale Hecate's Team* (New York:

Humanities Press, 1962), Diane Purkiss, *The Witch in History* (London: Routledge, 1996) and Diane Purkiss, 'Charming Witches'.

116 William Carr, *The Dialect of Craven, in the West Rising of the County of York* (London: Wm. Crofts: 1828), p. 212.

117 Not to be confused with a paternoster, which is a string of prayer beads similar to a rosary.

118 Anon., *'Pater Noster' (Our Father) in Latin and English*, undated, *Glorian* https://glorian.org/connect/blog/pater-noster-our-father?highlight=WyJwYXRlcil sInBhdGVycyIsIm5vc3RlciIsInBhdGVyIG5vc3RlciJd

119 *Enchiridion Leonis Pape* is a mysterious work, associated with the Affair of the Poisons, and purported to have been published in 1523, although the earliest extant text is dated 1633. The first known literary reference to the Pater Noster appears in Chaucer's *The Miller's Tale*, in the mid-fourteenth century, when three characters recite it during a flood.

120 Anna Edith Gottschall, 'The Pater Noster and the Laity in England c.700–1560' (University of Birmingham, thesis, 2014), p. 199.

121 John White, *A Defence of the Way to the True Church* (London: Felix Kyngston for William Barret, 1624), p. 75.

122 Joseph Ames, *Typographical Antiquities: Being an Historical Account of Printing in England* (London: Printed for W. Faden, 1749), p. 109.

123 Ibid.

124 Ibid, p. 110.

125 The original 1685 title is given in the text, but quotations are taken from the 1814 edition of George Sinclair's work, *Satan's Invisible World Discovered: Or a Choice Collection of Modern Relations* (London: James Clarke, 1814), p. 16.

126 Anna Edith Gottschall, 'The Pater Noster and the Laity in England c.700–1560' (University of Birmingham, thesis, 2014), p. 200.

127 Sinclair, p. 144.

128 Ibid, p. 145.

129 Gottschall, p. 202.

130 Gottschall, p. 204.

131 J. S. Forsyth, *Demonologia or Natural Knowledge Revealed* (London: John Bumpus, 1827), pp. 269–70.

132 Reay, *Popular Culture in Seventeenth Century England* (London: St Martin's Press, 1985), p. 113.

133 Ibid, p. 114.

134 E. C. Vansittart, 'The White Pater Noster', in *The Antiquary: A Magazine Devoted to the Study of Past,* Vol. XL., January-December 1904 (London: Elliot Stock, 1904), online edition:
https://archive.org/stream/antiquary40slsniala/antiquary40slsniala_djvu.txt

CHAPTER FOUR: MUCH BLOOD SPILT *or* ANNE REDFEARN

135 Fred Redwood, 'Casting a Spell', *Mail on Sunday*, 8 July 2017. In 1976, writer Richard Catlow suggested the extended family lived near Pendle Hill Farm, close to the footbridge at the bottom of Ightenhill Lane where a ruined building was known locally as the witches' cottage.

136 Potts, *Discoverie*, p. 127.

137 Clayton points out a baptism on 12 August 1571, which may be relevant, and also the burial of a child of Jane Boothman's on 8 December 1581 at Burnley.

138 Potts, *Discoverie*, p. 202.

139 Ibid, p. 203.

140 Ibid, p. 131.

141 The Museum of Witchcraft and Magic, Boscastle, 'Betwixt and Between: Isobel Gowdie, The Witch of Auldearn', exhibition 1 April – 31 October 2019:
https://museumofwitchcraftandmagic.co.uk/exhibitions/betwixt-and-between-isobel-gowdie-the-witch-of-auldearn-2/

142 Christina Hole, 'Some Instances of Image-Magic in Great Britain', essay in Venetia Newall (ed.), *The Witch Figure* (Routledge & Kegan Paul, 1973), p. 81.

143 When he came to draft Elizabeth's examination, Nowell attached her description of image magic immediately after the section regarding the death of miller Richard Baldwin's daughter, implying that Elizabeth had killed the girl in just such a manner.

144 Michael P. Conroy, *The Shuttleworths of Gawthorpe* (Bury: The Lancashire Family History and Heraldry Society, 1999), p. 30.

145 James Sharpe, *Instruments of Darkness: Witchcraft in England 1550–1750* (London: Penguin, 1997), p. 202.

CHAPTER FIVE: HE WERE BUT YOUNG *or* JAMES DEVICE

146 Walter Bennett, *The Pendle Witches* (Burnley: The County Borough of Burnley Libraries and Arts Committee, 1957), p. 6.

147 Jonathan Lumby, *The Lancashire Witch Craze* (Lancaster: Carnegie Publishing Ltd, 1999), p. 83.

148 Crossley: 'Of an aghendole of meal. Since writing the Note, I am indebted to Miss Clegg, of Hallfoot, near Clitheroe, for information as to the exact quantity contained in an aghendole, which is eight pounds. This measure, she informs me, is still in use in Little Harwood, in the district of Pendle. The Archdeacon of Manchester considers that an aghendole, or more properly, as generally pronounced, a nackendole, is a kneading-dole, the quantity of meal, &c. usually taken for kneading at one time. There can be no doubt that this is the correct derivation.' James Crossley, Introduction, Potts, *Discoverie*, p57.

149 In *The Lancashire Parish Register Society: Vol. 154: The Indexes and Registers of Newchurch-in-Pendle, 1574-1754* (Manchester: Lancashire Parish Register Society, 2002), Jennet appears as 'Jenneta Denis'.

150 Christopher Haigh, *Reformation and Resistance in Tudor Lancashire* (London: Cambridge University Press, 1975), p. 47.

151 *Gawthorpe Hall and Witches in Lancashire (Part One)* by Museum Assistant Jessica Young in Lancashire Museum Stories: https://lancashiremuseumsstories.wordpress.com/2024/04/19/gawthorpe-hall-and-witches-in-lancashire-part-one/

Referring back to the possibility that Anne Whittle's surname was Chadwick at some point, or that the family were related, perhaps through the Redfearns to the Chadwicks, there is an entry in the Padiham Parish registers for the baptism of an illegitimate child named Elizabeth to one Alicia Chadwick in 1593 – the only entry under that surname in many years, and which would give that child the nickname Bess Chattox.

152 It is often stated, wrongly, that Bessie broke into Malkin Tower, but the Device family home was a separate structure and Alizon is clear in her pronouncement to Roger Nowell that it was their home that was ransacked. Her statement also leaves no doubt that her father had passed away before the break-in and therefore Bessie's actions were not intended to frighten John Device into making an agreement with them, nor from revenge for missed payments. It could, however, have been a warning that the Devices were fair game to their enemies now that John Device was dead.

153 Walter Bennett, Kathleen Eyre and Donald Foster have each suggested another sequence of events, largely due to Potts's interchanging of the dates of Alizon's depositions of 13 March ('xiii' in the *Discoverie* text) and 30 March, and to an entry in the account books belonging to the Shuttleworths of Gawthorpe, which was believed to state that Bessie was imprisoned in 1613. This latter has now been corrected; Bessie was not in gaol in 1613, which weakens the argument put forward by Bennett, Eyre and Foster that Bessie's breaking into the Device family home occurred about a week before Alizon's encounter with the pedlar. For further information see: Walter Bennett, Kathleen Eyre, *Witchcraft in Lancashire* (Dalesman Books, 1986), Donald Foster with Tobian Banton (eds.), *Women's Works Vol 3: 1605–1625* (New York: Wicked Good Books, 2013).

154 Licence, *Woodsmoke*, p. 342.

155 Haigh, *Reformation and Resistance*, p. 46.

156 Ibid.

157 Ibid.

158 Ibid.

159 Ibid.

160 Ibid, p. 89.

161 Ibid, p. 48.

162 Ibid, pp. 44–5.

163 John Anthony Hilton, *Catholic Lancashire: from Reformation to Renewal, 1559–1991* (Phillimore: Chichester, 1994), p. 16.

164 Margaret Baker, *Folklore and Customs of Rural England* (Totowa: Rowman and Littlefield, 1974), p. 69.

165 According to Clayton.

166 George Lyman Kittredge, *Witchcraft in Old and New England* (Pennsylvania: Harvard University Press, 1929), p. 167.

167 Margaret Baker, *Folklore and Customs of Rural England* (Totowa: Rowman and Littlefield, 1974), p. 50.

168 Ibid.

169 Ibid.

170 Kittredge, *Witchcraft in Old and New England*, p. 150.

CHAPTER SIX: BROUGHT UP IN THIS DETESTABLE COURSE OF LIFE *or* ALIZON DEVICE

171 Christina Hole, *English Home-Life 1500 to 1800* (London: B. T. Batsford Ltd, 1949), p. 41.

172 Alizon remembered the incident as several years before, but Demdike stated it was in 1611, just before Christmas; Alizon was correct.

173 The exact location of Baldwin's mill at Wheathead is no longer known, but James Crossley states that the explorer, 'a little distance from Rough Lee, pursuing the course of the stream, he will find the foundations of an ancient mill, and the millstones still unremoved, though the building itself has been pulled down long ago. This was, doubtless, the mill of Richard Baldwin ...' Crossley, Introduction in Potts, *Discoverie*, p. 63.

174 Kittredge, *Witchcraft in Old and New England*, p. 170.

175 Upon her marriage to John Moore, Elizabeth inherited her childhood home, Greenhead. It is thought that the couple built the present Greenhead Manor.

176 Clayton, *The Pendle Witch Fourth Centenary Handbook*, pp. 280-1.

177 Purkiss: 'Charming Witches', in *Preternature*, loc. 370.

178 Thomas, *Decline*, pp. 186–7.

179 Hasted, Rachel, 'The New Myth of the Witch', *Trouble and Strife: A Radical Feminist Magazine*, Issue 2, Spring 1984, (Manchester: Amazon Press, 1984), p. 15.

180 Thomas, *Decline*, pp. 186–7.

181 Kittredge, *Witchcraft in Old and New England*, p. 39.

182 Ibid.

183 Ibid.

184 John C. Hirsh, 'Credulity and Belief: The Role of Postconditions in the Late Medieval Charm', in *Preternature: Critical and Historical Studies on the Preternatural*, Volume I, Number I, 2012: https://muse.jhu.edu/article/470477

185 Ibid.

186 Ibid.

187 Ibid.

188 Deborah Lea, 'Witchcraft, Possession and Confessional Tension', p. 58.

189 Lancashire Record Office QSB 1/139/81.

190 Kittredge, *Witchcraft in Old and New England*, p. 39.

191 Sir Jonas Moore (1617–1679), astronomer and mathematician, was born at White Lee and is closely related to this family, but there is some confusion over the matter. Moore's biographer, Frances Willmoth, and a number of other sources pin him as the son of Hugh Moore (1591–1649) of White Lee (now Higher White Lee Farm). However, the Borough of Pendle's walking guide, *On The Trail of the Father of Time*, describes Jonas as the son of John Moore, making him the elder brother of the boy alleged to have been killed by Anne Whittle.

CHAPTER SEVEN: DRAWN TO FALL *or* ALICE NUTTER

192 Jean Fielding, 'Lancashire Witches', *Liverpool Daily Post*, 31 October 1963, p. 10.

193 'Bergan', 'Holiday Fellowship Rambles', *The Rochdale Observer*, 19 November 1932, p. 14.

194 Frances Willmoth, *Sir Jonas Moore: Practical mathematics and Restoration Science* (Woodbridge: Boydell Press, 1993), p. 12.

195 Ibid.

196 Ibid.

197 Clifford Byrne, *Newchurch-in-Pendle*, p. 25.

198 Jesse Blakey, *The Annals and Stories of Barrowford* (Nelson: Blakeys, 1929), p. 193.

199 J. A. Hilton, *Catholic Lancashire: from Reformation to Renewal, 1559–1991* (Phillimore: Chichester, 1994), p. 12.

200 Ibid.

201 Henry, born in 1541, was the son of Lawrence and Hellen Hesketh. He died in 1616. Anna Catterall was the daughter of Thomas Catterall and Margaret Tempest, of Catterall and Little Mitton. Henry and Anna married on 2 December 1559.

CHAPTER EIGHT: LAME HIM

202 Potts, *Discoverie*, p. 229.

203 Ibid, p. 235.

204 Margaret Spufford, *The Great Reclothing of Rural England: Petty Chapman and their Wares in the Seventeenth Century* (London: Hambledon Press, 1984), p. 4.

205 Spufford, p. 33.

206 Spufford, 8, footnote 27.

207 The trunk was later exhibited at both the British Museum and Samlesbury Hall.

208 Another possibility, popular with town guides, is that Law ended up at The Greyhound on the eastern end of Market Street. Owned by Charles Ayre, it was demolished in 1790. However, that would have been a longer walk, and given Law's poor state of health, it seems unlikely.

209 Colne Town Council refer to this building, situated at what is now 14–16 Keighley Road, on their website regarding the town's heritage assets. https://colnetowncouncil.org.uk/ctc/wp-content/uploads/2020/10/Colne-Local-Heritage-List-2020-10-26_compressed.pdf

210 Frances Dolan, *Dangerous Familiars: Representations of Domestic Crime in England, 1550–1700* (New York: Cornell University Press, 1994), p. 186.

CHAPTER NINE: PRICKING THUMBS

211 Macfarlane, *Witchcraft in Tudor and Stuart England*, p. 110.

212 Haigh, *Reformation and Resistance*, p. 321.

213 Ibid, pp. 321–2.

214 Kittredge, *Witchcraft in Old and New England*, p. 287.

215 Ibid.

216 Marion Gibson, *Witchcraft and Society in England and America 1550–1750* (New York: Cornell University Press, 2003), pp. 5–6.

217 Ibid.

218 Christina Larner, *Witchcraft and Religion: The Politics of Popular Belief* (New York: Blackwell, 1984), p. 87.

219 Sara Mendelson and Patricia Crawford, *Women in Early Modern England, 1550–1720* (Oxford: Clarendon, 1998), p. 69.

220 C. L'Estrange Ewen, *Witch Hunting and Witch Trials: The Indictments for Witchcraft from the Records of the 1373 Assizes Held from the Home Court 1559-1736* (London: Routledge, 1929), p. 67.

221 William Andrews, *Old-Time Punishments* (Corner House,1975), pp. 2–3.

222 Ibid, p. 39.

223 E. J. Burford and Sandra Shulman, *Of Bridles and Burnings: The Punishment of Women* (London: Robert Hale, 1992) p. 58.

224 Ibid.

225 Silvia Federici, *Witches, Witch-Hunting, and Women* (PM Press, Oakland, 2018), p. 26.

226 James Brown, 'Margaret Alcock's Evil Eye: Witchcraft Defamations in Early Modern England', 31 October 2016, Inner Lives: Emotions, Identity, and the Supernatural 1300-1900 blog: https://innerlivesblog.wordpress.com/2016/10/31/margaret-alcocks-evil-eye-witchcraft-defamation-suits-in-early-modern-england/

227 James Sharpe, *Instruments of Darkness: Witchcraft in England 1550–1750* (London: Penguin, 1997), p. 99.

228 Jonathan Lumby, *The Lancashire Witch-Craze* (Lancaster: Carnegie Publishing Ltd, 1999), p. 48.

229 Roy S. Hickey, 'Radical Religion and the Background to the Development of the Quaker Movement in the area of Pendle, the Ribble Valley, Craven, Westmoreland and the Yorkshire Dales, c1570 to 1652', thesis, University of Manchester, 2020, pp. 53–4.

230 Keith Thomas, *Decline*, pp. 456–7.

231 Lancashire Quarter Sessions records 1589–1607, Preston Record Office.

232 Another row broke out about the pew around 1800, when the inhabitants of Read Hall and Moreton Hall quarrelled about its ownership. The resulting lawsuit, which cost several thousand pounds, led to the court's decision to divide the pew into two halves. Both parties reluctantly agreed, but each built their own separate gallery and staircase in the south aisle of the church. The decision in this dispute is marked by the initials J.F.R. (John Fort, Read 1830) and I.T.M. (John Taylor, Moreton) 1830, inscribed on panels over the two entrance doors on the north side. The galleries have long since disappeared.

CHAPTER TEN: THE LANCASHIRE SEVEN

233 Kathleen Eyre, *Witchcraft in Lancashire* (Dalesman Publishing Co. Ltd., 1974), p. 38.

234 Judith Bonzol, 'The Medical Diagnosis of Demonic Possession in an Early Modern English Community', *Parergon*, Volume 26, Number 1, 2009, p. 124.

235 Kathleen Eyre, *Witchcraft*, p. 38.

236 Ibid, p. 39.

237 Citation from Joyce Froome, *Wicked Enchantments*, p. 120.

238 Ibid, p. 122.

239 Ibid, p. 125.

240 Citation from Philip C. Almond, *Demonic Possession and Exorcism in Early Modern England: Contemporary Texts and Their Cultural Contexts* (Cambridge: Cambridge University Press, 2004) p. 207.

241 Ibid, p. 205.

242 Luca Baratta, 'Lancashire: A Land of Witches in Shakespeare's Time', in *Journal of Early Modern Studies 2* (March 2013), pp. 187-8: https://www.researchgate.net/publication/307651576_Lancashire_a_Land_of_Witches_in_Shakespeare%27s_Time

In an unrelated incident, in February 1612, Nowell's son, who had followed him into the judiciary, was among a group of men against whom a Bill of Complaint had been presented to the Lord Chancellor. The matter concerned 'alleged fraud and unlawful retention of documents relating to the office of Clerk of the Peace' and was part of an ongoing legal dispute involving the Clerk of the Peace and his family, in which Roger Nowell the younger had become embroiled due to his position within the judiciary. It would not be resolved in haste, but is unlikely to have had any influence on the witch trials involving his father. Unpublished papers: the Nowells of Read, Lancashire Records Office, Preston.

243 Luca Baratta, 'A Land of Witches', pp. 187-8.

244 B. W. Quintrell (ed.), *Proceedings of the Lancashire Justices of the Peace at the Sheriff's Table During Assize Week, 1578-1694* (The Record Society of Lancashire and Cheshire, 1981), p. 72.

245 There are two potentially relevant entries in the parish registers. The first shows Henry Hargreaves marrying Jeneta Fearnesyd or Feirnside at Whalley in December 1598; if correct, then that would make Constable Hargreaves the brother-in-law of Anthony Nutter and uncle to Anthony's daughter Anne (Alizon Device's close friend), who was recorded as having been bewitched to death by Anne Whittle. The second entry shows Henry Hargreaves marrying Elizabeth Lawe at Colne on 24 October 1602 – which raises the equally remarkable possibility that he was then related, albeit perhaps distantly, to John and Abraham Law.

246 *Bannister of Altham Papers*, Lancashire Record Office.

247 John A. Clayton, *The Pendle Witch Fourth Centenary Handbook: History and Archaeology in Fact and Fiction* (Barrowford: Barrowford Press, 2012), Kindle edition, loc. 1141.

248 John A. Clayton, *The Lancashire Witch Conspiracy: A History of Pendle Forest and the Pendle Witch Trials* (Barrowford: Barrowford Press, 2007), p. 229.

CHAPTER ELEVEN: A CURSTE QUEANE

249 Lyndal Roper, *Witch Craze: Terror and Fantasy in Baroque Germany* (New Haven and London: Yale University Press, 2004), p. 58.

250 Robert Neill, *Mist Over Pendle* (London: Hutchinson, 1951), back cover matter.

251 Reginald Scot, *The Discoverie of Witchcraft* (London: Elliot Stock, 1886), p. 40.

252 Marion Gibson, *Witchcraft: A History in Thirteen Trials* (London: Simon & Schuster, 2023), p. xvi.

253 Wilby, *Cunning Folk*, p. 30.

254 There is a possibility that from this day onwards, Alizon and her grandmother were both held in custody, along with Elizabeth and James Device, but kept in insolation from each other until Nowell was ready to interrogate them again.

CHAPTER TWELVE: FOR THE CARRIAGE OF THE WITCHES

255 Anonymous, 'Rambles in Witchland by Boshemengro: Chapter III – To Cock Clough', *The Nelson Leader*, 10 June 1921.

256 Anonymous, 'Rambles in Witchland by Boshemengro: Chapter VIII – Lilac Farm', *The Nelson Leader*, 15 July 1921.

257 James was not, however, the son of Sir Thomas, as has been suggested elsewhere.

258 Potts wrongly gives the name of the owner of Ashlar House as James Wilsey when it was in fact James Walmsley.

259 Potts implies that it was on 2 April that James gave his evidence regarding spotting Anne Whittle and her family making the clay pictures. However, he mentions that this evidence was taken by Nowell and Nicholas Bannister, with the latter having taken no role on that date in any other examinations. Bannister was certainly present with Nowell when James was questioned at Ashlar House on 27 April, and therefore the most logical explanation is that it was on this later date when James discussed the clay pictures.

260 The newly transcribed account books belonging to the Shuttleworths of Gawthorpe Hall present us with a puzzle: the date of the prisoners' transportation to Lancaster is given as 16 April. This seems strange, given that Nowell had evidently completed his interviews with Anne Whittle and Anne Redfearn on 2 April, which is also the date Potts gives as them leaving Fence. Furthermore, the date in the account book is both a fortnight after their final questioning, and a week after the meeting at Malkin Tower – which we can be certain neither Anne Whittle nor her daughter attended. How to account for the disparity? It may simply refer to the greave being paid on that date for a transport that had taken two weeks prior. Or might there be a discrepancy with the date in the account book? A more intriguing idea is that the entry might refer to other suspects from West Close who were sent to Lancaster on that date. Perhaps the Redfearns and Bessie were expected to be tried after all, yet the case against them collapsed.

261 *Gawthorpe Hall and Witches in Lancashire (Part One)* by Museum Assistant Jessica Young in Lancashire Museum Stories: https://lancashiremuseumsstories.wordpress.com/2024/04/19/gawthorpe-hall-and-witches-in-lancashire-part-one/

262 Clitheroe's Moot Hall, as the old Town Hall was sometimes called, was built in 1610 on Church Street. The centre of justice for the Hundred of Blackburn, it contained prison cells with barrel-vaulted ceilings cut out of solid rock; these were frequently used to accommodate petty criminals on their way to prison in Lancaster Castle. It is possible that Alizon Device, Elizabeth Southerns and the rest of the group from Pendle were held there briefly before being sent on to Lancaster. Records from later in the seventeenth century describe how several families had to share a cell in the Moot Hall: 'It was a small, dark, unventilated room without furniture, and prisoners could not take exercise and had to find their own bedding or go without' (cited in Jessica Lofthouse, *Three Rivers*, London: Robert Hale, 1946, p.40). The Moot Hall was demolished in the nineteenth century and a new building erected, but the old prison cells below ground level were retained. Today, the Carnegie Library stands on the spot; access to the cells – now used as store rooms – is through a medieval wooden door on York Street.

263 Jessica Lofthouse, *Lancashire's Fair Face* (Robert Hale Ltd., 1976) pp. 174–5.

264 Ibid.

CHAPTER THIRTEEN: A WITNESS UNEXPECTED *or* JENNET DEVICE

265 Lisa A. Martin, 'Children, Adolescents and English Witchcraft', thesis, University of North Texas, December 2005, p. 66.

266 Potts, *Discoverie*, p. 142.

CHAPTER FOURTEEN: MALICE OF HEARTS *or* JENNET PRESTON

267 Henry Lyttleton Lyster Denny, *Memorials of an Ancient House: A History of the Family of Lister or Lyster* (Edinburgh: Ballantyne, Hanson & Co., 1913), p. 12.

268 Ibid.

269 Ibid.

270 Indenture: John Pudsey of Arnford, Yorkshire to Richard Preston, late of Dudland, 28 October 1612, WARD 2/54/180/32, National Archives.

271 M. Gaskill, 'Reporting Murder: Fiction in the Archives in Early Modern England', *Social History, 23* (1), 1-30 (1998), p. 25. https://doi.org/10.1080/03071029808568018

272 Richard Bernard, *A Guide to Grand-Jury Men, Divided into Two Bookes* (London: Felix Kingston, 1627), pp. 199–200.

273 Dalton, *The Countrey Justice*, p. 384.

274 Quoted in Owen Davies, 'The Nightmare Experience, Sleep Paralysis, and Witchcraft Accusations', in *Folklore* 114 (2003), p. 188.

275 Potts, *Discoverie*, p. 235.

276 Reginald Scot, *The Discoverie of Witchcraft* (London: Elliot Stock, 1886), p. 303.

277 G. B. Harrison (ed.), *King James the First: Daemonologie (1597) Newes From Scotland (1591)*, (London, John Lane, The Bodley Head, 1924), pp. 80–1.

278 M. Gaskill, 'Reporting Murder: Fiction in the Archives in Early Modern England', *Social History, 23* (1), 1-30 (1998), p. 9.

279 Bolton Parish Registers. These, and other Lancashire parish registers, can now be viewed online via the Online Parish Clerks database at: https://www.lan-opc.org.uk/indexp.html

The name Dodgson appears elsewhere in the case when Margaret Pearson of Padiham was charged with causing the death of a horse owned by 'Dodgson of Padiham', but they are extremely unlikely to have been the same family.

CHAPTER FIFTEEN: UPON A WITCH-FREQUENTED GREEN *or* KATHERINE HEWITT *and* JANE AND JOHN BULCOCK

280 Kittredge, *Witchcraft in Old and New England*, p. 243.

281 Ibid.

282 Ibid, p. 248.

283 Ibid, p. 271.

284 In his study of the history of witchcraft, Wallace Notestein suggests that the meeting at Malkin Tower never occurred, and that it was simply the invention of one of the accused, or developed due to suggestive questions from a justice. But had that been the case, then we might expect the meeting to be far more aligned with those depicted in Continental witch trials.

285 Also spelled Howgate.

286 Jennet Hargreaves, Christopher Hargreaves and his wife Elizabeth clearly all shared the same surname as Constable Henry Hargreaves; they were not prosecuted. Jonathan Lumby includes a photograph of One Tree Farm, Under Pendle in his book *The Lancashire Witch Craze* (Carnegie Publishing Ltd, 1999), which he states was the home of Jennet Hargreaves.

287 Her surname is spelled a variety of ways, including Hewitt.

288 Also spelled Cronkshaw.

289 James Carr, *Annals and Stories of Colne and Neighbourhood* (Manchester: John Heywood, 1878), p. 212.

290 Phyllis Bentley, *Colne Valley Cloth: From the Earliest Times to the Present Day* (Huddersfield: The Huddersfield and District Woollen Export Group, 1947), p. 20.

291 John A. Clayton, *The Lancashire Witch Conspiracy*, p.171.

292 Jonathan Lumby disputes the idea that the Moss End mentioned is the same Moss End that lies just west of Newchurch-in-Pendle today. He points out that a Christopher Bulcock is mentioned living further north-east in Wheatley Booth, in a list of tenants dated 1608–9. However, names were repeated with great frequency throughout the region and it is my firm belief that the reference is to Moss End Farm within the Saddlers Triangle.

293 Anon, *Newes from Scotland, Declaring the Damnable Life and Death of Doctor Fian* (London: William Wright, 1591), p. 16.

294 Potts, *Discoverie*, p. 166.

295 This seems to be a mistake on Potts's part since there was no such place, unless it was their own name for a particular location. It has been suggested that James Device might actually have been referring to Rombalds Moor, in West Yorkshire, but it was quite a distance, some twenty miles away.

296 Potts, *Discoverie*, p. 166.

297 Deborah Lea, 'Witchcraft, Possession and Confessional Tension', p. 99.

CHAPTER SIXTEEN: ONE FOR SORROW

298 Anon., 'Epitaph in Lancaster Church', *The Lancaster Gazette*, 21 May 1884.

299 *Henry Burton, A Narration of the Life of Mr Henry Burton* (London: John Bothwell, 1643), p. 15.

300 Ibid.

301 Ibid, p 17.

302 Jonathan Slinger, 'An Impeachment of Covell', *Lancaster Standard and County Advertiser*, 19 September 1902.

303 Cross Fleury, *Time Honoured Lancaster* (Lancaster: Eaton & Bulfield, 1891), p. 109.

304 J. S. Cockburn, *A History of English Assizes, 1558–1714* (Cambridge: Cambridge University Press, 1972), p. 107.

305 Ibid.

306 William Hewitson, 'A Lancaster Worthy – Thomas Covell', chapter in Ernest Axon, *Bygone Lancashire* (Wakefield: S. R. Publishers, 1971), pp. 63–4.

307 Ibid, in Axon, p. 60.

308 Ibid, in Axon, pp. 63–4.

309 Ibid.

310 Cross Fleury, *Time-Honoured Lancaster* (Lancaster: Eaton & Bulfield, 1891), pp. 61–2.

311 Dr Colin Penny, author interview, Lancaster Castle, 15 August 2023. Lancashire University conducted an archaeological survey of the building in the 1990s, and discovered a pair of eighteenth-century shoes bricked into one of the walls. But this is quite common, given the work carried out by prisoners, and not believed to have any sinister significance, despite claims that they were placed there to protect against witchcraft. Dr Penny confirms: 'There have been excavations in the well tower but nothing of interest regarding the witches concerned.'

312 Cross Fleury, *Time-Honoured Lancaster* (Lancaster: Eaton & Bulfield, 1891), pp. 67–8.

313 Edward W. Cox, 'Lancaster Castle', 5 November 1895, in *Transactions of the Historic Society of Lancashire and Cheshire Vol. 48* (The Historic Society of Lancashire and Cheshire, 1896), p. 114.

314 Ibid.

315 E. J. Burford and Sandra Shulman, *Of Bridles and Burnings: The Punishment of Women* (London: Robert Hale, 1992), p. 112.

316 Joanna J. Kucinski, *Representations of Witches in Popular Literature in England, 1566–1645* (Sweet Briar: Sweet Briar College, 1998), p. 25.

317 James Anderton, reader's letter, *The Nelson Leader*, 10 June 1932.

CHAPTER SEVENTEEN: THE WITCH IN THE WOODPILE *and* THE WINDLE WITCH *or* MARGARET PEARSON AND ISABEL ROBEY

318 Some so-called 'hag-ridden' horses were said to be found alive but severely fatigued and drenched in sweat after witches or fairies had taken them during the night and ridden them to the point of death. In order to avoid such horrors, hag-stones (stones with a naturally occurring hole) would be hung at the stable door, in the stalls, or around the neck of each horse. Later the term hag-ridden came to mean sleep paralysis, when a person wakes at night, utterly unable to move, with the sensation of something heavy on their stomach or chest, and a sense of someone else unexpectedly present. In the past, although other supernatural entities were sometimes blamed (depending largely upon where and when the sufferer lived), it was usually said to be the fault of a witch. In the west country, several cases were recorded of elderly women being attacked as a result. Again, hag-stones would be used to ward off any further occurrences. In one instance during the Victorian era, a Somerset man tied a nail-studded board to his chest, hoping to give any malicious witch a painful surprise of her own.

319 The Padiham parish registers; see above for details.

320 The Padiham parish registers record the marriage of Margaret Bouker and Eduardus Peersonne.

321 The examination of Jennet Booth, witness against Margaret Pearson, in Thomas Potts, *Discoverie*, p. 242.

322 Ibid, p 241.

323 Information collated from the Clitheroe Court Rolls and the National Archives. Thomas Childers, who left a will, is mentioned in *The Spending of the Money of Robert Nowell*. Dean Nowell was Robert's brother and Roger Nowell's great-uncle; he was related by marriage to Sir John Towneley, who was the grandfather of Henry Towneley, husband of Ann, whom James Device was charged with having murdered. Thomas's father, Lawrence Childers, was constable of Padiham but died in 1560, before the accusations of witchcraft were levelled at Margaret.

324 Thomas Childers himself died in 1604, outliving his wife by around twenty years, but his death does not appear to have been attributed to Margaret in any sense.

325 John Harland (ed.), *The House and Farm Accounts of the Shuttleworths of Gawthorpe Hall in the County of Lancaster, September 1582–October 1621* (Manchester: Chetham Society, 1856), p. 201.

326 Potts relates Jennet Booth's evidence with two clear but puzzling errors. First he states that Jennet dates the toad in the woodpile incident as occurring 'the Friday next after, the said Pearson's wife was committed to the gaol at Lancaster'. This makes no sense, unless he means that Margaret Pearson was sent to prison the Friday after the incident took place. More obviously, he wrongly names Margaret as 'Margerie' on three occasions within a single paragraph.

327 Potts, *Discoverie*, p. 242.

328 Ibid.

329 E. H. Wormwood, *Toadlore: The Natterjack at the Edges of Occult History*, 6 April 2023, *The MIT Press Reader* website: https://thereader.mitpress.mit.edu/toad-lore-the-natterjack-at-the-edges-of-occult-history/

330 Ibid.

331 The name came from the belief that a royal personage could cure a sufferer simply by touch.

332 'Toadlore' endured: the association of toads with witchcraft fuelled a commonly held belief in the early twentieth century that it was bad luck for a toad to enter a house, although some regarded it as quite the opposite. As late as the 1930s, Toadmen cults existed in the British Isles, with the most well-known in Cambridgeshire. Members believed that they held a supernatural power over horses by making a pact with the devil in a ritual that varied slightly from location to location. Most required catching a toad, hanging it on a thorn tree until only the skeleton remained, then throwing the bones into a stream by the light of a full moon until one bone detached from the rest; this then gave the horseman his power.

333 William Shakespeare, *Macbeth*, Act IV, Scene I.

334 Shakespeare also refers to another magical aspect of toads in *As You Like It*, when he describes the 'ugly and venomous' creature who 'wears yet a precious jewel in his head'. This was the belief, common to Northern European folklore, that within the toad's head is a form of philosopher's stone. It offers an antidote to poison, changing colour in its presence, and has a number of other healing properties.

CHAPTER EIGHTEEN: CITY OF SCAFFOLDS

335 James Raine (ed.), *Depositions from the Castle of York: Relating to Offenses Committed in the Northern Counties in the Seventeenth Century* (Durham: Frances Andrews, 1861), p. xxxii, footnote.

336 Ibid.

337 John Nichols, *The Progresses, Processions and Magnificent Festivities of King James the First* (London: J. B. Nichols, 1828), pp. 333–4.

338 W. R. Prest (ed.), *The Diary of Sir Richard Hutton, 1614–39* (London: Selden Society, 1991), p. 17.

339 Harrison, *King James the First: Daemonologie*, p. 78.

340 William Andrews, *Old-Time Punishments* (London: Corner House, 1975), p. 230.

341 Late eighteenth-century references to the 'old gallows' outside Micklegate Bar suggest there may have been two gallows operational.

342 William Knipe, *Tyburn Tales: The Criminal Chronology of York Castle* (London: The History Press, 2010), p. 27.

343 Ibid, p. 29.

344 Parish records for Pocklington state that 'Old Wife Green' was hanged as a witch in 1630 in the market square. This seems to have been mob action rather than a judicial execution. There is no indication of what she was alleged to have done. Twelve years later, Petronella Haxley, the wife of the blacksmith, was hanged in the same market square. Again, there is no record of her crimes.

345 The Assize Courts' gallows was last used in 1896 and dismantled in 1930. A 'drop' behind the city prison was in use in 1809 and 1821.

CHAPTER NINETEEN: WICKED PERSUASIONS

346 N. G. Jones, 'Bromley, Sir Edward', in *Oxford Dictionary of National Biography* website:
https://doi.org/10.1093/ref:odnb/66565

347 B. W. Quintrell (ed.), *Proceedings of the Lancashire Justices of the Peace at the Sheriff's Table During Assize Week, 1578–1694* (The Record Society of Lancashire and Cheshire, 1981), p. 62.

348 Ibid.

349 According to John Champness, *Lancaster Castle, A Brief History* (Preston: Lancaster County Books, 1993), p. 15: 'There were no holding cells on the ground floor then; the stables were there until 1796, when the area was remodelled. The Crown Court became the Library and Barristers' Robing Room and the stables were converted into cells. 'The courts of the Earls and Dukes of Lancaster must have been held in the hall of the medieval castle. This was a largish building (about 15 metres long by 8 metres wide) which stood on the site of the present Barristers' Library and Robing Room, to the south of the present Crown Court. Its basement remains – the so-called Dungeons which one can visit after Adrian's Tower – but most of the rest was demolished or hidden by new masonry at the end of the 18th century; we only know of its appearance from a few unclear drawings of that period. It was, however, the scene of a number of notorious trials whose records survive [inc. Pendle].'

350 J. S. Cockburn, *A History of English Assizes, 1558–1714* (Cambridge: Cambridge University Press, 1972), p. 74.

351 Indictments could also go before a Quarter Sessions jury for them to make the decision.

352 J. S. Cockburn, *A History of English Assizes, 1558–1714* (Cambridge: Cambridge University Press, 1972), p. 108.

353 Potts, *Discoverie*, p. 200.

CHAPTER TWENTY: THE AXE LAID TO THE TREE

354 Thomas Dunham Whitaker, *An History of the Original Parish of Whalley and Honor of Clitheroe* (London: Routledge, 1876), p. 351.

355 Lea, 'Witchcraft, Possession and Confessional Tension', p. 95.

356 David Brazendale, *Lancashire's Historic Halls*, (Carnegie Publishing, 1994) p. 95.

357 Glen Clayton, *The Famous Witches of Samlesbury* (Glen Clayton, 2012), p. 9.

358 Alistair Hodge, *A Short History of Samlesbury* (Carnegie Publishing, 1986), p. 31.

359 Ibid, p. 32.

360 Eaton, Robert, *A History of Samlesbury in the Hundred of Blackburn, County of Lancaster* (J. Dickinson & Sons Ltd., 1936), p. 162.

361 Potts tells us that Grace was 'further sworn and examined', suggesting a second examination.

362 Potts, *Discoverie*, p. 178.

363 Kramer, Heinrich, *Malleus Maleficarum* (London: John Rodker, 1928), p. 101.

364 Potts, *Discoverie*, p. 184. Although we cannot be certain that Grace's recollection of the date (4 April) for this incident was correct, it seems more likely than Thomas Walshman's statement that it was 15 April – if only because this was the day on which William Alker gave his evidence about Jane Southworth. The fifteenth of April was also a Wednesday. Were Walshman's date correct, this would have made a very long period of 'unconsciousness'. The evidence given by Grace also mentions 4 April correctly as a Saturday.

365 Potts, *Discoverie*, p. 179. This is Friday 10 April, thus we know that the first examination must have taken place after this date.

366 Ibid.

367 Glen Clayton, *The Famous Witches of Samlesbury* (Glen Clayton, 2012), p. 29.

368 Potts, *Discoverie*, p186. The heading of the examination refers to Jane Bierley, which must be a misprint for Jane Southworth; the text of the deposition refers to the 'said wife of John Southworth, now Prisoner in the Gaole'.

369 Potts, *Discoverie*, p.185.

370 Stephen Wright, 'Leigh, William', *Oxford Dictionary of National Biography* website: https://doi.org?10.1093/ref:0dnb/16394

371 Luca Baratta, 'A Land of Witches', p. 201. There is another witch story associated with Samlesbury; in fact, there are two versions of it. In the church near the south wall and a yew tree, not far from the sundial, is a flat gravestone, cracked across its surface but held in place by several long iron spikes driven into the stone itself. The first version of the story holds that it is the grave of a local woman who swore on her deathbed that she would haunt her husband if he married again. After her death, the widower disregarded his first wife's threat and married the woman who kept the ale store at the Boat House near the ferry (which implies that he was related to the Bierleys of Grace's tales). The widower then heard that his first wife's grave slab had moved. Remembering her last words, he piled heavy stones on her grave. But the stone slab moved again. This time the widower drove iron spikes through the grave. Cracks appeared in the stone slab but the spikes held it firm and the widower lived peacefully with his second wife. In another version of the story, we are told that the woman beneath the stone was a witch and the villagers drove spikes into her grave to keep her buried. A more prosaic explanation for the iron spikes is that they were added for safety during the time of the resurrectionists, when graves would be plundered for bodies to be sold for dissection. Hence why so many graves bear spikes, grilles or iron gratings known as 'mortsafes'.

CHAPTER TWENTY-ONE: DOLLS OF CLAY

372 Peter Haining (ed.), *The Witchcraft Papers* (London: Robert Hale & Co., 1974), p. 27.

373 Thomas Darling was later punished for promoting papistry and criticising the Bishop of London. He was whipped and had his ears cropped.

374 Joanna J. Kucinski, *Representations of Witches in Popular Literature in England, 1566–1645* (Sweet Briar: Sweet Briar College, 1998), pp. 27–8.

375 Stephen J. Ceci, *Jeopardy in the Courtroom: A Scientific Analysis of Children's Testimony* (Washington: American Psychological Association, 1995), p. 8

376 David J. Skal, *Death Makes a Holiday: A Cultural History of Halloween* (Bloomsbury: New York, 2003), p. 65.

377 Stephen J. Ceci, *Jeopardy in the Courtroom: A Scientific Analysis of Children's Testimony* (Washington: American Psychological Association, 1995), p. 304.

378 Ibid.

379 Cockburn, *A History of English Assizes, 1558–1714*, p. 124.

CHAPTER TWENTY-TWO: PLACE OF SKULLS

380 William Andrews, *Old-Time Punishments* (London: Corner House, 1975), p. 64.

381 Ibid, p. 71.

382 Ibid, p. 75.

383 Ibid, p. 85.

384 Ibid, p. 86.

385 The church is mainly from 1766 but the tower and part of the original chancel of the c.1520 building survive.

386 Thomas J. Farrow, *Gallows and Golgotha: Morbid Conventions in the Inherited Place-names of Seventeenth Century Quaker Burial Grounds*, (Liverpool: Liverpool University Press, June 2021), p. 142.

387 Thomas Cruddas Porteus, *A History of the Parish of Standish* (J. Starr & Sons Ltd, 1927), p. 102.

388 Ibid.

389 William Leigh, *The Dampe of Death: Beaten Back with the Glorious Light and Life of Jesus Christ*, sermon preached at Lancaster Assizes (Thomas Creede for Arthur Johnson, 1613):
https://quod.lib.umich.edu/e/eebo2/A72540.0001.001?rgn=main;view=fulltext

390 Ibid.

391 Ibid.

392 The Golden Lion pub on Moor Lane bears a plaque to the Lancashire Witches. In its earlier days, the pub was known as the Whittle Springs. There was a tradition, during the latter days of public hangings on Gallows Hill, whereby the execution cart would stop to allow the condemned prisoners to have a last drink at the Whittle Springs before the final leg of the journey. But this post-dates the witch trials.

393 Hurren, E. T., *Dissecting the Criminal Corpse: Staging Post-Execution Punishment in Early Modern England* (Palgrave Macmillan, 2016), p. 108.

394 Ibid.

395 Ibid, p. 109.

396 Ibid, p. 111.

397 Sharpe, *Crime in Early Modern England 1550–1750* (London: Routledge, 1998), p. 231.

398 Ibid.

399 William Leigh, *The Dampe of Death: Beaten Back with the Glorious Light and Life of Jesus Christ*, sermon preached at Lancaster Assizes (Thomas Creede for Arthur Johnson, 1613):
https://quod.lib.umich.edu/e/eebo2/A72540.0001.001?rgn=main;view=fulltext

400 Headsman, '1705: John "Half-Hanged" Smith', 24 December 2008, *Executed Today* website:
https://www.executedtoday.com/2008/12/24/1705-john-half-hanged-smith-half-hanged

401 Thomas J. Farrow, *Gallows and Golgotha: Morbid Conventions in the Inherited Place-names of Seventeenth Century Quaker Burial Grounds* (Liverpool: Liverpool University Press, June 2021), p. 139.

402 Lancaster City Museum, Facebook post, 7 June 2020.

EPILOGUE

403 Basil Fuller and John Cornes, *No. 10 Downing Street* (New York: Greenberg Publishers, 1936), pp. 76–7.

404 Ibid.

405 Hasted, Rachel, *The Pendle Witch-Trial 1612* (Lancashire County Books, 1993), p. 44.

406 Ibid.

407 Kittredge, *Witchcraft in Old and New England*, p. 287.

408 Ibid.

409 Potts, *Discoverie*, p. 244.

410 Wallace Notestein, *A History of Witchcraft in England from 1558 to 1718* (The American Historical Association, 1911), p. 130.

411 Robert Neill, *Mist Over Pendle* (London: Hutchinson, 1951), back cover matter.

412 This is the Londesborough manuscript; Lord Londesborough (1805-60) was an antiquarian who collected early manuscripts. He obtained a copy of a supposedly contemporary document describing the 1634 depositions, along with the results of their examinations, alleged crimes, list of the accused, and the outcome of their physical examinations.

413 Clifford Moorhouse, *Sabden: The Forgotten Valley* (Clifford Moorhouse, 1978), p. 95.